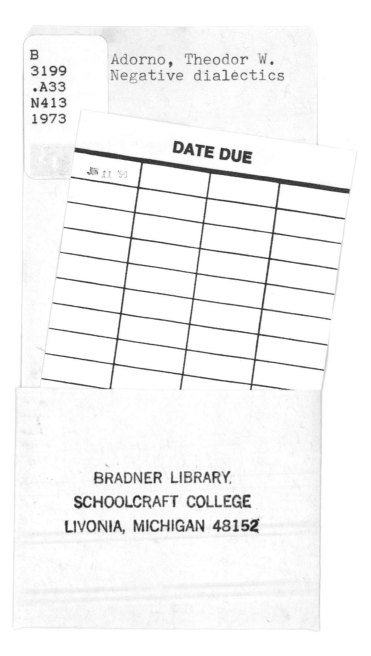

NEGATIVE DIALECTICS

NEGATIVE DIALECTICS

by Theodor W. Adorno

Translated by E. B. Ashton

A Continuum Book

THE SEABURY PRESS • NEW YORK

THE SEABURY PRESS
815 Second Avenue, New York 10017

English translation copyright © 1973 by The Seabury Press, Incorporated.
Printed in the United States of America.

Original edition: *Negative Dialektik,* © 1966 by Suhrkamp Verlag, Frankfurt am Main

LIBRARY OF CONGRESS CATALOGING IN PUBLICATION DATA

Adorno, Theodor W.   1903–1969
Negative dialectics

Includes bibliographical references.
1. Philosophy—Addresses, essays, lectures.   I. Title.
B3199.A33N413   1973   193   72–11720
ISBN 0–8164–9129–1

CONTENTS

TRANSLATOR'S NOTE   ix

PREFACE   xix

INTRODUCTION   3
The Possibility of Philosophy *3*   Dialectics Not a Standpoint *4*
Reality and Dialectics *6*   The Concern of Philosophy *8*   The
Antagonistic Entirety *10*   Disenchantment of the Concept *11*
"Infinity" *13*   The Speculative Moment *15*   Presentation *18*
Attitude Toward Systems *20*   Idealism as Rage *22*   The Two-
fold Character of the System *24*   The Antinomical Character of
Systems *26*   Argument and Experience *28*
Vertiginousness *31*   Fragility of Truth *33*   Against Relativ-
ism *35*   Dialectics and Solidity *37*
The Privilege of Experience *40*   Qualitative Moment of Ration-
ality *43*   Quality and Individual *44*   Substantiality and
Method *47*   Existentialism *49*   Thing, Language, History *52*
Tradition and Knowledge *53*   Rhetoric *55*

PART ONE: RELATION TO ONTOLOGY

I. THE ONTOLOGICAL NEED   61
Question and Answer *61*   Affirmative Character *65*   Incapaci-
tation of the Subject *66*   Being, Subject, Object *69*   Ontologi-
cal Objectivism *70*
The Disappointed Need *72*   "Deficiency = Profit" *76*   No Man's
Land *77*
Unsuccessful Realism *78*   On Categorical Vision *80*   Being
θέσει *83*
"Sense of Being" *85*   Ontology Prescribed *87*   Protest Against
Reification *89*   The Wrong Need *92*   Weakness and Support *94*

II. BEING AND EXISTENCE

Immanent Critique of Ontology 97   Copula 100   No Transcendence of Being 105   Expressing the Inexpressible 108
The Child's Question 110   The Question of Being 112   Looping the Loop 115   Mythology of Being 117
Ontologization of the Ontical 119   Function of the Concept of Existence 122   "Dasein in Itself Ontological" 124   The Nominalistic Aspect 126   Existence Authoritarian 127   "Historicality" 128

PART TWO: NEGATIVE DIALECTICS. CONCEPT AND CATEGORIES

The Indissoluble "Something" 134   Compulsory Sustantiveness 136
"Peephole Metaphysics" 137   Noncontradictoriness Not to be Hypostatized 139   Relation to Left-wing Hegelianism 143
"Logic of Disintegration" 144   On the Dialectics of Identity 146
Cogitative Self-reflection 148   Objectivity of Contradiction 151
Starting Out from the Concept 153   Synthesis 156   Critique of Positive Negation 158
Individuality Not the Ultimate Either 161   Constellation 162
Constellation in Science 164
Essence and Appearance 166   Indirectness by Objectivity 170
Particularity and the Particular 173   Subject-Object Dialectics 174
Reversal of the Subjective Reduction 176   Interpreting the Transcendental 178   "Transcendental Delusion" 180
The Object's Preponderance 183   The Object Not a Datum 186
Objectivity and Reification 189
Passage to Materialism 192   Materialism and Immediacy 194
Dialectics Not a Sociology of Knowledge 197   The Concept of Mind 198   Pure Activity and Genesis 200   Suffering Physical 202   Materialism Imageless 204

PART THREE: MODELS

I. FREEDOM

On The Metacritique of Practical Reason   211
"Pseudoproblems" 211   A Split in the Concern with Freedom 214
Freedom, Determinism, Identity 216   Freedom and Organized Society 217   The Impulse Before the Ego 221   Experimenta crucis 223   The Addendum 226

The Fiction of Positive Freedom *231*   Unfreedom of Thought *233*
'Formalism" *235*   The Will as a Thing *237*
Objectivity in the Antinomy *239*   Dialectical Definition of the
Will *241*   Contemplation *244*
Structure of the Third Antinomy *246*   Kant's Concept of Causality *247*   The Plea for Order *249*   The Antithetical Argument *252*   Ontical and Ideal Moments *255*   Repressive Character of the Doctrine of Freedom *260*   Self-experience of Freedom
and Unfreedom *261*   The Crisis of Causality *265*   Causality
as a Spell *269*
Reason, Ego, Super-ego *270*   Potential of Freedom *274*
Against Personalism *276*   Depersonalization and Existential Ontology *279*   Universal and Individual in the Philosophy of Morals *281*   On the State of Freedom *285*
Kant's "Intelligible Character" *287*   Intelligibility and the Unity
of Consciousness *292*   Truth Content of the Doctrine of Intelligibility *297*

II. WORLD SPIRIT AND NATURAL HISTORY.
An Excursion to Hegel   300

Trend and Facts *300*   Construction of the World Spirit *303*
"Harmonizing with the World Spirit" *305*   The Unleashing of
Productive Forces *306*   Group Spirit and Dominion *307*   The
Legal Sphere *309*   Law and Equity *310*   Individualistic
Veil *312*   Dynamics of Universal and Particular *313*
Spirit as a Social Totality *314*   Historical Reason Antagonis-
tic *317*
Universal History *319*   Antagonism Contingent? *321*
The Supramundance Character of the Hegelian World Spirit *323*
Hegel Siding with the Universal *326*   Relapse into Platonism *329*
Detemporalization of Time *331*   Dialectics Cut Short by
Hegel *334*
The Role of the Popular Spirit *338*   Popular Spirit Obsolete *340*
Individuality and History *342*   The Spell *344*   Regression
Under the Spell *347*
Subject and Individual *349*   Dialectics and Psychology *351*
"Natural History" *354*   History and Metaphysics *358*

III. MEDITATIONS ON METAPHYSICS 361

After Auschwitz *361*   Metaphysics and Culture *365*   Dying Today *368*   Happiness and Idle Waiting *373*   "Nihilism" *376* Kant's Resignation *381*   Rescuing Urge and Block *384*   Mundus intelligibilis *390*   Neutralization *393*   "Only a Parable" *399* The Semblance of Otherness *402*   Self-Reflection of Dialectics *405*

NOTES 409

TRANSLATOR'S NOTE

This book—to begin with an admission—made me violate what I consider the Number One rule for translators of philosophy: never to start translating until you think you know what the author means by every sentence, indeed by every word. It was done unwittingly. I had read the book in German, not too thoroughly but never unsure of its theses. I clearly recalled the thrust of what it conveys in a polished prose that had seemed eminently translatable. And so it turned out to be, not only because most of Theodor Adorno's philosophical vocabulary is of Latin or Greek stock and identical in English and German. His syntax rarely needs disentangling like that of most German philosophers since Kant; he is not as addicted to making up words as they are; and the few neologisms he does use are borrowed from English.

In the early stages of translation I wondered now and then what one sentence might have to do with the preceding one and that with the one before. But other readers told of the same experience, and Adorno's own Preface promised that what seemed baffling at first would be clarified later. Besides, I felt, there was no mistranslating his text. His sentences were clear. The words (his own, that is; his discussions of other men's words are a different matter) were unequivocal. Their English equivalents were beyond doubt. I plodded on, oblivious of my Number One rule.

But the enigmas piled up. I found myself translating entire pages without seeing how they led from the start of an argument to the conclusion. I was about to return the book as untranslatable—for me, at least—when my favorite translators' story crossed my mind. A colleague, commissioned to translate a certain book, was asked whether he had had a chance to read it yet. "I do not read; I translate," was his reply.

I put my nascent translation aside and did what I ought to

have done in the first place. I reread *Negative Dialectics*—not at a fast clip, not for an overall view of the intellectual edifice, but examining brick after brick to see whether they were really thrown together helter-skelter or there was some method in the madness. I found not one method but several.

Let me inject here that both ways of reading this book are legitimate, in my opinion. A writer as facile and literate as Adorno will make his points on two levels: line by line, and impression by impression. What he wants to say comes through even if you read as I first read it and as probably many of its German readers have—if you savor the nuggets of wit, the darts of sarcasm, and get the drift while floating over problems on the ripples of a style that may, at best, approximate the smoothness of the German.

If you do want to get to the bottom and dig, however, there are, I believe, three keys—not to Adorno's philosophy, but to his presentation. They will unlock, not the substance of his thinking, but the formidable formal gates along the way to it. Carried in mind, they will greatly ease one's path through *Negative Dialectics*.

The first key is the title. In his Preface, Adorno calls it paradoxical, explaining that one of his aims is to rid dialectics of such traditional affirmative traits as trying "to achieve something positive by way of negation." But this logical sense of negativity is not the only one in which it is here pursued. In this book the word "negative" has all the meanings found in an unabridged dictionary, and then some—logical, ethical, utilitarian, political, socio-economic. It may be used, or its use may be implied, in a purely vernacular sense at one moment, and the next moment in the esoteric sense of running counter to the philosophies of identity and noncontradictoriness. It is the implied use of "negative," the multitude of passages avidly hunting the thing without mentioning the word, that perplexes readers who do not keep reminding themselves of the title.

Its second word also has implications beyond philosophical usage. Much of this book is dialectical in the traditional sense of Platonic, Kantian, Hegelian dialectics; but all of it is dialectics in the popular, commonplace sense of skilled argumentation. It never addresses itself to philosophical problems, always to other philosophies. There is a chapter against Heidegger (with a few swipes at Husserl and Jaspers), another against Hegel, a third against Kant. The targets cover an impressive range; Adorno spares neither idealists nor positivists of the eighteenth and nineteenth century, and he savages the neo-ontologists, intuitionists, and existentialists of the twentieth. Sub rosa, he polemicizes also against the twentieth-century Marxist establishment—which brings us to the second of the three keys.

"The author," Adorno ends his Preface, "is prepared for the attacks to which *Negative Dialectics* will expose him. He feels no rancor and does not begrudge the joy of those in either camp who will proclaim that they knew it all the time and now he was confessing." The two camps—"*hüben und drüben*"—are East and West, Marxists and anti-Marxists. To the latter, Adorno had nothing new to confess; he had never made a secret of his convictions. But he had striven long and hard against his doubts, and when he could not repress them any more he felt obliged to defend them. At bottom, this book is an apologia for deviationism, a Marxist thinker's explication of his inability to toe the lines laid down today for proper Marxist thinking.

The deviations to which he pleads guilty are numerous. He accords primacy to facts over concepts, and to substance over form. He holds that dark realities can eclipse dazzling ideas, and that theory, however noncontradictory, cannot undo a contradictory practice. He contends that if nonidentical objects belie the identity of subjectivism—even of collective subjectivism—that identity is not truth but a lie. And his defense of all this, the reason why a believer feels compelled to disavow articles of his own creed, is that the negativity of the concrete particular, of things as we see and experience them in our time, makes his the true, the "negative" dialectics.

Concretely, all of these sins are epitomized in one: in the contention that history, all reinterpretations to the contrary notwithstanding, has failed to take the course predicted for it as a scientific necessity. Directly following the Preface, the book itself opens with a flat statement of this cardinal heresy: "Philosophy, which once seemed obsolete, lives on because the moment to realize it was missed. The summary judgment that it had merely interpreted the world, that resignation in the face of reality had crippled it in itself, becomes a defeatism of reason after the attempt to change the world miscarried"—two sentences one may be at a loss to understand unless he remembers Marx's famous dictum about the philosophers who were content to interpret the world: "What matters is to change it."

What matters here is the third key to reading this book. It overflows with such allusions, with paraphrases of renowned and not so renowned quotations from men presupposed as familiar. Adorno has several ways of handling these. The original may be quoted at length, in the text or in footnotes, leaving the parallel to be figured out by the reader. Or the authors—modern ones in particular—are named, assuming only that the reader will know them sufficiently to understand what specific line or aspect of their work is here referred to. But sometimes such aids are dispensed with altogether, on the assumption that whoever reads *Negative Dialectics* will instantly have the source in mind.

The last procedure, I believe, will be responsible for most of the problems one may have in reading; it certainly was responsible for most of mine. To follow the line of thought from detail to detail, you need to know Kant near-perfectly, Hegel perfectly, and Marx-Engels viscerally—not just "by heart." If you twitch whenever a phrase in this book resembles one from the Marxist Founding Fathers, then and not until then can you think along with Adorno.

Besides, you should have a working knowledge of moderns from a variety of fields, of such philosophers as Bergson, Husserl, Scheler, Walter Benjamin (an anthology of whose work has lately appeared in English and who may be the one object of Adorno's unqualified admiration), of prominent sociologists and psychiatrists, of seminal poets (Beckett) and composers (Schönberg—Adorno is not only a philosopher but one of the most knowledgeable musicologists of our time). And you should at least have heard of Karl Kraus of Vienna, the consummate intellectual and jack-of-all-literary-trades whose influence covered the German language area after the first World War and had a revival of sorts after the second.

You do not need to know Heidegger. The principal target of Adorno's polemics is the only one where he presupposes nothing, where every line he scorns is quoted in full, preliminary to dissection. The duels with Heidegger in the first half of this book will not stump the reader, as a rule, although some did stump the translator. For Martin Heidegger has always struck me as untranslatable, and despite the talent and effort invested in recent English versions of his works, he still does. He is a man who chose to put the gist of his philosophizing into the form of an argument with language. Being a German, he argues with the German language. To reproduce his plays on German words, his translators invented ingenious English words and word combinations, but the very point of the method is that in the source language the words are neither ingenious nor invented. Like the means used to vary them, they are all commonplace, almost all Germanic, and carefully selected for both traits. Heidegger's most abstruse texts can be skimmed with a sense of familiarity by German readers, and this plays a major role in the philosophy.

That a vocabulary of linguistic oddities will not produce the same illusion is clear. With Heidegger, time and again, there is simply no way to the equivalence that is the crux of translation. In two or three such cases, therefore, a few lines of the original have been omitted from this volume. They are not vital, merely reenforcing other exemplifications of the same points, and the alternative—to quote the German and to append footnotes with a translation bound to miss the point, an explanation of the inadequacy, and a further explanation of Adorno's comments on the mistranslated quotes—seemed to me too horrible to contemplate.

The passages Adorno quotes or paraphrases from Kant, Hegel, or Marx-Engels posed a different problem. There are many Kant translations and some excellent ones, but in the concrete case their wording would not often lend itself to the Adorno variations. There are not many good Hegel translations, though the Josiah Royce version of *Die Vernunft in der Geschichte,* a work analyzed extensively in this book, ranks with the best; looking forward to this chance to draw upon the late Professor Royce's English, I spent hours searching for his rendering of every quoted line. In vain; most of them were undiscoverable. To capture Hegel's spirit, the translator had stripped away the weak Hegelian flesh. But it is the flesh, unfortunately, that Adorno picks on.

The official, canonical English version of the works of Marx and Engels is in the opposite category. The flesh is there, but the spirit is that of the Leninist revision. The greatest translations have not escaped from such ideological service; after all, in one of our English Bibles the Christmas message promises "good will toward men" while the other limits it to "men of good will." In the standard English Marx-Engels, the original tenets are ever so slightly nudged in the direction of meanings given to them, as Adorno's heretical opening puts it, "after the attempt to change the world miscarried." (Three little words repeated over and over in this book—"*nach wie vor*," now as before—keep us mindful of that miscarriage.)

Finally, it should be noted that each of these wellsprings of thought has its own variant of German philosophical usage, its own somewhat different understanding of the same terms, and that in English each new translation led inevitably to new differences within Hegel, for instance, besides adding to the original ones between Hegel and others. In *Negative Dialectics* the consistent use of existing translations would have produced an unintelligible hodgepodge. What I decided to do instead, after much soul-searching, was to orient my work to the man I was translating. Wherever someone else is quoted, paraphrased, discussed, or alluded to, I would take Adorno's terminology, construction, and meaning as the base on which to synthesize my own renderings of the texts he refers to, regardless of how they may have been rendered elsewhere.

It was he, after all, who dealt with them, who reasoned and argued with them, and here, to my mind, these dealings rather than their objects are of the essence. My responsibility, as I saw it, was to put Adorno's thought into English, not to keep his examples of other philosophers' thought in line with the English forms lent to them by other translators. If a reader has studied the German thinkers in English and fails to find here the expressions he has come to be familiar with, I ask him to remember that this is Adorno's book—and to take my word for it that a comparison with the original text of the others will show that they were translated faithfully.

"I often wonder," a noted translator and critic wrote to me years ago, "how far writers like Benjamin, Lukács, Adorno, say, are ever going to make much mark in the English-speaking world . . . as long as translators do not risk their lives and *think* them into English. What does the reader with a quite different philosophical background, and often very little philosophical background of any sort, really make of them?"

For readers with no philosophical background of any sort, I am afraid, the answer has to be: Not much—in any language. And Lukács and Benjamin may indeed force a translator to take his life in his hands even for a well-trained audience. But I like to believe that Adorno, who often seems to do his own thinking in English, requires no such valor. If you are aware that he is defending himself against attacks from "either camp"; if you recall that his armor is a dialectics built on relentless pursuit of the negative in every possible sense; and if you know the philosophies he uses (negatively, as a rule) for his concretions and models, the encounter with his "anti-system," as the German book jacket calls it, may prove a challenging and intriguing experience— even, I hope, in English.

E. B. A.

NEGATIVE
DIALECTICS

PREFACE

Negative Dialectics is a phrase that flouts tradition. As early as Plato, dialectics meant to achieve something positive by means of negation; the thought figure of a "negation of negation" later became the succinct term. This book seeks to free dialectics from such affirmative traits without reducing its determinacy. The unfoldment of the paradoxical title is one of its aims.

What would be the foundation, according to the dominant view of philosophy, will here be developed long after the author has discussed things of which that view assumes that they grow out of a foundation. This implies a critique of the foundation concept as well as the primacy of substantive thought—a thought of whose movement the thinker becomes aware only as he performs it. What it needs is secondary under the rules of the intellectual game, which always remain applicable.

A methodology of the author's material works is not all there is to this book; no continuum exists between those works and it, according to the theory of negative dialectics. The discontinuity will be dealt with, however, and so will the directions for thought to be read in it. The procedure will be justified, not based on reasons. To the best of his ability the author means to put his cards on the table—which is by no means the same as playing the game.

In 1937, when the author had completed his *Metakritik der Erkenntnistheorie,* the last chapter of that publication moved Walter Benjamin to remark that one had to "cross the frozen waste of abstraction to arrive at concise, concrete philosophizing." *Negative Dialectics* now charts such a crossing in retrospect. In contemporary philosophy, concretion would mostly be obtained on the sly. By contrast, this largely abstract text seeks no less to serve authentic concretion than to explain the author's concrete procedure. As the latest esthetic discussions feature the "anti-drama" and the "anti-hero," this *Negative Dialectics* in which all esthetic topics are shunned might be called an "anti-system." It attempts by means of logical consistency to substitute for the unity principle, and for the paramountcy of the supra-ordinated concept, the idea of what would be outside the sway of such unity. To use the strength of the subject to break through the fallacy of constitutive subjectivity—this is what the author felt to be his task ever since he came to trust his own mental impulses; now he did not wish to put it off any longer. Stringently to transcend the official separation of pure philosophy and the substantive or formally scientific realm was one of his determining motives.

The Introduction expounds the concept of philosophical experience. Part One starts out from the current state of the ontology reigning in Germany; rather than judged from above, this ontology is understood and immanently criticized out of the need for it, which is a problem of its own. From the results, Part Two proceeds to the idea of a negative dialectics and to its position on several categories which are retained as well as qualitatively altered. Part Three elaborates models of negative dialectics. They are not examples; they do not simply elucidate general reflections. Guiding into the substantive realm, they seek simultaneously to do justice to the topical intention of what has initially, of necessity, been generally treated—as opposed to the use of examples which Plato introduced and philosophy repeated ever since: as matters of indifference in themselves. The models are to make plain what negative dialectics is and to bring it into the realm of reality, in line with its own concept. At the same time—not unlike the so-called "exemplary method"—they serve the purpose of discussing key concepts of philosophical disciplines and centrally intervening in those disciplines. For philosophical ethics this will be done by a dialectics of freedom, and for the philosophy of history, by "World Spirit and Natural History." The last chapter, groping its way around metaphysical questions, tries by critical self-reflection to give the Copernican revolution an axial turn.

The author is prepared for the attacks to which *Negative Dia-*

lectics will expose him. He feels no rancor and does not begrudge the joy of those in either camp who will proclaim that they knew it all the time and now he was confessing.

Frankfurt am Main
Summer 1966

THEODOR W. ADORNO

INTRODUCTION

INTRODUCTION

THE POSSIBILITY OF PHILOSOPHY

Philosophy, which once seemed obsolete, lives on because the moment to realize it was missed. The summary judgment that it had merely interpreted the world, that resignation in the face of reality had crippled it in itself, becomes a defeatism of reason after the attempt to change the world miscarried. Philosophy offers no place from which theory as such might be concretely convicted of the anachronisms it is suspected of, now as before. Perhaps it was an inadequate interpretation which promised that it would be put into practice. Theory cannot prolong the moment its critique depended on. A practice indefinitely delayed is no longer the forum for appeals against self-satisfied speculation; it is mostly the pretext used by executive authorities to choke, as vain, whatever critical thoughts the practical change would require.

Having broken its pledge to be as one with reality or at the point of realization, philosophy is obliged ruthlessly to criticize itself. Once upon a time, compared with sense perception and every kind of external experience, it was felt to be the very opposite of naïveté; now it has objectively grown as naïve in its turn as the seedy scholars feasting on subjective speculation seemed to Goethe, one hundred and fifty years ago. The introverted thought architect dwells behind the moon that is taken over by extroverted technicians. The conceptual shells that were to house the whole, according to philosophical custom, have in view of the immense expansion of society and of the strides made by positive natural science come to seem like relics of a simple barter economy amidst the late stage of industrial capitalism. The discrepancy (since decayed into a commonplace) between power and any sort of spirit has grown so vast as to foil whatever attempts to understand the preponderance might be inspired by

3

the spirit's own concept The will to this understanding bespeaks a power claim denied by that which is to be understood. The most patent expression of philosophy's historical fate is the way the special sciences compelled it to turn back into a special science. If Kant had, as he put it, "freed himself from the school concept of philosophy for its world concept,"[1] it has now, perforce, regressed to its school concept. Whenever philosophers mistake that for the world concept, their pretensions grow ridiculous. Hegel, despite his doctrine of the absolute spirit in which he included philosophy, knew philosophy as a mere element of reality, an activity in the division of labor, and thus restricted it. This has since led to the narrowness of philosophy, to a disproportionateness to reality that became the more marked the more thoroughly philosophers forgot about the restriction—the more they disdained, as alien, any thought of their position in a whole which they monopolized as their object, instead of recognizing how much they depended on it all the way to the internal composition of their philosophy, to its immanent truth.

To be worth another thought, philosophy must rid itself of such naïveté. But its critical self-reflection must not halt before the highest peaks of its history. Its task would be to inquire whether and how there can still be a philosophy at all, now that Hegel's has fallen, just as Kant inquired into the possibility of metaphysics after the critique of rationalism. If Hegel's dialectics constituted the unsuccessful attempt to use philosophical concepts for coping with all that is heterogeneous to those concepts, the relationship to dialectics is due for an accounting insofar as his attempt failed.

DIALECTICS NOT A STANDPOINT

No theory today escapes the marketplace. Each one is offered as a possibility among competing opinions; all are put up for choice; all are swallowed. There are no blinders for thought to don against this, and the self-righteous conviction that my own theory is spared that fate will surely deteriorate into self-advertising. But neither need dialectics be muted by such rebuke, or by the concomitant charge of its superfluity, of being a method slapped on outwardly, at random. The name of dialectics says no more, to begin with, than that objects do not go into their concepts without leaving a remainder, that they come to contradict the traditional norm of adequacy. Contradiction is not what Hegel's absolute idealism was bound to transfigure it into: it is not of the essence in a Heraclitean sense. It indicates the untruth of identity, the fact that the concept does not exhaust the thing conceived.

Yet the appearance of identity is inherent in thought itself, in its pure form. To think is to identify. Conceptual order is content to screen what thinking seeks to comprehend. The semblance and the truth of thought entwine. The semblance cannot be decreed away, as by avowal of a being-in-itself outside the totality of cogitative definitions. It is a thesis secretly implied by Kant—and mobilized against him by Hegel—that the transconceptual "in itself" is void, being wholly indefinite. Aware that the conceptual totality is mere appearance, I have no way but to break immanently, in its own measure, through the appearance of total identity. Since that totality is structured to accord with logic, however, whose core is the principle of the excluded middle, whatever will not fit this principle, whatever differs in quality, comes to be designated as a contradiction. Contradiction is nonidentity under the aspect of identity; the dialectical primary of the principle of contradiction makes the thought of unity the measure of heterogeneity. As the heterogeneous collides with its limit it exceeds itself.

Dialectics is the consistent sense of nonidentity. It does not begin by taking a standpoint. My thought is driven to it by its own inevitable insufficiency, by my guilt of what I am thinking. We are blaming the method for the fault of the matter when we object to dialectics on the ground (repeated from Hegel's Aristotelian critics on[2]) that whatever happens to come into the dialectical mill will be reduced to the merely logical form of contradiction, and that (an argument still advanced by Croce[3]) the full diversity of the noncontradictory, of that which is simply differentiated, will be ignored. What we differentiate will appear divergent, dissonant, negative for just as long as the structure of our consciousness obliges it to strive for unity: as long as its demand for totality will be its measure for whatever is not identical with it. This is what dialectics holds up to our consciousness as a contradiction. Because of the immanent nature of consciousness, contradictoriness itself has an inescapably and fatefully legal character. Identity and contradiction of thought are welded together. Total contradiction is nothing but the manifested untruth of total identification. Contradiction is nonidentity under the rule of a law that affects the nonidentical as well.

REALITY AND DIALECTICS

This law is not a cogitative law, however. It is real. Unquestionably, one who submits to the dialectical discipline has to pay dearly in the qualitative variety of experience. Still, in the administered world the impoverishment of experience by dialectics, which outrages healthy opinion, proves appropriate to the abstract monotony of that world. Its agony is the world's agony raised to a concept. Cognition must bow to it, unless concretion is once more to be debased into the ideology it starts becoming in fact.

Another version of dialectics contented itself with a debilitated renascence: with its intellectual-historical derivation from Kant's *aporias* and from that which the systems of his successors projected but failed to achieve. It can be achieved only negatively. Dialectics unfolds the difference between the particular and the universal, dictated by the universal. As the subject-object dichotomy is brought to mind it becomes inescapable for the subject, furrowing whatever the subject thinks, even objectively—but it would come to an end in reconcilement. Reconcilement would release the nonidentical, would rid it of coercion, including spiritualized coercion; it would open the road to the multiplicity of different things and strip dialectics of its power over them. Reconcilement would be the thought of the many as no longer inimical, a thought that is anathema to subjective reason.

Dialectics serves the end of reconcilement. It dismantles the coercive logical character of its own course; that is why it is denounced as "panlogism." As idealistic dialectics, it was bracketed with the absolute subject's predominance as the negative impulse of each single move of the concept and of its course as a whole. Historically, such primacy of the subject has been condemned even in the Hegelian conception that eclipsed the individual human consciousness as well as the transcendental one of Kant and Fichte. Subjective primacy was not only supplanted by the impotence of the weakening thought, which the world's overpowering course deters from construing it; but none of the reconcilements claimed by absolute idealism—and no other kind remained consistent— has stood up, whether in logic or in politics and history. The inability of consistent idealism to constitute itself as anything but the epitome of contradiction is as much the logical consequence of its truth as it is the punishment incurred by its logicity *qua* logicity; it is appearance as much as necessity.

Yet reopening the case of dialectics, whose non-idealistic form has since degenerated into a dogma as its idealistic one did into a cultural asset, will not decide solely about the actuality of a traditional mode of philosophizing, nor about the actuality of the philosophical structure of cognitive objects. Through Hegel, philosophy had regained the right and the capacity to think substantively instead of being put off with the analysis of cognitive forms that were empty and, in an emphatic sense, null and void. Where present philosophy deals with anything substantive at all, it lapses either into the randomness of a weltanschauung or into that formalism, that "matter of indifference," against which Hegel had risen. There is historical evidence of this in the evolution of phenomenology, which once was animated by the need for contents and became an invocation of being, a repudiation of any content as unclean.

The fundament and result of Hegel's substantive philosophizing was the primacy of the subject, or—in the famous phrase from the Introduction to his *Logic*—the "identity of identity and non-identity."[4] He held the definite particular to be definable by the mind because its immanent definition was to be nothing but the mind. Without this supposition, according to Hegel, philosophy would be incapable of knowing anything substantive or essential. Unless the idealistically acquired concept of dialectics harbors experiences contrary to the Hegelian emphasis, experiences independent of the idealistic machinery, philosophy must inevitably do without substantive insight, confine itself to the methodology of science, call that philosophy, and virtually cross itself out.

THE CONCERN OF PHILOSOPHY

The matters of true philosophical interest at this point in history are those in which Hegel, agreeing with tradition, expressed his disinterest. They are nonconceptuality, individuality, and particularity—things which ever since Plato used to be dismissed as transitory and insignificant, and which Hegel labeled "lazy Existenz." Philosophy's theme would consist of the qualities it downgrades as contingent, as a *quantité négligeable*. A matter of urgency to the concept would be what it fails to cover, what its abstractionist mechanism eliminates, what is not already a case of the concept.

Bergson and Husserl, carriers of philosophical modernism, both have innervated this idea but withdrawn from it to traditional metaphysics. Bergson, in a tour de force, created another type of cognition for nonconceptuality's sake. The dialectical salt was washed away in an undifferentiated tide of life; solidified reality was disposed of as subaltern, not comprehended along with its subalternity. The hater of the rigid general concept established a cult of irrational immediacy, of sovereign freedom in the midst of unfreedom. He drafted his two cognitive modes in as dualistic an opposition as that of the Cartesian and Kantian doctrines he fought had ever been; the causal-mechanical mode, as pragmatistic knowledge, was no more affected by the intuitive one than the bourgeois establishment was by the relaxed unself-consciousness of those who owe their privileges to that establishment.

The celebrated intuitions themselves seem rather abstract in Bergson's philosophy; they scarcely go beyond the phenomenal time consciousness which even Kant had underlying chronological-physical time—spatial time, according to Bergson's insight. Although it takes an effort to develop, the intuitive mode of mental conduct does continue to exist in fact as an archaic rudiment of mimetic reactions. What preceded its past holds a promise beyond the ossified present. Intuitions succeed only desultorily, however.

Every cognition including Bergson's own needs the rationality he scorns, and needs it precisely at the moment of concretion. Absolutized duration, pure becoming, the pure act—these would recoil into the same timelessness which Bergson chides in metaphysics since Plato and Aristotle. He did not mind that the thing he groped for, if it is not to remain a mirage, is visible solely with the equipment of cognition, by reflection upon its own means, and that it grows arbitrary in a procedure unrelated, from the start, to that of cognition.

Husserl the logician, on the other hand, would indeed sharply distinguish the mode of apprehending the essence from generalizing abstraction—what he had in mind was a specific mental experience capable of perceiving the essence in the particular—but the essence to which this experience referred did not differ in any respect from the familiar general concepts. There is a glaring discrepancy between the arrangements of essence perception and its *terminus ad quem*. Neither attempt to break out of idealism was successful: Bergson's bearings, like those of his positivistic arch-enemies, came from the *données immédiates de la conscience;* Husserl's came in similar fashion from phenomena of the stream of consciousness. Both men stay within range of immanent subjectivity.[5] To be insisted upon, against both, would be the goal they pursue in vain: to counter Wittgenstein by uttering the unutterable.

The plain contradictoriness of this challenge is that of philosophy itself, which is thereby qualified as dialectics before getting entangled in its individual contradictions. The work of philosophical self-reflection consists in unraveling that paradox. Everything else is signification, secondhand construction, pre-philosophical activity, today as in Hegel's time. Though doubtful as ever, a confidence that philosophy can make it after all—that the concept can transcend the concept, the preparatory and concluding element, and can thus reach the nonconceptual—is one of philosophy's inalienable features and part of the naïveté that ails it. Otherwise it must capitulate, and the human mind with it. We could not conceive the simplest operation; there would be no truth; emphatically, everything would be just nothing. But whatever truth the concepts cover beyond their abstract range can have no other stage than what the concepts suppress, disparage, and discard. The cognitive utopia would be to use concepts to unseal the non-conceptual with concepts, without making it their equal.

THE ANTAGONISTIC ENTIRETY

Such a concept of dialectics makes us doubt its possibility. However varied, the anticipation of moving in contradictions throughout seems to teach a mental totality—the very identity thesis we have just rendered inoperative. The mind which ceaselessly reflects on contradiction in the thing itself, we hear, must be the thing itself if it is to be organized in the form of contradiction; the truth which in idealistic dialectics drives beyond every particular, as onesided and wrong, is the truth of the whole, and if that were not preconceived, the dialectical steps would lack motivation and direction. We have to answer that the object of a mental experience is an antagonistic system in itself—antagonistic in reality, not just in its conveyance to the knowing subject that rediscovers itself therein. The coercive state of reality, which idealism had projected into the region of the subject and the mind, must be retranslated from that region. What remains of idealism is that society, the objective determinant of the mind, is as much an epitome of subjects as it is their negation. In society the subjects are unknowable and incapacitated; hence its desperate objectivity and conceptuality, which idealism mistakes for something positive.

The system is not one of the absolute spirit; it is one of the most conditioned spirit of those who have it and cannot even know how much it is their own. The subjective preconception of the material production process in society—basically different from its theoretical constitution—is the unresolved part, the part unreconciled with the subjects. Their own reason, unconscious like the transcendental subject and establishing identity by barter, remains incommensurable with the subjects it reduces to the same denominator: the subject as the subject's foe. The preceding generality is both true and untrue: true, because it forms that "ether" which Hegel calls spirit; untrue, because its reason is no reason yet, because its universality is the product of particular interests. This is why a philosophical critique of identity transcends philosophy. But the ineffable part of the utopia is that what defies subsumption under identity—the "use value," in Marxist terminology—is necessary anyway if life is to go on at all, even under the prevailing circumstances of production. The utopia extends to the sworn enemies of its realization. Regarding the concrete utopian possibility, dialectics is the ontology of the wrong state of things. The right state of things would be free of it: neither a system nor a contradiction.

DISENCHANTMENT OF THE CONCEPT

Philosophy, Hegel's included, invites the general objection that by inevitably having concepts for its material it anticipates an idealistic decision. In fact no philosophy, not even extreme empiricism, can drag in the *facta bruta* and present them like cases in anatomy or experiments in physics; no philosophy can paste the particulars into the text, as seductive paintings would hoodwink it into believing. But the argument in its formality and generality takes as fetishistic a view of the concept as the concept does in interpreting itself naïvely in its own domain: in either case it is regarded as a self-sufficient totality over which philosophical thought has no power. In truth, all concepts, even the philosophical ones, refer to nonconceptualities, because concepts on their part are moments of the reality that requires their formation, primarily for the control of nature. What conceptualization appears to be from within, to one engaged in it—the predominance of its sphere, without which nothing is known—must not be mistaken for what it is in itself. Such a semblance of being-in-itself is conferred upon it by the motion that exempts it from reality, to which it is harnessed in turn.

Necessity compels philosophy to operate with concepts, but this necessity must not be turned into the virtue of their priority—no more than, conversely, criticism of that virtue can be turned into a summary verdict against philosophy. On the other hand, the insight that philosophy's conceptual knowledge is not the absolute of philosophy—this insight, for all its inescapability, is again due to the nature of the concept. It is not a dogmatic thesis, much less a naïvely realistic one. Initially, such concepts as that of "being" at the start of Hegel's *Logic* emphatically mean nonconceptualities; as Lask put it, they "mean beyond themselves." Dissatisfaction with their own conceptuality is part of their meaning, although the inclusion of nonconceptuality in their meaning makes it tendentially their equal and thus keeps them trapped within themselves. The substance of concepts is to them both immanent, as far as the mind is concerned, and transcendent as far as being is concerned. To be aware of this is to be able to get rid of concept fetishism. Philosophical reflection makes sure of the nonconceptual in the concept. It would be empty otherwise, according to Kant's dictum; in the end, having ceased to be a concept of anything at all, it would be nothing.

A philosophy that lets us know this, that extinguishes the autarky of the concept, strips the blindfold from our eyes. That the concept is a concept even when dealing with things in being does not change the fact that on its part it is entwined with a nonconceptual whole. Its only insulation from that whole is its reification—that which establishes it as a concept. The concept is an element in dialectical logic, like any other. What survives in it is the fact that nonconceptuality has conveyed it by way of its meaning, which in turn establishes its conceptuality. To refer to nonconceptualities—as ultimately, according to traditional epistemology, every definition of concepts requires nonconceptual, deictic elements—is characteristic of the concept, and so is the contrary: that as the abstract unit of the noumena subsumed thereunder it will depart from the noumenal. To change this direction of conceptuality, to give it a turn toward nonidentity, is the hinge of negative dialectics. Insight into the constitutive character of the nonconceptual in the concept would end the compulsive identification which the concept brings unless halted by such reflection. Reflection upon its own meaning is the way out of the concept's seeming being-in-itself as a unit of meaning.

"INFINITY"

Disenchantment of the concept is the antidote of philosophy. It keeps it from growing rampant and becoming an absolute to itself. An idea bequeathed to us by idealism—and corrupted by it, more than any other—needs a change in its function: the idea of the infinite. It is not up to philosophy to exhaust things according to scientific usage, to reduce the phenomena to a minimum of propositions; there are hints of that in Hegel's polemic against Fichte, whom he accused of starting out with a "dictum." Instead, in philosophy we literally seek to immerse ourselves in things that are heterogeneous to it, without placing those things in prefabricated categories. We want to adhere as closely to the heterogeneous as the programs of phenomenology and of Simmel tried in vain to do; our aim is total self-relinquishment. Philosophical contents can only be grasped where philosophy does not impose them. The illusion that it might confine the essence in its finite definitions will have to be given up.

The fatal ease with which the word "infinite" rolled off the idealistic philosophers' tongues may have been due only to a wish to allay gnawing doubts about the meager finiteness of their conceptual machinery—including Hegel's, his intentions notwithstanding. Traditional philosophy thinks of itself as possessing an infinite object, and in that belief it becomes a finite, conclusive philosophy. A changed philosophy would have to cancel that claim, to cease persuading others and itself that it has the infinite at its disposal. Instead, if it were delicately understood, the changed philosophy itself would be infinite in the sense of scorning solidification in a body of enumerable theorems. Its substance would lie in the diversity of objects that impinge upon it and of the objects it seeks, a diversity not wrought by any schema; to those objects, philosophy would truly give itself rather than use them as a mirror in which to reread itself, mistaking its own image for concretion. It would be nothing but full, unreduced experience in the medium of conceptual reflection, whereas even the "science of empirical consciousness" reduced the contents of such experience to cases of categories. What makes philosophy risk the strain of its own infinity is the unwarranted expectation that each individual and particular puzzle it solves will be like Leibniz's monad, the ever-elusive entirety in itself—although, of course, in line with a pre-established disharmony rather than a pre-established harmony. The metacritical turn against the *prima philosophia* is at the same time a turn against the finiteness of a philosophy that prates about infinity without respecting it.

No object is wholly known; knowledge is not supposed to prepare the phantasm of a whole. Thus the goal of a philosophical interpretation of works of art cannot be their identification with the concept, their absorption in the concept; yet it is through such interpretation that the truth of the work unfolds. What can be envisioned, however—whether as the regularly continued abstraction or as an application of the concepts to whatever comes under their definition—may be useful as technology in the broadest sense of the word; but to philosophy, which refuses to fit in, it is irrelevant. In principle, philosophy can always go astray, which is the sole reason why it can go forward. This has been recognized in skepticism and in pragmatism, most recently in Dewey's wholly humane version of the latter; but we ought to add it as a ferment to an emphatic philosophy instead of renouncing philosophy, from the outset, in favor of the test it has to stand.

As a corrective to the total rule of method, philosophy contains a playful element which the traditional view of it as a science would like to exorcise. For Hegel, too, this was a sensitive point; he rejects "types and distinctions determined by external chance and by play, not by reason."[6] The un-naïve thinker knows how far he remains from the object of his thinking, and yet he must always talk as if he had it entirely. This brings him to the point of clowning. He must not deny his clownish traits, least of all since they alone can give him hope for what is denied him. Philosophy is the most serious of things, but then again it is not all that serious. A thing that aims at what it is not a priori and is not authorized to control—such a thing, according to its own concept, is simultaneously part of a sphere beyond control, a sphere tabooed by conceptuality. To represent the mimesis it supplanted, the concept has no other way than to adopt something mimetic in its own conduct, without abandoning itself.

The esthetic moment is thus not accidental to philosophy, though on grounds quite different from Schelling's; but it is no less incumbent upon philosophy to void its estheticism, to sublimate the esthetic into the real, by cogent insights. Cogency and play are the two poles of philosophy. Its affinity to art does not entitle it to borrow from art, least of all by virtue of the intuitions which barbarians take for the prerogatives of art. Intuitions hardly ever strike in isolation, as lightning from above; they do not strike the artist's work like that either. They hang together with the formal law of the work; if one tried to extract and preserve them, they would dissolve. Finally, thought is no protector of springs whose freshness might deliver us from thinking. We have no type of cognition at our disposal that differs absolutely from the disposing type, the type which intuitionism flees in panic and in vain.

A philosophy that tried to imitate art, that would turn itself into a work of art, would be expunging itself. It would be postulating the demand for identity, claiming to exhaust its object by endowing its procedure with a supremacy to which the heterogeneous bows a priori, as material—whereas to genuine philosophy its relation to the heterogeneous is virtually thematic. Common to art and philosophy is not the form, not the forming process, but a mode of conduct that forbids pseudomorphosis. Both keep faith with their own substance through their opposites: art by making itself resistant to its meanings; philosophy, by refusing to clutch at any immediate thing. What the philosophical concept will not abandon is the yearning that animates the nonconceptual side of art, and whose fulfillment shuns the immediate side of art as mere appearance. The concept—the organon of thinking, and yet the wall between thinking and the thought—negates that yearning. Philosophy can neither circumvent such negation nor submit to it. It must strive, by way of the concept, to transcend the concept.

THE SPECULATIVE MOMENT

Even after breaking with idealism, philosophy cannot do without speculation, which was exalted by idealism and tabooed with it—meaning speculation, of course, in a sense broader than the overly

15

positive Hegelian one.* For positivists it is not difficult to attribute speculation to Marxian materialism, which starts out from laws of objective being, by no means from immediate data or protocol statements. To cleanse himself of the suspicion of ideology, it is now safer for a man to call Marx a metaphysician than to call him a class enemy.

But the safe ground is a phantasm where the claims of truth demand that one rise above it. Philosophy is not to be put off with theorems that would talk it out of its essential concern instead of satisfying that concern, albeit with a No. In the counter-movements to Kant, from the nineteenth century on, this was sensed but always compromised again by obscurantism. The resistance of philosophy needs to unfold, however. Even in music—as in all art, presumably—the impulse animating the first bar will not be fulfilled at once, but only in further articulation. To this extent, however much it may be phenomenal as a totality, music is a critique of phenomenality, of the appearance that the substance is present here and now. Such a mediate role befits philosophy no less. When it presumes to say things forthwith it invites Hegel's verdict on empty profundity. Mouthing profundities will no more make a man profound than narrating the metaphysical views of its characters will make a novel metaphysical.

To ask philosophy to deal with the question of being, or with other cardinal themes of Western metaphysics, shows a primitive

---

* "Moreover, if skepticism even nowadays is frequently considered an irresistible enemy of all positive knowledge, and thus of philosophy insofar as it is a matter of positive cognition, we have to counter by saying that it is indeed only finite, abstractly intellectual thought that need fear skepticism and cannot withstand it, while philosophy contains the skeptical as one of its own elements, namely, as dialectics. But then philosophy will not halt at the merely negative result of dialectics, as is the case in skepticism. Skepticism misconceives its result, holding on to pure (i.e., abstract) negation. As dialectics has the negative for its result, this negative, being a result, is simultaneously positive, since it contains sublimated within itself that from which it results and without which it is not. This is the basic definition of the third form of logic, namely, of speculation or positive reason." (Hegel, Works 8, p. 194ff.)

topical faith. The objective worth of those themes is indeed inescapable in philosophy, but neither can we rely on our ability to cope with the great topics. We must be so wary of the beaten tracks of philosophical reflection that our emphatic interest will seek refuge in ephemeral objects not yet overdetermined by intentions. Though chained to the questions of traditional philosophical problematics, we certainly must negate that problematics. A world that is objectively set for totality will not release the human consciousness, will ceaselessly fasten it to points it wants to get away from; but a thinking that blithely begins afresh, heedless of the historic form of its problems, will so much more be their prey.

That philosophy shares in the idea of depth is due to its cogitative breath alone. A prime example from the modern age is the Kantian deduction of pure intellectual concepts, which the author, with abysmally apologetic irony, called "somewhat profoundly arranged."[7] Profundity, as Hegel did not fail to note, is another element of dialectics, not an isolated trait. A dreadful German tradition equates profound thoughts with thoughts ready to swear by the theodicy of death and evil. A theological *terminus ad quem* is tacitly passed over and passed under, as if the worth of a thought were decided by its result, the confirmation of transcendence, or by its immersion in inwardness, its sheer being-for-itself; as if withdrawal from the world were flatly tantamount to consciousness of the world ground. As for the phantasms of profundity—which in the history of the human spirit have always been well-disposed toward an existing state of affairs they find insipid—resistance would be their true measure.

The power of the status quo puts up the façades into which our consciousness crashes. It must seek to crash through them. This alone would free the postulate of depth from ideology. Surviving in such resistance is the speculative moment: what will not have its law prescribed for it by given facts transcends them even in the closest contact with the objects, and in repudiating a sacrosanct transcendence. Where the thought transcends the bonds it tied in resistance—there is its freedom. Freedom follows the subject's urge to express itself. The need to lend a voice to suffering is a condition of all truth. For suffering is objectivity that weighs upon the subject; its most subjective experience, its expression, is objectively conveyed.

PRESENTATION

This may help to explain why the presentation of philosophy is not an external matter of indifference to it but immanent to its idea. Its integral, nonconceptually mimetic moment of expression is objectified only by presentation in language. The freedom of philosophy is nothing but the capacity to lend a voice to its unfreedom. If more is claimed for the expressive moment, it will degenerate into a weltanschauung; where the expressive moment and the duty of presentation are given up, philosophy comes to resemble science.

To philosophy, expression and stringency are not two dichotomous possibilities. They need each other; neither one can be without the other. Expression is relieved of its accidental character by thought, on which it toils as thought toils on expression. Only an expressed thought is succinct, rendered succinct by its presentation in language; what is vaguely put is poorly thought. Expression compels stringency in what it expresses. It is not an end in itself at the latter's expense; rather, expression removes the expressed from the materialized mischief which in its turn is an object of philosophical criticism. Speculative philosophy without an idealistic substructure requires observance of stringency to break the authoritarian power claim of stringency. Benjamin, whose original draft of his passage theory combined incomparable speculative skill with micrological proximity to factual contents, later remarked in a correspondence about the first properly metaphysical stratum of this work that it could be accomplished only as an "impermissible 'poetic' one."[8] This admission of surrender denotes as much the difficulty of a philosophy loath to decline as the point at which its concept can be carried further. It was probably due to Benjamin's acceptance of dialectical materialism as a weltanschauung, so to speak, with closed eyes. But the fact that he could not bring himself to put the definitive version of the passage theory in writing reminds us that philosophy is more than bustle only where it runs the risk of total failure—this in reply to the absolute certainty that has traditionally been obtained by stealth. Benjamin's defeatism about his own thought was conditioned by the undialectical positivity of which he carried a formally unchanged remnant from his theological phase into his materialistic phase. By comparison, Hegel's equating negativity with the thought that keeps philosophy from both the positivity of science and the contingency of dilettantism has empirical substance.

Thought as such, before all particular contents, is an act of negation, of resistance to that which is forced upon it; this is what thought has inherited from its archetype, the relation between labor and material. Today, when ideologues tend more than ever to encourage thought to be positive, they cleverly note that positivity runs precisely counter to thought and that it takes friendly persuasion by social authority to accustom thought to positivity. The effort implied in the concept of thought itself, as the counterpart of passive contemplation, is negative already—a revolt against being importuned to bow to every immediate thing. Critical germs are contained in judgment and inference, the thought forms without which not even the critique of thought can do: they are never definite without simultaneously excluding what they have failed to achieve, and whatever does not bear their stamp will be denied—although with questionable authority—by the truth they seek to organize. The judgment that a thing is such and such is a potential rebuttal to claims of any relation of its subject and predicate other than the one expressed in the judgment. Thought forms tend beyond that which merely exists, is merely "given." The point which thinking aims at its material is not solely a spiritualized control of nature. While doing violence to the object of its syntheses, our thinking heeds a potential that waits in the object, and it unconsciously obeys the idea of making amends to the pieces for what it has done. In philosophy, this unconscious tendency becomes conscious. Accompanying irreconcilable thoughts is the hope for reconcilement, because the resistance of thought to mere things in being, the commanding freedom of the subject, intends in the object even that of which the object was deprived by objectification.

ATTITUDE TOWARD SYSTEMS

Traditional speculation has developed the synthesis of diversity
—which it conceived as chaotic, on Kantian grounds—and its
ultimate aim was to divest itself of any kind of content. By contrast, the *telos* of philosophy, its open and unshielded part, is
as anti-systematic as its freedom to interpret the phenomena with
which it joins unarmed issue. Philosophy retains respect for systems to the extent to which things heterogeneous to it face it in the
form of a system. The administered world moves in this direction.
It is the negative objectivity that is a system, not the positive subject. In a historical phase in which systems—insofar as they deal
seriously with contents—have been relegated to the ominous realm
of conceptual poetry and nothing but the pale outline of their
schematic order has been retained, it is difficult to imagine vividly
what used to attract a philosophical spirit to the system.

When we contemplate philosophical history, the virtue of partisanship must not keep us from perceiving how superior the system,
whether rationalistic or idealistic, has been to its opponents for
more than two centuries. Compared with the systems, the opposition seems trivial. Systems elaborate things; they interpret the
world while the others really keep protesting only that it can't
be done. The others display resignation, denial, failure—if they
had more truth in the end, it would indicate the transience of
philosophy. In any case, it would be up to philosophy to elevate
such truth from its subaltern state and to champion it against the
philosophies which not only boast of their "higher" rank: materialism in particular shows to this day that it was spawned in
Abdera. According to Nietzsche's critique, systems no longer
documented anything but the finickiness of scholars compensating
themselves for political impotence by conceptually construing
their, so to speak, administrative authority over things in being.
But the systematic need, the need not to put up with the *membra
disiecta* of knowledge but to achieve the absolute knowledge that
is already, involuntarily, claimed in each succinct individual
judgment—this need was more, at times, than a pseudomorphosis

of the spirit into the irresistibly successful method of mathematical and natural science.

In the philosophy of history, the systems of the seventeenth century especially served a compensatory purpose. The *ratio* which in accordance with bourgeois class interests had smashed the feudal order and scholastic ontology, the form of the intellectual reflection of that order—this same *ratio* no sooner faced the ruins, its own handiwork, than it would be struck by fear of chaos. It trembled before the menace that continued underneath its own domain, waxing stronger in proportion to its own power. This fear shaped the beginnings of a mode of conduct constitutive for bourgeois existence as a whole: of the neutralization, by confirming the existent order, of every emancipatory step. In the shadow of its own incomplete emancipation the bourgeois consciousness must fear to be annulled by a more advanced consciousness; not being the whole freedom, it senses that it can produce only a caricature of freedom—hence its theoretical expansion of its autonomy into a system similar to its own coercive mechanisms.

Out of itself, the bourgeois *ratio* undertook to produce the order it had negated outside itself. Once produced, however, that order ceased to be an order and was therefore insatiable. Every system was such an order, such an absurdly rational product: a posited thing posing as being-in-itself. Its origin had to be placed into formal thought divorced from content; nothing else would let it control the material. The philosophical systems were antinomical from the outset. Their rudiments entwined with their own impossibility; it was precisely in the early history of the modern systems that each was condemned to annihilation at the hands of the next. To prevail as a system, the *ratio* eliminated virtually all qualitative definitions it referred to, thus coming into an irreconcilable conflict with the objectivity it violated by pretending to grasp it. The *ratio* came to be removed from objectivity—the farther removed, the more completely objectivity was subjected to its axioms, and finally to the one axiom of identity. The pedantries of all systems, down to the architectonic complexities of Kant—and even of Hegel, despite the latter's program—are the marks of

21

an a priori inescapable failure, noted with incomparable honesty in the fractures of the Kantian system; Molière was the first to show pedantry as a main feature of the ontology of the bourgeois spirit.

Whenever something that is to be conceived flees from identity with the concept, the concept will be forced to take exaggerated steps to prevent any doubts of the unassailable validity, solidity, and acribia of the thought product from stirring. Great philosophy was accompanied by a paranoid zeal to tolerate nothing else, and to pursue everything else with all the cunning of reason, while the other kept retreating farther and farther from the pursuit. The slightest remnant of nonidentity sufficed to deny an identity conceived as total. The excrescences of the systems, ever since the Cartesian pineal gland and the axioms and definitions of Spinoza, already crammed with the entire rationalism he would then deductively extract—by their untruth, these excrescences show the untruth, the mania, of the systems themselves.

IDEALISM AS RAGE

The system in which the sovereign mind imagined itself transfigured, has its primal history in the pre-mental, the animal life of the species. Predators get hungry, but pouncing on their prey is difficult and often dangerous; additional impulses may be needed for the beast to dare it. These impulses and the unpleasantness of hunger fuse into rage at the victim, a rage whose expression in turn serves the end of frightening and paralyzing the victim. In the advance to humanity this is rationalized by projection. The "rational animal" with an appetite for his opponent is already fortunate enough to have a superego and must find a reason. The more completely his actions follow the law of self-preservation, the less can he admit the primacy of that law to himself and to others; if he did, his laboriously attained status of a *zoon politikon* would lose all credibility.

The animal to be devoured must be evil. The sublimation of this anthropological schema extends all the way to epistemology. Idealism—most explicitly Fichte—gives unconscious sway to the ideology that the not-I, *l'autrui,* and finally all that reminds us of nature is inferior, so the unity of the self-preserving thought may devour it without misgivings. This justifies the principle of the thought as much as it increases the appetite. The system is the belly turned mind, and rage is the mark of each and every idealism. It disfigures even Kant's humanism and refutes the aura of higher and nobler things in which he knew how to garb it. The view of man in the middle is akin to misanthropy: leave nothing unchallenged. The august inexorability of the moral law was this kind of rationalized rage at nonidentity; nor did the liberalistic Hegel do better with the superiority of his bad conscience, dressing down those who refused homage to the speculative concept, the hypostasis of the mind.* Nietzsche's liberating act, a true turning point of Western thought and merely usurped by others later, was to put such mysteries into words. A mind that discards rationalization—its own spell—ceases by its self-reflection to be the radical evil that irks it in another.

Yet the process in which the systems decomposed, due to their own insufficiency, stands in counterpoint to a social process. In the form of the barter principle, the bourgeois *ratio* really approximated to the systems whatever it would make commensurable with itself, would identify with itself—and it did so with increasing, if potentially homicidal, success. Less and less was left outside. What proved idle in theory was ironically borne out in practice. Hence the ideological popularity of talk about a "crisis of the system" among all the types who earlier could not spout enough stentorian rancor at the "aperçu," according to the system's own, already obsolete ideal. Reality is no longer to be construed, because it would be all too thoroughly construable. Pretexts are furnished by its irrationality, intensifying under the

---

* "The thought or conception which has before it only a definite being, existence, is to be relegated to the aforementioned beginning of science that was made by Parmenides, who purified and exalted his conceiving—and thus the conceiving of subsequent times as well— into the pure thought of being as such, and thus created the element of science." (Hegel, Works 4, p. 96.)

pressure of particular rationality: there is disintegration by way of integration. If society could be seen through as a closed system, a system accordingly unreconciled to the subjects, it would become too embarrassing for the subjects as long as they remain subjects in any sense.

Angst, that supposed "existential," is the claustrophobia of a systematized society. Its system character, yesterday still a shibboleth of academic philosophy, is strenuously denied by initiates of that philosophy; they may, with impunity, pose as spokesmen for free, for original, indeed, for unacademic thinking. Criticism of the systems is not vitiated by such abuse. A proposition common to all emphatic philosophy—as opposed to the skeptical one, which refrained from emphasis—was that only as a system could philosophy be pursued; this proposition has done hardly less to cripple philosophy than have the empiricisms. The things philosophy has yet to judge are postulated before it begins. The system, the form of presenting a totality to which nothing remains extraneous, absolutizes the thought against each of its contents and evaporates the content in thoughts. It proceeds idealistically before advancing any arguments for idealism.

THE TWOFOLD CHARACTER OF THE SYSTEM

In criticism we do not simply liquidate systems, however. At the peak of the Enlightenment, d'Alembert rightly distinguished between *l'esprit de système* and *l'esprit systématique,* and the method of the Encyclopédie took account of the distinction. Speaking for the *esprit systématique* is not only the trivial motive of a cohesion that will tend to crystallize in the incoherent anyway; it does not only satisfy the bureaucrats' desire to stuff all things into their categories. The form of the system is adequate to the world, whose substance eludes the hegemony of the human thought; but unity and unanimity are at the same time an oblique projection of pacified, no longer antagonistic conditions upon the coordinates of supremacist, oppressive thinking. The double meaning of philosophical systematics leaves no choice but to transpose the power of thought, once delivered from the systems, into the open realm of definition by individual moments.

To Hegelian logic this procedure was not altogether alien. The microanalysis of individual categories, which simultaneously appears as their objective self-reflection, was to let each concept pass into its otherness without regard to an overlay from above; to Hegel, the totality of this movement meant the system. There is contradiction as well as kinship between this concept of the system—a concept that concludes, and thus brings to a standstill —and the concept of dynamism, of pure, autarkic, subjective generation, which constitutes all philosophical systematics. Hegel could adjust the tension between statics and dynamics only by construing his unitarian principle, the spirit, as a simultaneous being-in-itself and pure becoming, a resumption of the Aristotelian-scholastic *actus purus;* and that the implausibility of this construction—in which subjective generation and ontology, nominalism and realism, are syncopated at the Archimedean point— will prevent the resolution of that tension is also immanent in the system.

And yet, such a concept of the philosophical system towers above a merely scientific systematics that call for orderly organization and presentation of thoughts, for a consistent structure of topical disciplines, without insisting strictly, from the object's point of view, upon the inner unity of its aspects. The postulate of this unity is bound up with the presupposition that all things in being are identical with the cognitive principle; but on the other hand, once burdened as it is in idealistic speculation, that postulate legitimately recalls the affinity which objects have for each other, and which is tabooed by the scientific need for order and obliged to yield to the surrogate of its schemata. What the objects communicate in—instead of each being the atom it becomes in the logic of classification—is the trace of the objects' definition in themselves, which Kant denied and Hegel, against Kant, sought to restore through the subject.

To comprehend a thing itself, not just to fit and register it in its system of reference, is nothing but to perceive the individual moment in its immanent connection with others. Such anti-subjectivism lies under the crackling shell of absolute idealism; it

25

stirs in the tendency to unseal current issues by resorting to the way they came to be. What the conception of the system recalls, in reverse, is the coherence of the nonidentical, the very thing infringed by deductive systematics. Criticism of systems and asystematic thought are superficial as long as they cannot release the cohesive force which the idealistic systems had signed over to the transcendental subject.

THE ANTINOMICAL CHARACTER OF SYSTEMS

The ego principle that founds the system, the pure method before any content, has always been the *ratio*. It is not confined by anything outside it, not even by a so-called mental order. Idealism, attesting the positive infinity of its principle at every one of its stages, turns the character of thought, the historic evolution of its independence, into metaphysics. It eliminates all heterogeneous being. This defines the system as pure becoming, a pure process, and eventually as that absolute engendering which Fichte—in this respect the authentic systematizer of philosophy—declared thinking to be. Kant had already held that the emancipated *ratio,* the *progressus ad infinitum,* is halted solely by recognizing nonidentities in form, at least. The antinomy of totality and infinity—for the restless *ad infinitum* explodes the self-contained system, for all its being owed to infinity alone—is of the essence of idealism.

It imitates a central antinomy of bourgeois society. To preserve itself, to remain the same, to "be," that society too must constantly expand, progress, advance its frontiers, not respect any limit, not remain the same.[9] It has been demonstrated to bourgeois society that it would no sooner reach a ceiling, would no sooner cease to have noncapitalist areas available outside itself, than its own concept would force its self-liquidation. This makes clear why, Aristotle notwithstanding, the modern concept of dynamics was inappropriate to Antiquity, as was the concept of the system. To Plato, who chose the aporetical form for so many of his dialogues, both concepts could be imputed only in retrospect. The reprimand which Kant gave the old man for that reason is not, as he put it, a matter of plain logic; it is historical, modern through and through. On the other hand, systematics is so deeply ingrained in the modern consciousness that even Husserl's anti-systematic efforts—which began under the name of ontology, and from which "fundamental ontology" branched off later—reverted irresistibly to a system, at the price of formalization.

Thus intertwined, the system's static and dynamic characters keep clashing. No matter how dynamically a system may be conceived, if it is in fact to be a closed system, to tolerate nothing outside its domain, it will become a positive infinity—in other words, finite and static. The fact that it sustains itself in this manner, for which Hegel praised his own system, brings it to a standstill. Bluntly put, closed systems are bound to be finished. Eccentricities like the one constantly held up to Hegel—of world history being perfected in the Prussian state—are not mere aberrations for ideological purposes, nor are they irrelevant vis-à-vis the whole. Their necessary absurdity shatters the asserted unity of system and dynamics. By negating the concept of the limit and theoretically assuring itself that there always remains something outside, dynamics also tends to disavow its own product, the system.

An aspect under which it might well be fruitful to treat the history of modern philosophy is how it managed to cope with the antagonism of statics and dynamics in its systems. The Hegelian system in itself was not a true becoming; implicitly, each single definition in it was already preconceived. Such safeguards condemn it to untruth. Unconsciously, so to speak, consciousness would have to immerse itself in the phenomena on which it takes a stand. This would, of course, effect a qualitative change in dialectics. Systematic unanimity would crumble. The phenomenon would not remain a case of its concept, as it does to Hegel, despite all pronouncements to the contrary. The thought would be burdened with more toil and trouble than Hegel defines as such, because the thought he discusses always extracts from its objects only that which is a thought already. Despite the program of self-yielding, the Hegelian thought finds satisfaction in itself; it goes rolling along, however often it may urge the contrary. If the thought really yielded to the object, if its attention were on the object, not on its category, the very objects would start talking under the lingering eye.

Hegel had argued against epistemology that one becomes a smith only by smithing, by the actual cognition of things that resist cognition—of things which are, so to speak, atheoretical. There we have to take him at his word; nothing else would return to philosophy what Hegel calls the "freedom to the object"— what philosophy had lost under the spell of the concept "freedom," of the subject's sense-determining autonomy. But the speculative power to break down the gates of the insoluble is the power of negation. The systematic trend lives on in negation alone. The categories of a critique of systems are at the same time the categories in which the particular is understood. What has once legitimately transcended particularity in the system has its place outside the system. The interpretive eye which sees more in a phenomenon than it is—and solely because of what it is— secularizes metaphysics. Only a philosophy in fragment form would give their proper place to the monads, those illusory idealistic drafts. They would be conceptions, in the particular, of the totality that is inconceivable as such.

ARGUMENT AND EXPERIENCE

The thought, to which a positive hypostasis of anything outside actual dialectics is forbidden, overshoots the object with which it no longer simulates being as one. It grows more independent than in the conception of its absoluteness, in which sovereignty and complaisance mingle, each inwardly depending on the other. This may have been the end to which Kant exempted the intelligible sphere from all immanence. An aspect of immersion in particularity, that extreme enhancement of dialectical immanence, must also be the freedom to step out of the object, a freedom which the identity claim cuts short. Hegel would have censured that freedom; he relied upon complete mediation by the objects. In cognitive practice, when we resolve the insoluble, a moment of such cogitative transcendence comes to light in the fact that for our micrological activity we have exclusively macrological means.

The call for binding statements without a system is a call for thought models, and these are not merely monadological in kind. A model covers the specific, and more than the specific, without letting it evaporate in its more general super-concept. Philosophical thinking is the same as thinking in models; negative dialectics is an ensemble of analyses of models. Philosophy would be debasing itself all over again, into a kind of affirmative solace, if it were to fool itself and others about the fact that it must, from without, imbue its objects with whatever moves them within it. What is waiting in the objects themselves needs such intervention to come to speak, with the perspective that the forces mobilized outside, and ultimately every theory that is brought to bear on the phenomena, should come to rest in the phenomena. In that sense, too, philosophical theory means that its own end lies in its realization.

There is no lack of related intentions in history. The French Enlightenment got a formally systematic touch from its supreme concept, that of reason; yet the constitutive entanglement of its idea of reason with that of an objectively rational arrangement of society deprived the idea of a pathos which it was not to recover until the realization of reason as an idea was renounced, until it was absolutized into the spirit. Encyclopedic thinking—rationally organized and yet discontinuous, unsystematic, loose—expressed the self-critical spirit of reason. That spirit represented something which later departed from philosophy, due as much to its increasing distance from practical life as to its absorption in the academic bustle: it represented mundane experience, that eye for reality of which thought, too, is a part.

The free spirit is nothing else. The element of the *homme de lettres,* disparaged by a petty bourgeois scientific ethos, is indispensable to thought; and no less indispensable, of course, is the element abused by a philosophy garbed as science: the meditative contraction—the argument, which came to merit so much skepticism. Whenever philosophy was substantial, both elements would coincide. At a distance, dialectics might be characterized as the elevation to self-consciousness of the effort to be saturated with dialectics. Otherwise the argument deteriorates into the technique of conceptless specialists amid the concept, as it is now spreading academically in the so-called "analytical philosophy," which robots can learn and copy.

The immanently argumentative element is legitimate where the reality that has been integrated in a system is received in order to oppose it with its own strength. The free part of thought, on the other hand, represents the authority which already knows about the emphatic untruth of that real-systematic context. Without this knowledge there would be no eruption; without adopting the power of the system, the outbreak would fail. That the two elements will not merge without a rift is due to the real power of the system, which includes even what potentially excels it. The untruth of the immanent context itself, however, shows in the overwhelming experience that the world—though organized as systematically as if it were Hegel's glorified realization of reason —will at the same time, in its old unreason, perpetuate the impotence of the seemingly almighty spirit. The immanent critic of idealism defends idealism by showing how much it is defrauded of its own self—how much the first cause, which according to idealism is always the spirit, is in league with the blind predominance of merely existing things. The doctrine of the absolute spirit immediately aids that predominance.

A scientific consensus tends to admit that experience also implies theory. It holds, however, that experience is a "standpoint," hypothetically at best. Conciliatory representatives of scientivism demand that what they call "decent" or "clean" science should account for premises of the sort. Precisely this demand is incompatible with the mind's experience. Any standpoint it were asked to have would be that of the diner regarding the roast. Experience lives by consuming the standpoint; not until the standpoint is submerged in it would there be philosophy. Until then, theory in mental experience embodies that discipline which already pained Goethe in relation to Kant. If experience were to trust solely to its dynamics and good fortune, there would be no stopping.

Ideology lies in wait for the mind which delights in itself like Nietzsche's Zarathustra, for the mind which all but irresistibly becomes an absolute to itself. Theory prevents this. It corrects the naïve self-confidence of the mind without obliging it to sacrifice its spontaneity, at which theory aims in its turn. For the difference between the so-called subjective part of mental experience and its object will not vanish by any means, as witness the necessary and painful exertions of the knowing subject. In the unreconciled condition, nonidentity is experienced as negativity. From the negative, the subject withdraws to itself, and to the abundance of its ways to react. Critical self-reflection alone will keep it from a constriction of this abundance, from building walls between itself and the object, from the supposition that its being-for-itself is an in-and-for-itself. The less identity can be assumed between subject and object, the more contradictory are the demands made upon the cognitive subject, upon its unfettered strength and candid self-reflection.

Theory and mental experience need to interact. Theory does not contain answers to everything; it reacts to the world, which is faulty to the core. What would be free from the spell of the world is not under theory's jurisdiction. Mobility is of the essence of consciousness; it is no accidental feature. It means a doubled mode of conduct: an inner one, the immanent process which is the properly dialectical one, and a free, unbound one like a stepping out of dialectics. Yet the two are not merely disparate. The unregimented thought has an elective affinity to dialectics, which as criticism of the system recalls what would be outside the system; and the force that liberates the dialectical movement in cognition is the very same that rebels against the system. Both attitudes of consciousness are linked by criticizing one another, not by compromising.

VERTIGINOUSNESS

A dialectics no longer "glued"[10] to identity will provoke either the charge that it is bottomless—one that ye shall know by its fascist fruits—or the objection that it is dizzying. In great modern poetry, vertigo has been a central feeling since Baudelaire; the anachronistic suggestion often made to philosophy is that it must

31

have no part in any such thing. Philosophy is cautioned to speak to the point; Karl Kraus had to learn that no matter how precisely each line of his expressed his meaning, a materialized consciousness would lament that this very precision was making its head swim. A usage of current opinion makes such complaints comprehensible. We like to present alternatives to choose from, to be marked True or False. The decisions of a bureaucracy are frequently reduced to Yes or No answers to drafts submitted to it; the bureaucratic way of thinking has become the secret model for a thought allegedly still free.

But the responsibility of philosophical thought in its essential situations is not to play this game. A given alternative is already a piece of heteronomy. The legitimacy of alternative demands has yet to be judged by the very consciousness that is moralistically asked to make its decision beforehand. To insist on the profession of a standpoint is to extend the coercion of conscience to the realm of theory. With this coercion goes a coarsening process in which not even the great theorems retain their truth content after the adjuncts have been eliminated. Marx and Engels, for instance, objected to having their dynamic class theory and its knife-edged economic expression diluted by substituting the simpler antithesis of rich and poor. The essence is falsified by a résumé of essentials. If philosophy were to stoop to a practice which Hegel already mocked, if it were to accommodate its kind reader by explaining what the thought should make him think, it would be joining the march of regression without being able to keep up the pace.

Behind the worry where to take hold of philosophy lies mostly pure aggression, a desire to take hold of it the way the historical schools used to devour each other. The equivalence of guilt and penance has been transposed to the sequence of thoughts. It is this very assimilation of the spirit to the reigning principle through which we see in philosophical reflection. Traditional thinking, and the common-sense habits it left behind after fading out philosophically, demand a frame of reference in which all things have their place. Not too much importance is attached to the intelligibility of the frame—it may even be laid down in dogmatic axioms—if only each reflection can be localized, and if unframed thoughts are kept out. But a cognition that is to bear fruit will throw itself to the objects *à fond perdu*. The vertigo which this causes is an *index veri;* the shock of inconclusiveness, the negative as which it cannot help appearing in the frame-covered, never-changing realm, is true for untruth only.

FRAGILITY OF TRUTH

The dismantling of systems, and of the system at large, is not an act of formal epistemology. What the system used to procure for the details can be sought in the details only, without advance assurance to the thought: whether it is there, or what it is. Not until then would the steadily misused word of "truth as concreteness" come into its own. It compels our thinking to abide with minutiae. We are not to philosophize about concrete things; we are to philosophize, rather, out of these things. But if we surrender to the specific object we are suspected of lacking an unequivocal position. What differs from the existent will strike the existent as witchcraft, while thought figures such as proximity, home, security hold the faulty world under their spell. Men are afraid that in losing this magic they would lose everything, because the only happiness they know, even in thought, is to be able to hold on to something—the perpetuation of unfreedom. They want a bit of ontology, at least, amidst their criticism of ontology—as if the smallest free insight did not express the goal better than a declaration of intention that is not followed up.

Philosophy serves to bear out an experience which Schoenberg noted in traditional musicology: one really learns from it only how a movement begins and ends, nothing about the movement itself and its course. Analogously, instead of reducing philosophy to categories, one would in a sense have to compose it first. Its course must be a ceaseless self-renewal, by its own strength as well as in friction with whatever standard it may have. The crux is what happens in it, not a thesis or a position—the texture, not the deductive or inductive course of one-track minds. Essentially, therefore, philosophy is not expoundable. If it were, it would be superfluous; the fact that most of it can be expounded speaks against it. But if a mode of conduct shields no primacy, harbors no certainty, and yet—because of its definite presentation, if on no other grounds—concedes so little to relativism, the twin of absolutism, that it approaches a doctrine, such a mode will give offense. It goes beyond, and to the point of breaking with, the dialectics of Hegel, who wanted his dialectics to be all things, including *prima philosophia,* and in fact made it that in his principle of identity, his absolute subject.

By dissociating thought from primacy and solidity, however, we do not absolutize it as in free suspense. The very dissociation fastens it to that which it is not. It removes the illusion of the autarky of thought. The falsehood of an unleashed rationality running away from itself, the recoil of enlightenment into mythology, is rationally definable. To think means to think something. By itself, the logically abstract form of "something," something that is meant or judged, does not claim to posit a being; and yet, surviving in it—indelible for a thinking that would delete it—is that which is not identical with thinking, which is not thinking at all. The *ratio* becomes irrational where it forgets this, where it runs counter to the meaning of thought by hypostasizing its products, the abstractions. The commandment of its autarky condemns thinking to emptiness, and finally to stupidity and primitivity. The charge of bottomlessness should be lodged against the self-preserving mental principle as the sphere of absolute origins; but where ontology, Heidegger in the lead, hits upon bottomlessness—there is the place of truth.

Truth is suspended and frail, due to its temporal substance; Benjamin sharply criticized Gottfried Keller's arch-bourgeois dictum that the truth can't run away from us. Philosophy must do without the consolation that truth cannot be lost. A truth that cannot plunge into the abyss which the metaphysical fundamentalists prate about—it is not the abyss of agile sophistry, but that of madness—will at the bidding of its certainty principle turn analytical, a potential tautology. Only thoughts that go the limit are facing up to the omnipotent impotence of certain accord; only a cerebral acrobatics keeps relating to the matter, for which, according to the *fable convenu,* it has nothing but disdain for the

sake of its self-satisfaction. No unreflected banality can remain
true as an imprint of the wrong life.

Any attempt to bring thought—particularly for its utility's sake
—to a halt with the hackneyed description of it as smugly exaggerated and noncommittal is reactionary nowadays. The argument
might be reduced to a vulgar form: "If you want me to, I'll make
innumerable analyses like that, rendering each one worthless."
Peter Altenberg gave the appropriate reply to a man who cast
the same sort of aspersion on his abbreviated literary forms: "But
I don't want you to." The open thought has no protection against
the risk of decline into randomness; nothing assures it of a sat-
uration with the matter that will suffice to surmount that risk.
But the consistency of its performance, the density of its texture,
helps the thought to hit the mark. There has been an about-face
in the function of the concept of certainty in philosophy. What
was once to surpass dogmas and the tutelage of self-certainty has
become the social insurance of a cognition that is to be proof
against any untoward happening. And indeed, to the unobjec-
tionable nothing happens.

AGAINST RELATIVISM

In the history of philosophy we repeatedly find epistemological
categories turned into moral ones; the most striking instance, although by no means the only one, is Fichte's interpretation of
Kant. Something similar happened with logical-phenomenological
absolutism. To fundamental ontologists, relativism is the offense
of bottomless thinking. Dialectics is as strictly opposed to that as
to absolutism, but it does not seek a middle ground between the
two; it opposes them through the extremes themselves, convicts
them of untruth by their own ideas. Against relativism this procedure is overdue because most of its criticism has been so formal in nature as to leave the fiber of relativistic thinking more or
less untouched. The popular argument against Spengler, for example—that relativism presupposes at least one absolute, its own
validity, and thus contradicts itself—is shabby; it confuses the

35

general denial of a principle with the denial's own elevation to affirmative rank, regardless of the specific difference in the positional value of both.

More fruitful might be the recognition of relativism as a limited form of consciousness. It began as that of bourgeois individualism, in which the individual consciousness is taken for the ultimate and all individual opinions are accorded equal rights, as if there were no criterion of their truth. Proponents of the abstract thesis that every man's thought is conditioned should be most concretely reminded that so is their own, that it is blind to the supra-individual element which alone turns individual consciousness into thought. The attitude behind that thesis is one of disdaining the mind and respecting the predominance of material conditions, considered the only thing that counts. A father's retort to his son's decidedly uncomfortable views is that all things are relative, that money makes the man, as in the Greek proverb. Relativism is a popularized materialism; thought gets in the way of money-making.

Such a flatly anti-intellectual posture must necessarily remain abstract. The relativity of all cognition can always be asserted only from without, for as long as there is no act of concrete cognition. Consciousness no sooner enters into some definite thing, no sooner faces its immanent claim to be true or false, than the thought's allegedly subjective accidentality will dissolve. Relativism is nugatory for another reason: the things it considers random and accidental, on the one hand, and irreducible on the other— those things themselves are brought forth by an objectivity, by an objective individualist society, and can be deduced from it as socially necessary phenomena. The reactive modes which relativistic doctrine holds to be peculiar to each individual are pre-established; they are never far from the bleating of sheep, the stereotype of relativity in particular. And indeed, cannier relativists such as Pareto have extended the individualistic phenomenality to group interests. But the bounds of objectivity which sociology has drawn, the bounds which are specific to its strata, are on their part only so much more deducible from the whole of society, from the objective realm. In Mannheim's late version of sociological relativism, which fancies that scientific objectivity might be distilled from the different perspectives of the strata of a "freely suspended" intelligence, the factors are reversed: the conditioning becomes the conditioned.

In fact, the law that governs the divergent perspectives is the structure of the social process as a preordained whole. Knowledge of the whole makes the perspectives binding. An entrepreneur who wants to stay competitive must calculate so that the uncompensated portion of the yield of other people's labor will go to him as profit, and he must believe that what he is doing is a fair exchange of labor against the cost of its reproduction. It can be just as stringently shown, however, why this objectively necessary belief is an objective falsehood. The dialectical relation voids its particular elements in itself. The alleged social relativity of views obeys the objective law of social production under private ownership of the means of production. Bourgeois skepticism, of which relativism is the doctrinal embodiment, is obtuse.

But the perennial anti-intellectualism is more than an anthropological trait of bourgeois subjectivity. It is due to the fact that under the existing conditions of production the concept of reason, once emancipated, must fear that its consistent pursuit will explode those conditions. This is why reason limits itself; throughout the bourgeois era, the spirit's accompanying reaction to the idea of its autonomy has been to despise itself. The spirit cannot forgive itself for being barred, by the constitution of the existence it guides, from unfolding the freedom inherent in its concept. The philosophical term for this prohibition is relativism. No dogmatic absolutism need be summoned against it; it is crushed by being proved narrow. Relativism, no matter how progressive its bearing, has at all times been linked with moments of reaction, beginning with the sophists' availability to the more powerful interests. To intervene by criticizing relativism is the paradigm of definite negation.

DIALECTICS AND SOLIDITY

Unleashed dialectics is not without anything solid, no more than is Hegel. But it no longer confers primacy on it. Hegel did not overstress the solid features in the origin of his metaphysics: they were to emerge from it at the end, as a translucent entirety. This lends a peculiar duplicity to his logical categories. They are structures that have originated, structures that void themselves, and at the same time they are a priori, invariant structures. With dynamism they are made to accord by the doctrine of an immediacy newly restored in each dialectical stage. The theory of second nature, to which Hegel already gave a critical tinge, is not lost to a negative dialectics. It assumes, *tel quel,* the abrupt immediacy, the formations which society and its evolution present to our thought; and it does this so that analysis may bare its mediations to the extent of the immanent difference between phenomena and that which they claim to be in themselves.

The self-preserving solidity, the young Hegel's "positive," is to such analysis, as it was to him, the negative. In the Preface to *Phenomenology* he still characterized thought, the arch-enemy of that positivity, as the negative principle.* The road to this is the simplest of reflections: what does not think, what surrenders to visibility, is inclined toward the badly positive by that passive nature which in the critique of reason marks the sensory source of the rights of knowledge. To receive something as it is offered at a time, dispensing with reflection, is potentially always tantamount to recognizing it the way it is; virtually all thoughts, on the other hand, cause a negative motion.

Of course, all his statements to the contrary notwithstanding, Hegel left the subject's primacy over the object unchallenged. It is disguised merely by the semi-theological word "spirit" with its indelible memories of individual subjectivity. The bill for this is presented in the excessive formality of Hegel's logic. According

---

* "The activity of distinguishing is the force and the work of the intellect, the most marvelous and greatest or, rather, the absolute power. The closed circle, which rests in itself and substantially contains its elements, is the immediate and therefore not marvelous relation. But that accidental things as such, apart from their extent, dependent things which are real only in connection with others—that these obtain an existence of their own and a separate freedom is the enormous power of the negative; it is the energy of thought, of the pure I." (Hegel, Works 2, p. 33f.)

to its own concept it would have to be substantial, but the endeavor to make it all things at once, metaphysics as well as a doctrine of categories, resulted in the elimination of the definite being that might have legitimized its rudiment. In this respect Hegel is not so far removed from Kant and Fichte, whom he never tires of denouncing as spokesmen for abstract subjectivity. For its part, the science of logic is abstract in the simplest sense of the word: the reduction to general concepts is an advance elimination of the counter-agent to those concepts, of that concrete element which idealistic dialectics boasts of harboring and unfolding.

The spirit wins its fight against a nonexistent foe. Hegel's derogatory remark about contingent existence—the Krugianism which philosophy may, and must, scorn to deduce from itself—is a cry of "Stop thief!" Having always dealt with the medium of the concept, and reflecting only generally on the relation between the concept and its conceptual content, Hegelian logic has advance assurance of what it offers to prove: that the concept is absolute. The more critically we see through the autonomy of subjectivity, however, and the clearer our awareness of its own mediated nature, the more incumbent is it upon our thinking to take on what lends it the solidity it does not have in itself. Otherwise we would not even have the dynamics with which dialectics moves its solid burden.

Not every experience that appears as primary can be denied point-blank. If conscious experience were utterly lacking in what Kierkegaard defended as naïveté, thought would be unsure of itself, would do what the establishment expects of it, and would become still more naïve. Even terms such as "original experience," terms compromised by phenomenology and neo-ontology, denote a truth while pompously doing it harm. Unless resistance to the façade stirs spontaneously, heedless of its own dependencies, thought and activity are dull copies. Whichever part of the object exceeds the definitions imposed on it by thinking will face the subject, first of all, as immediacy; and again, where the subject feels altogether sure of itself—in primary experience—it will be least subjective. The most subjective, the immediate datum, eludes the subject's intervention. Yet such immediate consciousness is neither continuously maintainable nor downright positive; for consciousness is at the same time the universal medium and cannot jump across its shadow even in its own *données immédiates*. They are not the truth.

The confidence that from immediacy, from the solid and downright primary, an unbroken entirety will spring—this confidence is an idealistic chimera. To dialectics, immediacy does not maintain its immediate pose. Instead of becoming the ground, it becomes a moment. At the opposite pole, the same thing happens to the invariants of pure thought. Nothing but a childish relativism would deny the validity of formal logic and mathematics and treat them as ephemeral because they have come to be. Yet the invariants, whose own invariance has been produced, cannot be peeled out of the variables as if all truth were at hand, then. Truth has coalesced with substance, which will change; immutability of truth is the delusion of *prima philosophia*. The invariants are not identically resolved in the dynamics of history and of consciousness, but they are moments in that dynamics; stabilized as transcendence, they become ideology. By no means will ideology always resemble the explicit idealistic philosophy. Ideology lies in the substruction of something primary, the content of which hardly matters; it lies in the implicit identity of concept and thing, an identity justified by the world even when a doctrine summarily teaches that consciousness depends on being.

THE PRIVILEGE OF EXPERIENCE

In sharp contrast to the usual ideal of science, the objectivity of dialectical cognition needs not less subjectivity, but more. Philosophical experience withers otherwise. But our positivistic *zeitgeist* is allergic to this need. It holds that not all men are capable of such experience; that it is the prerogative of individuals destined for it by their disposition and life story; that calling for it as a premise of cognition is elitist and undemocratic.

Granted, philosophical experiences are indeed not equally accessible to everyone, not the way all men of comparable I.Q.

should be able to repeat experiments in the natural sciences, for instance, or to grasp the cogency of mathematical deductions, although current opinion regards these faculties as requiring even more of a specific talent. In any case, compared with the virtually subjectless rationality of a scientific ideal that regards all men as interchangeable, the subjective share in philosophy retains an irrational adjunct. It is not a quality of nature. While the argument pretends to be democratic, it ignores what the administered world makes of its compulsory members. Only a mind which it has not entirely molded can withstand it. Criticizing privilege becomes a privilege—the world's course is as dialectical as that. Under social conditions—educational ones, in particular —which prune and often cripple the forces of mental productivity, and considering the prevailing dearth of images and the pathogenic processes in early childhood which psychoanalysis diagnoses but cannot really change, it would be fictitious to assume that all men might understand, or even perceive, all things. To expect this would be to make cognition accord with the pathic features of a mankind stripped of its capacity for experience—if it ever had this capacity—and by a law of perpetual sameness. The construction of truth in analogy to a *volonté de tous,* which is the final consequence of the concept of subjective reason, would in all men's name defraud all men of what they need.

If a stroke of undeserved luck has kept the mental composition of some individuals not quite adjusted to the prevailing norms —a stroke of luck they have often enough to pay for in their relations with their environment—it is up to these individuals to make the moral and, as it were, representative effort to say what most of those for whom they say it cannot see or, to do justice to reality, will not allow themselves to see. Direct communicability to everyone is not a criterion of truth. We must resist the all but universal compulsion to confuse the communication of knowledge with knowledge itself, and to rate it higher, if possible—whereas at present each communicative step is falsifying truth and selling it out. Meanwhile, whatever has to do with language suffers of this paradoxicality.

Truth is objective, not plausible. It falls into no man's lap; it does take objective conveyance; but just as applicable to its web is what Spinoza over-enthusiastically claimed for each single truth: that it is its own index. As for the privileged character which rancor holds against it, truth will lose that character when men stop pleading the experiences they owe it to—when they let it enter instead into configurations and causal contexts that help to make it evident or to convict it of its failings. Elitist pride would be the last thing to befit the philosophical experience. He who has it must admit to himself how much, according to his possibilities in existence, his experience has been contaminated by existence, and ultimately by the class relationship. In philosophical experience, chances which the universal desultorily affords to individuals turn against the universal that sabotages the universality of such experience. If this universality were established, the experience of all individuals would change accordingly, losing much of the accidental character which until then incurably disfigures it even where it keeps stirring. Hegel's doctrine of the self-reflecting object survives its idealistic version because in a changed dialectics the subject's divestment of sovereignty turns it even more into a reflexive form of its object.

The less definitive and all-encompassing a theory is claimed to be, the less of an object will it become to the thinker. As the compulsion of the system evaporates, he will be free to rely more frankly on his own consciousness and experience than was permitted by the pathos-filled conception of a subjectivity whose abstract triumph would exact the price of renouncing its specific substance. This price was in line with the emancipation of individuality that occurred between the great age of idealism and the present, and whose achievements—despite, and because of, the present pressure of collective regression—are theoretically as irrevocable as the impulses of the dialectics of 1800. Nineteenth century individualism has indeed weakened the objectifying power of the mind, its capacity for insight into objectivity and for its construction; but it has also equipped the mind with a discriminating sense that strengthened its experience of the object.

I

THE QUALITATIVE MOMENT OF RATIONALITY

To yield to the object means to do justice to the object's qualitative moments. Scientific objectification, in line with the quantifying tendency of all science since Descartes, tends to eliminate qualities and to transform them into measurable definitions. Increasingly, rationality itself is equated *more mathematico* with the faculty of quantification. While perfectly corresponding to the primacy of a triumphant natural science, this faculty is by no means inherent in the concept of the *ratio* itself, which is blinded mainly when it balks at the idea that qualitative moments on their part are susceptible of rational conception. *Ratio* is not merely συναγογή, an ascent from the scattered phenomena to the concept of their species,[11] it calls just as much for an ability to discriminate. Without this, the synthetic function of thought—abstract unification—would not be possible: to aggregate what is alike means necessarily to segregate it from what is different. But what is different is the qualitative; a thinking in which we do not think qualitatively is already emasculated and at odds with itself.

At the very dawn of the European philosophy of reason, the qualitative moment of the *ratio* was still vigorously expressed by Plato, the first to install mathematics as a model of method. Next to συναγογή, with equal rights, he put διαίρεσις—which amounts to the commandment that consciousness, mindful of the Socratic and sophistical separation of φύσει and θέσει, should adhere to the nature of things and not deal with them arbitrarily. And qualitative distinction is not only incorporated in Plato's dialectics, in his doctrine of thought, but interpreted as a corrective for the violence of unleashed quantification. A parable from *Phaedrus* leaves no doubt of it; there, organizing thought and nonviolence strike a balance. The principle, reversing the conceptual motion of synthesis, is that of "division into species according to the natural formation, where the joints are, not breaking any part as a bad carver might."[12]

The qualitative moment is preserved in all quantification, as the substrate of that which is to be quantified. This is what Plato cautions us not to destroy, lest the *ratio,* impairing the object it should attain, recoil into unreason. In a second reflection—an antidote, as it were—rational operations are accompanied by the same quality that was dismissed in the first, narrowly scientific reflection of a philosophy as alien to science as it is beholden to it. There is no quantified insight whose point, whose *terminus ad quem,* can be reached without qualitative retranslation. Even in statistics the cognitive goal is qualitative; quantification is nothing but the means. Absolutizing the *ratio's* tendency to quantify agrees with its lack of self-reflection, which serves an insistence on the qualitative; it does not raise the specter of irrationality. Later, Hegel alone seemed aware of this without any romantic-retrospective leanings—at a time, of course, when quantification did not yet enjoy its present undisputed supremacy. He did agree with the scientivistic tradition that "the truth of quality itself is quantity,"[13] but in *System of Philosophy* he recognizes quantity as a "definition indifferent to Being and extraneous to it,"[14] and according to *Logic,* quantity is "itself a quality." It retains its relevance in quantitative form; and the quantum returns to quality.[15]

QUALITY AND INDIVIDUAL

Corresponding to the quantifying tendency on the subjective side was the reduction of the knower to a purely logical universal without qualities. True, the qualities would be free only at an objective stage no longer limited to quantification, no longer having quantification drilled into the man who must make a mental adjustment. But quantification is not the timeless being it is made to seem by mathematics, its instrument. When it claimed exclusiveness it became transient. What awaits the qualitative subject in the matter is the potential of its qualities, not the transcendental residue of this potential—although the subject's restriction by the division of labor strengthens it for that residue alone. Yet as more of the subject's reactions are tabooed as allegedly merely subjective, more qualitative definitions of the object will escape cognition.

The ideal of discrimination, of the nuance—an ideal which in cognition, including the latest developments, has never been quite forgotten, despite all "Science is measurement"—refers not only to an individual faculty which objectivity can do without. A discriminating man is one who in the matter and its concept can distinguish even the infinitesimal, that which escapes the concept; discrimination alone gets down to the infinitesimal. Its postulate of a capacity to experience the object—and discrimination is the experience of the object turned into a form of subjective reaction —provides a haven for the mimetic element of knowledge, for the element of elective affinity between the knower and the known.

In the total process of enlightenment this element gradually crumbles. But it cannot vanish completely if the process is not to annul itself. Even in the conception of rational knowledge, devoid of all affinity, there survives a groping for that concordance which the magical delusion used to place beyond doubt. If this moment were extinguished altogether, it would be flatly incomprehensible that a subject can know an object; the unleashed rationality would be irrational. In being secularized, however, the mimetic element in turn blends with the rational one. The word for this process is discrimination. It contains the faculty of mimetic reaction as well as the logical organ for the relation of genus, species, and *differentia specifica*. In the process, the differentiating faculty keeps as accidental a character as does any undiminished individuality compared with the universal of its reason.

Yet this element of chance is not radical enough for the criteria of scientivism. Hegel was oddly inconsistent when he arraigned the individual consciousness, the stage of the mental experience that animates his work, as accidental and narrow. The only explanation is an urge to incapacitate the critical element that entwines with the individual mind. Particularizing this, he came to feel the contradictions between the concept and the particular. The individual consciousness is almost always the unhappy one, and with good reason. In his aversion to it, Hegel refuses to face the very fact he underscores where it suits him: how much universality is inherent in that individuality. According to his strategic requirements he treats the individual as if it were the immediacy whose semblance he is destroying; with that, however, the semblance of an absolute contingency of individual experience will disappear as well.

Without concepts, that experience would lack continuity. By definition, the part it takes in the discursive medium makes it always more than purely individual. The individual becomes a subject insofar as its individual consciousness objectifies it, in the unity of the self as well as in the unity of its experiences; to animals, presumably, both unities are denied. Because it is general in itself, and to the extent to which it is general, individual experience goes as far as the universal. Even in epistemological reflection, logical universality and the unity of the individual consciousness are mutually interdependent. Yet this does not only refer to the subjective-formal side of individuality: every content of individual consciousness is brought to it by its carrier for the sake of his self-preservation, and is reproduced along with that self-preservation.

Self-reflection may free the individual consciousness from that dependence and expand it. Spurring that expansion is the agonizing fact that logical universality tends to predominate in individual experience. As the "test of reality," experience does not simply double the individual's wishes and whims; it also denies them for the sake of his survival. The subject has no way at all to grasp universals other than in the motion of individual human consciousness. The result of cropping the individual would not be a higher subject cleansed of the dross of accidentality; the only subject to emerge from such an operation would be an unconsciously imitative one. In the East, the theoretical short circuit in the views of individuality has served as a pretext for collective oppression. The party, even if deluded or terrorized, is deemed a priori superior in judgment to each individual because of the number of its members. Yet the isolated individual unhampered by any ukase may at times perceive objectivities more clearly than the collective, which is no more than the ideology of its functionaries, anyway.

Brecht's line—that the party has a thousand eyes while the individual has but two—is as false as any bromide ever. A dissenter's exact imagination can see more than a thousand eyes peering through the same pink spectacles, confusing what they see with universal truth, and regressing. Against this stands the individuation of knowledge. Not only the way the object is perceived depends upon that individuation and differentiation; the differentiation itself is determined by the object, which demands therein its *restitutio in integrum,* so to speak. Just the same, the modes of subjective reaction which the object needs require ceaseless objective correction in their turn. This occurs in self-reflection, in the ferment of mental experience. Metaphorically speaking, the process of philosophical objectivation would be vertical and intratemporal as opposed to the horizontal, abstractly quantifying one of science. This much of Bergson's metaphysics of time is true.

SUBSTANTIALITY AND METHOD

Bergson's generation—also Simmel, Husserl, and Scheler—yearned in vain for a philosophy receptive to the objects, a philosophy that would substantialize itself. What tradition tells, tradition wanted. Yet this does not relieve us of methodical reflection on the relative positions of substantial individual analysis and dialectical theory. The idealistic-identitarian avowals that the first absorbs the second are unconvincing; but objectively—not just through the knowing subject—the whole which theory expresses is contained in the individual object to be analyzed. What links the two is a matter of substance: the social totality.

But the link is also a matter of form, of the abstract legality of the totality itself: the legality of barter. It was from this that idealism distilled its absolute spirit, simultaneously encoding the truth that the linkage happens to phenomena as a coercive mechanism; this lies behind the so-called "constitutive problem." In a philosophical experience we do not have this universal immediately, as a phenomenon; we have it as abstractly as it is objective. We are constrained to take our departure from the particular, without forgetting what we know but do not have. The path of philosophical experience is twofold, like that of Heraclitus, one leading upward, one downward. Assured of the real determination of phenomena by their concept, our experience cannot propound this concept ontologically, as truth-in-itself. The concept is fused with untruth, with the oppressive principle, thus lessening even the dignity of its epistemological criticism. It does not constitute a positive *telos* that would quench cognition. The negativity of the universal in turn welds cognition to the particular as that which is to be saved. "Only thoughts which cannot understand themselves are true."

All philosophy, even that which intends freedom, carries in its inalienably general elements the unfreedom in which society prolongs its existence. Coercion is inherent in philosophy, yet coercion alone protects it from regressing into license. The coercive character that is immanent in our thinking can be critically known; the coercion of thought is the medium of its deliverance. Hegel's "freedom to the object," the net result of which was the subject's incapacitation, has yet to be achieved. Until then, the divergence between dialectics as a method and substantial dialectics will go on. The principle of dominion, which antagonistically rends human society, is the same principle which, spiritualized, causes the difference between the concept and its subject matter; and that difference assumes the logical form of contradiction because, measured by the principle of dominion, whatever does not bow to its unity will not appear as something different from and indifferent to the principle, but as a violation of logic.

The remnant of divergence between philosophical conception and execution, on the other hand, also denotes some of the nonidentity that allows the method neither quite to absorb the contents—though it is supposed to be in the contents alone—nor to immaterialize them. The precedence of the matter shows as a necessary insufficiency of the method. What must be said methodically, in the form of general reflection, in order not to be defenseless against the philosophers' philosophy, can be legitimized solely in execution, thus denying the method in turn. A surplus of method, compared with the substance, is abstract and false; even Hegel had to put up with the discrepancy between his Preface to *Phenomenology* and phenomenology itself. The philosophical ideal would be to obviate accounting for the deed by doing it.

EXISTENTIALISM

The most recent attempt to break out of conceptual fetishism—out of academic philosophy, without relinquishing the demand for commitment—went by the name of Existentialism. Like fundamental ontology, from which it split off by entering into political commitments, Existentialism remained in idealistic bonds; besides, compared with the philosophical structure, it retained an accidental touch replaceable by politics to the contrary, provided only the politics satisfied the Existentialist *characteristica formalis.* Each bloc has its partisans. There is no theoretical dividing line from decisionism. And yet the idealistic component of Existentialism is a political function. As social critics, Sartre and his friends were unwilling to limit themselves to theoretical criticisms, and it did not escape them that wherever communism had seized power it was digging in as a bureaucracy. The institution of a centralized state party makes a mockery of all past thinking about men's relation to the state. Hence Sartre's total stress upon the moment which the reigning practice will no longer tolerate—on spontaneity, philosophically speaking. He would urge Kierkegaard's category of decision the more exclusively, the smaller the objective chances left to it by the distribution of social power. Kierkegaard drew the meaning of the category from Christology, its *terminus ad quem;* Sartre made it the absolute it was to serve.

Despite his extreme nominalism,* Sartre's philosophy in its

---

* By the rules of the game as played under an unreflected Enlightenment, Hegel's restitution of conceptual realism, down to his provocative defense of the ontological argument for the existence of God, was reactionary. Meanwhile, the course of history has justified his anti-nominalist intention. In contrast to the crude schema of Scheler's sociology of knowledge, nominalism on its part has turned into ideology—into the ideology of an eye-blinking "There isn't any such thing," which official science likes to use as soon as mention is made of such embarrassing entities as class or ideology or, nowadays, society at large. A genuinely critical philosophy's relation to nominalism is not invariant; it changes historically with the function of skepticism. To ascribe any *fundamentum in re* of concepts to the subject is idealism.

most effective phase was organized according to the old idealistic category of the free act of the subject. To Existentialism as to Fichte, any objectivity is a matter of indifference. Consequently, social conditions came in Sartre's plays to be topical adjuncts, at best; structurally, they do hardly more than provide an occasion for the action. The irrationality to which Sartre's philosophical nonobjectiveness condemned his plots was surely the last thing in the obdurate Enlightenment apostle's mind. The notion of absolute freedom of choice is as illusionary as that of the absolute I as the world's source has ever been. As for the situations that were built up as foils for heroic decisions, a modicum of political experience would make them wobble like stageprops. Not even dramaturgically could such a sovereign choice be postulated at a concrete historic juncture. A general who resolved, as irrationally as he used to revel in atrocities, to allow no more of them to be committed; a general who raised the siege of a city already given into his hands by traitors and set up a utopian community instead—such a general would have been promptly killed by mutinous soldiers or else recalled by his superiors even in the furious, farcically romanticized times of the German Renaissance.

Fitting in only too well with this is the fact that Götz, bragging like Nestroy's Holofernes who had at least been enlightened about his free act by the massacre of the City of Light, puts himself at the disposal of an organized people's movement, a transparent likeness of the ones against which Sartre plays off his absolute spontaneity. And indeed—although now clearly with philosophy's blessing—the Renaissance man promptly recommits the atrocities he had so freely forsworn. The absolute subject cannot get out of its entanglements: the bonds it would have to tear, the bonds of dominion, are as one with the principle of absolute subjectivity. It honors Sartre that this shows up in his plays, against his philosophical chef d'oeuvre. The plays disavow the philosophy with whose theses they deal. There is, however, a philosophical reason for the follies of political Existentialism, as

---

Nominalism parted company with it only where idealism made objective claims. The concept of a capitalist society is not a *flatus vocis*.

there is for the phraseology of the nonpolitical German one. Existentialism raises the inevitable, the sheer existence of men, to the status of a mentality which the individual is to choose, without his choice being determined by any reason, and without there really being another choice. Whenever they go beyond such a tautology, Existentialist teachings join hands with subjectivity as a being-for-itself, and as the sole substantial being.

The schools that take derivatives of the Latin *existere* for their device would cite the realities of tangible experience against the alienated special sciences. For fear of materialization they withdraw from substance. Unwittingly they turn it into an example. What they subsume under ἐποχή will avenge itself by enforcing its power behind the back of philosophy, in decisions which philosophy deems irrational. A thinking purged of substantialities is not superior to a special science stripped of concepts; all versions of such thinking will relapse into the very formalism they combat for the sake of philosophy's vital concern. Afterwards it will be replenished with accidental loans, from psychology in particular. The intent of Existentialism, at least in its radical French form, would not be realizable at a distance from the substantial contents, but in menacing proximity to those contents. The dichotomy of subject and object is not to be voided by a reduction to the human person, not even to the absolutely isolated person. The question of man, a question whose present popularity extends all the way to Marxism of the Lukács persuasion, is ideological because its pure form dictates the invariant of the possible answer, even if that invariant is historicity itself.

What man ought to be as such is never more than what he has been: he is chained to the rock of his past. He is not only what he was and is, however, but equally what he can come to be, and to anticipate that, no definition suffices. The schools grouped around Existenz, even the utterly nominalistic ones, are incapable of the self-relinquishment they long for in their recourse to the individual human Existenz; and they confess that incapacity by philosophizing in general concepts about things not absorbed in their concepts, things running counter to their concepts—instead of thinking them through. They illustrate *Existenz,* the concept, by *Existenz,* the condition.

THING, LANGUAGE, HISTORY

How one should think instead has its distant and vague archetype in the various languages, in the names which do not categorically cover the thing, albeit at the cost of their cognitive function. In undiminished cognition we want what we have been drilled to resign ourselves to, what the names that come too close will blind us to—resignation and delusion are ideological complements. An idiosyncratic precision in the choice of words, as if they were to designate the things, is one of the major reasons why presentation is essential to philosophy. The cognitive reason for much expressive insistence on the τόδε τι is its own dialectics, its conceptual mediation within itself; this is the point of attack for conceiving its nonconceptual side.

For mediation in the midst of nonconceptuality is not a remainder after accomplished subtraction, nor something pointing to a bad infinity of such procedures. Rather, the mediation of the ὕλη is its implicit history. It is from a negative that philosophy draws whatever legitimacy it still retains: from the fact that, in being so and not otherwise, those insolubles which forced philosophy to capitulate and from which idealism declines are another fetish—the fetish of the irrevocability of things in being. What dissolves the fetish is the insight that things are not simply so and not otherwise, that they have come to be under certain conditions. Their becoming fades and dwells within the things; it can no more be stabilized in their concepts than it can be split off from its own results and forgotten. Similar to this becoming is temporal experience. It is when things in being are read as a text of their becoming that idealistic and materialistic dialects touch. But while idealism sees in the inner history of immediacy its vindication as a stage of the concept, materialism makes that inner history the measure, not just of the untruth of concepts, but even more of the immediacy in being.

The means employed in negative dialectics for the penetration of its hardened objects is possibility—the possibility of which their reality has cheated the objects and which is nonetheless visible in each one. But no matter how hard we try for linguistic expression of such a history congealed in things, the words we use will remain concepts. Their precision substitutes for the thing itself, without quite bringing its selfhood to mind; there is a gap between words and the thing they conjure. Hence, the residue of arbitrariness and relativity in the choice of words as well as in the presentation as a whole. Benjamin's concepts still tend to an authoritarian concealment of their conceptuality. Concepts alone can achieve what the concept prevents. Cognition is a τρώσας ἰάσεται. The determinable flaw in every concept makes it necessary to cite others; this is the font of the only constellations which inherited some of the hope of the name. The language of philosophy approaches that name by denying it. The claim of immediate truth for which it chides the words is almost always the ideology of a positive, existent identity of word and thing. Insistence upon a single word and concept as the iron gate to be unlocked is also a mere moment, though an inalienable one. To be known, the inwardness to which cognition clings in expression always needs its own outwardness as well.

TRADITION AND KNOWLEDGE

In the mainstream of modern philosophy we can no longer— pardon the odious word—be in the swim. The hitherto dominant philosophy of the modern age wants to eliminate the traditional moments of thinking. It would dehistoricize the contents of thought and assign history to a special, fact-gathering branch of science. Ever since the fundament of knowledge came to be sought in supposedly immediate subjective data, men have been enthralled by the idol of a pure present. They would endeavor to strip thought of its historic dimension. The fictitious, one-dimensional Now became the cognitive ground of all inner meaning. On this point there is agreement between patriarchs of modernity who are officially considered antipodes: between Descartes' autobiographical statements on the origin of his method and Bacon's idol theory. What is historic in thought, instead of heeding the timelessness of an objectified logic, was equated with superstition—and to cite ecclesiastically institutional traditions against inquiring thought was indeed superstition. Men had every reason to criticize authority. But their critique misconceived that tradition is immanent in knowledge itself, that it serves to mediate between known objects. Knowledge no sooner starts from scratch, by way of a stabilizing objectification, than it will distort the objects. Knowledge as such, even in a form detached from substance, takes part in tradition as unconscious remembrance; there is no question which we might simply ask, without knowing of past things that are preserved in the question and spur it.

From the outset, thinking as an intratemporal, motivated, progressive motion is the microcosmic equivalent of the macrocosmic motion of history that was internalized in the structure of thinking. Among the achievements of Kantian deduction, one ranging foremost is that even in the pure cognitive form, in the unity of the "I think" at the stage of imaginative reproduction, Kant perceived remembrance, the trace of historicity. Because there is no time without its content, however, that which Husserl in his late phase called "inner historicity" cannot remain internal, a pure form. The inner historicity of thought is inseparable from its content, and thus inseparable from tradition; the pure, perfectly sublimated subject, on the other hand, would be absolutely devoid of tradition. A knowledge wholly conforming to the idol of that purity, of total timelessness—a knowledge coincident with formal logic—would become a tautology; there would be no more room in it even for transcendental logic. Timelessness, the goal which the bourgeois mind may be pursuing in order to compensate for its own mortality, is the acme of its delusion. Benjamin innervated this when he strictly foreswore the ideal of autonomy and submitted his thought to tradition—although to a voluntarily installed, subjectively chosen tradition that is as unauthoritative as it accuses the autarkic thought of being. Although reflecting the transcendental moment, the traditional moment is quasi-transcendental: it is not a point-like subjectivity but the properly constitutive factor, what Kant called "the mechanism hidden in the depths of the soul." There is one variant that should not be missing from the excessively narrow initial questions in the *Critique of Pure Reason,* and that is the question how a thinking obliged to relinquish tradition might preserve and transform tradition.[16] For this and nothing else is the mental experience. It was plumbed by Bergson in philosophy, and even more by Proust in the novel, though both men were kept under the spell of immediacy by their disgust with the bourgeois timelessness that will use conceptual mechanics to anticipate the end of life. Yet philosophy's methexis in tradition would only be a definite denial of tradition. Philosophy rests on the texts it criticizes. They are brought to it by the tradition they embody, and it is in dealing with them that the conduct of philosophy becomes commensurable with tradition. This justifies the move from philosophy to exegesis, which exalts neither the interpretation nor the symbol into an absolute but seeks the truth where thinking secularizes the irretrievable archetype of sacred texts.

RHETORIC

In its dependence—patent or latent—on texts, philosophy admits its linguistic nature which the ideal of the method leads it to deny in vain. Like tradition, this nature has been tabooed in recent philosophical history, as rhetoric. Severed and degraded into a means to achieve effects, it became the carrier of the lie in philosophy. In despising rhetoric, philosophy atoned for a guilt incurred ever since Antiquity by its detachment from things, a guilt already pointed out by Plato. But the persecutors of the rhetorical element that saved expression for thought did just as much for the technification of thought, for its potential abolition, as did those who cultivated rhetoric and ignored the object.

In philosophy, rhetoric represents that which cannot be thought except in language. It holds a place among the postulates of contents already known and fixed. Rhetoric is in jeopardy, like any substitute, because it may easily come to usurp what the thought cannot obtain directly from the presentation. It is incessantly corrupted by persuasive purposes—without which, on the other hand, the thought act would no longer have a practical relation. The fact that all approved traditional philosophy from Plato down to the semanticists has been allergic to expression, this fact accords with a propensity of all Enlightenment: to punish undisciplined gestures. It is a trait extending all the way to logic, a defense mechanism of the materialized consciousness.

The alliance of philosophy and science aims at the virtual abolition of language and thus of philosophy, and yet philosophy cannot survive without the linguistic effort. Instead of splashing around in the linguistic cascade, a philosopher reflects upon it. There is a reason why sloppy language—inexactness, scientifically speaking —tends to be leagued with the scientific mien of incorruptibility by language. For to abolish language in thought is not to demythologize thought. Along with language, philosophy would blindly sacrifice whatever is not merely significative in dealing with its object; it is in language alone that like knows like. Yet we cannot ignore the perpetual denunciation of rhetoric by nominalists to whom a name bears no resemblance to what it says, nor can an unbroken rhetoric be summoned against them.

Dialectics—literally: language as the organon of thought— would mean to attempt a critical rescue of the rhetorical element, a mutual approximation of thing and expression, to the point where the difference fades. Dialectics appropriates for the power of thought what historically seemed to be a flaw in thinking: its link with language, which nothing can wholly break. It was this link that inspired phenomenology to try—naïvely, as always— to make sure of truth by analyzing words. It is in the rhetorical quality that culture, society, and tradition animate the thought; a stern hostility to it is leagued with barbarism, in which bourgeois thinking ends. The vilification of Cicero and even Hegel's aversion to Diderot bear witness to the resentment of those whom the trials of life have robbed of the freedom to stand tall, and who regard the body of language as sinful.

In dialectics, contrary to popular opinion, the rhetorical element is on the side of content. Dialectics seeks to mediate between random views and unessential accuracy, to master this dilemma by way of the formal, logical dilemma. But dialectics inclines to content because the content is not closed, not predetermined by a skeleton; it is a protest against mythology. Mythical is that which never changes, ultimately diluted to a formal legality of thought. To want substance in cognition is to want a utopia. It is this consciousness of possibility that sticks to the concrete, the undis-figured. Utopia is blocked off by possibility, never by immediate reality; this is why it seems abstract in the midst of extant things. The inextinguishable color comes from nonbeing. Thought is its servant, a piece of existence extending—however negatively—to that which is not. The utmost distance alone would be proximity; philosophy is the prism in which its color is caught.

PART ONE

RELATION TO ONTOLOGY

ONE

THE ONTOLOGICAL NEED

QUESTION AND ANSWER

The ontologies in Germany, Heidegger's in particular, remain effective to this day. Traces of the political past are no deterrent. Tacitly, ontology is understood as readiness to sanction a heteronomous order that need not be consciously justified, and that such interpretations are denied in higher places—as misconceptions, declines to the ontical sphere, deficient radicalism in formulating the question—serves but to enhance the dignity of their appeal. Ontology seems the more numinous the less it can be laid down in definite contents that would give the meddlesome intellect something to latch on to. Intangibility comes to be unassailability. He who refuses to follow suit is suspect, a fellow without a spiritual fatherland, without a home in Being—not so much different from the "baseness" for which the idealists Fichte and Schelling used to excoriate resisters to their metaphysics. In all its embattled trends, which mutually exclude each other as false versions, ontology is apologetical. Yet its effect would be unintelligible if it did not meet an emphatic need, a sign of something missed, a longing that Kant's verdict on a knowledge of the Absolute should not be the end of the matter.

The need was crudely but openly manifest in the early days of the neo-ontological movements, when theological sympathizers would talk of the resurrection of metaphysics. There was a touch of it in Husserl's will to replace the *intentio obliqua* with the *intentio recta;* what had delimited the cognitive possibilities in the critique of reason was nothing but the recollection of the cognitive powers themselves, a recollection which the phenomenological platform initially meant to dispense with. Plainly stirring in the "draft" of the ontological constitution of topical fields and regions, and finally of the "world as the entirety of all there is," was the will to grasp the whole without any limits being placed on its cognition. Husserl's εἴδη—later turned into *"existentialia"* by the Heidegger of *Being and Time*—were to anticipate encompassingly what those regions were, up to the highest. The implication behind them was that rational drafts might pre-design the structure of all the abundance of Being. It was a second reprise of the old philosophies of the Absolute, their first reprise having been post-Kantian idealism.

Yet the critical trend remained at work at the same time, though not so much as counter to dogmatic concepts. It continued as an effort in which the absolutes, now deprived of their systematic unity and delimited from each other, would no longer be posited or construed but received, accepted, and described in a posture following the lines of the positivistic scientific ideal. Once again, as for Schelling, absolute knowledge became intellectual visuality. One hoped to delete the transmissions instead of reflecting them. The nonconformist motive that philosophy need not resign itself within the bounds of an organized, usable science recoiled into conformism. The categorial structure that had been uncritically accepted as such, as the skeleton of extant conditions, was confirmed as absolute, and the unreflective immediacy of the method lent itself to any kind of license. The critique of criticism became pre-critical. Hence the mental posture of a permanent "back to." The Absolute became what it would least like to be, and what critical truth does call it: a matter of natural history that would quickly and crudely provide the norm of adjustment.

In comparison, the idealistic academic philosophy denied what will be expected of philosophy by anyone who goes in for it unprepared. That was the reverse of its Kant-enforced scientific self-responsibility. The awareness that a philosophy carried on as a specialty no longer has anything to do with people—with the people it trains to stop asking, as futile, the only questions for whose sake they turn to it—this awareness was already stirring in German idealism; it was voiced without professional discretion by Schopenhauer and Kierkegaard, and Nietzsche challenged any kind of accord with academicism. But what the present ontologies have done under this aspect is not simply to adopt the anti-academic philosophical tradition by asking, as Paul Tillich phrased it once, about that which concerns one absolutely. They have taken the nonacademic pathos and established it academically. They combined a pleasant shudder at the world's imminent end with a soothing sense of operating on solid ground, perhaps even on philologically fortified ground. Audacity, ever the prerogative of youth, knew itself covered by general agreement and by the most powerful educational institution. The movement as a whole became the opposite of what its germs seemed to promise: the treatment of relevant things relapsed into an abstractness unsurpassed by any neo-Kantian methodology.

This development is inseparable from the problematics of the ontological need itself. It can no more be quenched by that sort of philosophy than it could once be quenched by the transcendental system. This is why ontology has become shrouded in vapors. In line with an older German tradition, it puts the question above the answer; where it keeps owing what it promised, it has consolingly raised failure as such to existential rank. The weight of questions in philosophy differs indeed from the weight they have in special sciences, where the solution of questions removes them, while in philosophical history their rhythm would be more that of duration and oblivion. But this does not mean that—as some keep parroting Kierkegaard—the truth lies in the questioner's existence, in his mere futile search for an answer. Rather, in philosophy the authentic question will somehow almost always include its answer. Unlike science, philosophy knows no fixed sequence of question and answer. Its question must be shaped by its experience, so as to catch up with the experience. Its answers are not given, not made, not generated: they are the recoil of the unfolded, transparent question.

This is precisely what idealism would drown out in its constant endeavor to produce, to "deduce," its own form and, if possible, its every content. But thought does not preserve itself as an origin, and it ought not to hide the fact that it does not generate— that it merely returns what it already has as experience. The expressive moment in thought keeps it from proceeding *more mathematico* and serving up problems followed by pseudo-solutions. In philosophy, words like "problem" and "solution" have a mendacious ring because they postulate the thought's independence from thinking precisely where thinking and the thought transmit each other. Only the truth can really be philosophically understood. Our fulfilling concurrence in the judgment in which we understand something is the same as a decision about True or False. If we do not personally judge the stringency or nonstringency of a theorem, we do not understand it. The theorem's claim of such stringency is its own content of meaning, the very thing that is to be understood.

This distinguishes the relation of understanding and judgment from the usual order of time. The fact that we can no more understand without judging than we can judge without understanding invalidates the schema that the solution is the judgment and the problem is only the question, based on understanding. What is transmitted here is the fiber of the so-called philosophical demonstration, a mode of proof that contrasts with the mathematical model. And yet that model does not simply disappear, for the stringency of a philosophical thought requires its mode of proceeding to be measured by the forms of inference. Philosophical proof is the effort to give statements a binding quality by making them commensurable with the means of discursive thinking. But it does not purely follow from that thinking: the critical reflection of such cogitative productivity is itself a philosophical content.

In Hegel's case, despite the extreme enhancement of his claim to derive the nonidentical from identity, the thought structure of the great *Logic* implies the solutions in the way the problems are put, instead of presenting results after striking a balance. While Hegel's critique of analytical judgments is exacerbated to the thesis of their "falseness," everything is to him an analytical judgment, a turning to and fro of the thought without citation of anything extraneous to it. It is a moment of dialectics that the new is the old, and otherness is familiarity. The connection of that moment with the identity thesis is evident, but it is not circumscribed by the thesis. Paradoxically, the more a philosophical thought yields to its experience, the closer its approach to an analytical judgment. To grow fully aware of a desideratum of cognition is mostly to achieve the cognition itself; this is the counterpart of the idealistic principle of perpetual production. That it is by no means the Absolute is asserted in philosophy by doing without the traditional machinery of proof, by accentuating a knowledge that is known already.

AFFIRMATIVE CHARACTER

The ontological need can no more guarantee its object than the agony of the starving assures them of food. But no doubts of such guarantees plague a philosophical movement once destined for better things; it was for this reason as much as for any other that it became untruthfully affirmative. "Dimming the world never takes us to the light of Being."[1] In the categories to which fundamental ontology owes its echo—and which it therefore either denies or sublimates until they will no longer serve for any unwelcome confrontation—we can read how much they are the imprints of something missing that is not to be produced, how much they are its complementary ideology. Yet the cult of Being, or at least the attraction of the word as of something superior, lives by the fact that in reality, as once upon a time in epistemology, concepts denoting function have more and more replaced the concepts denoting substance. Society has become the total functional context which liberalism used to think it was: to be is to be relative to other persons and things, and to be irrelevant in oneself. This frightening fact, this dawning awareness that it may be losing its substantiality, prepares the subject to listen to avowals that its unarticulated being—equated with that substantiality—cannot be lost, that it will survive the functional context.

What the conjurers of ontological philosophizing strive, as it were, to awaken is undermined by real processes, however: by the production and reproduction of social life. The effort to justify "man" and "being" and "time" theoretically, as primal phenomena, cannot stay the fate of the resurrected ideas. Concepts whose substrate is historically at an end have always been duly criticized as dogmatic hypostases, even in the specifically philosophical realm— as Kant, for example, criticized the transcendence of the empirical soul, the aura of the word *Dasein,* in his chapter on paralogisms, and the immediate recourse to Being in his chapter on the amphiboly of reflexive concepts. But the exponents of the new

65

ontology do not make that Kantian critique their own. They do not carry it forward by reflection. Instead, they act as if that critique belonged to a rationalistic consciousness of whose flaws genuine thought had to be cleansed as in a ritual bath.

Despite this, trying to hitch their wagon to critical philosophy as well, they directly impute to this philosophy an ontological content. Heidegger's reading of the anti-subjectivist and "transcending" element in Kant was not quite unwarranted: in the Preface to the *Critique of Pure Reason* Kant does programmatically stress his objective way to pose questions, and leaves no doubt of it as he performs the deduction of pure intellectual concepts. The Copernican turn registered in conventional philosophical history does not exhaust him; the objective interest retains primacy over the subjective interest in the mere occurrence of cognition, in a dismembering of consciousness in empiricist style. By no means, however, can we equate this objective interest with a hidden ontology. Arguing against such an equation is not only Kant's critique of rationalist ontology—which might allow for the conception of another, if need be—but the train of thought of the critique of reason itself. Following this train of thought, we find that objectivity, the objectivity of knowledge as well as that of the totality of all things known, is subjectively transmitted. It allows us to assume an "in itself" beyond the subject-object polarity, but it intentionally leaves this assumption so indefinite that no sort of interpretation whatsoever would be able to extract an ontology from it. If Kant meant to rescue that *kosmos noetikos* which the turn to the subject was attacking, and if, therefore, there is an ontological element in his work, it is still an element, and not the central one. His philosophy is an attempt to accomplish the rescue by means of that which menaces what he would save.

INCAPACITATION OF THE SUBJECT

A fact supporting the objectivistic resuscitation of ontology would indeed be the least compatible with its idea: the fact that to a great extent the subject came to be an ideology, a screen for society's objective functional context and a palliative for the subjects' suffering under society. In this sense—and not just today —the not-I has moved drastically ahead of the I. In Heidegger's philosophy the fact is detoured but registered; in his hands that historical primacy becomes an ontological precedence of "Being" pure and simple over all ontical and real things. He prudently refrained from reversing the Copernican turn, the turn to the idea, in plain view of all. He zealously set off his version of ontology from objectivism, and his anti-idealistic stand from realism, whether critical or naïve.[2] Unquestionably, the ontological need could not be planed down to an anti-idealism along the battle lines of academic debate. And yet, of all the impulses given by that need the most enduring may have been the disavowal of idealism.

The anthropocentric sense of life has been shaken. The subject in its philosophical self-reflection has, so to speak, made the centuries-old critique of geocentrism its own. This motive is more than a matter of weltanschauung, however easy it was to exploit as a weltanschauung. Extravagant syntheses between developments in philosophy and in the natural science are odious, of course; they ignore the increasingly independent language of physical-mathematical formulas, a language that has long ceased to be retrievable into visuality or any other categories directly commensurable to the consciousness of man. And yet, the results of recent cosmology have radiated far and wide. All notions to make the universe resemble the subject, if not indeed to derive it as positing the subject, have been relegated to a naïveté comparable to that of Boeotians or paranoiacs who regard their hamlet as the center of the world. The ground of philosophical idealism, the control of nature, has lost the certainty of its omnipotence precisely because of its immense expansion during the first half of the twentieth century; also because human consciousness has limped behind, leaving the order of human affairs irrational, and finally because it took the magnitude of the attainments to let us measure their infinitesimality in comparison with the unattainable. There is a universal feeling, a universal fear, that our progress in controlling nature may increasingly help to weave the very calamity it is supposed to protect us from, that it may be weaving that second nature into which society has rankly grown.

Ontology and the philosophy of Being are modes of reaction in which—along with other and cruder modes—consciousness hopes to escape from that entanglement. But they contain a fatal dialectics. The truth that expels man from the center of creation and reminds him of his impotence—this same truth will, as a subjective mode of conduct, confirm the sense of impotence, cause men to identify with it, and thus reinforce the spell of the second nature. Faith in Being, a dim weltanschauung derived from critical premonitions, really degenerates into a bondage to Being, as Heidegger incautiously defined it once. Feeling face to face with the cosmos, the believer clings without much ado to any kind of particular, if only it is forceful enough in convicting the subject of its weakness. The subjects' readiness to cringe before the calamity that springs from the subjective context itself is the punishment for their futile wish to fly the prison of their subjectivity. The philosophical leap, the primal gesture of Kierkegaard, is the very license from which the subject dreams it may escape by its submission to Being.

The spell is diminished only where the subject, in Hegel's language, is "involved"; it is perpetuated in whatever would be the subject's downright otherness, just as the *deus absconditus* always carried some of the irrational features of mythical deities. The corny exoticism of such decorative world views as the astonishingly consumable Zen Buddhist one casts light upon today's restorative philosophies. Like Zen, they simulate a thinking posture which the history stored in the subjects makes impossible to assume. Restricting the mind to thoughts open and attainable at the historical stage of its experience is an element of freedom; nonconceptual vagary represents the opposite of freedom. Doctrines which heedlessly run off from the subject to the universe, along with the philosophy of Being, are more easily brought into accord with the world's hardened condition and with the chances of success in it than is the tiniest bit of self-reflection by a subject pondering upon itself and its real captivity.

BEING, SUBJECT, OBJECT

The popular success of ontology feeds on an illusion: that the
state of the *intentio recta* might simply be chosen by a consciousness full of nominalist and subjectivist sediments, a consciousness
which self-reflection alone has made what it is. Heidegger, of
course, saw through this illusion. He circumvents the alternative by
way of the doctrine of Being that prevails beyond *intentio recta*
and *intentio obliqua,* beyond subject and object, beyond concept
and entity. Being is the supreme concept—for on the lips of him
who says "Being" is the word, not Being itself—and yet it is said
to be privileged above all conceptuality, by virtue of moments
which the thinker thinks along with the word "Being" and which
the abstractly obtained significative unity of the concept does not
exhaust.

Presupposed by the talk of Being—though no longer referred
to by the mature Heidegger, at least—is Husserl's doctrine of
categorial visuality or essence perception. It is solely by such
perception that the structure which Heidegger's philosophy
ascribes to Being could, in the terminology of the school, be "un-
sealed" or "unveiled"; Heidegger's emphatic Being would be the
ideal of what yields to ideation. The critique that lies in Husserl's
doctrine—of a classifying logic as the significative unity of whatever the concept covers—remains in force. But Husserl wished to
have his cake and eat it too: he kept his philosophy within the
bounds of the division of labor and left the concept of strict
science alone until his late phase, despite all of the so-called
"foundation questions," and yet he sought to apply the strict rules
of the scientific game to whatever critique of these rules has its
own meaning. What his explicitly propounded method sought to
do to classifying concepts, by the mode of their cognitive ascertainment, was to imbue them with that which as classification, as the
mere arrangement of given things, they cannot have—to imbue
them with what they would have only by grasping the thing itself,
which in Husserl's case oscillates between an intramental thing
and one contrary to the immanence of consciousness. Husserl

cannot, as was customary in his lifetime, be accused of irrationalism on the ground that his categorial vision is unscientific; his work as a whole is a stand against irrationalism. But what can be held against his work is its contamination with science.

Heidegger noticed this and took the step Husserl shrank from. However, in doing so he discarded the rational moment which Husserl preserved, and—more like Bergson in this respect—he tacitly followed a procedure in which the relation to the discursive concept, an inalienable element of thought, was sacrificed. At the same time he covered Bergson's weakness, his juxtaposition of two disconnected, disparate modes of cognition: Heidegger, mobilizing the alleged higher dignity of the part of categorial vision, removes the epistemological-critical question as pre-ontological, along with the question whether that part is legitimate. Discontent with the preliminary epistemological question comes to justify its outright elimination; dogmatics simply turns into a higher truth, as against the traditional critique of dogmatics. This is the root of Heidegger's archaicism. The ambiguity of the Greek words for "being"—an ambiguity that dates back to the Ionians' failure to distinguish between materials, principles, and the pure essence—is not listed as a defect but as original superiority. Its mission is to heal the concept "Being" of the wound of its conceptuality, of the split between thoughts and their content.

ONTOLOGICAL OBJECTIVISM

What appears as if it were located in the eon before the Fall, however—the Fall of both subjectifying and objectifying metaphysics—will turn, *contre coeur,* into a stark "in itself." A self-denying subjectivity recoils into objectivism. No matter how painstakingly such thinking shuns the criticist controversy by adding the two antithetical positions alike to the loss of Being, the sublimation of its concepts will be a ceaseless continuance of Husserl's reductions. What is meant by Being is stripped as much of all individuated existence as of all traces of rational abstraction. This Being ends up in a tautology from which the subject has been evicted: "But Being—what is Being? It is Itself."[3] There is no way for Being to avoid the tautology, and we do not improve it if with prudent candor we opt for it and pronounce it a pledge of profundity.

Intentionally or not, every judgment—even an analytical one, as shown by Hegel—carries with it the claim to predicate something that is not simply identical with the mere concept of the subject. If it ignores this requirement, the judgment breaks the contract it has previously signed by its form. But the concept of Being as handled by the new ontology cannot help breaking that contract. In this ontology, Being must be defined by itself alone because it is held to be neither comprehensible in concepts—in other words, neither "transmitted"—nor immediately demonstrable after the model of sensory ascertainment. In lieu of any critical authority for Being we get a reiteration of the mere name. The residue, the supposedly undisfigured essence,[4] is like an ἀρχή of the type which the motivated thought movement had to reject.

As Heidegger once pointed out against Sartre,[5] a philosophy's denial that it is metaphysics does not settle the question whether or not it is, but it does justify the suspicion that untruth may hide in the refusal to admit its metaphysical content. A new beginning at an alleged zero point is the mask of strenuous forgetfulness—an effort to which sympathy with barbarism is not extraneous. The decay of the older ontologies, of the scholastic ones as well as of their rationalistic successors, was not a contingent change in weltanschauung or thinking style; to believe in that change is the same historical relativism to which the ontological need used to take exception. No sympathy with Plato's enthusiasm as against Aristotle's touch of resignation to the special sciences can refute the objection that the doctrine of ideas duplicates the world of things; no plea for the blessings of order will remove the difficulties caused in Aristotelian metaphysics by the relation of τόδε τι and πρώτη οὐσία. These difficulties spring from the disjoint definitions of Being and entity, which the new ontology resolutely and naively restores. Nor would the demand, however legitimate, for objective reason alone enable us to think Kant's critique of the ontological argument for God out of existence. Compared with hylozoism, the Eleatic turn to the presently glorified concept of Being was already a sort of Enlightenment, something less appreciated by Heidegger. But to wipe this all out by regressing to sacred primordiality, behind the reflection of critical thought—this intention would solely circumvent philosophical compulsions which, once understood, barred the quenching of the ontological need. The will not to accept evasions, the will to learn essential things from philosophy, is deformed by answers tailored to the need, by answers that lie in twilight between the legitimate duty to provide bread, not stones, and the illegitimate conviction that there must be bread because it must be.

THE DISAPPOINTED NEED

That a philosophy based on the primacy of method will acquiesce in so-called preliminary questions—and that, therefore, it may possibly even feel secure as a basic science—serves only to deceive us about the fact that the preliminary questions and philosophy itself have virtually no cognitive consequences any more. Reflections on the instrument of scientific knowledge have long ceased to touch its substance; they only touch upon what may be cognoscible at all, on the validity of scientific judgments. To such reflection, any definite knowledge is subaltern, a mere *constitutum*. While resting its claims on its immersion in the general constitution of knowledge, the reflection leaves knowledge indifferent.

The first formula to express this was Kant's famous line that the "transcendental idealist" is an "empirical realist."[6] Admirers of the critic of pure reason, and of his attempt to find reasons for experience, were deaf to this admission of bankruptcy: that the immeasurable strain of that critique was ἀδιάφορον with respect to the content of experience. Encouraged are only the normally functioning intellect and the corresponding view of reality—Heidegger, by the way, still opts for the "normally thinking human being."[7] Few of the intramundane views and judgments of common sense are withdrawn from circulation. "What Kant wished to prove, in a way that would offend 'all the world,' was that 'all the world' was right—this was that soul's secret joke. He wrote against the scholars and in favor of the prejudices of the people, but he wrote for scholars, and not for the people."[8] Defeatism paralyzes the specifically philosophical impulse to blast a hidden truth out from behind the idols of conventional consciousness. The chapter on amphibolies mocks the brazen desire to know the inside of things, and this self-satisfied, manly resignation of a philosophy settling down in the external *mundus sensibilis* is not just the Enlightenment's No to a metaphysics that confuses the concept with its own reality; it is also the obscurantist No to every refusal to capitulate to the façade.

Surviving in the ontological need is some remembrance of this greatest virtue, which critical philosophy did not so much forget as zealously eliminate in honor of the science it sought to establish—a remembrance of the will not to let thoughts be robbed of that for the sake of which men think them. Since the sciences' irrevocable farewell to idealistic philosophy, the successful sciences are no longer seeking to legitimize themselves otherwise than by a statement of their method. Their self-exegesis makes a *causa sui* of science. It accepts itself as given and thereby sanctions also its currently existing form, its division of labor, although in the long run the insufficiency of that form cannot be concealed. The intellectual sciences in particular, due to their borrowed ideal of positivity, lapse into the irrelevance and nonconceptuality of countless special investigations. The cuts between special disciplines such as sociology, economics, and history make the cognitive interest vanish in pedantically drawn, inflatedly defended trenches.

Ontology recalls this, but it has become cautious enough not to try to breathe the essence into the thing by speculative thinking. The essence is to spring forth like something given, rather, in tribute to the rules of positivity, which the need would transcend. Some initiates of science expect it to be decisively supplemented by ontology without their having to touch the scientific procedures. If Heidegger, in the later phase of his philosophy, claims to rise above the traditional distinction of essence and fact, he is reflecting a justified irritation at the divergence of essential and factual sciences, of mathematical-logical and substantive disciplines, which in scientific activity thrive side by side, disconnected, although the cognitive ideal of one group would be irreconcilable with that of the other.

But the antagonism between exclusive scientific criteria and the absolute claim of a doctrine of essence—or, later, of Being —will not vanish at the doctrine's bidding. The doctrine opposes its counterpart abstractly, displaying the same flaws of a labor-dividing consciousness which it pretends to cure. What it enlists against science is not scientific self-reflection, nor, as some seem to think, is it something qualitatively different whose necessary motion would superimpose it on science. According to the old parable Hegel used against Schelling, the doctrine comes out of a gun: it is an addition to science, a summary disposal that effects no valid change in science itself.

The doctrine's noble turn away from science finally serves only to confirm the universal rule of science, not unlike the way irrationalist slogans under fascism served as a counterpoint to scientific-technological activities. To pass from a critique of the sciences to their essential concerns—as to Being—is to disregard in turn whatever might be of the essence in the sciences; it is a move that robs those in need of ontology of what ontology appears to give them. With a detachment from all things substantive that is more anxious than Kant's ever was, ontological philosophizing permits less unregimented insight than Schelling's idealism, or even Hegel's. Especially tabooed as heterodoxy, as dealing with mere entity and μετάβασις εἰς ἄλλο γένος, is social consciousness, which precisely in the ontologies of Antiquity was inseparable from the philosophical one. In his hermeneutics, Heidegger adopts the turn against epistemology which Hegel inaugurated in the Preface to *Phenomenology of the Mind*.[9] But the reservations of transcendental philosophy against a substantive philosophy that forbids substance to cross its threshold as merely empirical— these reservations survive, for all protestations to the contrary, in Heidegger's program to distinguish Being from entity and to explicate Being itself.[10]

Not the last reason for the aloofness of fundamental ontology is that an ideal of the "purity" of Being in contrast to entity—an ideal derived from the methodologization of philosophy, with Husserl as the last connecting link—will be maintained, and yet philosophizing will go on as though about matters of substance. This habitude and that purity could be reconciled only in a realm that blurs all definite distinctions, indeed every content. Scared by

Scheler's weaknesses, Heidegger refuses to have the *prima philosophia* crassly compromised by the contingency of material things, by the transciency of the eternities of the moment. But neither will he do without the concretion originally promised by the word existence.* The distinction of concept and matter is called the original sin while it perpetuates itself in the pathos of Being.

Not to be underestimated among the many functions of Being is that, while flaunting its higher worth against entity, it simultaneously carries with it the memory of the entity from which it wants to be set off, as a memory of something precedent to differ-

---

* Years ago, Günther Anders already pilloried the pseudo-concreteness of fundamental ontology ("On the Pseudo-Concreteness of Heidegger's Philosophy," *Philosophical and Phenomenological Research,* vol. VIII, Nr. 3, pp. 337ff.). The word "concretion," most affectively occupied in German philosophy between the two World Wars, was drenched with the spirit of the times. Its magic used the feature of Homer's *nekyia,* when Ulysses feeds blood to the shadows to make them speak. Presumably it was not at all as an appeal to roots that "Blood and Soil" was so effective. The ironic undertone that accompanied the formula from the beginning shows a sense of the threadbareness of such archaicism at the finance-capitalistic stage of industrial production. Even *Das Schwarze Korps* snickered at the old Teutonic beards. Instead, the lure was the semblance of concreteness as noninterchangeability, as nonfungibility. This was the phantasm that rose amidst a world bound for monotony. It was a phantasm because it left the basis of the barter relationship untouched—else the longing ones would have felt even more menaced by what they called equalitarianism, by the capitalist principle of which they were unaware while taxing its opponents with it. Obsession with the concept of concreteness joined with inability to reach it in thought. The conjuring word replaced the thing. Heidegger's philosophy, of course, exploits even the *pseudos* of that sort of concretion: because τόδε τι and οὐσία are undistinguishable, he proceeds—as Aristotle projected already—to substitute one for the other, according to requirement and *thema probandum.* Mere entity becomes nonentity; rid of the stain of being an entity, it is raised up to Being, to its own pure concept. Being, on the other hand, devoid of any content that would restrict it, no longer needs to appear as a concept. It is held to be immediate like τόδε τι, in other words, to be concrete. Once isolated absolutely, the two moments have no *differentia specifica* from each other and become interchangeable. This *quid pro quo* is a main feature of Heidegger's philosophy.

entiation and antagonism. The lure of Being is as eloquent as the rustle of leaves in the wind of bad poems. But what that rustle praises will slide out of reach rather harmlessly, while in philosophy it is insisted on like a possession over which the thought that thinks it has no power. Dialectics—in which pure particularization and pure generality pass into each other, both equally indistinct—is shrouded in silence and exploited in the doctrine of Being. Indistinctness makes a mythical cuirass.

"DEFICIENCY = PROFIT"

Heidegger's philosophy is like a highly developed credit system: one concept borrows from the other. The state of suspense thus created gives an ironic touch to the bearing of a philosophy that feels close enough to the soil to prefer the Germanic "thinking" to the foreign word "philosophy." The debtor, says a faded joke, has it all over the creditor, who must depend upon the debtor's will to pay—and so, for Heidegger, blessings flow from everything he owes. That Being is neither a fact nor a concept exempts it from criticism. Whatever a critic would pick on can be dismissed as a misconception. The concept borrows from the factual realm an air of solid abundance, of something not just cogitatively and unsolidly made—an air of being "in itself." From the mind which synthesizes it, entity borrows the aura of being more than factual: the sanctity of transcendence. And this very structure hypostatizes itself as superior to the reflective intellect, which is accused of dissecting entity and concept with a scalpel.

The very meagerness of what all this leaves in Heidegger's hands is recoined into an advantage. One of the invariants that pervade his philosophy (though never called invariants, of course) is that each substantive deficiency, each absence of a cognition, will be revalued into a sign of profundity. Involuntary abstractness is presented as a voluntary vow. "Thinking," it says in the tract on Plato's doctrine of truth, "is on its descent to the poverty of its provisional essence"[11]—as if the emptiness of the concept of Being were the fruit of original monastic chastity, not of conditioning by cogitative aporias. And yet, this Being which is supposed to be no concept at all, or at least a very special concept, is the aporetical concept pure and simple.[12] It transforms that which is more abstract into that which is more concrete and thus more true. Heidegger's own language confesses, in phrasings that are more critical of him than the most malevolent critic, what his asceticism is about: "Thinking, by its saying, lays unobtrusive furrows into the language. They are even less obtrusive than the furrows drawn through the field by the slow-gaited yeoman."[13]

Despite such affectations of humility, not even theological risks will be taken. The attributes of Being do indeed, like those of the absolute idea of old, resemble the traditional attributes of the deity; but the philosophy of Being bewares of divine existence. The whole, however archaicist, is not to be an admission of being unmodern. Instead, it participates in modernity as an alibi of entity— of that to which Being transcended, but which is to be sheltered in Being just the same.

NO MAN'S LAND

Since Schelling, substantive philosophizing has been based on the thesis of identity. Unless the essence of entity, and ultimately entity itself, was a mental element reducible to subjectivity—unless concept and thing were identical on the superior level of the mind —there was no chance to proceed according to Fichte's maxim that the a priori is at the same time the a posteriori. Yet the judgment which history passed on the identity thesis upsets Heidegger's conception also. To his phenomenological maxim that the thought must bow to what is given or, finally, "sent" to it (as if the thought could not penetrate the conditions of such sending) the possibility of construction, of the speculative concept that was ingrained in the identity thesis, is taboo. Husserl's phenomenology already suffered from a desire to transcend epistemology under the slogan "Back to things." Husserl expressly described his doctrine as non-epistemological,* as Heidegger later called his own doctrine non-

---

* In the phenomenological "fundamental consideration" of *Ideas* [*Ideas—General Introduction to Pure Phenomenology*, trans. by W. R. Boyce Gibson, London, 1931] Husserl expounds his method as a struc-

metaphysical; but the thought of passing into subject-matter was more chilling to Husserl than to any neo-Kantian of the University of Marburg who might find the infinitesimal method helpful in such a passage.

Heidegger, like Husserl, sacrifices empiricism and ascribes to the unphilosophical factual sciences whatever would not be eidetic phenomenology, in Husserl's language. But Heidegger extends the proscription even to Husserl's εἴδη, those supreme, fact-free, conceptual units of a factuality with which traces of subject-matter are commingled. Being is the contraction of essences. Ontology's own consistency takes it to a no man's land. It must eliminate each a posteriori; it is not supposed to be logic either, in the sense of a doctrine of thought and a particular discipline; each thinking step would necessarily take ontology beyond the only point where it may hope to be sufficient unto itself. In the end, there is hardly anything it would dare aver any longer, not even about Being. What shows in this ontology is not so much mystical meditation as the distress of a thinking that seeks its otherness and cannot make a move without fearing to lose what it claims. Tendentially, philosophy becomes a ritualistic posture. Yet there is a truth stirring in that posture as well: the truth of philosophy falling silent.

UNSUCCESSFUL REALISM

The historic innervation of realism as a mode of mental conduct is not foreign to the philosophy of Being. Realism seeks to breach the walls which thought has built around itself, to pierce the interjected layer of subjective positions that have become a second

---

ture of operations, without deducing it. The arbitrariness he thus concedes—and sought to remove only in his late phase—is inevitable. If it were deduced, the procedure would reveal itself precisely as that "from above" which Husserl did not want, which at all costs he wished to prevent it from being. It would violate his quasi-positivistic "Back to things." Yet things do by no means compel the phenomenological reductions, which therefore get a touch of being posited at random. In spite of all the preserved "jurisdiction of reason" they lead to irrationalism.

nature. There are vibrations of this in Husserl's program, and Heidegger agreed with it.[14] The performance of the subject, which establishes idealistic cognition, has the irritating quality of a dispensable ornament after idealism has declined. In this respect fundamental ontology remains, like phenomenology, an involuntary heir to positivism.[15] Heidegger's realism turns a somersault: his aim is to philosophize formlessly, so to speak, purely on the ground of things, with the result that things evaporate for him. Weary of the subjective jail of cognition, he becomes convinced that what is transcendent to subjectivity is immediate for subjectivity, without being conceptually stained by subjectivity. In analogy to such romantic currents as the later "*Jugendbewegung*," fundamental ontology mistakes its protest against the confining and dimming subjective element for anti-romanticism; it wants to conquer subjectivity by belligerent speech, from which Heidegger does not shrink either.[16]

Since the transmissions of our subjectivity cannot be thought out of the world, we want to return to stages of consciousness that lie before the reflection upon subjectivity and transmission. This effort fails. When we believe we are, so to speak, subjectlessly clinging to the phenomenality of things, are original and neo-realistic and at the same time doing justice to the material, we are in fact eliminating all definitions from our thought, as Kant once eliminated them from the transcendent thing-in-itself. Definitions would be equally offensive to us as works of mere subjective reason and as descendants of a particular entity. Contradictory desiderata collide and destroy one another. Because we are neither to think speculatively, to have any thoughts that posit anything whatever, nor the other way round to admit an entity—a bit of the world, which would compromise the precedence of Being—we really dare not think anything but a complete vacuum, a capital X far emptier than the ancient transcendental subject which always carried "egoity," the memory of a consciousness in being, as its unit of consciousness.

This new X, absolutely ineffable and removed from all predicates, becomes the *ens realissimum* under the name of Being. In the inevitability of aporetical concept formation the philosophy of Being becomes the unwilling victim of Hegel's judgment about

Being: it is indistinguishably one with nothingness. Heidegger did not deceive himself about this. But what should be held against existential ontology[17] is not the nihilism which the left-wing Existentialists later interpreted into it, to its own horror; to be held against that ontology is its positive presentation of the downright nihility of its supreme word.

ON CATEGORIAL VISION

No matter how nondimensional we may make Being, how we may compress it into a point by the permanent exercise of caution in both directions, the procedure does have its *fundamentum in re.* Categorial vision, the growing awareness of a concept, reminds us that categorially constituted facts, which traditional epistemology knew as syntheses only, must always have a corresponding moment beyond the sensory ὕλη. They always have something immediate about them, something resembling visuality. A simple mathematical theorem would not apply without the synthesis of the figures between which the equation is set up, and neither—this is what Kant neglects—would a synthesis be possible if the relation of elements were not in line with this synthesis, regardless of the trouble in which such a manner of speaking entangles us, according to current logic.

To put it drastically, in a way that invites misunderstanding: there could be no synthesis if the two sides of the equation were not actually alike. To talk sensibly about this link apart from the cogitative synthesis is no more possible than a rational synthesis could be without that correspondence. It is a classic case of "transmission," as suggested by the fact that in reflection we waver whether thought is an activity or whether the very strain of it does not make it a self-adjustment, rather.

Inseparably therefrom, spontaneous thoughts are phenomena. Heidegger's stress on their phenomenal aspect against its total reduction to thought would be a salutary corrective of idealism. But his procedure is to isolate the factual moment, to conceive it, in Hegel's terminology, as abstractly as idealism conceives the synthetic moment. Hypostatized, it ceases to be a moment and comes to be what ontology in its protest against the split between concept and entity would least like it to be: it becomes a thing. And yet, its own character is genetical. The mental objectivity which Hegel taught, that product of the historic process, allows something like a visual relation to things of the mind, as some idealists (the late Rickert, for instance) were to rediscover. The more intensely our consciousness feels assured of such an evolved objectivity of the mental sphere—instead of attributing it as a "projection" to the contemplating subject—the closer its approach to a binding physiognomy of the mind. To a thinking which does not draw all definitions to its side, which does not disqualify its vis-à-vis, structures of the mind turn into a second immediacy.

This is what the doctrine of categorial vision too naïvely relies upon: it confuses that second immediacy with a first immediacy. Hegel's logic of essences went much farther; it treated the essence equally as grown out of Being and as independent of Being, as a kind of Dasein. By the demand which Husserl set forth and Heidegger tacitly adopted, on the other hand, that mental facts be purely described—that they be accepted as what they claim to be, and as nothing else—by this demand such facts are so dogmatized as if reflecting on things of the mind, re-thinking them, did not turn them into something else. The unhesitant supposition is that thinking, an inalienable activity, can really have an object that will not be made a product by the mere thought. Idealism, already conserved in the concept of the purely mental fact, is thus potentially reshaped into ontology. With the substruction of purely acceptant thought, however, the phenomenological thesis to which the entire school owed its effect broke down: that phenomenology is exploring and describing things rather than thinking them up; that it is not epistemology; in short, that it does not bear the stigma of a reflecting intelligence. Yet Being, the arcanum of fundamental ontology, is nothing but the categorial fact, offered in alleged purity and raised to the supreme formula.

To phenomenological analysis it was long known that there is something receptive about a synthesizing consciousness. What belongs together in a judgment is recognized in examples, not merely in comparisons. The immediacy of insight as such is not deniable, only its hypostasis. Primary clarity about some side of a specific object throws the clearest light upon the species, a light that dissolves the tautology of knowing nothing of the species save its definition. Without the moment of immediate insight, Hegel's line that the particular is the universal would remain pure avowal. Phenomenology, from Husserl on, has saved that line, albeit at the cost of the reflecting element that complements the line.

Its essence perception, however—the late Heidegger carefully shuns the slogan of the school that made him—involves contradictions that cannot be settled for the sake of peace and quiet, neither in the nominalistic direction nor in the realistic one. On the one hand, ideation has an elective affinity for ideology, for the surreptitious acquisition by indirect things of a directness vested with the authority of absolute, unimpeachable, subjectively evident being-in-itself. On the other hand, essence perception is our word for the physiognomic view of mental facts—a legitimate view because things of the mind are not constituted by the cognitive intentionality of consciousness but are based objectively, far beyond the individual author, on the collective life of the mind, in accordance with its imminent laws.

That mental objectivity corresponds to the moment of direct vision. Pre-shaped in itself, it can be viewed like things of the senses. Only, this view is no more absolute and irrefutable than our view of sensory things. Husserl, without much ado, credits both the physiognomic flash and Kant's synthetic a priori judgments with scientific necessity and generality; but what categorial vision contributes to—fallibly enough—would be the understanding of the thing itself, not its classification. The $\psi\epsilon\tilde{\upsilon}\delta o\varsigma$ of categorial vision is its dogmatic scientification, not its unscientific nature. Astir beneath the ideating view is the transmission that had congealed in the seeming directness of mentally given things; in this respect, essence perception is close to allegorical consciousness. As the experience of what has come into being in things which supposedly merely are, essence perception would be the almost diametrical opposite of the end it is used for. Rather than a faithful acceptance of Being, it would be its critique; rather than a sense of the thing's identity with its concept, it would be an awareness of the break between them. What the philosophy of Being boasts about, as if it were the organ of positivity pure and simple, has its truth in negativity.

Heidegger's stress on Being, which is not to be a mere concept, can be based upon the indissoluble content in judgments, as Husserl previously based himself on the ideal unity of the species. The positional value of such an exemplary consciousness is apt to rise historically. Günther Anders remarked that the more socialized the world, and the more tightly the network of general definitions covers its objects, the greater will be the tendency of individual facts to be direct transparencies of their universals, and the greater the yield a viewer obtains precisely by micrological immersion. This, of course, is a nominalistic kind of fact directly contrary to the ontological intention, although the essence perception may unwittingly have been occasioned by it. If the procedure nonetheless keeps exposing itself to the special-scientific objection, to the long since automatized charge of false or premature generalization, the fault lies not only with thought habits that have long caused men to misuse their scientific ethos, to use the principle of arranging facts modestly from outside as a rationalization of their failure to understand those facts from within. Insofar as the anticipations of the concept, the medium of exemplary thought, are confronted by empirical inquiry with concrete proof that the quasi-direct categorial view of a particular is not universal, the Husserl-Heidegger method—which avoids this test and yet flirts with a scientific language that sounds as if the test were submitted to—stands convicted of its failing.

BEING θέσει

It is asserted that Being, precedent to each abstraction, is no concept, or at most a qualitatively eminent concept. Ignored in this assertion is the fact that no immediacy—of which Hegel's *Phenomenology* already taught that in all its transmissions it keeps reproducing itself—is the whole of cognition. Each immediacy is a moment. No ontological draft can do without absolutizing single, culled-out moments. If cognition is an interaction of the synthetic cogitative function and that which it is to synthesize, with neither independent of the other, the direct insight stipulated by Heidegger as the sole title to a philosophy worthy of Being will not succeed either, unless by the spontaneity of thought which Heidegger disdains. If there were no substantial reflection without immediacy, the immediacy would linger non-committally and arbitrarily without reflection—without the thinking, distinguishing definition of what is meant by the Being that is alleged to show purely to a passive, nonthinking thought. The decorative sound of the pronouncements about things "unhiding" or "clearing" is due to the fictitious character of the claims. If the alleged primal word cannot be defined and fulfilled in thinking, if it cannot be critically confronted with its aims, the impossibility indicts all talk of Being. It has not been conceived because in the indistinctness it requires it cannot be conceived.

But that the philosophy of Being turns the unworkability into untouchability, that it turns the exemption from the rational process into a transcendence of the reflecting intellect—this is an act of violence as desperate as it is prudent. More resolute than phenomenology, which stops halfway, Heidegger wants to break out of the immanence of consciousness. But his outbreak is an outbreak into the mirror. Blinded to the moment of synthesis in the substrate, he ignores the fact that the mind—which in Heidegger's adored Eleatic philosophy of Being confessed to identity with Being—is already implied in the meaning of what it presents as the pure selfhood it would be confronting. Objectively, Heidegger's critique of philosophical tradition comes to run counter to its own promise. This critique tacitly ignores the subjective mind and thus necessarily the material, the factuality which any synthesis acts upon; it feigns a unity and absoluteness of what is articulated in it along these lines; and so it turns into the reverse of "destruction"—of the challenge to disenchant the manmade concepts.

Instead of recognizing human conditions in the concepts, Heidegger's critique confuses the conditions with the *mundus sensibilis*. It conserves, by repetition, what it is rising against: the screening thought structures for whose removal its own program calls. On the pretext of bringing to light what underlies them, those structures are once more, imperceptibly, turned into the "in itself" which a reified consciousness makes of them anyway. What pretends to crush fetishes is crushing nothing but the conditions of their recognition as fetishes. The seeming jailbreak terminates in what the flight is from; the Being it flows into is θέσει. As Being, which the mind transmits, is ceded to receptive vision, philosophy converges with a flatly irrationalist view of life.

A sign of irrationality would not by itself be the same as philosophical irrationalism. Irrationality is the scar which the irremovable nonidentity of subject and object leaves on cognition—whose mere form of predicative judgment postulates identity; it is also the hope of withstanding the omnipotence of the subjective concept. Like the concept, however, irrationality itself remains a function of the *ratio* and an object of its self-criticism: what slips through the net is filtered by the net. The philosophemes of irrationalism too depend on concepts, and thus on a rational element incompatible with them. One of the motives of dialectics is to cope with that which Heidegger evades by usurping a standpoint beyond the difference of subject and object—the difference that shows how inadequate the *ratio* is to thought. By means of reason, however, such a leap will fail. We cannot, by thinking, assume any position in which that separation of subject and object will directly vanish, for the separation is inherent in each thought; it is inherent in thinking itself. This is why Heidegger's moment of truth levels off into an irrationalist weltanschauung. Today as in Kant's time, philosophy demands a rational critique of reason, not its banishment or abolition.

"SENSE OF BEING"

When men are forbidden to think, their thinking sanctions what simply exists. The genuinely critical need of thought to awaken from the cultural phantasmagoria is trapped, channeled, steered into the wrong consciousness. The culture of its environment has broken thought of the habit to ask what all this may be, and to what end; it has enfeebled the question what it all means—a question growing in urgency as fewer people find some such sense self-evident, as it yields more and more to cultural bustle. Enthroned instead is the being-thus-and-not-otherwise of whatever may, as culture, claim to make sense. The weight of existing culture ends all insistence on the reality of its asserted meaning, or on the legitimacy of that meaning. On the other hand, fundamental ontology makes its appearance as spokesman for the pilfered interest, for all that has been "forgotten." This is not the least of its reasons for being averse to epistemology, which tends to list that interest among the prejudices.

Even so, fundamental ontology cannot annul epistemology at will. The doctrine of Dasein—of subjectivity—as the royal road to ontology resurrects the old subjective inquiry that had been humbled by ontological pathos. The phenomenological method claims to strip the tradition of Western philosophizing of its power, but it is at home in that tradition and well aware of the fact; for its main effect, its seeming originality, it has to thank the strides of obliviousness among the ones it appeals to. Phenomenology is the source of a turn in the question what Being means, or in its traditional variant: "Why is there anything at all? Why not nothing?" The question is now ceded to the analyzers of the meaning of a word: "Being." What this word, or the word "Dasein," might possibly mean is said to be one with the meaning of Being or Dasein: an immanent cultural component such as the meaning which semanticists decipher in the various languages is treated as if it had escaped from the relativity of products as well as from the senselessness of a mere entity. This is the function of Heidegger's version of the doctrine of the primacy of language.

That the sense of the word "Being" should be the direct sense of Being is bad equivocation. True, equivoques are not merely imprecise expressions.[18] The consonance of words always points to a sameness. The two meanings of "meaning" are entwined. Concepts, instruments of human thought, cannot make sense if sense itself is a negation, if every memory of an objective meaning beyond the mechanisms of concept formation has been expelled from the concepts. Positivism, to which concepts are nothing but accidental, interchangeable tokens, took the consequence and honored truth by extirpating truth. Taking the contrary position, the philosophy of Being does indeed rebuke positivism for the folly of its reason, but the unity of equivoques can be seen only through the veil of their implicit differences. In Heidegger's talk of "sense" this is discarded. He follows his inclination to hypostasis: findings made in the conditioned sphere have a semblance of unconditionality conferred upon them by the mode of their expression.

What makes this possible is the oscillating character of the word "Being." If we conceive true Being radically χωρίς from entity, it is identical with its meaning: we need only state the sense of the essence, "Being," to have the sense of Being itself. We do not notice that in following this schema the attempt to break out of idealism is revoked and the doctrine of Being turned back into one of thought, a doctrine which strips Being of everything other than pure thought. In order to get it to make any sort of sense—now felt by its absence—a compensatory summons goes out to the field which in analytical judgment is set up from the outset as the realm of sense: to the theory of meanings. It is a fact that if concepts are to be concepts at all they must mean something, and this fact serves as a vehicle for the thesis that their ὑποκείμενον, Being itself, must be meaningful because it is not given otherwise than as a concept, a linguistic meaning. That this concept is not to be a concept, that it is supposed to be immediate, rather, shrouds the semantic sense in ontological dignity. "Our talk of 'Being' never understands this name in the sense of a species to whose empty generality the historically offered doctrines of entity belong as individual cases. 'Being' speaks ever and ever as sent and hence pervaded by tradition."[19] This is the source from which such a philosophy draws its comfort. It is the magnet of fundamental ontology, far beyond its theoretical substance.

ONTOLOGY PRESCRIBED

Out of the human mind, ontology wants to restore the order shattered by the mind, along with the authority of that order. Its tendency freely to deny freedom shows when the expression *Entwurf* (draft, design) is traced to the verb *werfen* (to throw):

transsubjective commitment is placed into a subjectively positing act—an all too tangible absurdity which Heidegger could later put down only in dogmatic fashion, when the memory of subjectivity was eliminated from the concept.[20] Added to the mythologization of Being as the sphere of "sending"[21] was Heidegger's mythical *hubris,* his proclamation of the subject's decree as a plan of supreme authority and his disguise of his own voice as that of Being. Any consciousness that fails to go along was disqualified as "oblivious of Being."[22]

Such a claim, such a prescription of order, is in full accord with Heidegger's thought structure. Its only chance is to do violence to thinking; for the loss that echoes in the corny tremolo of the phrase "obliviousness of Being" was no stroke of fate. It was motivated. The mourned object, a legacy from the early ἀρχαί, dissipated for a consciousness wresting itself from nature. The myth itself showed up as a delusion; delusion alone, and command, can bring it to mind. The self-stylization of Being as a Beyond, a thing beyond the critical concept, is supposed, after all, to give the myth the legal title which heteronomy requires as long as a residue of the Enlightenment survives.

Suffering under that which Heidegger's philosophy calls "loss of Being" is not merely untrue; else he would scarcely look to Hölderlin for succor. Society's own concept says that men want their relations to be freely established; but no freedom has been realized in their relations to this day, and society remains as rigid as it is defective. All qualitative moments whose totality might be something like a structure are flattened in the universal barter relationship. The more immense the power of the institutional forms, the more chaotic the life they hem in and deform in their image. The production and reproduction of life, along with whatever the name superstructure covers, are not transparencies of reason—of that reason whose reconciled realization alone would be as one with a nonviolent order, an order worthy of men. The old, nature-spawned orders have either passed away or outlived their legitimacy in the direction of evil. By no means is the course of society anywhere as anarchic as it appears in the accidental and always irrational form of an individual fate. But its objectified legality is the converse of a state of Dasein in which men could live without fear.

This is felt in the ontological drafts. They project it on the victims, the subjects, and they frantically drown out premonitions of objective negativity with their message of order-in-itself, up to the most abstract order, the structure of Being. In place after place the world is set to shift to the horrors of order—not, as apologetic philosophy overtly or covertly complains, to the opposite. That freedom has largely remained an ideology; that men are powerless against the system, cannot rationally determine their lives and the life of the whole, cannot even think of such a determination without adding to their torment—this is what forces their rebellion into the wrong, invidious form of preferring the bad to a semblance of the better. And this is what the up-to-date philosophies are glad to toil for. The tragic Hitlerian pose of lonely valor makes them feel already in tune with the dawning order of the most powerful interests. Their posturing as metaphysically homeless and nothingness-bound is ideology, an attempt to justify the very order that drives men to despair and threatens them with physical extinction. The resonance of the resurrected metaphysics is anticipatory consent to an oppression whose potential triumph is inherent in Western society, and which has long triumphed in the East, where the thought of having gained freedom is twisted into unfreedom. Heidegger promotes slave thinking. With the standard gesture against the marketplace of public opinion he spurns the word "humanism," taking his place in the united front of thunderers against all "isms." The current talk of humanism is awful enough, but one may well ask whether Heidegger would not end the talk solely because his doctrine would end the matter.

PROTEST AGAINST REIFICATION

Despite its authoritarian intentions, however, the new ontology, now several experiences richer, will seldom be as frank in its praise of hierarchy as in the days when a disciple of Scheler's published a treatise on "The Medieval World and We." The tactics of covering every flank is in harmony with a social phase whose states of dominion are only half-heartedly based on a past stage of society. Those who seize power reckon with the anthropological end products of bourgeois society. They need those products. As the Führer rises above an atomized nation, as he thunders against social prejudice and, to perpetuate himself, will change the guard on occasion, so will the hierarchic leanings from the early days of the ontological renaissance fade out in the omnipotence and solitude of Being.

This too is more than ideology. The anti-relativism that goes back to Husserl's *Prolegomena to Pure Logic,* the work that established logical absolutism, blends with an aversion to static, reified thought—an aversion expressed in German idealism and by Marx, but initially neglected by the early Scheler and the first rudiments of the new ontology. Anyway, relativism has gone somewhat out of style. You do not hear so much twaddle about it either. An imperceptible change has taken place in the philosophical need: from a need for substance and solidity it has turned into a need to avoid the spiritual reification which society has carried out and categorically dictated to its members. And the means to avoid this is a metaphysics that condemns such reification, limits it by appealing to an origin we cannot lose, but actually does no more serious harm to reification than ontology does to the scientific bustle.

Of the compromised eternal values nothing remains but trust in the sanctity of Being, the essence before all things. Because in view of Being—which is supposed to be dynamic in itself, to be "happening"—the reified world is contemptibly unintrinsic, it is considered not worth changing, so to speak; the critique of relativism is enhanced to branding the progressive rationality of Western thought, and all subjective reason, as heresy. The affection against the subversive intellect, tried and tested and already rekindled by public opinion, combines with that against material alienation. There has always been an interaction between the two. Heidegger is anti-thing and anti-functional in one. Under no circumstances is Being to be a thing, and yet, as the metaphors keep indicating, it is to be the "ground" and something solid.[23]

Coming to light in this is the fact that subjectification and reification do not merely diverge. They are correlates. The more knowledge is functionalized and made a product of cognition, the more perfectly will its moment of motion be credited to the subject as its activity, while the object becomes the result of the labor that has congealed in it—a dead thing.

The reduction of the object to pure material, which precedes all subjective synthesis as its necessary condition, sucks the object's own dynamics out of it: it is disqualified, immobilized, and robbed of whatever would allow motion to be predicated at all. Not in vain did Kant call a class of categories "dynamics."[24] Even devoid of dynamics, however, the material is not flatly immediate. Despite its seeming absolute concreteness it is transmitted by abstraction—impaled, as it were, to begin with. Life becomes polarized, wholly abstract and wholly concrete, although it would be only in the tension between them. The two poles are equally reified, and what is left of the spontaneous subject, the pure apperception, ceases to be a subject; in the hypostatized logicity of a Kantian *cogito,* detached from any living I, it is covered by the all-controlling rigidity.

Only, in Heidegger's critique of reification, what originates in reality is placed without much ado upon the shoulders of whichever intellect repeats the cogitative performance—although this intellect itself, along with the world of its experience, is reified by the reality. What the mind does is not the fault of presumptuous irreverence; rather, the mind passes on what it is forced to pass on by the real context in which it is but a moment. It takes untruthfulness to push reification back into Being and into a history of Being, to mourn and consecrate as "fate" what might perhaps be changed by self-reflection and by the action it kindles. The doctrine of Being does indeed—legitimately, insofar as it goes against positivism—hand down the fundament of the entire philosophical history it slanders, notably Kant's and Hegel's: the view that the dualisms of within and without, of subject and object, of essence and appearance, of concept and fact, are not absolute. But their reconcilement is projected into the irretrievable origin, and thus dualism itself, the target of the whole conception, is steeled against the reconciling impulse. The dirge about obliviousness of Being sabotages reconcilement; a mythically impervious history of Being, to which hope may cling, denies reconcilement. Its fateful character could and should be dispelled as a context of delusions.

THE WRONG NEED

This delusive context extends not only to the ontological drafts, however. It extends equally to the needs which the drafts are to meet, to the needs into which the drafts inexplicitly read something like a warrant for their theses. The need itself—the spiritual no less than the material—is subject to criticism now that even hardboiled naïveté can no longer depend on it that social processes will go directly by supply and demand, and thus by needs. Needs are not invariant and undeducible, and neither do they guarantee their satisfaction. The semblance and the illusion that they must be met wherever they appear can be traced back to the same faulty consciousness. Be they ever so tangible, needs that are heteronomously produced participate in ideology.

Nothing real, of course, can be neatly peeled out of its ideological shell if the critique itself is not to succumb to ideology: to the ideology of a simple natural life. Real needs can objectively be ideologies without entitling us to deny them. For in the needs of even the people who are covered, who are administered, there reacts something in regard to which they are not fully covered—a surplus of their subjective share, which the system has not wholly mastered. Material needs should be respected even in their wrong form, the form caused by overproduction. The ontological need too has its real moment in a state in which men can neither recognize nor admit the rationality, the sense, of the necessity that rules their conduct. The faulty consciousness of their needs aims at things not needed by subjects, human beings who have come of age, and thus it compromises every possible fulfillment.

Added to the faulty consciousness is that it makes us believe in the attainability of unattainable things, complementary to the possibility of meeting needs the fulfillment of which is denied us.

At the same time, inverted needs of that sort also spiritualize our unconscious suffering under the material denial. This suffering is as bound to press us to reverse the denial as the need alone will not reverse it. A thought without a need, a thought that wished for nothing, would be like nothing; but a thought based on a need becomes confused if our conception of the need is purely subjective. Needs are conglomerates of truth and falsehood; what would be true is the thought that wants the right thing. If there is any truth to the doctrine that human needs cannot be told by a state of nature, only by the so-called cultural standard, the conditions of social production along with their bad irrationality are also part of that standard. Its irrationality must be ruthlessly criticized against the needs of the mind, the substitute for all that has been withheld.

The new ontology in itself is a substitute: what is promised as lying beyond the idealistic approach remains a latent idealism and a barrier to the incisive critique of idealism. Not only the primitive wish fulfillments which the cultural industry feeds to the masses—who do not really believe in them—are generally substitutes. Delusion is boundless in the field in which the official culture canon deposits its assets, in the supposedly sublime field of philosophy. Its most urgent need today appears to be the need for something solid. This need inspires the ontologies; it is what they adjust to. Its right lies in the will of people to be safe from being buried by a historical dynamics they feel helpless against. The immovable is to conserve the old and condemned. The more hopeless this longing, blocked by the extant forms of society, the more irresistible the trend of desperate self-preservation to a philosophy that is to be both in one: desperate and self-preserving. The invariant frames are made in the image of an omnipresent terror, of the dizziness that overcomes a society threatened by total destruction. If the threat vanished, its positive reversal—itself nothing but its abstract negation—would probably vanish with it.

WEAKNESS AND SUPPORT

A more specific need is that for a structure of invariants as a reaction to an idea drafted by conservative culture critics in the nineteenth century and popularized since: that the world has become formless. The idea fed on art-historical theses like the one of an extinguished style-building force; originating in aesthetics, it spread as a view of the whole. The basic assumption of the art historians—that this loss is in fact a loss, and not indeed a powerful step toward unshackling the productive forces—is by no means established. Esthetically revolutionary theoreticians such as Adolf Loos still dared to say so at the beginning of the century;[25] it has been forgotten only by the frightened culture critics, oathbound since to the existing culture. The lament about the loss of ordering forms increases with their very power. Institutions are more powerful than ever; they have long since produced something like the neon-lit style of the culture industry, a style that covers the world as the turn to the baroque did once upon a time. The conflict between subjectivity and forms is undiminished, but under the universal rule of forms a consciousness that feels impotent, that has lost confidence in its ability to change the institutions and their mental images, will reverse the conflict into identification with the aggressor.

The lament about a world-wide loss of forms is the arsis to the call for a binding order, which the subject tacitly expects to come heteronomously, from outside. That loss, insofar as its assertion is more than mere ideology, is not the fruit of the subject's emancipation; it is the fruit of the failure of emancipation. What appears as the formlessness of a Dasein modeled solely after subjective reason is in fact that which enslaves the subjects: the pure principle of being-for-something-else, of being merchandise. For the sake of universal equivalence and comparability this principle depreciates qualitative definitions everywhere; its tendency is to bring all things down to one level. Yet the same merchandise character—the indirect rule of men over other men—consolidates the subjects' state of tutelage. Their coming of age and their freedom to think qualitatively would go together.

Under the searchlight of modern art, style itself reveals its repressive moments. The need for form that has been borrowed from style fools people about the bad, coercive side of form. If a form does not prove by itself, by its transparent function, that it is entitled to live—if it is merely posited in order that there be form—such a form is untrue and thus inadequate even as a form. The mind which is to be persuaded that it is sheltered in forms is potentially beyond them. The effort so to arrange the world that it would stop obeying formal categories contrary to the most advanced consciousness has failed, and it is only because of this failure that the prevailing consciousness must frantically champion those categories as its own cause. Because the mind cannot wholly repress their inadequacy, however, it opposes the present, starkly visible heteronomy with another heteronomy, whether past or abstract, with values that are viewed as *causae sui,* and with the phantasm of their reconcilement with the living.

Radical modern art is hated—with restorative conservatism and fascism always in blissful accord—because it reminds us of missed chances, but also because by its sheer existence it reveals the dubiousness of the heteronomous structural ideal. The subjective consciousness of men is socially too enfeebled to burst the invariants it is imprisoned in. Instead, it adapts itself to them while mourning their absence. The reified consciousness is a moment in the totality of the reified world. The ontological need is the metaphysics of that consciousness even when its doctrinal content leads it to exploit the critique of reification that has nowadays become so cheap. The form of invariance as such is the projection of what has congealed in the reified consciousness. Incapable of experiencing things not already contained in the repertory of eversameness, that consciousness recoins immutability into the idea of something eternal—of transcendence.

In a state of unfreedom no one, of course, has a liberated consciousness. But such a consciousness which would have power over itself, which would really be as autonomous as it so far always only pretended to be, would not need to be continually afraid of losing itself to something else—secretly, to the powers that rule it. The need for support, for a supposed substantiality, is not so substantial as its self-righteousness would have it be.

It is a sign of the weakness of the I, rather, known to psychologists as a presently typical human impairment. A man no longer oppressed from without and within himself would not be looking for support, perhaps not even for himself. Subjects who managed to save some of their freedom even under heteronomous conditions suffer less of a lack of support than do the unfree, who are only too glad to charge that lack to freedom, as freedom's fault. If men no longer had to equate themselves with things, they would need neither a superstructure of things nor an invariant picture of themselves, after the model of things.

The doctrine of invariants perpetuates how little has changed; its positivity perpetuates what is bad about it. This is why the ontological need is wrong. It is probably not until after the invariants have fallen that metaphysics would dawn on the horizon. But this consolation does not help much. An idea whose time has come has no time to waste. To wait in the clutch is to go along with the separation of temporality and eternity. The separation is wrong, and yet the answers that would be required are blocked off at the historic hour—hence the antinomical character of all questions aimed at consolation.

TWO

BEING AND EXISTENCE

IMMANENT CRITIQUE OF ONTOLOGY

Our critique of the ontological need brings us to an immanent critique of ontology itself. We have no power over the philosophy of Being if we reject it generally, from outside, instead of taking it on in its own structure—turning its own force against it, in line with Hegel's desideratum. The motivations and results of Heidegger's thought movements can be construed even where they are not uttered; there is hardly a sentence of his without its positional value in the functional context of the whole. In that sense he is a successor to the deductive systems. Their history is already full of concepts spawned by cogitative progress, even if we cannot put a finger on the corresponding facts; the need to form these concepts is the source of philosophy's speculative element. The thought movement that congealed in them must be reliquified, its validity traced, so to speak, in repetition.

It is not enough to demonstrate to the philosophy of Being that what it calls Being does not exist, that there is no such thing. For it does not postulate this sort of "being there." Instead, such a blind Being would have to be deduced in reply to the irrefutable claim that exploits the blindness. The very senselessness whose establishment elicits yells of positivistic triumph is plausible from the viewpoint of philosophical history. Because the secularization of theological contents once deemed objectively binding is irrevocable, the apologist for those contents must strive to rescue them through subjectivity. The religious doctrine of the Reformation virtually did so; it surely was the thought figure of Kantian philosophy. Enlightenment has since made irresistible strides, with subjectivity itself drawn into the demythologizing process. This reduced the chances of rescue to a borderline value. Paradoxically, the hope for it has been ceded to its relinquishment, to an unreserved and at the same time self-reflecting secularization.

Heidegger's approach is true insofar as he accepts that and denies traditional metaphysics; he becomes untrue where—not unlike Hegel—he talks as if the contents we want to rescue were thus directly in our minds. The philosophy of Being fails as soon as it claims a sense in Being, a sense which its own testimony shows to have been dissolved by the thought to which Being itself, since its conception, is still attached as a conceptual reflection. The senselessness of the word "Being," at which common sense finds it so easy to sneer, cannot be laid to either thinking too little or irresponsibly thinking too fast. It is the sediment of the impossibility of grasping or producing any positive sense by the thought that was the medium of the objective evaporation of such sense. If we try to accomplish Heidegger's distinction of Being from the concept that circumscribes it logically, we are left—after deducting entity as well as the categories of abstraction—with an unknown quantity which nothing but the pathos of its invocation lifts above the Kantian concept of the transcendent thing-in-itself. Yet this makes the very word "thinking," which Heidegger will not renounce, as unsubstantial as the thing to be thought: thinking without a concept is not thinking at all.

The true philosophical task, according to Heidegger, would be to conceive Being, yet Being resists any cogitative definition. This makes the appeal to conceive it a hollow one. Heidegger's objectivism, the interdict he hurls against the thinking subject, is its faithful reverse image. Lines that a positivist finds bereft of sense present a promissory note to the eon; those lines are false only because they claim to make sense, because they sound like the echo of a substance. It is not sense that inhabits the inmost core of Heidegger's philosophy. Expounded as a knowledge of salvation, it is what Scheler called a "knowledge of dominion."

Heidegger's cult of Being, his polemics against the idealistic cult of the mind, does of course presuppose a critique of the deification of Being. But Heidegger's Being, all but indistinguishable from its antipode, the mind, is no less repressive than the mind. It is only less transparent than the mind, whose principle was transparency, and therefore even less capable of critical self-reflection on the nature of dominion than the philosophies of the mind had ever been. The electric charge of Heidegger's word Being goes well with the praise which a neutralized culture bestows upon the devout or faithful as such—as if their devotions and beliefs were merits in themselves, regardless of the truth of what they believe. This neutralization comes into its own in Heidegger: faith in Being strikes out all the substance that had been noncommittally dragged along in the half or fully secularized religions. Heidegger drills in religious customs, but all that he retains of them is the general confirmation of dependence and submissiveness as surrogates of the objective formal laws of thought. Like logical positivism, the structure clings to the initiate while permanently eluding him. With the facts stripped of all that makes them more than facts, Heidegger seizes upon the waste product, so to speak, of the evaporating aura. He assures philosophy of something like a post-existence, provided it will make the ἕν καὶ πᾶν its specialty.

The expression of Being is nothing but the feeling of this aura. It is an aura without a light-giving star, of course, one in which the indirect element becomes isolated and thus direct. But indirectness can no more be hypostatized than can the poles of subject and object; it is valid only in their constellation. Transmission is transmitted by what it transmits. Heidegger overstretches it into a sort of nonobjective objectivity. He settles in an imaginary realm between the obtuse *facta bruta* and the twaddle about weltanschauung. The concept of Being, whose transmissions are not to be put into words, becomes the "non-essence" which Aristotle recognized in the Platonic idea, the paragon of essence. It becomes a repetition of entity, from which Heidegger takes away whatever he gives to Being.

With the emphatic claim of Being to be purely essential thus voided, entity—indelibly inherent in Being without, in Heidegger's version, having to admit its ontical character—shares as a parasite in that ontological claim. That Being shows, and that the subject should accept it passively, is borrowed from the old epistemological data which were supposed to be factual, ontical in character. However, in the sacral domain of Being this ontical character simultaneously sheds the trace of contingency that used to permit its critique. By virtue of the logic of the philosophical aporia, and without waiting for the philosopher to add his ideology, Heidegger transposes the empirical superiority of the way things are into the realm of essence.

The idea of Being as an entity whose cognitive definition would inevitably miss the thought by dissecting and thus, to use the current political term, subverting it—what this idea amounts to is conclusiveness, as in the one-time closed Eleatic system and in today's closed world. Unlike the systems' intent, however, the conclusiveness is heteronomous: beyond achievement by either the rational will of individuals or that total social subject which has not been realized to this day. In the statically renewed society we see ahead, no more new motives seem to swell the stockpile of apologetic ideology. Rather, the current motives are diluted and rendered unrecognizable to such an extent that actual experience is hard put to refute them. If the flashbacks and other tricks of philosophy project an entity upon Being, the entity is satisfactorily justified; if it is treated with disdain, as "a mere entity," it may go on making mischief outside, without hindrance. There is little difference from the sensibility of dictators who avoid visits to concentration camps whose staff is honestly carrying out their directives.

COPULA

The cult of Being lives by the age-old ideology of the *idola fori,* by that which thrives in the darkness of the word "being" and of the forms derived from it. "Is" establishes a context of existential judgment between the grammatical subject and the predicate, thus suggesting something ontical. Taken purely by itself, however, as a copula, it means at the same time the general, categorical fact of a synthesis, without representing anything ontical. Hence it can be entered straightways on the ontological side of the ledger. From the logicity of the copula, Heidegger gets the ontological purity that suits his allergy to all things factual, and from existential judgment he gets the memory of things ontical

—which will permit the categorial achievement of the synthesis to be hypostatized, then, as given.

Even the word "is," of course, has a "state of facts" corresponding to it. In every predicative judgment, "is" has its meaning, as have the subject and the predicate. But the "state of facts" is a matter of intentionality, not of being. The copula, by definition, is fulfilled only in the relation between subject and predicate. It is not independent. Heidegger, in misplacing it beyond the sole source of its meaning, succumbs to that reified thought to which he took exception. His definition of that which is meant by "is" as the absolute, ideal "in itself"—in other words, as Being—would give the same right to the things represented by the judgment's subject and predicate, once detached from the copula. To both, synthesis by the copula would happen as a mere external occurrence; this was precisely what the concept of Being was thought up against. Once again, as in an obsolete logic, subject, copula, and predicate would be conclusive, completed details after the model of things.

In truth, however, predication is not an adjunct. In coupling the subject and the predicate it is also that which both would be in themselves if there were any way to conceive this "would be" without the synthesis of "is." Hence the ban on extrapolating from the copula, either to a preordained "being" or to a "becoming," a pure synthesis. This extrapolation rests on a confusion in the theory of meanings: the general meaning of the copula "is," the constant grammatical token for the synthesis of the judgment, is confused with the specific meaning acquired by "is" in every judgment. The two coincide by no means. In that sense, "is" might be likened to occasional expressions. Its generality is a promissory note on particularization, the general form in which to carry out particular acts of judgment. Nomenclature takes this into account by reserving the scientific term "copula" for that generality—and for the particular job required in each judgment it reserves the "is."

Heidegger ignores the difference. As a result, the particular job of "is" comes to be merely something like a phenomenal mode of the generality. The difference between the category and the substance of the existential judgment is blurred. The substitution of the general grammatical form for the apophantic content transforms the ontical task of "is" into an ontological one, a way of Being to be. Yet if the task that is postulated, transmitted, and transmitting in the sense of "is" were neglected in the particular, that "is" would retain no substrate of any kind; there would be nothing left but the abstract form of transmission in general. This "pure Becoming," in Hegel's word, is no more a primal principle than any other, unless one wishes to drive out Parmenides with Heraclitus.

The word Being has an overtone that can be missed in arbitrary definition only; it is what lends Heidegger's philosophy its timbre. Every entity is more than it is—as we are reminded by Being, in contrast to entity. There is no entity whose determination and self-determination does not require something else, something which the entity itself is not; for by itself alone it would not be definable. It therefore points beyond itself. "Transmission" is simply another word for this. Yet Heidegger seeks to hold on to that which points beyond itself, and to leave behind, as rubble, that beyond which it points. To him, entwinement turns into its absolute opposite, into the πρώτη οὐσία. In the word "Being," the totality of that which is, the copula has become an object.

We could, of course, not talk of an "is" without Being any more than we can talk of Being without an "is." The word points to the objective element which in each predicative judgment qualifies the very synthesis required for its own crystallization. Yet Being is no more independent of the "is" than that state of facts in a judgment is independent of it. The dependence of the forms of language—which Heidegger rightly takes to be more than mere signification—bears witness against the things he will squeeze out of language. If grammar couples the "is" with the substrate category "Being" as its asset—that something is—it will reciprocally use Being only in relation to all there is, rather than in itself. True, the appearance of ontological purity is strengthened by the fact that every analysis of judgments leads to two moments of which neither one can be reduced to the other—no more than, metalogically, subject and object can be so reduced.* A thought fascinated by the chimera that anything is absolutely "first" will eventually tend to claim that even this irreducible thing itself is the "last." The reduction to irreducibility vibrates in Heidegger's concept of Being. But it is a formali-

---

* A rigorous distinction has to be made, first, between the purely logical subject-object relation in a judgment and the relation of subject and object as an epistemological-material one. What the term subject means in the two cases is almost contradictory. In the theory of judgments it is the basic assumption of which something is predicated, as opposed to the act of judgment and to what is judged in the synthesis of the judgment; in a sense, it is the objectivity upon which thinking works. Epistemologically, however, "subject" means the thinking function, and frequently also the entity which thinks and cannot be excluded from the concept "I" except at the price of ceasing to mean what it means.

In spite of this, the distinction involves a close kinship of the things distinguished. The constellation of a state of facts covered by the judgment—"the judged as such," in the language of phenomenology—and of the synthesis, of which that state of facts is the basis as much as the product, recalls the material constellation of subject and object. These differ in the same way, cannot be brought to pure identity with one side or the other, and mutually qualify each other because no object is determinable without the subject, the determinant that makes an object of it, and because no subject can think anything it does not confront, not even that subject itself. Thinking is tied to entities.

The parallel between logic and epistemology is more than a mere analogy. The purely logical relation between fact and synthesis, a relation known irrespective of existence, of spatial-temporal factuality, is in truth an abstraction from the subject-object relation. It is on this abstraction that pure thought focuses, neglecting all particular ontical subject-matter, and yet the abstraction has no power over something that occupies the vacant place of the subject-matter—something which, however generally it may designate that vacant place, means substantive things and requires substantive things to become that which it means.

The methodological procedure of abstraction has its limit in the sense of what we imagine to have in our hands as a pure form. There is no extinguishing the trace of entity in the formal-logical "something." The form "something" is shaped after the model of material, of the $\tau\acute{o}\delta\epsilon$ $\tau\iota$; it is a material form and thus, after its own purely logical meaning, in need of that metalogical element for which epistemological reflection strove as the counter-pole of thought.

zation that does not jibe with what it formalizes. Taken by itself, it means no more than a negative: that whenever we judge, the moments of judgment will not go into each other on either side —in other words, that they are not identical. Outside this relation of the moments of judgment, irreducibility is nothing; there is nothing we can mean by it. Hence our inability to impute to it an ontological priority over the moments. The paralogism lies in the transformation of that negative—that one of the moments cannot be reduced to the other—into something positive.

Heidegger gets as far as the borderline of dialectical insight into the nonidentity in identity. But he does not carry through the contradiction in the concept of Being. He suppresses it. What can somehow be conceived as Being mocks the notion of an identity between the concept and that which it means; but Heidegger treats it as an identity, as pure Being itself, devoid of its otherness. The nonidentity in absolute identity is covered up like a skeleton in the family closet. Because "is" is neither a merely subjective function nor a thing, an entity—because to our traditional way of thinking it is no objectivity—Heidegger calls it "Being," that nonsubjective, nonobjective third. The transition ignores the intent of the term as whose humble interpreter Heidegger regards himself. The insight that "is" can be called neither a mere thought nor a mere entity does not permit its transfiguration into something transcendent in relation to those two definitions. Every attempt to conceive the "is" at all, even in the palest generality, leads to entities on the one side and to concepts on the other. The constellation of moments is not to be reduced to a singular essence; what is inherent in that constellation is not an essence. The unity promised by the word "Being" lasts only so long as it is not conceived, as its meaning is not analyzed in line with Heidegger's own method; any such analysis will bring to light what disappeared in the abyss of Being. But if the analysis becomes taboo, aporia turns into subreption. We are to conceive Being as the absolute, but it is to be the absolute only because we cannot conceive it. It shines beyond the moments only because it magically blinds our cognition of moments. A rationality that cannot do its best strikes itself as the worst.

NO TRANSCENDENCE OF BEING

Contrary to the linguistic atomization practiced by Heidegger, the believer in entirety, there is already a kind of coadunation between all single concepts in themselves and the judgments neglected by a classifying logic. The old tripartition of logic into concept, judgment, and conclusion is a relic like the system of Linné. Judgments are not a mere synthesis of concepts, for without judgment there is no concept—a fact which Heidegger overlooks, possibly under the influence of scholasticism. Yet within the indirectness, of Being as well as of "is," the subject lies hidden—another moment (idealistic, if you will) which Heidegger discards, thus enhancing subjectivity into the absolute that precedes all subject-object dualism. Every analysis of a judgment takes us to a subject and an object, but this fact does not create a region beyond those moments, a region that would be "in itself." The analysis results in the constellation of those moments, not in a third that would be superior, or at least more general.

One might, of course, say in Heidegger's sense that "is" is not a thing, not τὰ ὄντα, not an entity, not what we usually mean by objectivity. For "is" has no substrate without the synthesis; in the state of facts that we mean, there is no corresponding τόδε τι we might interpret it as being. Therefore, we conclude, "is" must indicate that third, which is Being. But our conclusion is wrong, a *tour de force* of self-sufficient semantics. The paralogism is evinced by the fact that we cannot conceive such a supposedly pure substrate of "is." Every attempt to do so runs into transmissions of which the hypostatized Being would be relieved. To Heidegger, however, its very inconceivability yields a profit, an addition to the metaphysical dignity of Being. Its refusal to submit to human thought is said to make it the Absolute. Because, in the best Hegelian manner, it cannot be reduced to either a subject or an object without leaving a remainder, it is regarded as beyond subject and object—although, independently of them, it would indeed not be at all. In the end, human reason, which cannot conceive Being, is itself disparaged—as if there were any way to separate thought from reason.

Undeniably, Being is not simply the totality of all there is, of all that is the case. With this anti-positivistic insight we do justice to the concept's surplus over factuality. No concept would be thinkable, indeed none would be possible without the "more" that makes a language of language. But what echoes in the word "Being" as opposed to τὰ ὄντα—that everything is more than it is—means entwinement, not something transcendent to entwinement. This is what Heidegger makes of it: something added to the individual entity. He pursues dialectics to the point of saying that neither the subject nor the object are immediate and ultimate; but he deserts dialectics in reaching for something immediate and primary beyond subject and object.

Thinking becomes archaistic as soon as whichever scattered entity is more than entity will be transfigured into a metaphysical ἀρχή. Heidegger reacts to the loss of the aura[1] by arranging its function, turning the fact that things point beyond themselves into a substrate, and thus making that fact itself like a thing. He prescribes a repristination of the shudder caused, long before the mythical nature religions, by intermingling: Mana[2] is raised up under the name of Being, as if our dawning impotence resembled that of pre-animistic primitives during a thunderstorm. Secretly, Heidegger obeys the law that the advancing rationality of their constantly irrational society makes men reach farther and farther into the past. Cautioned by trouble, he shuns the romantic Pelagianism of Klages and the powers of Oskar Goldberg; from the region of tangible superstition he flees to a dusk in which not even such mythologemas as that of the reality of images will take shape any longer. He eludes criticism, but without letting go of the advantages of originality: the origin is placed so far back that it will seem extratemporal and therefore omnipresent.

It does not work, however.[3] There is no other way to break out of history than regression. Its goal, the most ancient of goals, is not truth but absolute semblance, dull imprisonment in a nature we do not see through, a mere parody of the supernatural. Heidegger's transcendence* is an absolutized immanence, obdurate

---

* "Being, as the basic theme of philosophy, is no class or or genus of entities; yet it pertains to every entity. Its 'universality' is to be

against its own immanent character. That semblance needs an explanation: how Being, flatly deduced and transmitted, can commandeer the insignia of *ens concretissimum*. The semblance rests upon the fact that the two poles of traditional epistemology and metaphysics, the pure, present object and pure thought, are both abstract, both removed from so many definitions that little more is to be said about them if we want our judgment to go by what we judge. Thus the two poles seem indistinguishable from each other, and this permits the unnoticed substitution of one for the other, depending on what is to be proved. The concept of entity at large, ideally without any category, is stripped of all qualifications, so it need not let itself be confined to any particular entity and may call itself Being. Yet Being, as an absolute concept, need not legitimize itself as a concept: by any definition it would delimit itself and violate its own meaning. Hence it may as well be garbed in the dignity of immediacy as the τόδε τι in that of essentiality.

Heidegger's entire philosophy is set between these two extremes which are indifferent to one another.* Against his will, however,

---

sought higher up. Being and the structure of Being lie beyond every entity and every possible character which an entity may possess. Being is the *transcendens* pure and simple. And the transcendence of Dasein's Being is distinctive in that it implies the possibility and the necessity of the most radical individuation. Every disclosure of Being as the *transcendens* is transcendental knowledge. Phenomenological truth (the disclosedness of Being) is *veritas transcendentalis*." (Heidegger, *Being and Time*, trans. J. Macquarrie and E. S. Robinson, p. 62.)

* The fact that this philosophy detours around dialectics, despite its contact with Hegel, lends it the appeal of having reached transcendence. It is proof against dialectical reflection, though incessantly touching upon it; it makes do with traditional logic and follows the model of predicative judgment in procuring a solid and unconditional character for things which dialectical logic would consider mere moments. For example, according to an early phrasing (cf. Heidegger, *Being and Time*, trans. Macquarrie-Robinson, p. 33) "Dasein" is to be that ontical, existential thing which has the paradoxical—unadmittedly paradoxical—advantage of being ontological.

"Dasein" is an abashed German variant of subject. It did not escape Heidegger that it is both direct and the very principle of indirectness, that as a *constituens* it presupposes the constitutum, factuality. The entity comes to the fore in Being. Being gets its life from the forbidden fruit, as if the fruit were Freya's apples. Being, for its aural absoluteness' sake, must not be contaminated with any entity; yet nothing but such contamination can give Being the immediacy that furnishes the legal title for the claim of absoluteness: that "Being" always means also as much as "entity" pure and simple. As soon as the talk of Being adds anything to pure invocation, the addition will come from the ontical sphere. Heidegger's rudiments of material ontology are temporal; they have come to be, and they will pass as Scheler's did before.

EXPRESSING THE INEXPRESSIBLE

We fail to do justice to the concept of Being, however, until we also grasp the genuine experience that effects its instauration: the philosophical urge to express the inexpressible. The more anxiously a philosophy resists that urge, which is its peculiarity, the greater the temptation to tackle the inexpressible directly, without the labor of Sisyphus—which, by the way, would not be the worst definition of philosophy and does so much to bring ridicule upon it. Philosophy itself, as a form of the mind, contains a moment deeply akin to the state of suspense which Heidegger assigns to the topic of meditation—and which prevents meditation. For philosophy is form in a far more specific sense than the history of its concept

---

state of facts is dialectical; Heidegger proceeds at any cost to translate it into the logic of noncontradictoriness. The mutually contradictory moments of the subjects are turned into two attributes which he attaches to the subject as to a substance. But this is helpful to the ontological dignity: the undeveloped contradiction will assure a superiority as such, because it defies the conditions of discursive logic, the language into which it has been translated. By virtue of this projection, the substance called Being is to be something positive above both concept and fact. Such positivity would not withstand its dialectical reflection.

All fundamental ontology has schemata of this sort for its τόποι. Transcendence, both beyond thinking and beyond facts, is derived by this ontology from the undialectical expression and hypostasis of dialectical structures—as if these structures were simply to be named.

leads us to suspect. In that history (except in a Hegelian stratum) it is rare for philosophy to incorporate in its reflection the qualitative difference that sets it apart from science, from the theory of science, and from logic, for all its coadunation with all three of them.

Philosophy consists neither in *vérités de raison* nor in *vérités de fait*. Nothing it says will bow to tangible criteria of any "being the case"; its theses on conceptualities are no more subject to the criteria of a logical state of facts than its theses on factualities are to the criteria of empirical science. Its detachment adds to its fragility. It will not be nailed down. Its history is one of permanent failure insofar as, terrorized by science, it would keep searching for tangibility. It has earned the positivists' criticism by claiming to have a scientific approach—a claim rejected by science; but these critics are wrong when they confront philosophy with unphilosophical criteria as soon as these criteria are even slightly in line with the philosophical idea. Philosophy will not dispense with truth, however, but will illuminate the narrowness of scientific truth. The determinant of its suspended state is that even while keeping its distance from the verifying type of cognition it is not noncommittal—that the life it leads has a stringency of its own. Philosophy seeks stringency in that which it is not, in its opposite, and in the reflection on what, with a poor sort of naïveté, is viewed as binding by positive cognition.

Philosophy is neither a science nor the "cogitative poetry" to which positivists would degrade it in a stupid oxymoron. It is a form transmitted to those which differ from it as well as distinguished from them. Its suspended state is nothing but the expression of its inexpressibility. In this respect it is a true sister of music. There is scarcely a way to put the suspension into words, which may have caused the philosophers—except for Nietzsche, perhaps—to gloss it over. It is more the premise of understanding philosophical texts than it is their succinct quality. It may have sprung forth historically and may fall silent again, as music is in danger of doing. Heidegger has innervated this and literally transformed that specific trait of philosophy—perhaps because it is on the point of extinction—into a specialty, an objectivity of quasisuperior rank: a philosophy that knows it is judging neither facts nor concepts the way other things are judged, a philosophy that is not even sure what it is dealing with, would seek a positive content just the same, beyond facts, concepts, and judgments.

The suspended character of thought is thus raised to the very inexpressibility which the thought seeks to express. The nonobjective is enhanced into the outlined object of its own essence—and thereby violated. Under the weight of tradition, which Heidegger wants to shake off, the inexpressible becomes explicit and compact in the word "Being," while the protest against reification becomes reified, divorced from thinking, and irrational. By treating the inexpressible side of philosophy as his immediate theme, Heidegger dams up philosophy all the way back to a revocation of consciousness. By way of punishment, the well he wants to excavate dries up. It is a buried well, in his conception, oozing a scantier trickle then ever came from the insights of the allegedly destroyed philosophy that inclines indirectly to the inexpressible. What Heidegger attributes to the poverty of our time is the poverty of a thought that fancies itself beyond time. The direct expression of the inexpressible is void; where the expression carried, as in great music, its seal was evanescence and transitoriness, and it was attached to the process, not to an indicative "That's it." Thoughts intended to think the inexpressible by abandoning thought falsify the inexpressible. They make of it what the thinker would least like it to be: the monstrosity of a flatly abstract object.

THE CHILD'S QUESTION

If it were not too ontical-psychological for them, functional ontologists might argue that every child asks about Being. Reflection cures him of that habit, and as always in idealism, reflection on the reflection seeks to compensate for the cure. But the doubled reflection will hardly ask directly, as the child does. With the anthropomorphism of an adult, so to speak, philosophy pictures the conduct of the child as that of the childhood of the species, as before and above time. The child has trouble with his relation to words, which he appropriates with an effort that can scarcely be imagined any more at a later age; he has far less trouble with the world that is fairly familiar to him, in his early phases, as made up of objects of action. He wants to find out what the words mean, and the occupation with them—as well as an impish, nagging, psychoanalytically explicable stubbornness, perhaps—leads him to the relation of words and things. He may get on his mother's nerves with the awkward problem why a bench is called a bench. His naïveté is un-naïve. As language, culture has invaded his stirring consciousness very early, mortgaging the talk of originality. The meaning of the words and their truth content, their "attitude toward objectivity," are not yet sharply distinguished from each other. To know what the word "bench" means and to know what a bench really is—which does include an existential judgment—is one and the same to that consciousness, or not differentiated, at least. Besides, in countless cases, the distinction takes an effort.

It is thus precisely the childlike directness that is indirect in itself, with the acquired vocabulary for its orientation. The boring for the "why," for the first cause, is pre-formed. Language is taken for granted; it is experienced as φύσει, not as θέσει. At the outset there is fetishism, and the hunt for the outset remains always subject to it. That fetishism is hard to see through, of course, since whatever we think is also a matter of language. Unreflective nominalism is as wrong as the realism that equips a fallible language with the attributes of a revealed one. It is in Heidegger's favor that there is no speechless "in-itself"—that language, therefore, lies in truth, not truth in language, as something merely signified by language. But the constitutive share of language in truth does not establish an identity of truth and language.

The test of the power of language is that the expression and the thing will separate in reflection.[4] Language becomes a measure of truth only when we are conscious of the nonidentity of an expression with that which we mean. Heidegger refuses to engage in that reflection; he halts after the first step·of language-philosophical dialectics. His thinking is repristinative also in its aim to restore the "power of the Name" by a ritual of nomenclature. Yet in our secularized languages this power is not present in a way that would let the subject accomplish the restoration. By secularization, the subjects have withdrawn the Name from the languages, and the objectivity of language needs their intransigence, not a philosophical trust in God.

Language is more than a sign only where it shows significative strength, where it most exactly and succinctly covers what is meant. It "is" only insofar as it comes to be, in the constant confrontation of expression and thing—this was the premise Karl Kraus proceeded on, though himself probably leaning toward an ontological view of language. Heidegger's procedure, on the other hand, is a "Teutonizing cabbalism," in Scholem's phrase. He treats the historic languages as if they were those of Being, as romantically as any violent anti-romanticist. His kind of destruction halts before philological erudition—which he does not consider, but does suspend at the same time. Such a consciousness will affirm its environment, or will put up with it, at least; but a genuine philosophical radicalism, no matter what the form of its historical appearance, is a product of doubt. The radical question that will destroy nothing but the doubt is itself illusory.

THE QUESTION OF BEING

The fundament beneath Heidegger's emphatic expression of the word "Being" is an old category of his, one which later on goes all but unmentioned: authenticity. The transcendence of Being, as opposed to concept and entity, is to redeem the desideratum of authenticity as that which is not illusory, neither artificial nor moot. Protested against, with good reason, is the fact that the historic evolution of philosophy has leveled the distinction between essence and appearance, the inherent impulse of philosophy as θαυμάζειν, as discontent with the façade. Unreflecting enlighteners have negated the metaphysical thesis of essence as the true world behind the phenomena with an equally abstract counter-thesis: that essence, as the epitome of metaphysics, is itself mere appearance—as if appearance, therefore, were the same as essence. Because of the dichotomy in the world, its authentic element, the law of dichotomy, is hidden. The positivist who adjusts to this by deleting as myth and subjective projection whatever is not a datum, whatever is hidden, adds as much to the illusiveness as was once added by doctrines that consoled men for their suffering in the *mundus sensibilis* by avowing the noumenal. Heidegger did sense some of this mechanism. But the authenticity he misses will promptly recoil into positivity, into authenticity as a posture of consciousness—a posture whose emigration from the profane powerlessly imitates the theological habit of the old doctrine of essence. The hidden essence is rendered proof against the suspicion of being pure mischief. No one, for example, dares consider that the categories of the so-called mass trend—expounded in *Being and Time* as well as in Jaspers' paperback on the intellectual situation of our time[5]—may themselves be categories of that hidden mischief which makes men what they are; and they must let philosophy chide them to boot, then, for having forgotten the essence. The resistance to the reified consciousness, tremors of which linger in the pathos of authenticity, has been broken. The remaining criticism is unleashed against the phenomenon—in other words, against the subjects. The essence, whose self-reproducing guilt is merely represented by that of the subjects, remains undisturbed.

While refusing to be distracted from the θαυμάζειν, fundamental ontologists cut themselves off from an answer by the form in which they put the question what is authentic. Not for nothing is it dressed in the disgusting technical term "question of Being." This is mendacious because the appeal is to every individual's bodily concern—to the naked concern of Hamlet's soliloquy, whether in death the individual is obliterated absolutely or has the hope of the Christian *non confundar*—but what Hamlet means by being or not being is replaced by pure essence, in which existence is swallowed up. By making things thematical in accord with phenomenological custom, with a full array of descriptions and distinctions, existential ontology satisfies the concern and distracts from it. "The question of Being," says Heidegger, "aims therefore at ascertaining the a priori conditions not only for the possibility of the sciences which examine entities as entities of such and such a type, and, in so doing, already operate with an understanding of Being, but also for the possibility of those ontologies themselves which are prior to the ontical sciences and which provide their foundations. Basically, all ontology, no matter how rich and firmly compacted a system of categories it has at its disposal, remains blind and perverted from its ownmost aim, if it has not first adequately clarified the meaning of Being, and conceived this clarification as its fundamental task."[6]

What such lines, in complicated phenomenological fashion, rig up as the question of Being is so overstretched it will lose whatever can be conceived under the word; and the conception is further devalued, if possible, into so engrossing a bustle that the failure will commend itself as higher truth, as an authentic answer to the question that has been begged. Lest it be insufficiently authentic, the so-called question of Being condenses into a zero-dimensional point: into what it admits as the sole true-born meaning of Being. It turns into a ban on any step beyond this, and finally into a ban on any step beyond the tautology whose manifestation in Heidegger's prose is that time and again the self-uncovering Being says nothing else but "Being."[7]

If possible, Heidegger would pass off the tautological nature of Being as something superior to the rules of logic. But it can be derived from aporetics. As Husserl before him, Heidegger will blithely bow to desiderata of thinking which he juxtaposes although they have proved incompatible in the history of the metaphysics he withdrew from circulation, in overly sovereign fashion: to purity, the freedom from empirical admixtures that makes for absolute validity, and to the immediacy of flatly given things, irrefutable because they lack any conceptual adjunct. Thus Husserl combined his platform of a "pure"—i.e., eidetic—phenomenology with the postulate of a self-given phenomenal object. The title "Pure Phenomenology" is already a confluence of the contradictory norms. That it was to be no theory of knowledge but a position to be assumed at will, rather, relieved this phenomenology of the need to think through the interrelation of its categories. In this regard Heidegger differs from his mentor only insofar as he removes the contradictory program from consciousness, which was its stage for Husserl. Heidegger moves it into the transcendence of consciousness—a conception, by the way, that was already preformed in the preponderance of the *noema* in Husserl's middle period.

Yet the incompatibility of the pure and the visual compels us to choose the substrate of their unity so indefinitely that it will no longer contain any moment in which one of the two postulates might belie the other. Hence Heidegger's Being must be neither entity nor concept. The price it has to pay for thus becoming un-impeachable is its nihility—the fact that it defies fulfillment by any thought and any visuality, leaving us empty-handed but for the self-sameness of the mere name. Even the endless repetitions that abound in Heidegger's publications should not so much be laid to his garrulity as to aporetics. Definition alone brings a phenome-non beyond itself. What remains quite indefinite will compensate by being said over and over—just as a gesture that fails to impress its object will be made over and over, as an absurd ritual. The philosophy of Being shares this ritual of repetition with the mythus it would so much like to be.

LOOPING THE LOOP

The dialectics of Being and entity—that no Being can be con-ceived without an entity, and no entity without transmission—is suppressed by Heidegger. Moments that are not without one trans-mitting the other are to him directly one, and this one is positive Being. But the figures do not come out even. Categories also will be sued for debt. Though driven out with a pitchfork, entity re-turns: a Being purged of entity is a primal phenomenon only so long as the excluded entity lies nonetheless within it. Heidegger copes with this in a strategic masterpiece that is the matrix of his thinking as a whole. The term "ontological difference" permits his philosophy to lay hands even on the insoluble moment of entity. "What we are to understand by such a 'Being' alleged to be quite independent of the ontical sphere—this, of course, has to remain unsettled. Definition would involve it in the dialectics of subject and object, in the very thing from which it is to be exempt. This indefiniteness at the probably most central point of Heidegger's ontology is the reason why the extremes 'Being' and 'entity' must necessarily stay undefined toward each other as well, so that we cannot even say what the difference consists in. Talk of the 'ontological difference' comes down to the tautology that Being is not entity because it is Being. Thus Heidegger himself makes the mistake for which he upbraids Western metaphysics: that it always left unsaid what is meant by Being as distinct from entity."[8]

The breath of this philosophy turns entity into an ontological state of facts,* a dimmed and hypostatized expression of the impossibility to conceive Being without entity—just as entity, according to Heidegger's basic thesis, cannot be conceived without Being. This is how he loops the loop. The exigency that ontology cannot do without its opposite, the ontical—the ontological principle's dependence on its counterpart, the inalienable *skandalon* of ontology—becomes an element of ontology. The ontologization of the ontical is Heidegger's triumph over the other, less artful ontologists. The fact that there is no Being without entity is brought into the form that the being of entity is of the essence of Being. Thus a truth becomes an untruth, entity turns into essence. Being takes over what in the dimension of its being-in-itself it would not wish to be; it takes possession of entity, whose conceptual unity is always a connotation in the literal sense of Being.

The whole construction of the ontological difference is a fake, a "Potemkin's village." It is erected solely to permit a more sovereign rejection of doubts about absolute Being, by means of the thesis of entity as a mode of Being to be. As each individual entity is reduced to its concept, to the concept of the ontical, that

---

* Heidegger's doctrine of the distinction of Dasein as ontical and ontological at the same time—of the 'presence-at-hand' of Being—hypostatizes Being from the start. Unless Being is independent as preceding Dasein, as he would like it to be, Dasein will not become that transparency of Being which is supposed to uncover Being in turn. In that sense too, the alleged conquest of subjectivism has been surreptitious. In spite of Heidegger's reductive plan, the doctrine of the transcendence of Being served to smuggle back into entity the very same ontological primacy of subjectivity which the language of fundamental ontology abjures. Heidegger was consistent later, when he changed the course of the analysis of Dasein in the sense of an undiminished primacy of Being, a primacy that cannot rest on entity because, precisely in this sense, Being "is" not. With that, of course, all that had made Heidegger effective fell by the wayside, but the effect was already part of the authority of his later works.

which makes it an entity as opposed to the concept will disappear. The formal, generally conceptual structure of all talk of the ontical, and of all equivalents of this talk, takes the place of the substance of that concept, a substance heterogeneous to the conceptuality. What makes this possible is that the concept of entity—not at all unlike Heidegger's celebrated one of Being—is the concept which encompasses out-and-out nonconceptuality, that which is not exhausted by the concept, yet without ever expressing its difference from the encompassed. Because "entity" is the concept for all entities, entity itself becomes a concept, an ontological structure that is convertible without a break into the structure of Being. In *Being and Time,* the ontologization of entity is brought into a succinct formula: "The essence of Dasein lies in its existence."[9] The outcome of the definition of entities in Dasein, of existents *qua* existents, by the concepts of Dasein and existence is that precisely what is not essential in Dasein, precisely what is not ontological in it, *is* ontological. The ontological difference is removed by means of a conceptualization of the nonconceptual into nonconceptuality.

MYTHOLOGY OF BEING

The only time the ontical does not bother ontology is when it is of a kind with ontology. The subreption establishes the precedence of ontology over the ontological difference: "But here we are not dealing with an antithesis of *existentia* and *essentia,* because these two metaphysical definitions of Being, let alone their relationship, are not yet in question at all."[10] Heidegger, his assurances to the contrary notwithstanding, puts the alleged antecedent of the ontological difference on the side of essence: as the difference expressed in the concept of entity is denied, the concept is exalted by the nonconceptuality said to be beneath it. Another passage in the Plato tract makes this comprehensible. There Heidegger shifts the question of existence away from existence and transforms it into one about essence: "The statement, 'Man exists,' does not answer the question whether or not man is real; it answers the question about the 'essence' of man."[11]

117

The talk about "not yet," in the same passage in which the antithesis of existence and essence is rejected,[12] is not an accidental temporal metaphor for something other than temporal. Actually it is archaic thinking, Ionian hylozoistic far more than Eleatic; the scarce philosophemes of the former type that have come down to us show a murky mixture of existence and essence. The toil and trouble of the metaphysicists of Antiquity—from Parmenides, who had to split thinking and Being so that he might identify them, down to Aristotle—consisted in forcing the division. Demythologization is division; the myth is the deceptive unity of the undivided. But the primal principles did not suffice to explain the world which they always denoted also. It is because this insufficiency led to analysis—with the result that the magical extraterritoriality of Being as a vagrant between essence and fact was caught in the web of concepts—that Heidegger, to save the privilege of Being, must condemn the concept's critical labors as a history of decay, as if philosophy might occupy a historical standpoint beyond history while on the other hand obeying a history that is ontologized itself, as is existence.

Heidegger is anti-intellectualist under compulsion of the system and anti-philosophical on philosophical grounds, just as the present religious revivals do not get their inspiration from the truth of their doctrines but from the philosophy that religion would be good to have. As far back as we can trace it, the history of thought has been a dialectic of enlightenment. This is why Heidegger, resolutely enough, refuses to halt at any one stage of history, as he might perhaps have been tempted to do in his youth; it is why he takes a Wellsian time machine, rather, to plunge into the abyss of archaicism in which everything can be everything and mean everything. He reaches out for mythology, but his mythology too remains one of the twentieth century. It remains the illusion unmasked by history, an illusion made striking by the utter impossibility of reconciling the myths with the rationalized form of reality with which every possible consciousness is entwined. Heidegger's type of consciousness presumes to mythological status as if it could have that status without being mythological in kind.

Showing up, along with Heidegger's concept of Being, is the mythical concept of fate: "The advent of entity rests upon the fate of Being."[13] The eulogized undividedness of existence and essence in Being is thus called by name as what it is: the blind context of nature; the doom of concatenation; the absolute negation of the transcendence whose tremolo notes quiver in the talk of Being. The illusion in the concept of Being is this transcendence; but the reason for it is that Heidegger's definitions—deducted from Dasein, from the miseries of real human history to this day—dispense with the memory of those miseries. His definitions turn into moments of Being itself, and thus into things superior to that existence. Their astral power and glory is as cold to the infamy and fallibility of historic reality as that reality is sanctioned as immutable. The celebration of senselessness as sense is mythical; so is the ritualistic repetition of natural contexts in symbolic individual actions, as if that made these contexts supernatural. Categories such as *Angst*—of which, at least, we cannot stipulate that they must be everlasting—are transfigured into constituents of Being as such, into things superior to that existence, into its *a priori*. They are installed as the very "sense" which at the present state of history cannot be positively and immediately named. Absurdities are invested with sense, on the theory that the sense of Being will appear precisely in the form of its antithesis: in the form of mere existence.

ONTOLOGIZATION OF THE ONTICAL

Hegel anticipated the special ontological position of Dasein by means of the idealistic thesis that the subject takes precedence. He exploited the fact that the nonidentical on its part can be defined only as a concept. To him it was thereby removed from dialectics and brought to identity: the ontical was ontologized.

Shadings of language in the *Logic* make this quickly apparent. As the third Note to "Becoming" expounds, space and time are "explicitly defined as indefinite—which, to go back to its simplest form, is Being. Yet this very indefiniteness of Being is what makes out its definiteness; for indefiniteness is opposed to definiteness; so, as the opposite, it is itself defined as the negative, and as the purely, wholly abstractly negative at that. This indefiniteness or abstract negation, which Being has in itself, is what external as well as internal reflection expresses by equating Being with nothingness, by declaring it to be an empty thought figure, to be nothing. —Or one may express it thus: because Being is what lacks definition, it has not the (affirmative) being of definiteness; it is not Being, but nothingness."[14]

Tacitly, indefiniteness is used as a synonym for the undefined. Vanishing in the concept of indefiniteness is what it is the concept of; the concept is equated with the undefined as its definition, and this permits the undefined to be identified with nothingness. Thus the absolute idealism which logic would have to demonstrate first is in truth already presupposed. This is the point also of Hegel's refusal to begin with "something" rather than with Being. That the nonidentical is not immediate, that it is a matter of transmission, is trivial; but at central points Hegel fails to do justice to his own insight. The insight says that even though the nonidentical is identical—as self-transmitted—it is nonetheless nonidentical: it is otherness to all its identifications. Hegel does not carry the dialectics of nonidentity to the end, although his intention elsewhere is to defend the pre-critical usage against that of the philosophy of reflection. His own concept of nonidentity—to him a vehicle for turning it into identity, into equality with itself—inevitably has its opposite for its content; this he brushes aside in a hurry. What he explicitly stated in the tract on "difference," and promptly integrated in his own philosophy, becomes the most serious objection to that philosophy.

Hegel's absolute system, based upon the perennial resistance of the nonidentical, negates itself, contrary to his own understanding. There is truly no identity without something nonidentical—while in his writings identity, as totality, takes ontological precedence, assisted by the promotion of the indirectness of the nonidentical to the rank of its absolute conceptual Being. Theory, instead of bringing the indissoluble into its own in concepts, swallows it by subsumption under its general concept, that of indissolubility. Identity's dependence on the nonidentical, as Hegel almost achieved it, is the protest against any philosophy of identity. The Aristotelian category of *steresis* is the trump card of that protest, and its doom.

The abstract concept necessarily lacks the ability to be nonconceptual, and Hegel credits this lack to it as a merit, as something loftier, as the spirit—as opposed to that from which he unavoidably abstracts. What is less is supposed to be truer, as later on in Heidegger's self-righteous ideology of splendid homeliness.

The apologia for dearth is not merely one for a thinking that has once more shrunk to a point. It has its precise ideological function. The affectation of august simplicity warms up the dignity of indigence and frugal living; it suits the absurdity that real want is continuing in a society whose state of production no longer admits the plea that there are not enough goods to go around. Philosophy, barred from naïveté by its own concept, helps over this absurdity by flirting with the *Rhenish Home Companion:* in its history of Being, want has the radiance of superiority as such— at least *ad kalendas Graecas.* Hegel already gave a rating of greater substantiality to the results of abstraction. Under the same *topos* he deals with matter, also with the transition to existence.[15] That its concept is indefinite, that as a concept it lacks precisely what is meant by it, is supposed to be why all light is cast on its form. Hegel fits this into Western metaphysics, at its outermost limits; Engels saw that, but came to the opposite, equally undialectical conclusion: that matter is the first Being.[16]

Dialectical criticism is due the concept of the first Being itself. Heidegger repeats the Hegelian sleight-of-hand maneuver, except that Hegel's is practiced openly while Heidegger, not wanting to be an idealist, shrouds and beclouds the ontologization of the ontical. The mainspring for dressing up the deficiency of the concept as its surplus is in each case the old Platonic austerity: that whatever is nonsensual is more elevated. Logic achieves the utmost sublimation of the ascetic ideal and makes a fetish of it at the same time, devoid of the tension with the senses from which the ascetic ideal derives its truth as against the delusion of an authorized fulfillment. The concept, purified as its rejects its content, functions in secret as the model of a life that is arranged so no measure of mechanical progress—the equivalent of the concept—may ever, under any circumstances, do away with poverty.

If ontology were possible at all, it would be possible in an ironic sense, as the epitome of negativity. What remains equal to itself, the pure identity, is the worst. The mythical doom is timeless. Philosophy has been its secularization, in thrall to the doom insofar as its gigantic euphemisms would reinterpret the immutable as the good, down to the theodicies of Leibniz and Hegel. If one were drafting an ontology in accordance with the basic state of facts, of the facts whose repetition makes their state invariant, such an ontology would be pure horror. An ontology of culture, above all, would have to include where culture as such went wrong; a philosophically legitimate ontology would have more of a place in construing the culture industry than in construing Being. Good would be nothing but what has escaped from ontology.

FUNCTION OF THE CONCEPT OF EXISTENCE

The ontologization of the ontical is the primary goal of the doctrine of existence. According to the age-old argument, existence cannot be deduced from essence; hence it is said to be essential in itself. It is raised above Kierkegaard's model, but this very elevation blunts the cutting-edge it has for Kierkegaard. In the temple of existence, even the Bible word that "by their fruits ye shall know them" sounds like a profanation and must be silenced. As Being's mode to be, existence is no longer the antithetical opposite of the concept. Its poignancy has been removed. It is awarded the dignity of the Platonic idea, but also the bulletproof character of something that cannot otherwise be conceived because it is no conception, because it is simply there. On this point Heidegger is in accord with Jaspers, who guilelessly admits the neutralization of existence against Kierkegaard: "In his negative choices . . . I sensed the very opposite of everything I loved and wanted, of everything I was willing or unwilling to do."[17]

Though not infected by the *pater subtilis* in his construction of the concept of Being, Jaspers' own existentialism was understood from the outset as a "search for Being."[18] Without breaking faith with themselves, Jaspers and Heidegger both could make the sign of the cross at what was done in Paris in the sign of existence —at the phenomenon which all too quickly, for their taste, spread from the lecture halls to the *bistros*[19] where it sounded far less respectable. Of course, a critique confined to the thesis that the ontical cannot be ontologized will itself remain a judgment on invariant structural relations. It will remain too ontological, so to speak; this was the philosophical motive behind Sartre's turn to politics. There was something strengthless, something shadowy about the post-World War II movement that adopted the name "existentialism" and the bearing of an avant-garde. The existentialism which the German Establishment suspects of subversive leanings resembles the beards of its adherents. The beard is the oppositionist costume of juveniles acting like cavemen who refuse to play along with the cultural swindle, while in fact they merely don the oldfashioned emblem of the patriarchal dignity of their grandfathers.

What is true in the concept of existence is the protest against a condition of society and scientific thought that would expel unregimented experience—a condition that would virtually expel the subject as a moment of cognition. Kierkegaard's protest against philosophy was also one against the reified consciousness in which, as he put it, subjectivity has been extinguished: he opposed philosophy for philosophy's own sake. In the French existentialist schools this is anachronistically repeated. The subjectivity that has been really incapacitated and internally weakened in the meantime is isolated and—complementing Heidegger's hypostasis of its counter-pole, Being—hypostatized. Unmistakably in the Sartre of *Being and Nothingness,* the severance of the subject amounts, like that of Being, to the illusion that transmission is immediacy. As Being is transmitted by the concept, and thus by the subject, so is the subject transmitted by the world it lives in, and so powerless and merely inwardly is its decision. Such impotence helps the reified mischief to triumph over the subject.

The concept of existence impressed many as a philosophical approach because it seemed to combine divergent things: the reflection on the subject—said to constitute every cognition and thus every entity—and the concrete, immediate individuation of each single subject's experience. To the subjective approach, the divergence was an irritant *in toto:* the constitutive subject could be chided as a mere deduction from the empirical one, unfit to establish the empirical subject and any kind of empirical Dasein, while the individual could be upbraided as an accidental bit of the world, lacking the essential necessity required to encompass and, if possible, to establish entity. Existence—or man, in the demagogic jargon—seems to be both universal, the essence common to all men, and specific in the sense that this universal can be neither imagined nor even conceived otherwise than in particularization, in its distinct individuality.

Before all cognitive critique, however, in the simplest reflection on the concept of man *in intentione recta,* this *eureka* will lose its evidential character. We cannot say what man is. Man today is a function, unfree, regressing behind whatever is ascribed to him as invariant—except perhaps for the defenselessness and neediness in which some anthropologies wallow. He drags along with him as his social heritage the mutilations inflicted upon him over thousands of years. To decipher the human essence by the way it is now would sabotage its possibility. A so-called historical anthropology would scarcely serve any longer. It would indeed include evolution and conditioning, but it would attribute them to the subjects; it would abstract from the dehumanization that has made the subjects what they are, and that continues to be tolerated under the name of a *qualitas humana.* The more concrete the form in which anthropology appears, the more deceptive will it come to be, and the more indifferent to whatever in man is not at all due to him, as the subject, but to the de-subjectifying process that has paralleled the historic subject formation since time immemorial. That man is "open" is an empty thesis, advanced—rarely without an invidious side glance at the animal—by an anthropology that has "arrived." It is a thesis that would pass off its own indefiniteness, its *fallissement,* as its definite and positive side. Existence is a moment. It is not the whole it was conceived against, the whole from which, severed, it seized the unfulfillable pretension of entirety as soon as it styled itself philosophy. That we cannot tell what man is does not establish a peculiarly majestic anthropology; it vetoes any anthropology.

"DASEIN IN ITSELF ONTOLOGICAL"

While Kierkegaard nominalistically plays off existence against essence, as a wagon of theology against metaphysics, he does lend
to existence in the sense of the immediate individual a symbolic
character, if only in accordance with the dogma of the person as
created in God's image. He polemicizes against ontology, but the
attributes of ontology are absorbed by entity—by "that individual,"
in the realm of Dasein. The exaltation of existence in *Being and
Time* differs little from that in the initial reflections of *The Sick-
ness Unto Death*. Consciousness, Kierkegaard's "transparency" of
the subject, is the legal authority for ontologizing existence: "That
kind of Being towards which Dasein can comport itself in one
way or another, and always does comport itself somehow, we call
'existence,' "[20] or, literally: "Dasein is in itself 'ontological,' because existence is thus determinative for it."[21]

The concept of subjectivity oscillates no less than that of Being;
so it can be attuned at will to the concept of Being. Its ambiguity
permits Heidegger to equate Dasein with a mode of Being to be,
and it lets him remove the ontological difference by analysis.
Dasein is then called ontical by virtue of its spatial-temporal individuation, and ontological as the *logos*. The dubious part of
Heidegger's inference from Dasein to Being is the "simultaneity"
implied in his talk of a "multiple precedence" of Dasein "before
all other entity." The subject is determined by consciousness, but
that part of it from which consciousness cannot be split is not, for
that reason, fully conscious as well. It is not transparent and
"ontological."

In fact, nothing but propositions could be ontological. The
conscious individual (whose consciousness would not exist without
him) remains in space and time, a factuality, an entity; he is not
Being. In Being—since it is a concept, no immediate datum—
lies something of the subject; but in the subject lies the individual
human consciousness, and thus something ontical. That this
entity can think is not enough to strip it of its definition as an
entity, as if it were directly essential. It is precisely not "in itself"

that it is "ontological," for selfhood postulates the very onticality that is eliminated in the doctrine of ontological precedence.

THE NOMINALISTIC ASPECT

But criticism is not only due to the fact that the ontological concept of existence extirpates the nonconceptual by exalting it into a concept. There is also the positional value which the nonconceptual moment conquers in the concept. Nominalism, one of the roots of the existential philosophy of the Protestant Kierkegaard, gave Heidegger's ontology the attractiveness of the nonspeculative. Just as the concept of existence is a false conceptualization of existing things, the complementary precedence which these things are given over the concept allows the ontological concept of existence to profit in turn. If the individual is a socially transmitted phenomenon, so is his form of theoretical epistemological reflection. It is unfathomable why "my" individual consciousness should take precedence over anything else. By using the pronoun "my," the speaker of the moment presupposes the linguistic generality he would deny by the primacy of his particularization. What turns for him into a basis of necessity is the pure accident of having to start with his consciousness, with the consciousness he happens to have grown into.

And yet, as Hegel recognized quite early, the relation to the other, which the limitation to "my" is intended to exclude, is implied in the limitation. Society precedes the subject. That the subject mistakes itself for an antecedent of society is its necessary delusion, a mere negative statement about society. In the word "my," the proprietary relationship has been perpetuated in language, has all but turned into a logical form. Without the universal element to which this "my" points by setting itself apart from it, the pure $τόδε τι$ is as abstract as the universal which the isolated $τόδε τι$ brands empty and void.

What Kierkegaard's philosophical personalism—and perhaps Buber's distillate of it as well—sensed in nominalism was the latent chance for metaphysics. But where consistent enlighteners absolutize nominalism—instead of dialectically penetrating the nominalist thesis too—they recoil into mythology. Their philosophy becomes mythology at the point where, believing in some ultimate datum, they cut reflection short. To break off reflection, to take a positivist's pride in his own naïveté, is nothing else but thoughtless, stubbornly conceptualized self-preservation.

EXISTENCE ANTHORITARIAN

The concept of "existential" things—Heidegger prefers the already ontologized noun *existentialia* (Dasein *qua* Being)—is governed by the idea that the measure of truth is not its objectivity, of whichever kind, but the pure being-that-way and acting-that-way of the thinker. The subjective reason of the positivists is ennobled by divesting it of its rational element. Jaspers goes right along with Kierkegaard in this respect; the objectivist Heidegger would scarcely subscribe to the proposition that subjectivity is truth, and yet the analysis of *existentialia* in *Being and Time* has distinct overtones of that proposition. Contributing to its German popularity is the combination of radical bearing and sacred tone with a personality-directed ideology of genuineness and grit—qualities which individuals in the spirit of privilege have the doltish cunning to reserve to themselves. If subjectivity by its very nature, which Kant called functional, dissolves the preordained solid substances, its ontological affirmation dispels the fear of those substances. Subjectivity, the functional concept κατ' ἐξοχήν, becomes the one absolute solid—as already outlined, by the way, in Kant's doctrine of transcendental unity. But truth, the constellation of subject and object in which both penetrate each other, can no more be reduced to subjectivity than to that Being whose dialectical relation to subjectivity Heidegger tends to blur.

What is true in the subject unfolds in relation to that which it is not, by no means in a boastful affirmation of the way it is. Hegel knew this, but it bothers the repristinative schools. If truth were indeed subjectivity, if a thought were nothing but a repetition of the subject, the thought would be null and void. The existential exaltation of the subject eliminates, for the subject's sake, what might become clear to the subject. It thus falls prey to the relativism

127

to which it is deemed superior, and it brings the subject down to an opaque accidentality. The exponent of such an irrational existentialism will throw out his chest and agitate against the intellectuals by confessing that he is one, too: "But the philosopher will brave this sea of talk that knows no objective dividing line between genuine, originally philosophical parlance and empty intellectualism. While the man of science always has universally valid criteria for his results and derives his satisfaction from their inescapable validity, the philosopher has nothing but the ever-subjective criterion of his own being to tell empty talk from the talk that will awaken Existenz. The ethos of theoretical endeavors in the sciences and in philosophy is radically different."[22]

Devoid of its otherness, of what it renders extraneous, an existence which thus proclaims itself the criterion of thought will validate its mere decrees in authoritarian style, as in political practice a dictator validates the ideology of the day. The reduction of thought to the thinkers halts the progress of thought; it brings to a standstill what thought would need to be thought, and what subjectivity would need to live in. As the solid ground of truth, subjectivity is reified. In the ring of the old-fashioned word "personality" all this was heard already. Thinking becomes what the thinker has been from the start. It becomes a tautology, a regressive form of consciousness.

The utopian potential of thought would be, rather, to be conveyed by reason as embodied in the individual subjects, and to break through the narrowness of that other thinking. The best energy of thought is to outstrip the feeble and fallible thinker. This energy is paralyzed—since Kierkegaard, to obscurantist ends —by the existential truth concept. Obtundity is advertised as the strength for truth, which is why the existence cult thrives in the backwoods of all countries.

"HISTORICALITY"

Ontology has long cashiered the resistance to idealism which the concept of existence used to offer. Entity, once called upon to bear witness against the sanctity of the man-made idea, has been equipped with the far more ambitious sanctity of Being itself. This ether ennobles it from the outset, as compared with the conditions of material existence—the kind which the Kierkegaard of *The Present Age* meant when he confronted the idea with existence. What happens when the concept of existence is absorbed in Being, indeed what happens as soon as it is philosophically processed into a general concept fit for discussion, is another spiriting away of history—which Kierkegaard, who did not take a dim view of the left-wing Hegelians, had introduced into speculation under the theological sign of a paradox, the fusion of time and eternity. The ambivalence of the doctrine of Being, the fact that it deals with entity and at the same time ontologizes it—in other words, deprives it of all its nonconceptuality by resorting to its *characteristica formalis*—this ambivalence also determines the doctrine's relation to history.*

On the one hand, when history is transposed into the *existentiale* of historicality, the salt of the historical will lose its savor. By this transposition the claim of all *prima philosophia* to be a doctrine of invariants is extended to the variables: historicality immobilizes history in the unhistorical realm, heedless of the historical conditions that govern the inner composition and constellation of subject and object.** This, then, permits the verdict about soci-

---

* "Only an entity which, in its Being, is essentially futural so that it is free for its death and can let itself be thrown back upon its factical 'there' by shattering itself against death—that is to say, only an entity which, as futural, is equiprimordially in the process of having-been, can, by handing down to itself the possibility it has inherited, take over its own thrownness and be in the moment of vision for 'its time.' Only authentic temporality which is at the same time finite, makes possible something like fate—that is to say, authentic historicality." (Heidegger, *Being and Time*, trans. John Macquarrie and Edward Robinson, p. 437.)

** The linguistic form of fundamental ontology convicts it of a historical and social moment which in turn could not again be reduced to the pure *essentia* of historicality. The language-critical findings in the "jargon of authenticity" are therefore arguments against the philosophical content. The random nature dragged along in Heidegger's "draft" concept, a direct legacy of phenomenology since its transition to a material discipline, grows flagrant in the results: Heidegger's specific definitions of *Dasein* and existence, the things he attributes to

ology. As happened to psychology before, under Husserl, sociology is distorted into a relativism extraneous to the thing itself and held to injure the solid work of thinking—as if real history were not stored up in the core of each possible object of cognition; as if every cognition that seriously resists reification did not bring the petrified things in flux and precisely thus make us aware of history.

On the other hand, the ontologization of history permits one without a glance to attribute the power of Being to historical powers, and thus to justify submission to historical situations as though it were commanded by Being itself. This aspect of Heidegger's view of history has been stressed by Karl Löwith.* That history can be ignored or deified, depending on the circumstances, is a practicable political conclusion from the philosophy of Being. Time

---

the human condition and views as the key to a true doctrine of Being—these are not stringent, as he assumes, but deformed by accidental private factors. The false tone drowns that out and, by the same token, admits it.

* "The quotation marks in which Heidegger frames 'its time' in the above excerpt are presumably to indicate that what he is here referring to is not a random 'commitment' to a contemporary 'today' momentarily thrust upon us, but the decisive time of a genuine instant whose decisive character results from the difference between vulgar and existential time and history. Yet how can we tell unequivocally in a given case whether the time of decision is a 'primordial' moment or just an obtrusive 'today' in the course of world events? A resolve that does not know what it has resolved upon cannot answer this question. It has happened more than once that very resolute men would commit themselves to a cause that claimed to be fateful and decisive and yet was vulgar and not worth the sacrifice. How, in the framework of thoroughly historical thinking, should one be able at all to draw the line between 'authentic' events and those that happen 'vulgarly,' and to make an unequivocal distinction between man's self-chosen 'fate' and the unchosen 'vicissitudes' that befall him and lure him into momentary choices and decisions? And has not vulgar history avenged itself clearly enough for Heidegger's contempt of today's 'mere presence-at-hand,' when it induced him at a vulgarly decisive moment to assume the presidency of the University of Freiburg under Hitler, to transform his resolute 'ownmost *Dasein*' into a 'German *Dasein*,' and to practice the ontological theory of existential historicality on the ontical ground of really historical, i.e., political events?" (Karl Löwith, *Heidegger, Denker in dürftiger Zeit*, Göttingen 1953, p. 49.)

itself, and thus transiency, is both absolutized and transfigured as eternal by the existential-ontological drafts. The concept of existence as the essentiality of transience, the temporality of temporal things, keeps existence away by naming it. Once treated as the title of a phenomenological problem, existence is integrated. This is the latest type of philosophical solace, the type of mythical euphemism—a falsely resurrected faith that one might break the spell of nature by soothingly copying it.

Existential thinking crawls into the cave of a long-past mimesis. In the process it is nonetheless accommodating the most fatal prejudice from the philosophical history which it has laid off like a superfluous employee: the Platonic prejudice that the imperishable must be the good—which is to say no more than that in permanent warfare the stronger is always right. Yet if Plato's pedagogy cultivated martial virtues, the Gorgias dialogue still made these virtues answerable to the highest idea, to the idea of justice. In the darkened sky of the existence doctrine, however, no star is shining any more. Existence is sanctified without the sanctifying factor. Of the eternal idea in which entity was to share, or by which it was to be conditioned, nothing remains but the naked affirmation of what is anyway—the affirmation of power.

PART TWO

NEGATIVE DIALECTICS
CONCEPT AND CATEGORIES

THE INDISSOLUBLE "SOMETHING"

There is no Being without entities. "Something"—as a cogitatively indispensable substrate of any concept, including the concept of Being—is the utmost abstraction of the subject-matter that is not identical with thinking, an abstraction not to be abolished by any further thought process. Without "something" there is no thinkable formal logic, and there is no way to cleanse this logic of its metalogical rudiment.* The supposition of an absolute form, of "something at large" that might enable our thinking to shake off that subject-matter, is illusionary. Constitutive for the form of "subject-matter at large" is the substantive experience of subject-matter. Correlatively, at the subjective counter-pole, the pure concept, the function of thinking, is not to be radically segregated from the entity "I." Idealism's πρῶτον ψεῦδος ever since Fichte was that the movement of abstraction allows us to get rid of that from which we abstract. It is eliminated from our thought, banished from the realm where the thought is at home, but not annihilated in itself; the faith in it is magical.

---

* Hegel, in the first Note to the first Trias of his *Logic*, refuses to begin with Something instead of with Being (cf. Hegel, Works 4, especially p. 89, also p. 80). The entire work, which seeks to expound the primacy of the subject, is thus in a subjective sense idealistically prejudiced. Hegel's dialectics would scarcely take another course if— in line with the work's basic Aristotelianism—he were beginning with an abstract Something. The idea of such Something pure and simple may denote more tolerance toward the nonidentical than the idea of Being, but it is hardly less indirect. The concept of Something would not be the end either; the analysis of this concept would have to go on in the direction of Hegel's thought, the direction of nonconceptuality. Yet even the minimal trace of nonidentity in the approach to logic, of which the word "something" reminds us, is unbearable to Hegel.

Without specific thoughts, thinking would contravene its very concept, and these thoughts instantly point to entities—entities which absolute thinking in turn has yet to posit. This simple ὕστερον πρότερον would remain an offense to the logic of noncontradictoriness; dialectics alone can grasp it in the self-critique of the concept. This critique is objectively caused by epistemology, by the substance of what we discuss in the critique of reason, and it therefore survives the downfall of idealism, which culminated in it. The thought leads to the moment of idealism that runs counter to idealism; it cannot be evaporated once again, into the thought. The Kantian conception still allowed dichotomies such as the ones of form and substance, of subject and object, without being put off by the fact that the antithetical pairs transmit each other; the dialectical nature of that conception, the contradiction implied in its own meaning, went unnoticed. It took Heidegger's teacher Husserl so to sharpen the idea of apriority that—contrary to both his and Heidegger's intention—the dialectics of the εἴδη could be derived from their own claim.[1]

Once dialectics has become inescapable, however, it cannot stick to its principle like ontology and transcendental philosophy. It cannot be maintained as a structure that will stay basic no matter how it is modified. In criticizing ontology we do not aim at another ontology, not even at one of being nonontological. If that were our purpose we would be merely positing another downright "first"— not absolute identity, this time, not the concept, not Being, but nonidentity, facticity, entity. We would be hypostatizing the concept of nonconceptuality and thus acting counter to its meaning. A basic philosophy, πρώτη φιλοσοφία, necessarily carries with it the primacy of the concept; whatever withholds itself from the concept is departing from the form of allegedly basic philosophizing. The thoughts of transcendental apperception or of Being could satisfy philosophers as long as they found those concepts identical with their own thoughts. Once we dismiss such identity in principle, the peace of the concept as an Ultimate will be engulfed in the fall of the identity. Since the basic character of every general concept dissolves in the face of distinct entity, a total philosophy is no longer to be hoped for.

COMPULSORY SUBSTANTIVENESS

In the *Critique of Pure Reason,* sensation, as "something," occupies the place of the inextinguishably ontical. But sensation holds no higher cognitive rank than any other real entity. Its "my"—accidental to transcendental analysis and tied to ontical conditions —is mistaken for a legal title by experience, which is nearest to itself and the captive of its own reflective hierarchy. It is as if that which some individual human consciousness takes for the ultimate were an Ultimate in itself, as if every other human consciousness, individual and confined to itself, were not entitled to claim the same privilege for its own sensations. But if sensation were strictly required before the form, the transcendental subject, could function—in other words, before it could pass valid judgments—that subject would be quasi-ontologically tied, not only to pure apperception, but to matter, the counter-pole of apperception. This would have to undermine the entire doctrine of subjective constitution, to which matter, according to Kant, cannot be traced back.

With that, however, the idea of something immutable, something identical with itself, would collapse as well. This idea derives from the rule of the concept, from the concept's tendency to be constant as opposed to its contents, to "matter," and from its resulting blindness to matter. Sensations—the Kantian matter, without which forms would not even be imaginable, so that the forms also qualify the possibility of cognition—sensations have the character of transiency. Nonconceptuality, inalienable from the concept, disavows the concept's being-in-itself. It changes the concept. The concept of nonconceptuality cannot stay with itself, with epistemology; epistemology obliges philosophy to be substantive. Whenever philosophy was capable of substantiveness it has managed to deal with historic entities as its objects, long before Schelling and Hegel. Plato already did it, much against his will: it was he who gave to entity, to that which is, the name of "that which is not," and yet he wrote a doctrine of the state in which the eternal ideas are akin to such empirical definitions as the barter of equivalents and the division of labor.

In today's academic usage we have become inured to the difference between a regular, ordinary philosophy—said to have to do with the most sublime concepts, even though their conceptuality may be denied—and a merely genetical, extra-philosophical reference to society, the notorious prototypes of which are found in the sociology of knowledge and in the critique of ideology. The distinction is as invalid as the need for regular philosophy is suspect. A philosophy that fears too late for its purity is not only turning away from all that used to be its substance. Rather, what the philosophical analysis encounters immanently, in the interior of supposedly pure concepts and of their truth content, is that ontical element at which the purity claimants shudder, the element which, trembling with hauteur, they cede to the special sciences. The smallest ontical residue in the concepts that are vainly agitated by the regular philosophy compels that philosophy to include existing things in its own reflection, instead of making do with their mere concepts and feeling sheltered there from what the concept means. The contents of philosophical thinking are neither remnants after deducting space and time nor general findings about spatial-temporal matters. Philosophical thinking crystallizes in the particular, in that which is defined in space and time. The concept of entity pure and simple is the mere shadow of the false concept of Being.

"PEEPHOLE METAPHYSICS"

Wherever a doctrine of some absolute "first" is taught there will be talk of something inferior to it, of something absolutely heterogeneous to it, as its logical correlate. *Prima philosophia* and dualism go together. To escape from this, fundamental ontology must try to avoid defining what comes first to it. What was first to Kant, the synthetic unity of apperception, suffered the same fate. To Kant, every definition of the object is an investment of subjectivity in unqualitative diversity—regardless of the fact that the defining acts, which he takes for spontaneous achievements of transcendental logic, will adjust to a moment which they themselves are not; regardless of the fact that we can synthesize only what will allow and require a synthesis on its own. The active definition is not something purely subjective; hence the triumph of the sovereign subject which dictates its laws to nature is a hollow triumph. But as in truth subject and object do not solidly confront each other as in the Kantian diagram—as they reciprocally permeate each other, rather—Kant's degrading of the thing to a chaotic abstraction also affects the force that is to give it form.

The spell cast by the subject becomes equally a spell cast over the subject. Both spells are driven by the Hegelian fury of disappearance. The subject is spent and impoverished in its categorial performance; to be able to define and articulate what it confronts, so as to turn it into a Kantian object, the subject must dilute itself to the point of mere universality, for the sake of the objective validity of those definitions. It must cut loose from itself as much as from the cognitive object, so that this object will be reduced to its concept, according to plan. The objectifying subject contracts into a point of abstract reason, and finally into logical noncontradictoriness, which in turn means nothing except to a definite object. The absolute First remains necessarily as undefined as that which confronts it; no inquiry into something concrete and precedent will reveal the unity of abstract antithesis. Instead, the rigidly dichotomical structure disintegrates by virtue of either pole's definition as a moment of its own opposite. To philosophical thought, dualism is given and as inescapable as the continued course of thinking makes it false. Transmission—"mediation"—is simply the most general and inadequate way to express this.

Yet if we cancel the subject's claim to be first—the claim which surreptitiously keeps inspiring ontology—that which the schema of traditional philosophy calls secondary is no longer secondary either. It is no longer subordinate in a twofold sense. Its disparagement was the obverse of the trivium that all entity is colored by the observer, by his group or species. In fact, cognition of the moment of subjective mediation in the objective realm implies a critique of the notion that through that realm we get a glimpse of the pure "in-itself," a forgotten notion lurking behind that trivium. Except among heretics, all Western metaphysics has been peephole metaphysics. The subject—a mere limited moment—was locked up in its own self by that metaphysics, imprisoned for all eternity to punish it for its deification. As through the crenels of a parapet, the subject gazes upon a black sky in which the star of the idea, or of Being, is said to rise. And yet it is the very wall around the subject that casts its shadow on whatever the subject conjures: the shadow of reification, which a subjective philosophy will then helplessly fight again. Whatever experience the word "Being" may carry can only be expressed in configurations of entities, not by allergies to entity; otherwise the philosophical substance becomes the poor result of a process of subtraction, not unlike the one-time Cartesian certainty of the subject, the thinking substance.

There is no peeping out. What would lie in the beyond makes its appearance only in the materials and categories within. This is where the truth and the untruth of Kantian philosophy divide. It is true in destroying the illusion of an immediate knowledge of the Absolute; it is untrue in describing this Absolute by a model that would correspond to an immediate consciousness, even if that consciousness were the *intellectus archetypus*. To demonstrate this untruth is the truth of post-Kantian idealism; yet this in turn is untrue in its equation of subjectively mediated truth with the subject-in-itself—as if the pure concept of the subject were the same as Being.

NONCONTRADICTORINESS NOT TO BE HYPOSTATIZED

Such reflections come to seem paradoxical. Subjectivity, thinking itself, is called explicable not by itself but by facts, especially by social facts; but the objectivity of cognition in turn is said not to exist without thinking, without subjectivity. Such paradoxicality springs from the Cartesian norm of explication: reasons for what follows—for what follows logically, at least—have to be found in what goes before. This norm is no longer compulsory. Measured by it, the dialectical state of facts would be the plain logical contradiction. But the state of facts is not explicable by a hierarchic schema of order summoned from outside. If it were, the attempt to explain would presuppose the explication that remains to be found; it would presuppose noncontradictoriness, the principle of subjective thinking, as inherent in the object which is to be thought.

In a sense, dialectical logic is more positivistic than the positivism that outlaws it. As thinking, dialectical logic respects that which is to be thought—the object—even where the object does not heed the rules of thinking. The analysis of the object is tangential to the rules of thinking. Thought need not be content with its own legality; without abandoning it, we can think against our thought, and if it were possible to define dialectics, this would be a definition worth suggesting. The thinker's equipment need not remain ingrown in his thinking; it goes far enough to let him recognize the very totality of its logical claim as a delusion. The seemingly unbearable thesis that subjectivity presupposes facts while objectivity presupposes the subject—this thesis is unbearable only to one so deluded, to one who hypostatizes the relation of cause and effect, the subjective principle to which the experience of the object fails to bow.

Dialectics as a philosophical mode of proceeding is the attempt to untie the knot of paradoxicality by the oldest means of enlightenment: the ruse. Not by chance has the paradox been the decaying form of dialectics from Kierkegaard on. Dialectical reason follows the impulse to transcend the natural context and its delusion (a delusion continued in the subjective compulsion of the rules of logic) without forcing its own rule upon this context—in other words, without sacrifice and without vengeance. Dialectical reason's own essence has come to be and will pass, like antagonistic society. Antagonism, of course, is no more limited to society than is suffering. No more than dialectics can be extended to nature, as a universal principle of explication, can two kinds of truth be erected side by side, a dialectical one within society and one indifferent to society. The division of social and extra-social Being, a division that takes its bearings from the arrangement of the sciences, deceives us about the fact that heteronomous history perpetuates the blind growth of nature.[2]

The only way out of the dialectical context of immanence is by that context itself. Dialectics is critical reflection upon that context. It reflects its own motion; if it did not, Kant's legal claim against Hegel would never expire. Such dialectics is negative. Its idea names the difference from Hegel. In Hegel there was coincidence of identity and positivity; the inclusion of all nonidentical and objective things in a subjectivity expanded and exalted into an absolute spirit was to effect the reconcilement. On the other hand, the force of the entirety that works in every single definition is not simply its negation; that force itself is the negative, the untrue. The philosophy of the absolute and total subject is a particular one.* The inherent reversibility of the identity thesis counteracts the principles of its spirit. If entity can be totally derived from that spirit, the spirit is doomed to resemble the mere entity it means to contradict; otherwise, spirit and entity would not go together. It is precisely the insatiable identity principle that perpetuates antagonism by suppressing contradiction. What tolerates nothing that is

---

* In the history of modern philosophy, the word "identity" has had several meanings. It designated the unity of personal consciousness: that an "I" remains the same in all its experiences. This meant the Kantian "I think, which should be able to go with all my conceptions." Then, again, identity was what is legally the same in all rational beings—thought as logical universality—and besides, it was the equality with itself of every object of thought, the simple A = A. Finally, epistemologically, it meant that subject and object coincide, whatever their media.

Not even Kant keeps the first two layers of meaning strictly apart, and this is not due to a careless use of language. It is due to the fact that, in idealism, identity designates the point of indifference of the psychological and logical moments. Logical universality, as the universality of thought, is tied to individual identity, without which it would not come into being—for nothing past would be maintained in something present, and thus nothing would be maintained as the same at all. The recourse to this in turn presupposes logical universality; it is a recourse of thinking. The Kantian "I think," the moment of individual unity, always requires the supra-individual generality as well. The individual I is one I solely by virtue of the generality of the principle of numerical unity; the unity of consciousness itself is a form of reflection of the logical identity.

That an individual consciousness is one applies only on the logical premise of the excluded middle: that it shall not be able to be something else. In that sense its singularity, to be possible at all, must be supra-individual. Neither of the two moments has priority over the other. If there were no identical consciousness, no identity of particularization, there would be no universal—no more than there would be one the other way round. This is what lends epistemological legitimacy to the dialectical conception of particularity and universality.

not like itself thwarts the reconcilement for which it mistakes itself. The violence of equality-mongering reproduces the contradiction it eliminates.

RELATION TO LEFT-WING HEGELIANISM

The objection has been raised that, because of its immanently critical and theoretical character, the turn to nonidentity is an insignificant nuance of Neo-Hegelianism or of the historically obsolete Hegelian Left—as if Marxian criticism of philosophy were a dispensation from it, while at the same time the East, with its cultural propensities, refuses to do without a Marxist philosophy. The call for unity of theory and practice has irresistibly degraded theory to a servant's role, removing the very traits it should have brought to that unity. The visa stamp of practice which we demand of all theory became a censor's placet. Yet whereas theory succumbed in the vaunted mixture, practice became nonconceptual, a piece of the politics it was supposed to lead out of; it became the prey of power.

The liquidation of theory by dogmatization and thought taboos contributed to the bad practice; the recovery of theory's independence lies in the interest of practice itself. The interrelation of both moments is not settled once for all but fluctuates historically. Today, with theory paralyzed and disparaged by the all-governing bustle, its mere existence, however impotent, bears witness against the bustle. This is why theory is legitimate and why it is hated; without it, there would be no changing the practice that constantly calls for change. Those who chide theory anachronistic obey the *topos* of dismissing, as obsolete, what remains painful as thwarted. They thus endorse the world's course —defying which is the idea of theory alone—and the target is theoretically missed even if they succeeded in abolishing it, positivistically or by fiat.

Besides, this ranting at the recollection of a theory that carries weight is not far removed from the short-winded intellectual habits of the Western side. The fear of epigonality and of the academic odor that clings to any reprise of motives codified in philosophical history has long induced the various schools to advertise themselves as unprecedented. Precisely this confirms the fatal continuity of precedent. But for all the dubiousness of a procedure that will insist the more loudly on primal experience the more promptly it gets its categories from the social mechanism, thoughts cannot be equated with their source. This habit is another bit of "primal" philosophy. If a man resists oblivion (meaning, of course, historical oblivion rather than Heidegger's extra-historical one of a "history of Being")—if he resists the universally demanded sacrifice of a once-gained freedom of consciousness—he will not preach a Restoration in the field of intellectual history. The fact that history has rolled over certain positions will be respected as a verdict on their truth content only by those who agree with Schiller that "world history is the world tribunal." What has been cast aside but not absorbed theoretically will often yield its truth content only later. It festers as a sore on the prevailing health; this will lead back to it in changed situations. The remaining theoretical inadequacies in Hegel and Marx became part of historical practice and can thus be newly reflected upon in theory, instead of thought bowing irrationally to the primacy of practice. Practice itself was an eminently theoretical concept.

"LOGIC OF DISINTEGRATION"

The farewell to Hegel becomes tangible in a contradiction that concerns the whole, in one that cannot be resolved according to plan, as a particular contradiction. Hegel, the critic of the Kantian separation of form and substance, wanted a philosophy without detachable form, without a method to be employed independently of the matter, and yet he proceeded methodically. In fact, dialectics is neither a pure method nor a reality in the naïve sense of the word. It is not a method, for the unreconciled matter—lacking precisely the identity surrogated by the thought—is contradictory and resists any attempt at unanimous interpretation. It is the matter, not the organizing drive of thought, that brings us to dialectics. Nor is dialectics a simple reality, for contradictoriness is a category of reflection, the cogitative confrontation of concept and thing. To proceed dialectically means to think in contradictions, for the sake of the contradiction once experienced in the thing, and against that contradiction. A contradiction in reality, it is a contradiction against reality.

But such dialectics is no longer reconcilable with Hegel. Its motion does not tend to the identity in the difference between each object and its concept; instead, it is suspicious of all identity. Its logic is one of disintegration: of a disintegration of the prepared and objectified form of the concepts which the cognitive subject faces, primarily and directly. Their identity with the subject is untruth. With this untruth, the subjective pre-formation of the phenomenon moves in front of the nonidentical in the phenomenon, in front of the *individuum ineffabile*. The totality of identical definitions would correspond to the wish-fulfillment picture of traditional philosophy: to the a priori structure and to its archaistic late form, ontology. Yet before any specific content, this structure —as abstractly maintained—is negative in the simplest sense: it is spiritualized coercion. The power of that negativity holds real sway to this day. What would be different has not begun as yet.

This affects all individual definitions. Every definition that appears noncontradictory turns out to be as contradictory as the ontological models of "Being" and "Existenz." From philosophy we can obtain nothing positive that would be identical with its construction. In the process of demythologization, positivity must be denied all the way down to the reason that is the instrument of demythologization. The idea of reconcilement forbids the positive positing of reconcilement as a concept. And yet, in the critique of idealism we do not dismiss any insight once acquired from the concept by its construction, nor any energy once obtained from the method under the concept's guidance. The idealistic magic circle can be transcended only in thoughts still circumscribed by its figure, in thoughts that follow its own deductive procedure, call it by name, and demonstrate the disjointness, the untruth, of totality by unfolding its epitome. Pure identity is that which the subject posits and thus brings up from outside. Therefore, paradoxically enough, to criticize it immanently means to criticize it from outside as well. The subject must make up for what it has done to nonidentity. This is precisely what liberates it from the semblance of its absolute being-for-itself. That semblance in turn is a product of identifying thought—of the thought which depreciates a thing to a mere sample of its kind or species only to convince us that we have the thing as such, without subjective addition.

ON THE DIALECTICS OF IDENTITY

As the thinker immerses himself in what faces him to begin with, in the concept, and as he perceives its immanently antinomical character, he clings to the idea of something beyond contradiction. The antithesis of thought to whatever is heterogeneous to thought is reproduced in thought itself, as its immanent contradiction. Reciprocal criticism of the universal and of the particular; identifying acts of judgment whether the concept does justice to what it covers, and whether the particular fulfills its concept—these constitute the medium of thinking about the nonidentity of particular and concept.

And not of thinking only. If mankind is to get rid of the coercion to which the form of identification really subjects it, it must attain identity with its concept at the same time. In this, all relevant categories play a part. The barter principle, the reduction of human labor to the abstract universal concept of average working hours, is fundamentally akin to the principle of identification. Barter is the social model of the principle, and without the principle there would be no barter; it is through barter that nonidentical individuals and performances become commensurable and identical. The spread of the principle imposes on the whole world an obligation to become identical, to become total. But if we denied the principle abstractly—if we proclaimed, to the greater glory of the irreducibly qualitative, that parity should no longer be the ideal rule—we would be creating excuses for recidivism into ancient injustice. From olden times, the main characteristic of the exchange of equivalents has been that unequal things would be exchanged in its name, that the surplus value of labor would be appropriated. If comparability as a category of measure were simply annulled, the rationality which is inherent in the barter principle—as ideology, of course, but also as a promise—would give way to direct appropriation, to force, and nowadays to the naked privilege of monopolies and cliques.

When we criticize the barter principle as the identifying principle of thought, we want to realize the ideal of free and just barter. To date, this ideal is only a pretext. Its realization alone would transcend barter. Once critical theory has shown it up for what it is—an exchange of things that are equal and yet unequal—our critique of the inequality within equality aims at equality too, for all our skepticism of the rancor involved in the bourgeois egalitarian ideal that tolerates no qualitative difference. If no man had part of his labor withheld from him any more, rational identity would be a fact, and society would have transcended the identifying mode of thinking. This comes close enough to Hegel. The dividing line from him is scarcely drawn by individual distinctions. It is drawn by our intent: whether in our consciousness, theoretically and in the resulting practice, we maintain that identity is the ultimate, that it is absolute, that we want to reinforce it—or whether we feel that identity is the universal coercive mechanism which we, too, finally need to free ourselves from universal coercion, just as freedom can come to be real only through coercive civilization, not by way of any "Back to nature."

Totality is to be opposed by convicting it of nonidentity with itself—of the nonidentity it denies, according to its own concept. Negative dialectics is thus tied to the supreme categories of identitarian philosophy as its point of departure. Thus, too, it remains false according to identitarian logic: it remains the thing against which it is conceived. It must correct itself in its critical course— a course affecting concepts which in negative dialectics are formally treated as if they came "first" for it, too. It is one thing for our thought to close itself under compulsion of the form which nothing can escape from, to comply in principle, so as immanently to deny the conclusive structure claimed by traditional philosophy; and it is quite another thing for thought to urge that conclusive form on its own, with the intent of making itself "the first."

In idealism, the highly formal identity principle had, due to its formalization, an affirmative substance. This is innocently brought to light by terminology, when simple predicative sentences are called "affirmative." The copula says: It is so, not otherwise.

The act of synthesis, for which the copula stands, indicates that it shall not be otherwise—else the act would not be performed. The will to identity works in each synthesis. As an a priori task of thought, a task immanent in thought, identity seems positive and desirable: the substrate of the synthesis is thus held to be reconciled with the I, and therefore to be good. Which promptly permits the moral desideratum that the subject, understanding how much the cause is its own, should bow to what is heterogeneous to it.

Identity is the primal form of ideology. We relish it as adequacy to the thing it suppresses; adequacy has always been subjection to dominant purposes and, in that sense, its own contradiction. After the unspeakable effort it must have cost our species to produce the primacy of identity even against itself, man rejoices and basks in his conquest by turning it into the definition of the conquered thing: what has happened to it must be presented, by the thing, as its "in-itself." Ideology's power of resistance to enlightenment is owed to its complicity with identifying thought, or indeed with thought at large. The ideological side of thinking shows in its permanent failure to make good on the claim that the non-I is finally the I: the more the I thinks, the more perfectly will it find itself debased into an object. Identity becomes the authority for a doctrine of adjustment, in which the object— which the subject is supposed to go by—repays the subject for what the subject has done to it.

The subject is to see reason against its reason. The critique of ideology is thus not something peripheral and intra-scientific, not something limited to the objective mind and to the products of the subjective mind. Philosophically, it is central: it is a critique of the constitutive consciousness itself.

COGITATIVE SELF-REFLECTION

The force of consciousness extends to the delusion of consciousness. It is rationally knowable where an unleashed, self-escaping rationality goes wrong, where it becomes true mythology. The *ratio* recoils into irrationality as soon as in its necessary course it fails to grasp that the disappearance of its substrate—however diluted—is its own work, the product of its own abstraction. When thinking follows its law of motion unconsciously, it turns against its own sense, against what has been thought, against that which calls a halt to the flight of subjective intentions. The dictates of its autarky condemn our thinking to emptiness; in the end, subjectively, the emptiness becomes stupidity and primitivity. Regression of consciousness is a product of its lack of self-reflection. We can see through the identity principle, but we cannot think without identifying. Any definition is identification.

But definition also approaches that which the object itself is as nonidentical: in placing its mark on the object, definition seeks to be marked by the object. Nonidentity is the secret *telos* of identification. It is the part that can be salvaged; the mistake in traditional thinking is that identity is taken for the goal. The force that shatters the appearance of identity is the force of thinking: the use of "it is" undermines the form of that appearance, which remains inalienable just the same. Dialectically, cognition of nonidentity lies also in the fact that this very cognition identifies —that it identifies to a greater extent, and in other ways, than identitarian thinking. This cognition seeks to say what something is, while identitarian thinking says what something comes under, what it exemplifies or represents, and what, accordingly, it is not itself. The more relentlessly our identitarian thinking besets its object, the farther will it take us from the identity of the object. Under its critique, identity does not vanish but undergoes a qualitative change. Elements of affinity—of the object itself to the thought of it—come to live in identity.

To define identity as the correspondence of the thing-in-itself to its concept is *hubris;* but the ideal of identity must not simply be discarded. Living in the rebuke that the thing is not identical with the concept is the concept's longing to become identical with the thing. This is how the sense of nonidentity contains identity. The supposition of identity is indeed the ideological element of pure thought, all the way down to formal logic; but hidden in it is also the truth moment of ideology, the pledge that there should be no contradiction, no antagonism. In the simple identifying judgment, the pragmatist, nature-controlling element already joins with a utopian element. "A" is to be what it is not yet. Such hope is contradictorily tied to the breaks in the form of predicative identity. Philosophical tradition had a word for these breaks: "ideas." They are neither χωρίς nor an empty sound; they are negative signs. The untruth of any identity that has been attained is the obverse of truth. The ideas live in the cavities between what things claim to be and what they are. Utopia would be above identity and above contradiction; it would be a togetherness of diversity.

For the sake of utopia, identification is reflected in the linguistic use of the word outside of logic, in which we speak, not of identifying an object, but of identifying with people and things. Dialectics alone might settle the Greek argument whether like is known by like or by unlike. If the thesis that likeness alone has that capacity makes us aware of the indelible mimetic element in all cognition and all human practice, this awareness grows untrue when the affinity—indelible, yet infinitely far removed at the same time—is posited as positive. In epistemology the inevitable result is the false conclusion that the object is the subject. Traditional philosophy believes that it knows the unlike by likening it to itself, while in so doing it really knows itself only. The idea of a changed philosophy would be to become aware of likeness by defining it as that which is unlike itself.

The nonidentical element in an identifying judgment is clearly intelligible insofar as every single object subsumed under a class has definitions not contained in the definition of the class. But to a more emphatic concept, to one that is not simply the characteristic unit of the individual objects from which it was abstracted, the opposite applies as well. Emphatically conceived, the judgment that a man is free refers to the concept of freedom; but this concept in turn is more than is predicated of the man, and by other definitions the man is more than the concept of his freedom. The concept says not only that it is applicable to all individuals defined as free; it feeds on the idea of a condition in which individuals would have qualities not to be ascribed to anyone here and now. The specific of praising a man as free is the *sous-entendu* that something impossible is ascribed to him because it shows in him. This quality, striking and secret at the same time, animates every identifying judgment that is worth making.

The concept of freedom lags behind itself as soon as we apply it empirically. It is not what it says, then. But because it must always be also the concept of what it covers, it is to be confronted with what it covers. Such confrontation forces it to contradict itself. Whenever we try by a merely posited, "operational" definition to strip the concept of freedom of what philosophical terminology used to call its idea, we are arbitrarily diminishing the concept for utility's sake, in comparison with what it means in itself. The individual is both more and less than his general definition. But because the particular, the definite, would come to itself only by voiding that contradiction—in other words, by achieving an identity of the particular with its concept—the individual's concern is not only to hold on to that of which the general concept robs him; he is equally concerned with that "more" of the concept compared with his need. To this day, he will experience this "more" as his own negativity. The substance of the contradiction between universal and particular is that individuality is not yet—and that, therefore, it is bad wherever established. At the same time, that contradiction between the concept of freedom and its realization remains the insufficiency of the concept. The potential of freedom calls for criticizing what an inevitable formalization has made of the potential.

OBJECTIVITY OF CONTRADICTION

Such contradiction is not due to faulty subjective thinking. The embittering part of dialectics, notably for the reflexive philosophy that prevails now as in Hegel's day, is its objective contradictoriness. This, we say, is incompatible with flatly valid logic and removable by a formally unanimous judgment. As long as criticism sticks abstractly to the rules of logic, objective contradiction would be merely a pretentious way to put the fact that our subjective conceptual mechanism will inevitably claim truth for its judgment about the specific entity it judges, whereas this entity does coincide with the judgment only insofar as it is pre-formed in the definition of the concepts by the apophantic need. This would be easy to incorporate in the advanced logic of reflective philosophy. Yet objective contradictoriness does not designate only whatever entity remains outside our judgments; it also designates something in what we judge. For what we mean in the judgment is always the entity due to be judged *beyond* the particular that is included in the judgment—otherwise, according to its own intention, the judgment would be superfluous. And this intention is precisely what it does not satisfy. The negative motive of identitarian philosophy has remained in force: nothing particular is true; no particular is itself, as its particularity requires. Dialectical contradiction is neither the mere projection on the thing of a concept formation that miscarried nor a metaphysics running amuck.

Experience forbids the resolution in the unity of consciousness of whatever appears contradictory. For instance, a contradiction like the one between the definition which an individual knows as his own and his "role," the definition forced upon him by society when he would make his living—such a contradiction cannot be brought under any unity without manipulation, without the insertion of some wretched cover concepts that will make the crucial differences vanish.* Nor is it possible to unify the contradiction that the barter principle, which in present society enhances the productive forces, is simultaneously a growing threat to the existence of those forces. A subjective consciousness to which the contradiction is unbearable faces a desperate choice. Either such an individual must harmonistically stylize the contrary course of the world and heteronomously obey it, against his own better insight—or, doggedly loyal to his own definition, he must act as if the world's course did not exist and must perish by it. On his own, by conceptual dispositions, he cannot eliminate

---

* The classic case of such a cover concept, of the technique of logical subsumption for ideological purposes, is the current concept of industrial society. It ignores the social conditions of production by resorting to the technological productive forces—as if the state of these forces alone were the direct determinant of the social structure. This theoretical switch can of course be excused by the undeniable convergences of East and West in the sign of bureaucratic rule.

the objective contradiction and its emanations. He can comprehend it; everything else is idle protestation.

The contradiction weighs more heavily now than it did on Hegel, the first man to envision it. Once a vehicle of total identification, it has become the organon of its impossibility. The task of dialectical cognition is not, as its adversaries like to charge, to construe contradictions from above and to progress by resolving them—although Hegel's logic, now and then, proceeds in this fashion. Instead, it is up to dialectical cognition to pursue the inadequacy of thought and thing, to experience it in the thing. Dialectics need not fear the charge of being obsessed with the fixed idea of objective conflict in a thing already pacified; no single thing is at peace in the unpacified whole. The aporetical concepts of philosophy are marks of what is objectively, not just cogitatively, unresolved. To lay contradictions to incorrigible speculative obstinacy would be to shift the blame; a sense of shame bids philosophy not to repress George Simmel's insight that its history shows amazingly few indications of the sufferings of humankind.

Dialectical contradiction "is" not simply; it means—it has the subjective significance—that it cannot be talked out of this. In this meaning, this intention, dialectics aims at what is different. It is as philosophy's self-criticism that the dialectical motion stays philosophical.

STARTING OUT FROM THE CONCEPT

Because entity is not immediate, because it is only through the concept, we should begin with the concept, not with the mere datum. The concept's own concept has become a problem. No less than its irrationalist counterpart, intuition, that concept as such has archaic features which cut across the rational ones—relics of static thinking and of a static cognitive ideal amidst a consciousness that has become dynamic. The concept's immanent claim is its order-creating invariance as against the change in what it covers. The form of the concept—"false" in this respect also—would deny that change. Dialectics is a protest lodged by our

153

thinking against the archaicisms of its conceptuality. The concept in itself, previous to any content, hypostatizes its own form against the content. With that, however, it is already hypostatizing the identity principle: that what our thinking practice merely postulates is a fact in itself, solid and enduring. Identifying thought objectifies by the logical identity of the concept.

On its subjective side, dialectics amounts to thinking so that the thought form will no longer turn its objects into immutable ones, into objects that remain the same. Experience shows that they do not remain the same. The unstable character of traditional philosophy's solid identity can be learned from its guarantor, the individual human consciousness. To Kant, this is the generally predesigned unit underlying every identity. In fact, if an older person looking back has started early on a more or less conscious existence, he will distinctly remember his own distant past. It creates a unity, no matter how unreal the elusive picture of his childhood may seem. Yet the "I" which he remembers in this unreality, the I which he was at one time and potentially becomes again—this I turns simultaneously into another, into a stranger to be detachedly observed. Such ambivalence of identity and nonidentity extends even to logical problems of identity. For those, technical terminology stands ready with the customary formula of "identity in nonidentity"—a formula with which we would first have to contrast the nonidentity in identity. But such a purely formal reversal would leave room for the subreption that dialectics is *prima philosophia* after all, as *"prima dialectica."** The test of

---

* "If it does no more than re-process the yield of the several sciences and think it through to a whole, dialectics is a higher empiricism and really no more than the kind of reflection that would use experience to construe an overall harmony. But dialectics, then, must not break with the genetical view; it must not boast of immanent progress—which, after all, excludes the accidental acquisition of observation and discovery. Dialectics, then, works only in the same fashion and by the same means as other sciences and differs only in the goal of uniting the parts in the idea of the whole. We thus face another thought-provoking dilemma. Either the dialectical development is independent and solely self-determined; if so, it must indeed know everything by itself. Or it presupposes the finite sciences and empirical

the turn to nonidentity is its performance; if it remained declarative, it would be revoking itself.

In the traditional philosophies, even in the "constructive" ones of Schelling's slogan, the construction was in truth an imitation, a refusal to tolerate anything not pre-digested by the philosophies. By interpreting even heterogeneity as their own self and finally as the spirit, they already reconverted it into sameness, into the identity in which they would repeat themselves as in a vast analytical judgment, leaving no room for the qualitatively new. They got into a rut, into the habit of thinking that without such a structure of identity there could be no philosophy, that it would crumble into purely juxtaposed statements. The mere attempt to turn philosophical thought towards the nonidentical, away from identity, was called absurd. By such attempts the nonidentical was said to be a priori reduced to its concept, and thus identified.

Plausible considerations of this kind are too radical and, like most radical questions, are therefore not radical enough. Lashed by some of the driving ethos of labor, the form of tireless recourse takes us farther and farther from what we should see through, until in the end we leave it alone. The category of the root, the origin, is a category of dominion. It confirms that a man ranks first because he was there first; it confirms the autochthon against the newcomer, the settler against the migrant. The origin—seductive because it will not be appeased by the derivative, by ideology—is itself an ideological principle.

Karl Kraus's line "The origin is the goal" sounds conservative, but it also expresses something that was scarcely meant when the line was uttered: namely, that the concept "origin" ought to be stripped of its static mischief. Understood this way, the line does not mean that the goal had better make its way back to the origin, to the phantasm of "good" nature; it means that nothing is original except the goal, that it is only from the goal that the

---

knowledge—but then its immanent progress and continuous context is interrupted by that which has been received from outside, and besides, it is acting uncritically toward experience. Dialectics may choose. We see no third possibility." (F. A. Trendelenburg, *Logische Untersuchungen*, vol. I, Leipzig, 1870, p. 91f.)

origin will constitute itself. There is no origin save in ephemeral life.

SYNTHESIS

Idealistic dialectics also was an "origins' philosophy." Hegel compared it to a circle. By its return to the starting point of the motion, the result is fatally annulled; this was supposed to bring about a continuous identity of subject and object. The epistemological instrument of this dialectics was called synthesis. Its critique is not one of the individual act of thought which unites separate moments into their relation; it is a critique of synthesis as a guiding and supreme idea.

In general usage, meanwhile, the concept of synthesis—of construction as against decomposition—has assumed a patently different tenor, one whose most repulsive expression may be the invention of an alleged "psychosynthesis" against the Freudian psychoanalysis. Idiosyncrasy makes us balk at that usage; Hegel resorts to it far less often than the schema of triplicity—already convicted of rattling—leads us to expect. The actual structure of his thinking was probably in line with that idiosyncrasy. Predominating in it are definite negations of concepts visualized from close proximity and turned about. What such meditations formally characterize as synthesis keeps faith with negation: it intends to save what had succumbed to each preceding movement of the concept.

Throughout, the Hegelian synthesis is an insight into the insufficiency of that movement, into the cost of its reproduction, so to speak. As early as the Introduction to *Phenomenology of Mind,* Hegel comes close to a sense of the negativity of the dialectical logic he is expounding. That Introduction bids us purely observe each concept until it starts moving, until it becomes unidentical with itself by virtue of its own meaning—in other words, of its identity. This is a commandment to analyze, not to synthesize. For the concepts to satisfy themselves, their static side is to release their dynamic side, in a process comparable to the commotion in a drop of water under the microscope. This is why the method is called phenomenological, in passive relation to phenomena. As Hegel applied it, it was already what Benjamin would later call "dialectics at a standstill," far advanced beyond whatever would appear as phenomenology a hundred years later.

Objectively, dialectics means to break the compulsion to achieve identity, and to break it by means of the energy stored up in that compulsion and congealed in its objectifications. In Hegel, this meaning won a partial victory over Hegel—although Hegel, of course, could not admit the untruth in the compulsion to achieve identity. As the concept is experienced as nonidentical, as inwardly in motion, it is no longer purely itself; in Hegel's terminology, it leads to its otherness[3] without absorbing that otherness. It is defined by that which is outside it, because on its own it does not exhaust itself. As itself it is not itself alone. In Hegel's *Logic,* when he deals with Becoming,[4] the synthesis of the first triad, he waits until Being and Nothingness have been equated as wholly empty and indefinite before he pays attention to the difference indicated by the fact that the two concepts' literal linguistic meanings are absolutely contrary. He accentuates his early doctrine that nothing but the nonidentical can meaningfully—i.e., more than tautologically—predicate identity at all: it is not until their synthesis identifies them with each other that the moments will be nonidentical. This is where the claim of their identity obtains that restlessness, that inward shudder, which Hegel calls Becoming.

As a sense of nonidentity through identity, dialectics is not only an advancing process but a retrograde one at the same time. To this extent, the picture of the circle describes it correctly. The concept's unfoldment is also a reaching back, and synthesis is the definition of the differene that perished, "vanished," in the concept—almost like Hölderlin's anamnesis of the doomed naturalness. Only in the accomplished synthesis, in the union of contradictory moments, will their difference be manifested. Without the step that Being is the same as Nothingness, each of them would—to use one of Hegel's favorite terms—be "indifferent" to the other; only when they are to be the same do they become contradictory. Dialectics is not ashamed to recall the famous procession of Echternach: one jump forward, two jumps back. There is no question that Hegel, as opposed to Kant, restricted the priority of the synthesis: to Kant, multiplicity and unity were already categories side by side; Hegel, following the model of the late Platonic dialogues, recognized them as two moments of which neither is without the other.

Just the same, like Kant and the entire philosophical tradition including Plato, Hegel is a partisan of unity. An abstract denial of unity would not befit thinking either. The illusion of taking direct hold of the Many would be a mimetic regression, as much a recoil into mythology, into the horror of the diffuse, as the thinking of the One, the imitation of blind nature by repressing it, ends at the opposite pole in mythical dominion. The self-reflection of enlightenment is not its revocation; it is corrupted into revocation only for the sake of today's status quo. Even the self-critical turn of unitarian thinking depends on concepts, on congealed syntheses. The tendency of synthesizing acts is reversible by reflection upon what they do to the Many. Unity alone transcends unity. It is unity that grants the right to live to affinity, which was pushed back by the advancing unity and yet hibernated in it, secularized to the point of unrecognizability. As Plato knew only to well, the syntheses of the subject are indirect conceptual imitations of what that synthesis seeks on its own.

CRITIQUE OF POSITIVE NEGATION

The nonidentical is not to be obtained directly, as something positive on its part, nor is it obtainable by a negation of the negative. This negation is not an affirmation itself, as it is to Hegel. The positive which, to his mind, is due to result from the negation has more than its name in common with the positivity he fought in his youth. To equate the negation of negation with positivity is the quintessence of identification; it is the formal principle in its purest form. What thus wins out in the inmost core of dialectics is the anti-dialectical principle: that traditional logic which, *more arithmetico,* takes minus times minus for a plus. It was borrowed from that very mathematics to which Hegel reacts so idiosyncratically elsewhere. If the whole is the spell, if it is the negative, a negation of particularities—epitomized in that whole—remains negative.

Its only positive side would be criticism, definite negation; it would not be a circumventing result with a happy grasp on affirmation.

In reproducing an opaque immediacy—which, having come to be, is also phenomenal—the mature Hegel's very positivity bears features of what is bad, according to pre-dialectical usage. While his analyses destroy the semblance of the being-in-itself of subjectivity,* the institution which is to sublimate subjectivity, which is to bring subjectivity to itself, is therefore by no means the higher one as which he, all but mechanically, treats it. Rather, it is the expanded reproduction of whatever subjectivity has been denied for cause, no matter how abstract it may be in its suppressed condition. The negation practiced by the subject was legitimate; so is the negation practiced on the subject, and yet it is ideology. At each new dialectical step, Hegel goes against the intermittent insight of his own logic, forgets the rights of the preceding step, and thus prepares to copy what he chided as abstract negation: an abstract—to wit, a subjectively and arbitrarily confirmed—positivity.

In theory, this positivity springs from the method—not from the thing, as in Hegel's view it should—and its worldwide ideological dissemination has kept pace with its turn into a mockery that convicts itself of mischief-making unreality. Down to the vernacular of praising men who are "positive," and ultimately in the homicidal phrase of "positive forces," a fetish is made of the positive-in-itself. Against this, the seriousness of unswerving negation lies in its refusal to lend itself to sanctioning things as they are. To negate a negation does not bring about its reversal; it

---

* As almost each of Hegel's categories, that of the denied and thereby positive negation also has some empirical content—namely, for the subjective course of philosophical knowledge. If the knower knows precisely enough what an insight lacks or where it goes wrong, he will, by virtue of such definiteness, usually already have what he has missed. Only, this moment of definite negation on its part is subjective and must thus not be credited to objective logic, let alone to metaphysics. Still, that moment is the strongest argument for the adequacy of emphatic knowledge—for its ability to be definite after all—and this supports the possibility of a metaphysics beyond the Hegelian one.

proves, rather, that the negation was not negative enough. The other possibility for dialectics—one which in Hegel's case served to integrate it, at the cost of its potency—is to remain eventually indifferent to that which has been posited initially.

What is negated is negative until it has passed. This is the decisive break with Hegel. To use identity as a palliative for dialectical contradiction, for the expression of the insolubly nonidentical, is to ignore what the contradiction means. It is a return to purely consequential thinking. The thesis that the negation of a negation is something positive can only be upheld by one who presupposes positivity—as all-conceptuality—from the beginning. He reaps the benefit of the primacy of logic over the metalogical, of abstract philosophy's idealistic delusion, of vindication as such. The negation of negation would be another identity, a new delusion, a projection of consequential logic—and ultimately of the principle of subjectivity—upon the absolute. Oscillating between the most profound insight and the collapse of that insight is Hegel's line: "Truth also is positive, as knowledge coinciding with the object, but it is this self-sameness only if knowledge has reacted negatively to the Other, if it has penetrated the object and has voided the negation which it is."[5]

The qualification of truth as a negative reaction on the part of the knowledge that penetrates the object—in other words: extinguishes the appearance of the object being directly as it is—sounds like a program of negative dialectics as a knowledge "coinciding with the object." But the establishment of this knowledge as positivity abjures that program. By the formula of "self-sameness," of pure identity, the knowledge of the object is shown up as hocus-pocus, because this knowledge is no longer one of the object at all: it is the tautology of an absolutized νόησις νοήσεως. Irreconcilably, the idea of reconcilement bars its affirmation in a concept. The objection that critics of the positive negation of negation violate the vital nerve of Hegel's logic, that they would no longer permit any dialectical motion, shows a faith in authority whereby this motion is limited to Hegel's understanding of himself. The structure of his system would unquestionably fall without the principle that to negate negation is positive, but the empirical substance of dialectics is not the principle but the resistance which otherness offers to identity. Hence the power of dialectics. The subject too is hidden in dialectics, since its real rule brings forth the contradictions, but the contradictions have filtered into the object. If we attribute dialectics to the subject alone, removing contradiction by contradiction, so to speak, we also remove dialectics by broadening it into a totality. The system was the source of Hegel's dialectics, not its measure.

INDIVIDUALITY NOT THE ULTIMATE EITHER

Confusion about identity tends to make thinking capitulate to the indissoluble. Such thinking turns the object's indissolubility into a taboo for the subject. The subject is to resign itself, irrationalistically or scientifically, and not to touch whatever is unlike it. It is to surrender, even to pay homage, to the current cognitive ideal.

Such a thinking posture is by no means alien to this ideal. Throughout, the ideal combines an appetite for incorporation with an aversion to what cannot be incorporated, to the very thing that would need to be known. And indeed, theoretical resignation before individuality works no less for the status quo—to which it lends the nimbus and the authority of intellectual impenetrability and rigor—than does a voracious élan. The individual *Existenz* does not coincide with its cover concept of *Existenz* at large, but neither is it uninterpretable, another "last" thing against which cognition knocks its head in vain. The most enduring result of Hegelian logic is that the individual is not flatly for himself. In himself, he is his otherness and linked with others.

What is, is more than it is. This "more" is not imposed upon it but remains immanent to it, as that which has been pushed out of it. In that sense, the nonidentical would be the thing's own identity against its identifications. The innermost core of the object proves to be simultaneously extraneous to it, the phenomenon of its seclusion, the reflex of an identifying, stabilizing procedure. This is where insistent thinking leads us in regard to the individual: to his essence rather than to the universal he is said to represent. Communication with others crystallizes in the individual for whose existence they serve as media. In fact, as Husserl recognized, the universal dwells at the center of the individual; its constitution does not require comparison of an individual thing with others. For—and this is what Husserl failed to pay attention to—absolute individuality is a product of the very process of abstraction that is begun for universality's sake. The individual cannot be deduced from thought, yet the core of individuality would be comparable to those utterly individuated works of art which spurn all schemata and whose analysis will rediscover universal moments in their extreme individuation—a participation in typicality that is hidden from the participants themselves.

CONSTELLATION

The unifying moment survives without a negation of negation, but also without delivering itself to abstraction as a supreme principle. It survives because there is no step-by-step progression from the concepts to a more general cover concept. Instead, the concepts enter into a constellation. The constellation illuminates the specific side of the object, the side which to a classifying procedure is either a matter of indifference or a burden.

The model for this is the conduct of language. Language offers no mere system of signs for cognitive functions. Where it appears essentially as a language, where it becomes a form of representation, it will not define its concepts. It lends objectivity to them by the relation into which it puts the concepts, centered about a thing. Language thus serves the intention of the concept to express completely what it means. By themselves, constellations represent from without what the concept has cut away within: the "more" which the concept is equally desirous and incapable of being. By gathering around the object of cognition, the concepts potentially determine the object's interior. They attain, in thinking, what was necessarily excised from thinking.

The Hegelian usage of the term "concrete"—according to which the thing itself is its context, not its pure selfhood—takes note of this; and yet, for all the criticism of discursive logic, that logic is not ignored. But Hegelian dialectics was a dialectics without language, while the most literal sense of the word "dialectics" postulates language; to this extent, Hegel remained an adept of current science. He did not need language in an emphatic sense, since everything, even the speechless and opaque, was to him to be spirit, and the spirit would be the context. That supposition is past salvaging. Instead, what is indissoluble in any previous thought context transcends its seclusion in its own, as nonidentical. It communicates with that from which it was separated by the concept. It is opaque only for identity's claim to be total; it resists the pressure of that claim. But as such it seeks to be audible. Whatever part of nonidentity defies definition in its concept goes beyond its individual existence; it is only in polarity with the concept, in staring at the concept, that it will contract into that existence. The inside of nonidentity is its relation to that which it is not, and which its managed, frozen self-identity withholds from it. It only comes to in relinquishing itself, not in hardening—this we can still learn from Hegel, without conceding anything to the repressive moments of his relinquishment doctrine.

The object opens itself to a monadological insistence, to a sense of the constellation in which it stands; the possibility of internal immersion requires that externality. But such an immanent generality of something individual is objective as sedimented history. This history is in the individual thing and outside it; it is something encompassing in which the individual has its place. Becoming aware of the constellation in which a thing stands is tantamount to deciphering the constellation which, having come to be, it bears within it. The *chorismos* of without and within is historically qualified in turn. The history locked in the object can only be delivered by a knowledge mindful of the historic positional value of the object in its relation to other objects—by the actualization and concentration of something which is already known and is transformed by that knowledge. Cognition of the object in its constellation is cognition of the process stored in the object. As a constellation, theoretical thought circles the concept it would like to unseal, hoping that it may fly open like the lock of a well-guarded safe-deposit box: in response, not to a single key or a single number, but to a combination of numbers.

CONSTELLATION IN SCIENCE

How objects can be unlocked by their constellation is to be learned not so much from philosophy, which took no interest in the matter, as from important scientific investigations. The scientific accomplishment often ran ahead of its philosophical comprehension, ahead of scientivism. And we certainly need not start out from a work's own content, in line with such metaphysical inquiries as Benjamin's "Origin of German Tragedy" which take the very concept of truth for a constellation.[6] We must go back to a scholar of so positivistic a bent as Max Weber, who did—quite in the sense of subjectivist epistemology—understand "ideal types" as aids in approaching the object, devoid of any inherent substantiality and capable of being reliquefied at will. But as in all nominalism, however insignificant it may consider its concepts, some of the nature of the thing will come through and extend beyond the benefit to our thinking practice—not the least of our motivations for criticizing an unreflected nominalism!—so are Weber's material works far more object-directed than the South-West German methodology would lead us to expect.

Actually the concept is sufficient reason for the thing* insofar as the exploration of a social object, at least, is falsified if confined to dependencies within its domain, to dependencies that have established the object, and if its determination by the totality is ignored. Without the supraordinated concept, those dependencies conceal the most real among them, the dependence on society; and this dependence is not to be adequately compensated by the individual *res* which the concept covers. Yet it appears through the

---

* "This relationship of the whole as essential unity lies only in the concept, in the purpose. The mechanical causes do not suffice for this unity because they do not rest upon the purpose as the unity of definitions. Hence, by sufficient reason, Leibniz understood a reason that would suffice for this unity as well, one that accordingly would comprise in it not merely the direct causes but the final causes. This is not yet the place to define the reason thus, however; the teleological reason is a property of the concept and of mediation by the concept, i.e., by the *ratio*." (Hegel, Works 4, p. 555.)

individual alone, and thus the concept in turn is transformed in specific cognition. When Weber, in his treatise on Protestant ethics and the spirit of capitalism, raised the question of defining capitalism, he—in contrast with current scientific practice—was as well aware of the difficulty of defining historical concepts as previously only philosophers had been: Kant, Hegel, Nietzsche. He explicitly rejected the delimiting procedure of definition, the adherence to the schema *genus proximum, differentia specifica,*[7] and asked instead that sociological concepts be "gradually composed" from "individual parts to be taken from historic reality. The place of definitive conceptual comprehension cannot, therefore, be the beginning of the inquiry, only the end."[8]

Whether such a definition is always necessary at the end—or whether, even without a formal definitory result, what Weber calls "composing" can be equal to his epistemological goal—remains unsettled. Definitions are not the be-all and end-all of cognition, as popular scientivism holds; but neither are they to be banished. A thinking whose course made us incapable of definition, unable even for moments to have a succinct language represent the thing, would be as sterile, probably, as a thinking gorged with verbal definitions. More essential, however, is that to which Weber gives the name of "composing," a name which orthodox scientivists would find unacceptable. He is indeed looking only at the subjective side, at cognitive procedure; but the "compositions" in question are apt to follow similar rules as their analogue, the musical compositions. These are subjectively produced, but they work only where the subjective production is submerged in them. The subjectively created context—the "constellation"—becomes readable as sign of an objectivity: of the spiritual substance.

What resembles writing in such constellations is the conversion into objectivity, by way of language, of what has been subjectively thought and assembled. This element is not one of Max Weber's themes, but even a procedure as indebted as his to the traditional ideal and theory of science does not lack it. The most mature of his works seem at times to suffer from a glut of verbal definitions borrowed from jurisprudence, but a close look will show that these are more than definitions. They are not mere conceptual fixations. Rather, by gathering concepts round the central one that is sought, they attempt to express what that concept aims at, not to circumscribe it to operative ends. The concept of capitalism, for instance, which is so crucial in every respect is emphatically set off by Weber from such isolated and subjective categories as acquisitiveness or the profit motive—in a manner similar to Marx's, by the way. In capitalism, says Weber, the oft-cited profit motive must take its bearings from the principle of lucrativity and from the market chances; it must utilize the calculation of capital and interest; organized in the form of free labor, with household and business expenses separated, capitalism necessitates bookkeeping and a rationalistic legal system in line with its pervasive governing principle of rationality at large.[9]

The completeness of this list remains in doubt. We have to ask, in particular, whether Weber's stress on rationality, his disregarding of the class relation that reproduces itself by way of the barter of equivalents, will not as a mere method equate capitalism too much with its "spirit"—although that barter and its problematics would certainly be unthinkable without rationality. But the capitalist system's increasingly integrative trend, the fact that its elements entwine into a more and more total context of functions, is precisely what makes the old question about the cause—as opposed to the constellation—more and more precarious. We need no epistemological critique to make us pursue constellations; the search for them is forced upon us by the real course of history. In Weber's case the constellations take the place of systematics, which one liked to tax him with lacking, and this is what proves his thinking to be a third possibility beyond the alternative of positivism and idealism.

ESSENCE AND APPEARANCE

When a category changes, as those of identity and totality do in negative dialectics, a change occurs in the constellation of all categories, and thus again in each one. Paradigmatical for this phenomenon are the concepts of essence and appearance. They come from philosophical tradition and are maintained in negative dialectics, but their directional tendency is reversed. Essence can no longer be hypostatized as the pure, spiritual being-in-itself. Rather, essence passes into that which lies concealed beneath the façade of immediacy, of the supposed facts, and which makes the facts what they are. It comes to be the law of doom thus far obeyed by history, a law the more irresistible the more it will hide beneath the facts, only to be comfortably denied by them.

Such essence, to begin with, is the fatal mischief of a world arranged so as to degrade men to means of their *sese conservare,* a world that curtails and threatens their life by reproducing it and making them believe that it has this character so as to satisfy their needs. This essence too must come to appear like Hegel's: swathed in its own contradiction. It can be recognized only by the contradiction between what things are and what they claim to be. True, vis-à-vis the alleged facts this essence also is conceptual rather than immediate, but such conceptuality is no mere θέσει, no mere product of the cognitive subject, in which the subject ultimately finds itself confirmed. Instead, the conceptuality expresses the fact that, no matter how much blame may attach to the subject's contribution, the conceived world is not its own but a world hostile to the subject.

All but unrecognizably, this is attested by Husserl's doctrine of essence perception. What this amounts to is that the essence is totally alien to the consciousness that grasps it. The doctrine recalls—albeit in the fetishistic form of a downright absolute "ideal sphere"—that even the concepts with which it unhesitatingly equates its essentialities are not only products of syntheses and abstractions; they also represent a moment in the multiplicity which idealistic doctrine views as summoning the merely posited concepts. Husserl's idealism, an ontologization of the pure mind, was hypertrophied and therefore long unrecognizable even to Husserl himself. In his most effective writings it helped to give distorted expression to an anti-idealistic motive: to discontent with the thesis of the thinking subject's universal rule.

Phenomenology forbade the prescription of laws by a subject that was already obliged to obey them: in that sense, the subject experiences something objective in the laws. Yet because Husserl, like the idealists, put all mediations on the noetic side, on the subject's, he could not conceive the objective moment in the concept as anything but an immediacy sui generis, and he was forced to commit an act of epistemological violence and copy the mediations from sense perception. He frantically denied that essence on its part is another moment nonetheless, sprung from a source. Hegel, whom Husserl condemned with the hauteur of ignorance, had the superior insight that the essence categories in Volume II of his *Logic* are evolved—products of the self-reflection of the categories of Being—as well as objectively valid. This was beyond the thinking of anti-dialectical zealots, although Husserl's basic theme, his logical propositions, ought to have thrust dialectics upon him. For those propositions are no more objective in character, no more "laws of essence" in line with his theory, than (a fact he first passes over in silence) they are tied to thinking and centrally dependent upon that which they, in turn, are not.

The "absolute" of logical absolutism derives its title from the validity of formal theses and of mathematics; even so, it is not absolute because the claim of absoluteness in the sense of a positively achieved identity of subject and object is qualified itself, the precipitation of the claim of subjective totality. But the dialectics of essence, as of something which in its way, so to speak, simultaneously is and is not, can by no means be resolved as it is by Hegel: in the unity of the producing and produced mind. Hegel's doctrine of the objectivity of essence postulates that Being is the mind that has not yet come to itself. Essence recalls the nonidentity in the concept of that which, by the subject, is not posited but followed. Even the division of logic and mathematics from the ontical realm—the division upon which rests the appearance of their being-in-themselves, the ontological interpretation of formal categories—even this retains an ontical aspect, a recoil from the ontical, as it would have been called by Hegel. That ontical moment is reproduced in logic and mathematics. Since they cannot see themselves as separate and qualified—for to be separate is their very essence—they achieve a kind of existence.

Even more, however, do the essential laws of society and of its motion come to exist. They are more real than the facts in which they appear, the facts which deceive us about them. But they discard the traditional attributes of their essentiality. They might be called the reduction to a concept of the negativity that makes the world the way it is.

Nietzsche, the irreconcilable adversary of our theological heritage in metaphysics, had ridiculed the difference between essence and appearance. He had relegated the "background world" to the "backwoodsmen," concurring here with all of positivism. Nowhere else, perhaps, is it so palpable how an undefatigable enlightenment will profit the obscurantists. Essence is what must be covered up, according to the mischief-making law of unessentiality; to deny that there is an essence means to side with appearance, with the total ideology which existence has since become. If a man rates all phenomena alike because he knows of no essence that would allow him to discriminate, he will in a fanaticized love of truth make common cause with untruth. He will join hands with Nietzsche's despised scientific stupor that will not bother with the dignity of objects to be dealt with and will either parrot public opinion about this dignity or choose the criterion of whether, as they say, a thing "has not been worked upon as yet."

The scientific mentality cedes the decision about essentiality and unessentiality to the disciplines which deal with the object at the particular time. What is essential to one may be unessential to the other. Hegel, concurring, puts the difference into a third, which initially lies outside the thing's immanent motion.* Ironically, Husserl, who would not dream of any dialectics between essence and appearance, remains in the right against Hegel: there actually is a mental experience—fallible indeed, but immediate—of the essential and the unessential, an experience which only the scientific need for order can forcibly talk the subjects out of. Where

---

* "Insofar as an essential and an unessential part of an existence are differentiated, therefore, this difference is outwardly posited, a segregation of one part from another part of the existing thing, not touching its existence itself. It is a separation which falls into a third, and in which it is indefinite what belongs to the essential or to the unessential. It is some sort of external consideration and contemplation that makes the difference, and the same content is therefore to be regarded now as essential, now as unessential." (Hegel, ibid., p. 487.)

there is no such experience, knowledge stays unmoved and barren. Its measure is what happens objectively to the subjects, as their suffering.

The theoretical leveling of essence and appearance will be paralleled by subjective losses. Along with their faculty of suffering and happiness, the knowers lose the primary capacity to separate essentials and unessentials, without anyone really knowing what is cause and what is effect. The stubborn urge to check the accuracy of irrelevancies rather than to reflect on relevancy at the risk of error is one of the most widespread symptoms of a regressive consciousness. No background world annoys the latest type of backwoodsman; he happily buys what the foreground world will sell him on, in words or in silence. Positivism becomes ideology in eliminating first the objective category of essence and then, consistently, the concern with essentials. But it is by no means exhausted in its hidden universal law. Its positive potential survives in what the law affects, in what is flung aside as unessential to the verdict of the world's course. When we consider it, taking a far more than psychological view of that Freudian "dross of the phenomenal world," we mean the particular as the nonidentical. The essential runs counter to the prevailing generality, to the mischief of unessentiality, just as far as criticism will outstrip that generality.

INDIRECTNESS BY OBJECTIVITY

In negative dialectics not even the transmission of essence and phenomenality, of concept and thing, will remain what it was: the subjective moment in the object. What transmits the facts is not so much the subjective mechanism of their pre-formation and comprehension as it is the objectivity heteronomous to the subject, the objectivity behind that which the subject can experience. This objectivity is denied to the primary realm of subjective experience. It is preordinated to that realm. Wherever, in the current manner of speaking, judgment is too subjective at the present historical stage, the subject, as a rule, will automatically parrot the *consensus omnium*. To give the object its due instead of being content with the false copy, the subject would have to resist the average value of such objectivity and to free itself as a subject. It is on this emancipation, not on the subject's insatiable repression, that objectivity depends today. The superiority of objectification in the subjects not only keeps them from becoming subjects; it equally prevents a cognition of objectivity. This is what became of what used to be called "the subjective factor." It is now subjectivity rather than objectivity that is indirect, and this sort of mediation is more in need of analysis than the traditional one.

The subjective mechanisms of mediation serve to lengthen the objective ones to which each subject, including the transcendental one, is harnessed. The pre-subjective order (which in turn essentially constitutes the subjectivity that is constitutive for epistemology) sees to it that data are apperceived in this way and in no other, according to their claim. What in the Kantian deduction of categories remains ultimately "given" and, by Kant's own admission, accidental—that reason can have these and no other basic concepts at its disposal—is attributed to what the categories, according to Kant, have yet to establish. But the fact that indirectness is universal does not entitle us to reduce all things between heaven and earth to its level, as if transmitting an immediacy were the same as transmitting a concept. To concepts, mediation is essential; the concept itself is immediately, by nature, its own transmission; but the indirectness of something direct is a reflexive determination that makes sense only in regard to its opposite, the direct thing. There is nothing that is not transmitted, and yet, as Hegel emphasized, indirectness must always refer to some transmitted thing, without which there would be no indirectness. That there is no transmitted thing without indirectness, on the other hand, is a purely privative and epistemological fact, the expression of our inability to define "something" without mediation, and little more than the tautology that to think something is to think.

Conversely, there would be no mediation without "something." Directness does not involve being transmitted in the same sense in which indirectness involves something direct that would be transmitted. Hegel neglected this difference. The transmission of something direct refers to its mode: to knowledge of it, and to the bounds of such knowledge. Immediacy is no modality, no mere definition of the "how" for a consciousness. It is objective: its concept, the concept of immediacy, points to that which cannot be removed by its own concept. Mediation makes no claim whatever to exhaust all things; it postulates, rather, that what it transmits is not thereby exhausted. Directness itself, on the other hand, stands for a moment that does not require cognition—or mediation—in the same sense in which cognition necessitates immediacy.

As long as philosophers employ the concepts "direct" and "indirect"—concepts they cannot forgo for the time being—their language will bear witness to the facts denied by the idealist version of dialectics. That this version ignores the seemingly minimal difference serves to make it plausible. The triumphant finding that immediacy is wholly indirect rides roughshod over indirectness and blithely ends up with the totality of the concept, which nothing nonconceptual can stop any more. It ends up with the absolute rule of the subject.

In dialectics, however, it is not total identification that has the last word, because dialectics lets us recognize the difference that has been spirited away. Dialectics can break the spell of identification without dogmatically, from without, contrasting it with an allegedly realistic thesis. The circle of identification—which in the end always identifies itself alone—was drawn by a thinking that tolerates nothing outside it; its imprisonment is its own handiwork. Such totalitarian and therefore particular rationality was historically dictated by the threat of nature. That is its limitation. In fear, bondage to nature is perpetuated by a thinking that identifies, that equalizes everything unequal. Thoughtless rationality is blinded to the point of madness by the sight of whatsoever will elude its rule. For the present, reason is pathic; nothing but to cure ourselves of it would be rational. Even the theory of alienation, the ferment of dialectics, confuses the need to approach the heteronomous and thus irrational world—to be "at home everywhere," as Novalis put it—with the archaic barbarism that the longing subject cannot love what is alien and different, with the craving for incorporation and persecution. If the alien were no longer ostracized, there hardly would be any more alienation.

PARTICULARITY AND THE PARTICULAR

The equivocation in the concept of indirectness causes the opposite poles of cognition to be equated at the expense of their qualitative difference, the difference on which simply everything depends. This equivocation dates back to abstraction. The word "abstract" is still too abstract, however; it too is equivocal. The unity of that which general concepts cover differs fundamentally from the conceptually defined particular. The concept of the particular is always its negation at the same time; it cuts short what the particular is and what nonetheless cannot be directly named, and it replaces this with identity. This negative, wrong, and yet simultaneously necessary moment is the stage of dialectics. The core, which is also abstract in the idealist version, is not simply eliminated. Its distinction from "nothing" means that—contrary to Hegel—even the most indefinite "something" would not be downright indefinite. This refutes the idealist doctrine of the subjectivity of all definitions. The particular would not be definable without the universal that identifies it, according to current logic; but neither is it identical with the universal.

The idealist will not see that, however devoid of qualities "something" may be, this is no reason yet to call it "nothing." Hegel is constantly forced to shadow-box because he shrinks from his own conception: from the dialectics of the particular, which destroyed the primacy of identity and thus, consistently, idealism itself. For the particular he substitutes the general concept of particularization pure and simple—of "Existenz," for instance, in which the particular is not particular any more. He restores the thinking procedure which Kant rightly chided in an earlier rationalism, as the amphiboly of reflexive concepts. Hegel's dialectics turns sophistical where it miscarries. What makes a dialectical impulse of the particular—its indissolubility in the cover concept —is treated as a universal state of facts, as if the particular were its own cover concept and indissoluble for that reason. This is precisely what reduces the dialectics of nonidentity and identity to a mere semblance: identity wins over nonidentity. The shortcomings of a cognition that can make sure of no particular without the concept, which is anything but the particular—these shortcomings redound, legerdemain fashion, to the advantage of the mind that will rise above the particular and cleanse it of all that resists the concept. The general concept of particularity has no power over the particular which the concept means in abstracting.

SUBJECT-OBJECT DIALECTICS

The polarity of subject and object may well appear to be an undialectical structure in which all dialectics takes place. But the two concepts are resultant categories of reflection, formulas for an irreconcilability; they are not positive, primary states of fact but negative throughout, expressing nothing but nonidentity. Even so, the difference between subject and object cannot be simply negated. They are neither an ultimate duality nor a screen hiding ultimate unity. They constitute one another as much as—by virtue of such constitution—they depart from each other.

If the dualism of subject and object were laid down as a basic principle, it would—like the identity principle, to which it refuses to conform—be another total monism. Absolute duality would be unity. Hegel used this for the purpose of taking the subject-object polarity into his thinking after all; it was due to its bilateral unfoldment that he felt himself ranking above Fichte and Schelling. As the structure of Being, he held, the dialectics of subject and object comes to be the subject.* Both, as abstrac-

---

* "Indeed, the grasp of an object consists in nothing else but that an I will make the object its own, will penetrate it, and will bring it into its own form, i.e., into the universality which immediately is definition, or into definition, which immediately is universality. In visuality, or even in visualization, the object is still something external and strange. By grasping it, the being-in-and-for-itself which the object has in visuality and visualization is transformed into posited being; the I penetrates it in thought. Yet the object is in and for itself as it is in thought; it is phenomenal as it is in visuality and visualization; thinking voids the immediacy of our first encounter with it and thus turns it into a posited being; yet this posited being is its being-in-and-

tions, are thought products; the supposition of their antithesis inevitably declares thinking to be primary. Yet the dualism will not take the hint of a pure thought either. While this remains a thought, it will occur in line with the dichotomy that has become the thought form, and without which there might be no thought. Every concept, even that of Being, reproduces the difference of thinking and the thought. The difference has been seared into our theoretical awareness of the antagonistic state of reality; insofar as it expresses that condition, the falsehood of dualism is truth. Detached therefrom, on the other hand, the antagonism would become the philosophical excuse put forward to explain why dualism is eternal.

The only possible course is definite negation of the individual moments whereby subject and object are turned into absolute opposites and precisely thus are identified with each other. In truth, the subject is never quite the subject, and the object never quite the object; and yet the two are not pieced out of any third that transcends them. The third would be no less deceptive. The Kantian answer—withdrawing the third, as infinite, from positive, finite cognition and using its unattainability to spur cognition to untiring effort—falls short. The duality of subject and object must be critically maintained against the thought's inherent claim to be total. The division, which makes the object the alien thing to be mastered and appropriates it, is indeed subjective, the result of orderly preparation; but no critique of its subjective origin will reunify the parts, once they have split in reality.

Consciousness boasts of uniting what it has arbitrarily divided first, into elements—hence the ideological overtone of all talk of synthesis. It serves to cover up an analysis that is concealed from itself and has increasingly become taboo. The reason why a vulgar nobility of consciousness feels antipathetic to analysis is that

---

for-itself, or its objectivity. Thus the object has this objectivity in the concept, and the concept is the unity of the self-consciousness in which it has been received; its objectivity, or the concept itself, is therefore nothing but the nature of this self-consciousness and has no other moments or definitions than the I itself." (Hegel, Works, vol. 5, p. 16.)

the fragmentation for which the bourgeois spirit will upbraid its critics is that spirit's own unconscious work. The rational processes of labor are a model of that fragmentation. They need it as a condition of the production of goods, which resembles the general conceptual procedure of synthesis. If Kant's critique of reason had included the relation between his method and theory, the relation of the epistemologically examining subject to the examined subject, it would not have escaped him that the forms which are to synthesize diversity are products in turn of the operations on which the structure of his work, revealingly enough, bestows the title of "transcendental analytics."

REVERSAL OF THE SUBJECTIVE REDUCTION

The prevailing trend in epistemological reflection was to reduce objectivity more and more to the subject. This very tendency needs to be reversed. The means employed by philosophical tradition to distinguish the concept of subjectivity from entity are copied from entity. That philosophy, suffering of deficient self-reflection to this day, forgot the mediation in the mediating subject is no more indicative of meritorious sublimity than any forgetting. As though to punish it, the subject will be overcome by what it has forgotten. It no sooner turns into an object of epistemological reflection than it will share that objective character whose absence is so often cited as elevating it above the factual realm.

The subject's essentiality is an existence raised to the second potency and, as Hegel did not fail to state, presupposes the first potency: factuality. Factuality is a condition of the possibility —even though negated—of essentiality. The immediacy of primary reactions was broken, first, in the formation of the I; and broken with these reactions was the spontaneity which the pure I, according to transcendental custom, is to contract into. The centristic identity of the I is acquired at the expense of what idealism will then attribute to it. The constitutive subject of philosophy is more of a thing than the specific psychological content which it excreted, as naturalistic and reified. The more autocratically the I rises above entity, the greater its imperceptible objectification and ironic retraction of its constitutive role. Not only the pure I is ontically transmitted by the empirical I, the unmistakably pellucid model of the first version of the deduction of purely rational concepts; the transcendental principle itself, the supposed "first" of philosophy as against entity, is so transmitted.

Alfred Sohn-Rethel was the first to point out that hidden in this principle, in the general and necessary activity of the mind, lies work of an inalienably social nature. The aporetical concept of the transcendental subject—a nonentity which is nonetheless to act, a universal which is nonetheless to have particular experiences—would be a soap bubble, never obtainable from the autarkic immanent context of consciousness, which is necessarily individual. Compared with consciousness, however, the concept represents not only something more abstract; by virtue of its coining power it also represents something more real. Beyond the magic circle of identitarian philosophy, the transcendental subject can be deciphered as a society unaware of itself. Such unawareness is deducible. Ever since mental and physical labor were separated in the sign of the dominant mind, the sign of justified privilege, the separated mind has been obliged, with the exaggeration due to a bad conscience, to vindicate the very claim to dominate which it derives from the thesis that it is primary and original—and to make every effort to forget the source of its claim, lest the claim lapse.

Deep down, the mind feels that its stable dominance is no mental rule at all, that its *ultima ratio* lies in the physical force at its disposal. On pain of perdition, however, it must not put its secret into words. Abstraction—without which the subject would not be the *constituens* at large at all, not even according to such extreme idealists as Fichte—reflects the separation from physical labor, perceptible by confrontation with that labor. When Marx, in his critique of the Gotha Platform, told the Lassalleans that in contrast to the customary litany of popular socialists labor was not the sole source of social wealth,[10] he was philosophically—at a time when the official philosophical thematics lay already behind him—saying no less than that labor could not be hyposta-

177

tized in any form, neither in the form of diligent hands nor in that of mental production. Such hypostasis merely extends the illusion of the predominance of the productive principle. It comes to be true only in relation to that nonidentical moment which Marx in his disdain for epistemology called first by the crude, too narrow name of "nature," later on by that of "natural material" and by other less incriminated terms.[11]

The essence of the transcendental subject ever since the *Critique of Pure Reason* has been functionality, the pure activity that occurs in the achievements of individual subjects and surpasses them at the same time. It is a projection of freely suspended labor on the pure subject as its origin. In further restricting the subject's functionality by calling it empty and void without a fitting material, Kant undauntedly noted that social labor is a labor on something; his more consistent idealistic successors did not hesitate to eliminate this. Yet the generality of the transcendental subject is that of the functional context of society, of a whole that coalesces from individual spontaneities and qualities, delimits them in turn by the leveling barter principle, and virtually deletes them as helplessly dependent on the whole. The universal domination of mankind by the exchange value—a domination which a priori keeps the subjects from being subjects and degrades subjectivity itself to a mere object—makes an untruth of the general principle that claims to establish the subject's predominance. The surplus of the transcendental subject is the deficit of the utterly reduced empirical subject.

INTERPRETING THE TRANSCENDENTAL

As the extreme borderline case of ideology, the transcendental subject comes close to truth. The transcendental generality is no mere narcissist self-exaltation of the I, not the *hubris* of an autonomy of the I. Its reality lies in the domination that prevails and perpetuates itself by means of the principle of equivalence. The process of abstraction—which philosophy transfigures, and which it ascribes to the knowing subject alone—is taking place in the factual barter society.

The definition of the transcendental as that which is necessary, a definition added to functionality and generality, expresses the principle of the self-preservation of the species. It provides a legal basis for abstraction, which we cannot do without, for abstraction is the medium of self-preserving reason. It would not take much artifice to parody Heidegger by interpreting the general philosophical idea of necessity as the need to reverse want, to remedy the lack of foodstuffs by organized labor. Thereby, of course, Heidegger's language mythology itself would be unhinged—that apotheosis of the objective spirit in which reflection on the material process jutting into the spirit is banned from the outset, as inferior.

The unity of consciousness is that of the individual human consciousness. Even as a principle it visibly bears its traces, and thus the traces of entity. For transcendental philosophy, the ubiquity of individual self-consciousness will indeed turn it into a universal that may no longer boast of the advantages of concrete self-certainty; but insofar as the unity of consciousness is modeled after objectivity—that is to say, in so far as it is measured by the possibility of constituting objects—it is the conceptual reflex of the total, seamless juncture of the productive acts in society which the objectivity of goods, their "object character," requires if it is to come about at all.

Moreover, the solid, lasting, impenetrable side of the I mimics the outside world's impenetrability for conscious experience, as perceived by a primitive consciousness. The subject's real impotence has its echo in its mental omnipotence. The ego principle imitates its negation. It is not true that the object is a subject, as idealism has been drilling into us for thousands of years, but it is true that the subject is an object. The primacy of subjectivity is a spiritualized continuation of Darwin's struggle for existence. The suppression of nature for human ends is a mere natural relationship, which is why the supremacy of nature-controlling reason and its principle is a delusion. When the subject proclaims itself a Baconian master of all things, and finally their idealistic creator, it takes an epistemological and metaphysical part in this delusion. The practice of its rule makes it a part of what it thinks it is ruling; it succumbs like the Hegelian master. It reveals the extent to which in consuming the object it is beholden to the object. What it does is the spell of that which the subject believes under its own spell. The subject's desperate self-exaltation is its reaction to the experience of its impotence, which prevents self-reflection. Absolute consciousness is unconscious.

In Kantian ethics this is grandiosely attested by an unconcealed contradiction: as an entity, the very subject Kant calls free and exalted is part of that natural context above which freedom would lift it. Plato's doctrine of ideas, a great stride toward demythologization, reiterates the myth: under the name of essences it perpetuates the conditions of dominance which man took over from nature and is now practicing. If the control of nature was a condition of demythologization and a step in it, this dominance would have to spread to that other kind, lest it fall prey to the myth after all. But philosophy's stress on the constitutive power of the subjective moment always blocks the road to truth as well. This is how animal species like the dinosaur Triceratops or the rhinoceros drag their protective armor with them, an ingrown prison which they seem—anthropomorphically, at least—to be trying vainly to shed. The imprisonment in their survival mechanism may explain the special ferocity of rhinoceroses as well as the unacknowledged and therefore more dreadful ferocity of *homo sapiens*. The subjective moment is framed, as it were, in the objective one. As a limitation imposed on the subject, it is objective itself.

"TRANSCENDENTAL DELUSION"

All this, according to traditional norms of philosophy, whether idealistic or ontological, has a touch of ὕστερον πρότερον attached to it. One may say in a voice resonant with stringency that what we do in such reflections, without owning up to it, is to presuppose as transmitting what we would deduce as transmitted: the subject and its thought. Just by being definitions, one may say, all our definitions are already definitions of thought. But it is not the purpose of critical thought to place the object on the orphaned royal throne once occupied by the subject. On that throne the object would be nothing but an idol. The purpose of critical thought is to abolish the hierarchy.

The delusion that the transcendental subject is the Archimedean fixed point from which the world can be lifted out of its hinges—this delusion, purely in itself, is indeed hard to overcome altogether by subjective analysis. For contained in this delusion, and not to be extracted from the forms of cogitative mediation, is the truth that society comes before the individual consciousness and before all its experience. The insight into the fact that thinking is mediated by objectivity does not negate thinking, nor does it negate the objective laws that make it thinking. The further fact that there is no way to get out of thinking points to the support found in nonidentity—to the very support which thought, by its own forms, seeks and expresses as much as it denies it. Still transparent, however, is the reason for the delusion that is transcendental far beyond Kant: why our thinking in the *intentio obliqua* will inescapably keep coming back to its own primacy, to the hypostasis of the subject. For while in the history of nominalism ever since Aristotle's critique of Plato the subject has been rebuked for its mistake of reifying abstraction, abstraction itself is the principle whereby the subject comes to be a subject at all. Abstraction is the subject's essence. This is why going back to what it is not must impress the subject as external and violent.

To the subject, what convicts it of its own arbitrariness—and convicts its *prius* of aposteriority—will always sound like a transcendent dogma. When idealism is criticized strictly from within, it has the handy defense of thus being sanctioned by the critic—of virtually having the criticism within itself, by the critic's use of its own premises, and accordingly being superior to the criticism. Objections from without, on the other hand, will be dismissed by idealism as pre-dialectical, belonging to the philosophy of reflection. But there is no need for analysis to abdicate in view of this alternative. Immanence is the totality of those identitarian positions whose principle falls before immanent critique. As Marx put it, idealism can be made to "dance to its own tune." The nonidentity which determines it from within, after the criterion of identity, is at the same time the opposite of its principle, that which it vainly claims to be controlling. No immanent critique can serve its purpose wholly without outside knowledge, of course —without a moment of immediacy, if you will, a bonus from the subjective thought that looks beyond the dialectical structure. That moment is the moment of spontaneity, and idealists should be the last to ostracize it, because without it there would be no idealism. Spontaneity breaks through an idealism whose inmost core was christened "spontaneity."

The subject as ideology lies under a spell from which nothing but the name of subjectivity will free it, just as only the herb named "Sneezejoy" will free the enchanted "Dwarf Nose" in Wilhelm Hauff's fairy tale. This herb was kept a secret from the dwarf, and as a result he never learned to prepare "pâté Suzeraine," the dish that bears the name of sovereignty in decline. No amount of introspection would let him discover the rules governing his deformity and his labor; he needs an outside impulse, the wisdom of "Mimi the Goose."

To philosophy, and to Hegel's most of all, such an impulse is heresy. The limit of immanent critique is that the law of the immanent context is ultimately one with the delusion that has to be overcome. Yet that instant—truly the first qualitative leap—comes solely in the performance of immanent dialectics, which tends to transcend itself in a motion not at all unlike the passage from Platonic dialectics to the ideas, which "are in-themselves." If it became totally conclusive, dialectics would be the totality that goes back to the identity principle. This was the interest served—against Hegel—by Schelling, who thus invited jeers at the abdication of a thought in flight to mysticism. The materialistic moment in Schelling, who credited matter as such with something like a driving force, may contribute to that aspect of his philosophy. But neither can we hypostatize the leap, as Kierkegaard does, lest we blaspheme against reason.

Our sense of dialectics makes us restrict dialectics. Yet our disappointment at philosophy's failure to awaken from its dream by its own motion, without any leap—at its need for something else, for something new, for that which its spell keeps at a distance—this disappointment is none other than the disappointment of a child who reads Hauff's fairy tale and mourns because the dwarf, though no longer misshapen, did not get a chance to serve the duke his pâté Suzeraine.

THE OBJECT'S PREPONDERANCE

Carried through, the critique of identity is a groping for the preponderance of the object. Identitarian thinking is subjectivistic even when it denies being so. To revise that kind of thinking, to debit identity with untruth, does not bring subject and object into a balance, nor does it raise the concept of function to an exclusively dominant role in cognition; even when we merely limit the subject, we put an end to its power. Its own absoluteness is the measure by which the least surplus of nonidentity feels to the subject like an absolute threat. A minimum will do to spoil it as a whole, because it pretends to be the whole.

Subjectivity changes its quality in a context which it is unable to evolve on its own. Due to the inequality inherent in the concept of mediation, the subject enters into the object altogether differently from the way the object enters into the subject. An object can be conceived only by a subject but always remains something other than the subject, whereas a subject by its very nature is from the outset an object as well. Not even as an idea can we conceive a subject that is not an object; but we can conceive an object that is not a subject. To be an object also is part of the meaning of subjectivity; but it is not equally part of the meaning of objectivity to be a subject.

That the I is an entity is implicit even in the sense of the logical "I think, which should be able to accompany all my conceptions," because the sequence of time is a condition of its possibility and there is no sequence of time save in temporality. The pronoun "my" points to a subject as an object among objects, and again, without this "my" there would be no "I think." The being of a subject is taken from objectivity—a fact that lends a touch of objectivity to the subject itself; it is not by chance that the Latin word *subiectum,* the underlying, reminds us of the very thing which the technical language of philosophy has come to call "objective." The word "object," on the other hand, is not related to subjectivity until we reflect upon the possibility of its definition.

This does not mean that objectivity is something immediate, that we might forget our critique of naïve realism. To grant precedence to the object means to make progressive qualitative distinctions between things which in themselves are indirect; it means a moment in dialectics—not beyond dialectics, but articulated in dialectics. Kant still refused to be talked out of the moment of objective preponderance. He used an objective intention to direct the subjective analysis of the cognitive faculty in his *Critique of Pure Reason,*[12] and he stubbornly defended the transcendent thing-in-itself.* To him it was evident that being-in-itself did not run directly counter to the concept of an object, that the subjective indirectness of that concept is to be laid less to the object's idea than to the subject's insufficiency. The object cannot get beyond itself for Kant either, but he does not sacrifice the idea of otherness. Without otherness, cognition would deteriorate into tautology; what is known would be knowledge itself. To Kant's meditation this was clearly more irksome than the inconcinnity of the thing-in-itself being the unknown cause of phenomena even though the category of causality ends up on the subject's side in his critique of reason.

The construction of transcendental subjectivity was a magnifi-

---

* Literally, the preponderance of the object might be traced back to the point where a thought believes it has won its own absolute objectivity by rejecting any objectivity that is not thought—in other words, to formal logic. The "something" to which all logical propositions refer even when they are free to ignore it entirely is a copy of that which a thought means, and without which it could not be. The noncogitative is a logically immanent condition of the cogitative. In fact, the copula "is" always conveys some objectivity already, after the model of existential judgments. This disposes of all the hopes kindled by our craving for security: that in formal logic we might possess something downright unconditional as the sure foundation of philosophy.

cently paradoxical and fallible effort to master the object in its opposite pole; but in this respect too, the accomplishment of what was merely proclaimed in positive, idealistic dialectics requires a critique of that construction. An ontological moment is needed in so far as ontology will critically strip the subject of its cogently constitutive role without substituting it through the object, in a kind of second immediacy. The object's preponderance is solely attainable for subjective reflection, and for reflection on the subject. The state of facts is difficult to reconcile with the rules of current logic, and absurd in its abstract expression; it may clarify it to consider that one might write a primeval history of the subject—as outlined in *Dialectic of Enlightenment**— but one cannot write a primeval history of the object. Any such history would be dealing with specific objects.

Nor does an ontological supremacy of consciousness follow from the counter-argument that without a knowing subject nothing can be known about the object. Every statement to the effect that subjectivity "is," no matter what or how, includes an objectivity which the subject, by means of its absolute being, claims to have yet to establish. Only because the subject in turn is indirect—because it is not the radical otherness required to legitimize the object—is it capable of grasping objectivity at all. Rather than constitutive for objectivity, the subjective mediation is a block to objectivity; it fails to absorb entity, which objectivity is in essence. Genetically, the consciousness that has achieved independence, the epitome of what is done in cognitive performance, has branched off from the libidinous energy of the species. Human nature is not indifferent to this; it certainly does not define a "sphere of absolute origins," as Husserl thought. Consciousness is a function of the living subject, and no exorcism will expel this from the concept's meaning.

The objection that in the process the empirical moment of subjectivity would be mixed with its transcendental or essential moment is a feeble one. Without any relation to an empirical consciousness, to the living I, there would be no transcendental,

---

* Max Horkheimer and Theodor W. Adorno, *Dialektik der Aufklä- rung,* Amsterdam 1947 [*Dialectic of Enlightenment,* New York 1972].

purely mental consciousness. Analogous reflections on the object's genesis would be meaningless. Mediation of the object means that it must not be statically, dogmatically hypostatized but can be known only as it entwines with subjectivity; mediation of the subject means that without the moment of objectivity it would be literally nil. An index of the object's preponderance is the impotence of the mind—in all its judgments as well as, to this day, in the organization of reality. The negative fact that the mind, failing in identification, has also failed in reconcilement, that its supremacy has miscarried, becomes the motor of its disenchantment.

The human mind is both true and a mirage: it is true because nothing is exempt from the dominance which it has brought into pure form; it is untrue because, interlocked with dominance, it is anything but the mind it believes and claims to be. Enlightenment thus transcends its traditional self-understanding: it is demythologization—no longer merely as a *reductio ad hominem,* but the other way round, as a *reductio hominis,* an insight into the delusion of the subject that will style itself an absolute. The subject is the late form of the myth, and yet the equal of its oldest form.

THE OBJECT NOT A DATUM

That the object takes precedence even though indirect itself does not cut off the subject-object dialectics. Immediacy is no more beyond dialectics than is mediation. Epistemological tradition places anything immediate on the subject's side, but as the subject's datum or affection. The subject is said to have power to shape immediacy insofar as it is autonomous and spontaneous; but to be powerless in so far as the directly given thing flatly exists. The direct datum is as much the basic fact on which the doctrine of subjectivity rested—the doctrine of "mine," of the subject's substance as its possession—and it is the form of a kind of objective resistance, the Mene Tekel, as it were, of objectivity within the subject.

This is why Hume, in the name of immediacy, criticized identity, the principle of the I that would like to maintain itself as autochthonous in the face of immediacy. Yet immediacy cannot be fixed so as to please an epistemology gauged to standards of conclusiveness. In immediacy, the direct datum and the equally directly given forms are tailored so as to complement each other. Immediacy does call a halt to the idolatry of derivation, but it is also something abstracted from the object, a raw material for the subjective process of production that served as a model for epistemology. What is given in poor and blind form is not objectivity; it is merely the borderline value which the subject, having confiscated the concrete object, cannot fully master in its own domain. Here, for all its sensualistic reduction of things, empiricism registered some of the object's preponderance: from Locke onward, empiricists would insist that there is no content of consciousness other than that which comes from the senses, is "given."

The entire empiricist critique of naïve realism, culminating in Hume's abolition of the thing, was tied to the factitious character of immediacy and skeptical of the subject *qua* creator; in spite of everything, it remained rudimentarily "realistic." Once thought has been freed from the supposition of the subject's supremacy, however, empiricist epistemology is no longer entitled to transpose, as a residual definition, a kind of minimum object into the direct data by means of subjective reduction. Such a construction is nothing but a compromise between the dogma of the subject's preponderance and the impossibility to carry it through; the naked sense datum divested of its definitions is a product of that process of abstraction with which it is contrasted by Kant's epistemological subjectivism. And indeed, the more purified of its forms, the scantier and the more "abstract" the datum. The object's residue as that which remains given after subjective appendages have been subtracted is a delusion of *prima philosophia*. That the definitions which make the object concrete are merely imposed upon it— this rule applies only where the faith in the primacy of subjectivity remains unshaken. But the forms of subjectivity are not cognitive ultimates, as Kant taught; as its experience progresses, cognition can break through them.

If philosophy, fatally split off from the natural sciences, may refer to physics at all without causing a short circuit, it may do so in this context. With theoretical stringency, the evolution of physics since Einstein has burst the visual prison as well as that of the subjective apriority of space, time, and causality. In teaching the possibility of such a prison break, experience—subjective, according to the Newtonian principle of observation—argues for the primacy of the object, and against its own omnipotence. Involuntarily dialectical in spirit, it turns subjective observation against the doctrine of subjective constituents. The object is more than pure factuality; at the same time, the fact that factuality is irremovable forbids contentment with its abstract concept and with the dregs of factuality, the recorded sense data. The idea of a concrete object belongs to the critique of subjective-external categorization, and to the critique of its correlate, the fiction of a factuality without definitions. Nothing in the world is composed —added up, so to speak—of factuality and concept. The probative force of the Kantian example of the hundred imagined thalers, whose reality is not added to them as a further quality, affects the form-substance dualism of the *Critique of Pure Reason* itself and remains a force acting far beyond the example. What it really does is to disavow the distinction of diversity and unity which traditional philosophy has been making since Plato.

Neither the concept nor factuality is an addition to its complement. Hegel's presupposition that the subject might yield purely, unreservedly to the object, to the thing itself, since the process would show the thing to be what it already is in itself: a subject —this presupposition is presumptuously idealistic; but it does take note, against idealism, of a truth about the subject's mode of cogitative conduct. Because the subject does not make the object, it can really only "look on," and the cognitive maxim is to assist in that process. The measure of the subject's postulated passivity is the object's objective determination. But this determination needs a subjective reflection more lasting than the identifications of which Kant already taught that consciousness performs them, as it were, unconsciously and automatically. That the activity of the mind, and even more the activity which Kant ascribes to the problem of constitution, is something other than the automatism he equates it with—this, specifically, makes out the mental experience which the idealists discovered, albeit only in order to castrate it on the spot. What we may call the thing itself is not positively and immediately at hand. He who wants to know it must think more, not less, than the point of reference of the synthesis of diversity, which is the same, at bottom, as not to think at all. And yet the thing itself is by no means a thought product. It is nonidentity through identity. Such nonidentity is not an "idea," but it is an adjunct. The experiencing subject strives to disappear in it. The truth would be its demise—a demise merely feigned, to the greater glory of the subject objectified in a scientific method, by the subtraction of all specific subjectivity in that method.

OBJECTIVITY AND REIFICATION

Preponderance of the object is a thought of which any pretentious philosophy will be suspicious. Since Fichte, aversion to it has been institutionalized. Protestations to the contrary, reiterated and varied a thousandfold, seek to drown out the festering suspicion that heteronomy may be mightier than the autonomy of which Kant already taught that it cannot be conquered by that superior power. Such philosophical subjectivism is the ideological accompaniment of the emancipation of the bourgeois I. It furnishes reasons for that emancipation. Its tenacious vigor is drawn from a misdirected opposition to the status quo, from opposition to its thingness. In relativizing or liquefying that thingness, philosophy believes to be above the supremacy of goods, and above the form of subjective reflection on that supremacy, the reified consciousness.

In Fichte, that impulse is as unmistakable as the urge to universal rule. It was an anti-ideological impulse insofar as the world's being-in-itself, confirmed by a conventional, unreflected consciousness, was seen through as merely manufactured and unfit for self-preservation. Despite the preponderance of the object, the thingness of the world is also phenomenal. It tempts the subjects to ascribe their own social circumstances of production to the noumena. This is elaborated in Marx's chapter on fetishes, truly a piece from the heritages of classic German philosophy. Even its systematic motive survives in that chapter: the fetish character of goods is not laid to a subjectively errant consciousness, but objectively deduced from the social a priori, the exchange process.

Marx already expresses the difference between the object's preponderance as a product of criticism and its extant caricature, its distortion by the merchandise character. Barter as a process has real objectivity and is objectively untrue at the same time, transgressing against its own principle, the principle of equality. This is why, of necessity, it will create a false consciousness: the idols of the market. It is only in a sardonic sense that the barter society's natural growth is a law of nature, that the predominance of economics is no invariant. The thinker may easily comfort himself by imagining that in the dissolution of reification, of the merchandise character, he possesses the philosophers' stone. But reification itself is the reflexive form of false objectivity; centering theory around reification, a form of consciousness, makes the critical theory idealistically acceptable to the reigning consciousness and to the collective unconscious. This is what raised Marx's early writings—in contradistinction to *Das Kapital*—to their present popularity, notably with theologians.

There is a good deal of irony in the fact that the brutal and primitive functionaries who more than forty years back damned Lukács as a heretic, because of the reification chapter in his important *History and Class Consciousness,* did sense the idealistic nature of his conception. We can no more reduce dialectics to reification than we can reduce it to any other isolated category, however polemical. The cause of human suffering, meanwhile, will be glossed over rather than denounced in the lament about reification. The trouble is with the conditions that condemn mankind to impotence and apathy and would yet be changeable by human action; it is not primarily with people and with the way conditions appear to people. Considering the possibility of total disaster, reification is an epiphenomenon, and even more so is the alienation coupled with reification, the subjective state of consciousness that corresponds to it. Alienation is reproduced by anxiety; consciousness—reified in the already constituted society—is not the *constituens* of anxiety. If a man looks upon thing-ness as radical evil, if he would like to dynamize all entity into pure actuality, he tends to be hostile to otherness, to the alien thing that has lent its name to alienation, and not in vain. He tends to that nonidentity which would be the deliverance, not of consciousness alone, but of reconciled mankind. Absolute dynam-ics, on the other hand, would be that absolute action whose vio-lent satisfaction lies in itself, the action in which nonidentity is abused as a mere occasion.

Unbroken and all too human slogans lend themselves to new equations between the subject and what is not its like. Things congeal as fragments of that which was subjugated; to rescue it means to love things. We cannot eliminate from the dialectics of the extant what is experienced in consciousness as an alien thing: negatively, coercion and heteronomy, but also the marred figure of what we should love, and what the spell, the endogamy of consciousness, does not permit us to love. The reconciled con-dition would not be the philosophical imperialism of annexing the alien. Instead, its happiness would lie in the fact that the alien, in the proximity it is granted, remains what is distant and differ-ent, beyond the heterogeneous and beyond that which is one's own.

The tireless charge of reification resists that dialectics, and this indicts the constructions used in the philosophy of history to back up that charge. The meaningful times for whose return the early Lukács yearned were as much due to reification, to inhuman in-stitutions, as he would later attest it only to the bourgeois age. Contemporary representations of medieval towns usually look as if an execution were just taking place to cheer the populace. If any harmony of subject and object should have prevailed in those days, it was a harmony like the most recent one: pressure-born and brittle. The transfiguration of past conditions serves the pur-pose of a late, superfluous denial that is experienced as a no-exit situation; only as lost conditions do they become glamorous. Their cult, the cult of pre-subjective phases, arose in horror, in the age of individual disintegration and collective regression.

With the delivery of the natural sciences, reification and reified consciousness also brought about the possibility of worldwide freedom from want. Even earlier, humanity was conditioned by dehumanized things;[13] at least it went hand in hand with reified forms of consciousness, while indifference to things, appraising them as mere means and reducing them to the subject, helped to tear down humanity. In the realm of things there is an intermingling of both the object's unidentical side and the submission of men to prevailing conditions of production, to their own functional context which they cannot know. The mature Marx, in his few remarks on the character of a liberated society, changed his position on the cause of reification, the division of labor.[14] He now distinguished the state of freedom from original immediacy. In the moment of planning—the result of which, he hoped, would be production for use by the living rather than for profit, and thus, in a sense, a restitution of immediacy—in that planning he preserved the alien thing; in his design for a realization of what philosophy had only thought, at first, he preserved its mediation.

But that there could be no dialectics without the element of solid things, that without such things it would level off into a harmless doctrine of change—this was attributable neither to philosophical habit nor solely to the social compulsion of which consciousness receives such solid knowledge. It is up to philosophy to think the things which differ from the thought and yet make it a thought, exclusively, while their demon seeks to persuade the thought that it ought not to be.

PASSAGE TO MATERIALISM

It is by passing to the object's preponderance that dialectics is rendered materialistic. The object, the positive expression of nonidentity, is a terminological mask. Once the object becomes an object of cognition, its physical side is spiritualized from the outset by translation into epistemology, by a reduction of the sort which in the end, in general, was methodologically prescribed by the phenomenology of Husserl. When the categories of subject and object, both insoluble in the critique of knowledge, come to appear false—as not purely opposed to each other—this also means that the object's objective side, the part of it which cannot be spiritualized, is called "object" only from the viewpoint of a subjectively aimed analysis in which the subject's primacy seems beyond question. Viewed from outside, that which in reflecting upon the mind appears specifically as not mental, as an object, is material. The category of nonidentity still obeys the measure of identity. Emancipated from that measure, the nonidentical moments show up as matter, or as inseparably fused with material things. Sensation, the crux of all epistemology, needs epistemology to reinterpret it into a fact of consciousness, in contradiction to its own full character—which, after all, is to serve as authority for its cognition.

There is no sensation without a somatic moment. To this extent the concept of sensation, in comparison with that which it allegedly subsumes, is twisted so as to satisfy the demand for an autarkic connection of all cognitive steps. While sensation is a part of consciousness, according to the cognitive principle of styling, its phenomenology—unbiased, under the rules of cognition—would have to describe it equally as that which consciousness does not exhaust. Every sensation is a physical feeling also. The feeling does not even "accompany" it, for that would presuppose a tangibility of the sensation's *chorismos;* in fact, it gets this *chorismos* solely from the noological intent—from abstraction, strictly speaking. The linguistic shading of such words as "sensuous," "sensual," even "sensation" itself shows how little the designated facts are the pure moments of cognition as which they are treated in epistemology. To the subjectively immanent reconstruction of the world of things, sensation is the basis of its hierarchy, but it would not have that basis without the *physis* which an autarkic epistemology wants to build later, on top of it.

The somatic moment as the not purely cognitive part of cognition is irreducible, and thus the subjective claim collapses at the very point where radical empiricism had conserved it. The fact that the subject's cognitive achievements are somatic in accordance with their own meaning affects not only the basic relation of subject and object but the dignity of physicality. Physicality emerges at the ontical pole of subjective cognition, as the core of that cognition. This dethrones the guiding idea of epistemology: to constitute the body as the law governing the link between sensations and acts—in other words, to constitute it mentally. Sensations are already, in themselves, what the system would like to set forth as their formation by consciousness.

By tailoring its categories, traditional philosophy has bewitched what is heterogeneous to it. Neither the subject nor the object are merely "posited," in Hegel's manner of speaking. This alone explains fully why the antagonism which philosophy clothed in the words "subject" and "object" cannot be interpreted as a primal state of facts. If it could be so interpreted, the mind would be turned into the body's downright otherness, contradicting its immanent somatic side; but to have the mind alone void the antagonism is impossible, because that in turn would virtually spiritualize it. Showing equally in the antagonism are two things: that which seeks precedence over, and withdraws from, the subject and the fact that our time is unreconciled with the subject— the obverse form, as it were, of the precedence of objectivity.

MATERIALISM AND IMMEDIACY

Where the idealistic critique of materialism proceeds immanently, where it does not simply preach, it likes to make use of the doctrine of immediate data. Like all judgments about the world of things, the concept of matter is to be based upon facts of consciousness. If things of the mind were equated with cerebral processes, according to popular materialistic usage, our original sense perceptions would—so says the idealistic counter-argument —have to be perceptions of what goes on in the brain, not perceptions of color, for instance.

Such refutations are indisputably stringent because the straw men they are knocking down are arbitrary. The reduction to processes of consciousness clings to the apron strings of the scientific cognitive ideal, of the need to confirm the validity of scientific propositions methodically and without a gap. Verification, itself subject to philosophical problematics, comes to be the guideline of that problematics. Science is ontologized, so to speak, as if the criteria of the validity of judgments, the course pursued in their testing, were simply the same as the states of fact—whereas in truth judgments are retroactive treatments of already constituted facts, under the norms of their subjective intelligibility.

In testing scientific judgments we mostly have to make clear to ourselves, step by step, how we arrived at each judgment. The test is thus subjectively accentuated: what mistakes were made by the knowing subject when the judgment was made—one that conflicts with other propositions in the same field, for instance. But it is evident that such retroactive questioning does not coincide with the judged fact itself and its objective causes. If a man has miscalculated and his mistake is pointed out to him, this does not mean that either his arithmetic problem or the applicable mathematical rules can be reduced to "his" calculation, however indispensable subjective acts may be to that calculation, as moments of its objectivity.

The consequences of this distinction for the concept of a transcendental, constitutive logic are considerable. Kant repeated the mistake with which he charged his rationalistic predecessors: an amphiboly of the concepts of reflection. In place of the objective reasons for the judgment he put a reflection on the cognitive subject's course in judging. Here, again, the *Critique of Pure Reason* was revealed as a theory of science. To install that amphiboly as a philosophical principle, and to end up pressing metaphysical wine out of it, may have been the most fatal Freudian slip in the history of modern philosophy. And yet, from the viewpoint of a philosophy of history it is comprehensible. The Thomist *ordo* had presented objectivity as God's will; the destruction of that order seemed to result in a breakdown of objectivity. At the same time, however, scientific objectivity—as opposed to mere opinion —increased immensely, and with it the self-confidence of its organ, the *ratio*. The contradiction was soluble by letting the *ratio* induce one to reinterpret it from an instrument, an appeals court for reflection, into a constituent—by proceeding ontologically in the way in which the rationalist school of Wolff proceeded explicitly.

In that sense, Kantian criticism too remained enmeshed in precritical thinking, as did the whole doctrine of subjective constitution. The post-Kantian idealists made this manifest. Theoretically, the hypostasis of the medium—by now a matter of course in human custom—lay in the so-called "Copernican turn." Kant took care to introduce this as a metaphor whose substantial tendency is the very opposite of the astronomical turn; the traditional discursive logic that conducts the current argument against materialism would require criticizing the procedure as a *petitio principii.* The precedence of consciousness which is to legitimize science, as presupposed at the start of the *Critique of Pure Reason,* is then inferred from procedural standards that confirm or refute judgments in line with scientific rules. Such a logical circle indicates the wrong approach. It hushes up that in themselves, as doubtlessly and absolutely primary, pure facts of consciousness at large do not exist; this was the basic experience of the fin de siècle, of the Neo-Romanticist generation with its nervous horror of the reigning notion of the psyche as a flat factuality.

Ex post facto, in response to the dictates of validity control and a need for classification, facts of consciousness will be distinguished from their transitions, to physical innervations in particular—subtle borderline transitions that refute the supposed solidity of those facts. It is in keeping with this that no subject of immediate data, no "I" to which they might be given, is possible independently of the transsubjective world. He to whom something is given belongs a priori to the same sphere as the given thing. This confounds the thesis of subjective apriority. Materialism is not the dogma indicted by clever opponents, but a dissolution of things understood as dogmatic; hence its right to a place in critical philosophy. When Kant, in *Grundlegung zur Metaphysik der Sitten,* construed freedom as freedom from sensation he was paying involuntary homage to the very thing he wished to argue away. We can no more save the absolute segregation of body and mind (which is tantamount to a secret supremacy of the mind) than we can save the idealistic hierarchy of data. Historically, in the evolutionary course of rationality and ego principle, the two have come into opposition to each other; yet neither is without the other. The logic of noncontradictoriness may fault this, but that logic is brought to a halt by the state of facts. The phenomenology of facts of consciousness requires a transcending of their definitions.

DIALECTICS NOT A SOCIOLOGY OF KNOWLEDGE

It was Marx who drew the line between historic materialism and the popular-metaphysical kind. He thus involved the former in the problematics of philosophy, leaving popular materialism to cut its dogmatic capers this side of philosophy. Since then, materialism is no longer a counter-position one may resolve to take; it is the critique of idealism in its entirety, and of the reality for which idealism opts by distorting it. Horkheimer's phrasing, "critical theory," seeks not to make materialism acceptable but to use it to make men theoretically conscious of what it is that distinguishes materialism—distinguishes it from amateurish explications of the world as much as from the "traditional theory" of science.

A dialectical theory is bound—like Marx's, largely—to be immanent even if in the end it negates the whole sphere it moves in. This contrasts it with a sociology of knowledge that has been merely brought up from outside and is powerless against philosophy, as philosophy was quick to discover. A sociology of knowledge fails before philosophy: for the truth content of philosophy it substitutes its social function and its conditioning by interests, while refraining from a critique of that content itself, remaining indifferent toward it. It fails equally before the concept of ideology, which it will stir into its broad beggarly broth; for the concept of ideology makes sense only in relation to the truth or untruth of what it refers to. There can be no talk of socially necessary delusions except in regard to what would not be a delusion—although, of course, delusion is its index.

The task of criticizing ideology is to judge the subjective and objective shares and their dynamics. It is to deny the false objectivity of concept fetishism by reducing it to the social subject, and to deny false subjectivity, the sometimes unrecognizably

veiled claim that all being lies in the mind, by showing it up as
a fraud, a parasitical nonentity, as well as demonstrating its immanent hostility to the mind. The "all" of the indiscriminately
total concept of ideology, however, terminates in nothingness.
Once it has ceased to differ from any true consciousness it is
no longer fit to criticize a false one. In the idea of objective truth,
materialist dialectics necessarily turns philosophical—despite, and
because of, all its criticisms of philosophy.

A sociology of knowledge, on the other hand, denies not only
the objective structure of society but the idea of objective truth
and its cognition. To this sociology—as to the type of positivist
economics to which its founder Pareto belonged—society is nothing but the average value of individual reactive modes. The doctrine of ideology turns back into a doctrine of subjective idols,
similar to the early bourgeois one; in fact, this is a shyster's trick
to get rid of materialist dialectics as a whole, along with philosophy. Classification serves the *tel quel* localization of the mind.
Such a reduction of so-called "forms of consciousness" goes perfectly with philosophical apologetics. The excuse of the sociology
of knowledge—that the truth or untruth of philosophical teaching has nothing to do with social conditions—remains undisturbed; relativism allies itself with the division of labor. The late
Scheler did not hesitate to exploit this in his "two-worlds theory."
The only way to pass philosophically into social categories is to
decipher the truth content of philosophical categories.

THE CONCEPT OF MIND

We know that Hegel, in his chapter on master and servant, de-
velops the genesis of self-consciousness from the labor relation,
and that he does this by adjusting the I to its self-determined
purpose as well as to heterogeneous matter. The origin of "I" in
"Not I" remains scarcely veiled. It is looked up in the real living
process, in the legalities of the survival of the species, of provid-
ing it with nutriments. Thereafter, Hegel hypostatizes the mind,
but in vain. To succeed somehow, he must blow it up into a whole,
the total spirit—although according to the concept of the mind

its *differentia specifica* is that it is a subject and thus not the whole. Such subreption yields to no straining of the dialectical concept.

A mind that is to be a totality is nonsense. It resembles the political parties in the singular which made their appearance in the twentieth century, tolerating no other party beside them—the parties whose names grin in totalitarian states as allegories of the direct power of the particular. If we conceive the mind as a totality, eliminating every difference from the otherness it is to live by, according to Hegel, the mind turns for a second time into the nothingness which at the outset of dialectical logic is to reveal pure Being: the total spirit would evaporate in mere entity. At the time he wrote *Phenomenology of Mind,* Hegel would hardly have hesitated to designate the concept of the mind as self-transmitted, as both mind and not mind; he would not have followed up by casting off the chains of absolute identity.

Yet if the mind, in what it is, needs that which it is not, a recourse to labor is no longer what apologists for the philosophical field reiterate as their last wisdom; it is no longer a μετάβασις εἰς ἄλλο γένος. There remains the idealist insight that mental activity, as labor, is carried on as much by individuals as by the means they employ, and that performance of this activity degrades the individuals to its function. The idealist concept of the spirit exploits the passage to social labor: it is easy for the general activity that absorbs the individual actors to be transfigured into a noumenon while the individuals are ignored. The polemical answer to this is materialist sympathy with nominalism. Philosophically, however, the answer was too narrow; the thesis that individuality and individuals alone are the true reality was incompatible with Marx's Hegelian-trained theory of the law of value, which capitalism realizes over the heads of men.

The dialectical transmission of the universal and the particular does not permit a theory that opts for the particular to overzealously treat the universal as a soap bubble. Such treatment would let the theory grasp neither the universal's pernicious supremacy in the status quo nor the idea of conditions which in giving individuals their due would rid the universal of its wretched particularity. But even to imagine a transcendental subject without society, without the

199

individuals whom it integrates for good or ill, is just as impossible. This is what the concept of the transcendental subject founders on. Even Kant's universality seeks to be one for all, that is to say, for all rational beings; and the rational are a priori socialized. Scheler's attempt to banish materialism unceremoniously to the nominalist side was a tactical maneuver: first, and not without help from an undeniable lack of philosophical reflection, materialism was blackened as subaltern, and then its subalternity was gloriously conquered.

The loathing which materialist dialectics felt for any crude weltanschauung made it prefer an alliance with science, and yet, in its decline to a means of political rule, dialectics itself turned into such a weltanschauung. It conflicts with Brecht's suicidal demand for simplification to tactical ends. It remains dialectical in nature, philosophy and anti-philosophy at once. The line that consciousness depends on Being was not a metaphysics in reverse; it was pointed at the delusion that the mind is in itself, that it lies beyond the total process in which it finds itself as a moment. Yet the conditions of the mind are not a noumenon either. The term "Being" means altogether different things to Marx and to Heidegger, and yet there is a common trait: in the ontological doctrine of Being's priority over thought, in the "transcendence" of Being, the materialist echo reverberates from a vast distance. The doctrine of Being turns ideological as it imperceptibly spiritualizes the materialist moment in thought by transposing it into pure functionality beyond all entity—as it removes by magic whatever critique of a false consciousness resides in the materialist concept of Being. The word that was to name truth against ideology comes to be the most untrue: the denial of ideality becomes the proclamation of an ideal sphere.

PURE ACTIVITY AND GENESIS

It is the mind's definition as an activity which immanently compels philosophy to pass from the mind to its otherness. From Kant on, no idealism could escape this definition, not even Hegel's. Activity, however, involves the mind in the genesis which irks idealism as a contaminant. As the philosophers keep repeating, the mind as an activity is a sort of becoming; and therefore —almost more important to them yet—it is not χωρίς of history. The simple concept of mental activity makes it intratemporal and historic, becoming as well as that which has become and in which becoming has accumulated. As the most general notion of time takes something temporal, no activity is without a substrate, without an agent and that which is acted upon. The idea of absolute activity hides only what is to be active; the pure νόησις νοήσεως is the shamefaced, metaphysically neutralized belief in a divine Creator.

The idealist doctrine of the Absolute would absorb theological transcendence as a process, would bring it to an immanence that tolerates no absoluteness, no independence of ontical conditions. It may be idealism's most profound incongruity that on the one hand it must carry secularization to extremes lest it sacrifice its claim to totality, while on the other hand it cannot express totality, its phantom of the Absolute, except in theological categories. Torn out of religion, these categories come to be nonentities and are not fulfilled in that "experience of consciousness" into whose charge they are now given. Once humanized, mental activity can be attributed to no one and to nothing but the living. Thus a natural element infiltrates even the concept which most highly overshoots all naturalism: the concept of subjectivity as the synthetic unity of apperception.

Only if the I on its part is also not I does it react to the not-I. Only then does it "do" something. Only then would the doing itself be thinking. Thinking, in a second reflection, breaks the supremacy of thinking over its otherness, because it always is otherness already, within itself. Hence the supreme abstraction of all activity, the transcendental function, does not deserve to be ranked above the factual geneses. No ontological abyss yawns between the moment of reality in that function and the activity of real subjects, and neither, therefore, does one yawn between the mind and labor. It is true that labor, the production of something that was a conception but not yet a fact, is not exhausted in existence; the mind can no more be leveled down to existence than existence can be leveled down to the mind. But the mind's nonbeing moment is so intertwined with existence that to pick it out neatly would be the same as to objectify and falsify it.

The controversy about the priority of mind and body is a pre-dialectical proceeding. It carries on the question of a "first." All but hylozoistically aiming at an ἀρχή, it is ontological in form although the answer may sound materialistic in substance. Both body and mind are abstractions of their experience. Their radical difference is posited, reflecting the mind's historically gained "self-consciousness" and its rejection of what it denies for its own identity's sake. All mental things are modified physical impulses, and such modification is their qualitative recoil into what not merely "is." Urge, according to Schelling's insight,* is the mind's preliminary form.

SUFFERING PHYSICAL

The supposed basic facts of consciousness are something other than mere facts of consciousness. In the dimension of pleasure and displeasure they are invaded by a physical moment. All pain and all negativity, the moving forces of dialectical thinking, assume the variously conveyed, sometimes unrecognizable form of physical things, just as all happiness aims at sensual fulfillment and obtains its objectivity in that fulfillment. A happiness blocked off from every such aspect is no happiness. This dimension is the anti-spiritual side of the spirit, and in subjective sense data it is enfeebled, so to speak, into the spirit's epistemological copy—not so very different from Hume's curious theory that our ideas, facts

---

* "Being, too, is thus completely indifferent toward entity. But the closer, the more inherently pleasurable this relaxed state, the more inevitable is the inactive, unwitting creation in eternity of a quiet craving to come to oneself, a craving to find and to enjoy oneself, an urge to grow conscious of which nonetheless the relaxation does not make one conscious." (Schelling, *Die Weltalter,* Munich 1946, p. 136.) —"And thus, from the bottom stage on, we see Nature follow its inmost, most hidden desire to keep rising and advancing in its urge, until at last it has attracted the highest essentiality, the pure spirituality itself, and has made it its own." (Ibid., p. 140.)

of consciousness with an intentional function, are faded copies of our impressions.

This doctrine is easy to criticize as secretly expressing a naïve naturalism. In fact it is a last epistemological quiver of the somatic element, before that element is totally expelled. It is the somatic element's survival, in knowledge, as the unrest that makes knowledge move, the unassuaged unrest that reproduces itself in the advancement of knowledge. Conscious unhappiness is not a delusion of the mind's vanity but something inherent in the mind, the one authentic dignity it has received in its separation from the body. This dignity is the mind's negative reminder of its physical aspect; its capability of that aspect is the only source of whatever hope the mind can have. The smallest trace of senseless suffering in the empirical world belies all the identitarian philosophy that would talk us out of that suffering: "While there is a beggar, there is a myth," as Benjamin put it.[15] This is why the philosophy of identity is the mythological form of thought.

The physical moment tells our knowledge that suffering ought not to be, that things should be different. "Woe speaks: 'Go.'" Hence the convergence of specific materialism with criticism, with social change in practice. It is not up to the individual sufferer to abolish suffering or mitigate it to a degree which theory cannot anticipate, to which it can set no limit. This job is up solely to the species, to which the individual belongs even where he subjectively renounces it and is objectively thrust into the absolute loneliness of a helpless object. All activities of the species point to its continued physical existence, although they may be misconceptions of it, independent organizations whose business is done only by the way. Even the steps which society takes to exterminate itself are at the same time absurd acts of unleashed self-preservation. They are forms of unconscious social action against suffering even though an obtuse view of society's own interest turns their total particularity against that interest. Confronted with such steps, their purpose—and this alone makes society a society—calls for it to be so organized as the productive forces would directly permit it here and now, and as the conditions of production on either side relentlessly prevent it. The

203

telos of such an organization of society would be to negate the physical suffering of even the least of its members, and to negate the internal reflexive forms of that suffering. By now, this negation in the interest of all can be realized only in a solidarity that is transparent to itself and all the living.

MATERIALISM IMAGELESS

To those who do not want such realization, materialism has since done the favor to debase itself. The tutelage that caused this is not mankind's own fault, as Kant thought. In the meantime, at least, it has come to be systematically reproduced by men in power. The objective spirit, which they maneuver because they need its restraint, adjusts to a consciousness that has been restrained over thousands of years. A materialism come to political power is no less sold on such practices than the world it once wanted to change; it keeps fettering the human consciousness instead of comprehending it and changing it on its part. On the threadbare pretext of a dictatorship (now half a century old) of the proletariat (long bureaucratically administered), governmental terror machines entrench themselves as permanent institutions, mocking the theory they carry on their lips. They chain their vassals to their most direct concerns and keep them stupid.

Yet the depravation of theory could not have happened, had there been no apocryphal dregs in it. In their summary treatment of culture, from the outside, the functionaries who monopolize it would clumsily feign superiority to culture, thereby rendering aid to universal regression. Those whose expectations of imminent revolution made them wish to liquidate philosophy were impatient enough with its demands to lag behind philosophy even then. The apocryphal part of materialism reveals the one of high philosophy, the untruth in the sovereignty of the spirit which the reigning materialism disdains as cynically as bourgeois society used to do in secret. Idealistic majesty is the apocryphal imprint, a relationship which the texts of Kafka and Beckett glaringly illuminate.

The deficiencies of materialism are the unreflected deficiencies of the prevailing condition. What has been unable to keep up, due to the failing principle of spiritualization, is worse in comparison with that which is superior and shamed by the sight of the lastingly inferior. This extraterritoriality of the Fourth Estate is perpetuated by materialism's philistine and barbarian aspects—perpetuated into a culture which is now no longer confined to the Fourth Estate but has spread throughout culture itself. Materialism comes to be the very relapse into barbarism which it was supposed to prevent. To work against this is not the most irrelevant among the tasks of critical theory; otherwise the old untruth will continue with a diminished coefficient of friction and a more baneful effect. Subalternity increases, once the revolution has suffered the same fate as the Second Coming.

Materialist theory became not only aesthetically defective, as against the vacuous sublimity of bourgeois consciousness; it became untrue. This is theoretically determinable. Dialectics lies in things, but it could not exist without the consciousness that reflects it—no more than it can evaporate into that consciousness. If matter were total, undifferentiated, and flatly singular, there would be no dialectics in it. In official materialist dialectics, epistemology was skipped by fiat; epistemology's revenge has been the image doctrine. The thought is not an image of the thing (it becomes that only in an Epicurean-style materialist mythology which invents the emission by matter of little images); the thought aims at the thing itself. Demythologization, the thought's enlightening intent, deletes the image character of consciousness. What clings to the image remains idolatry, mythic enthrallment. The totality of images blends into a wall before reality. The image theory denies the spontaneity of the subject, a *movens* of the objective dialectics of productive forces and conditions. If the subject is bound to mulishly mirror the object—necessarily missing the object, which only opens itself to the subjective surplus in the thought—the result is the unpeaceful spiritual silence of integral administration.

Nothing but an indefatigably reified consciousness will believe, or will persuade others to believe, that it possesses photographs of objectivity. The illusions of such a consciousness turn into dogmatic immediacies. When Lenin, rather than go in for epistemology, opposed it in compulsively reiterated avowals of the noumenality of cognitive objects, he meant to demonstrate that subjective positivism is conspiring with the powers that be. His political requirements turned him against the goal of theoretical cognition. A transcendent argumentation disposes of things on the basis of its claim to power, and with disastrous results: the unpenetrated target of the criticism remains undisturbed as it is, and not being hit at all, it can be resurrected at will in changed constellations of power.

Brecht said once that the book on empirio-criticism obviated any further need to criticize the philosophy of immanence. It was a shortsighted remark. Materialist theory is subject to philosophical desiderata if it is not to succumb to the same provincialism that disfigures art in Eastern countries. The object of theory is not something immediate, of which theory might carry home a replica. Knowledge has not, like the state police, a rogues' gallery of its objects. Rather, it conceives them as it conveys them; else it would be content to describe the façade. As Brecht did admit, after all, the criterion of sense perception—overstretched and problematic even in its proper place—is not applicable to radically indirect society. What immigrated into the object as the law of its motion, inevitably concealed by the ideological form of the phenomenon, eludes that criterion.

Marx, disgusted with the academic squabbles, went rampaging through the epistemological categories like the proverbial bull in the china shop; he scarcely put too much weight on terms such as "reflection," where alleged supremacy is won at the cost of the subjective-critical moment. Living side by side with ideology in the stress on that moment is a bit of hostility to ideology, a bar to the subreption that products and conditions of production are immediate nature. No theory may, for agitatorial simplicity's sake, play the fool about objectively attained knowledge. Theory must reflect the state of this knowledge and promote its advance. The unity of theory and practice was not meant as a concession to weakness of thought, which is a teratism spawned by the repressive society. The computer—which thinking wants to make its own equal and to whose greater glory it would like nothing better than to eliminate itself—is the bankruptcy petition of consciousness in the face of a reality which at the present stage is not given visually but functionally, an abstraction in itself.

Representational thinking would be without reflection—an undialectical contradiction, for without reflection there is no theory. A consciousness interpolating images, a third element, between itself and that which it thinks would unwittingly reproduce idealism. A body of ideas would substitute for the object of cognition, and the subjective arbitrariness of such ideas is that of the authorities. The materialist longing to grasp the thing aims at the opposite: it is only in the absence of images that the full object could be conceived. Such absence concurs with the theological ban on images. Materialism brought that ban into secular form by not permitting Utopia to be positively pictured; this is the substance of its negativity. At its most materialistic, materialism comes to agree with theology. Its great desire would be the resurrection of the flesh, a desire utterly foreign to idealism, the realm of the absolute spirit. The perspective vanishing point of historic materialism would be its self-sublimation, the spirit's liberation from the primacy of material needs in their state of fulfillment. Only if the physical urge were quenched would the spirit be reconciled and would become that which it only promises while the spell of material conditions will not let it satisfy material needs.

PART THREE

MODELS

ONE

FREEDOM

On the Metacritique of Practical Reason

"PSEUDOPROBLEMS"

The talk of "pseudoproblems" comes from the Age of Enlightenment, when its point was to keep an unquestioned dogmatic authority from leading to considerations held to be impossible to decide for the very thought they were submitted to. There is a ring of this in the pejorative use of the word "scholasticism." But pseudoproblems have long ceased to be regarded as those that defy rational judgment and mock the rational interest. Instead, they are viewed as the problems in which the concepts used are unclearly defined. A semantical taboo chokes off questions of fact as if they were mere questions of meaning; preliminary considerations degenerate into a ban on consideration. What may or may not be reflected upon, however urgent, is regulated by a method blithely modeled after the current methods of exact science. Approved modes of proceeding, pure means, gain primacy over the ends, the goals of cognition. Experiences that balk at being unequivocally tagged get a dressing-down: the difficulties they cause are said to be due solely to lose, pre-scientific nomenclature.

The relevance of the question whether there is free will matches the technical terms' recalcitrance at the desideratum of stating clearly what they mean. With legal and penal process—and finally the possibility of that which throughout philosophical tradition has been called morality or ethics—depending upon the answer, our intellectual need does not allow us to be talked out of the naïve question as a pseudoproblem. A poor ersatz satisfaction is offered to that need by self-righteously tidy thinking; and yet the semantical critique cannot be carelessly ignored. A question's urgency cannot compel an answer if no true answer is obtainable; even less can the fallible need, however desperate, point the direction of the answer. We would not have to reflect on the topics under discussion by judging their being or nonbeing, but by expanding their definition so it will include the impossibility to nail them down, as well as the compulsion to conceive them.

This is what is attempted, with or without any such explicit intent, in the antinomy chapter of the *Critique of Pure Reason* and in long passages of the *Critique of Practical Reason*—although Kant, in the process, did not altogether avoid the dogmatic usage which, like Hume, he chides in other traditional concepts. He settled the conflict between facticity ("nature") and inescapable thoughts ("the intelligible world") in dichotomical fashion. Yet if we cannot point to freedom or the will as things in being, this does not mean—in analogy to simple, pre-dialectical epistemology—that specific impulses or experiences cannot be synthesized under concepts to which no naturalistic substrate corresponds, concept that reduce those impulses or experiences to a common denominator in similar fashion, for instance, as the Kantian "object" will reduce its phenomena. On that model, the will would be the lawful unity of all impulses that prove to be both spontaneous and rationally determined, as distinct from natural causality—although remaining in the framework of that causality, for outside the causal connection there can be no sequence of volitive acts. Freedom would be the word for the possibility of those impulses.

This agile epistemocritical solution does not suffice, however. The either-or exacted by the question of free will is both succinct and worth asking, and in the concept of the will as the lawful unity of its impulses it is indifferently glossed over. Above all, in the concept formation that takes its bearings from the model of the subjective philosophy of immanence we tacitly assume a monadological structure of both will and freedom. Yet this structure is contradicted by the simplest of things: by way of what analytical psychologists call the "test of reality," countless moments of external—notably social—reality invade the decisions designated by the words "will" and "freedom"; if the concept of rationality in the will means anything at all, it must refer precisely to that invasion, however obstinately this may be denied by Kant.

In fact, considering the actual decisions that permit us to ask whether they are free or unfree, what lends the immanently philosophical definition of those concepts its elegance and its autarky is an abstraction. The psychological moment left over by that abstraction is scant as compared with the real complexion of within and without. From this impoverished, chemically pure remnant we cannot tell what may be predicated about freedom, or about its opposite. To put it more strictly, and at the same time in more Kantian terms: the empirical subject that makes those decisions (and only an empirical one can make them; the transcendentally pure I would be incapable of impulses) is itself a moment of the spatial-temporal "external" world. It has no ontological priority before that world. This is why the attempt to localize the question of free will in the empirical subject must fail. In that attempt, the line between the intelligible and the empirical realm is drawn in the midst of empiricism.

This much of the thesis of the pseudoproblem is true. As soon as we ask about free will by asking about each individual decision, as soon as our question detaches these decisions from their context and the individual from society, the question will yield to the fallacy of absolute, pure being-in-itself: a limited subjective experience will usurp the dignity of the most certain of things. There is something fictitious about the substrate of the alternative. The supposedly noumenal subject is transmitted within itself by that from which it is distinguished, by the context of all subjects. The transmission makes it what in its sense of freedom it does not want to be: it becomes heteronomous. Even where unfreedom is positively assumed, the conditions of unfreedom, as those of an immanently conclusive psychological causality, are sought in the isolated individual—which essentially is not so isolated. Not even the individual can find the fact of freedom in himself, and neither can the naïve sense of acting arbitrarily be simply extinguished *post festum* by the theorem of determination. It was in a late phase only that the doctrine of psychological determinism was carried through.

A SPLIT IN THE CONCERN WITH FREEDOM

Ever since the seventeenth century, freedom had been defined as all great philosophy's most private concern. Philosophy had an unexpressed mandate from the bourgeoisie to find transparent grounds for freedom. But that concern is antagonistic in itself. It goes against the old oppression and promotes the new one, the one that hides in the principle of rationality itself. One seeks a common formula for freedom and oppression, ceding freedom to the rationality that restricts it, and removing it from empiricism in which one does not even want to see it realized. The dichotomy also refers to progressive scientification. The bourgeois class is in league with this insofar as it promotes production, but it must fear scientific progress as soon as that progress interferes with the belief that its freedom—already resigned to internality—is existent.

This is the real background of the doctrine of antinomies. In the works of Kant, and later in those of the idealists, the idea of freedom comes to be contrasted with the research of the individual sciences, of psychology in particular. Kant banishes the objects of this research to the realm of unfreedom; positive science is assigned its place beneath speculation—in Kant's case, beneath the doctrine of the noumena. With the flagging of speculative vigor and the correlative evolution of individual sciences, the antithesis has been exacerbated to the extreme. The sciences paid the price in narrowmindedness, and philosophy, in noncommittal vacuity. The more of its substance is confiscated by the individual sciences— as psychology, for instance, commandeered the genesis of character, on which even Kant still made wild guesses—the more embarrassingly will the philosophemes on freedom of the will deteriorate into declamations.

If the sciences keep searching for more legality, and if this search, ahead of any ideology, drives them to the side of determinism, philosophy becomes increasingly a depository of pre-scientific, apologetical views of freedom. The antinomics of freedom is an essential moment of Kant's philosophy, as the dialectics of freedom is an essential moment of Hegel's. Later on, oaths to the idol of a sublime realm above empiricism were taken by academic philosophy, at least. Praise of the intelligible freedom of the individuals allowed empirical individuals to be held more ruthlessly accountable, to be more effectively curbed with the prospect of punishment that could be metaphysically justified.

The alliance of libertarian doctrine and repressive practice removes philosophy farther and farther from genuine insight into the freedom and unfreedom of the living. Anachronistically, it approximates that jejune edification which Hegel diagnosed as the affliction of philosophy. But because an individual science— the prime example is criminal jurisprudence—cannot cope with the question of freedom and must reveal its own incompetence, it seeks help from the very philosophy whose bad, abstract antithesis to scientivism will not let it render that help. Where science finds problems insoluble and looks to philosophy for a decision, philosophy extends no more than the solace of a weltanschauung.

It is from this, then, that the scientists take their bearings— according to taste and, one must fear, according to the structure of their own psychological drives. The relation to the complex of freedom and determinism is laid into the hands of an arbitrary irrationality that wavers between dogmatic generalities and inconclusive, more or less empirical single determinations. In the end, one's position regarding that complex comes to depend upon his political creed, or upon the power he happens to recognize at the moment.

Reflections on freedom and determinism sound archaic, as though dating from the early times of the revolutionary bourgeoisie. But that freedom grows obsolete without having been realized— this is not a fatality to be accepted; it is a fatality which resistance must clarify. Not the least of the reasons why the idea of freedom lost its power over people is that from the outset it was conceived so abstractly and subjectively that the objective social trends found it easy to bury.

FREEDOM, DETERMINISM, IDENTITY

Indifference to freedom, to the concept and to the thing itself, is caused by the integration of society, which happens to the subjects as if it were irresistible. Their interest in being provided for has paralyzed the interest in a freedom which they fear would leave them unprotected. The mere mention of freedom sounds as bombastic as the appeal to it. This is what an intransigent nominalism adjusts to. Its relegation, by a logical canon, of objective antinomies to the realm of pseudoproblems has a social function: it serves to conceal contradictions by their denial. By holding on to data, or to their contemporary legatees, the protocol statements, one relieves the human consciousness of what runs counter to its outward situation.

Under the rules of that ideology, only modes of human conduct in different situations would have to be discussed and classified; talk of will or freedom would be concept fetishism. As actually proposed by the behaviorists, one would have simply to retranslate all definitions of the ego into reactive modes and individual reactions, which would then have solidified. No note is taken of the fact that what has been solidified brings forth new qualities, qualities distinct from the reflexes from which it may have arisen. Unconsciously, the positivists obey the dogma of the superior "first" which their metaphysical archenemies entertained: "For the most revered is the oldest, and the sworn witness is paid the highest homage."[1]

In Aristotle's case, the first is the mythus, of which the out-and-out anti-mythologists retain the conception that whatever is can be reduced to what once has been. The equality of their quantifying method leaves no more room for the evolving otherness than does the spell of fate. But what has been objectified in men, from their reflexes and against their reflexes—their character or their will, the potential organ of their freedom—this undermines freedom too. For it embodies the principle of dominion, to which men progressively submit. The identity of the self and its alienation are companions from the beginning; this is why the concept of self-alienation is poorly romanticist. Identity, the condition of freedom, is immediately and simultaneously the principle of determinism. There is a will insofar as a man objectified himself into a character. Toward himself—whatever that may be—he thus becomes something external, after the model of the outward world of things that is subjected to causality.

Besides, the positivistic concept of "reaction," a concept purely descriptive in intent, presupposes incomparably more than it admits. It presupposes a passive dependence on each given situation. The interaction of subject and object is spirited away, a priori, while spontaneity is excluded by the very method; it is in line with the ideology of adjustment that men, ever ready to serve the world's course, should once more be broken of that contrary habit, spontaneity. If passive reactions were all there is, all would —in the older philosophical terminology—be receptivity; there could be no thinking. If the will takes consciousness, we may presume, correlatively, that consciousness takes a will. On the other hand, self-preservation in its history calls for more than conditioned reflexes, and thus it prepares for what it would eventually transcend. In doing so, it presumably emulates the biological individual's prescription of the form of his reflexes; the reflexes scarcely would be without any unity. The strengthening moment is the self of self-preservation; it is to this that freedom opens as the difference that has evolved between the self and the reflexes.

FREEDOM AND ORGANIZED SOCIETY

Without any thought of freedom, theoretical reasons for an organized society would be hard to find. Society in its turn will then curtail freedom. Both might be shown on Hobbes' construction of the social contract. Unlike Hobbes, the determinist, a factually consistent determinism would sanction the *bellum omnium contra omnes;* if all men were equally predetermined and blind, every criterion of actions would fall by the wayside. The perspective of an extremity is unveiled: whether the demand for freedom, put forth so that men can live together, does not contain a paralogism —that freedom must be a reality lest there be horror.

In fact, there is horror because there is no freedom yet. Reflection on the question of free will does not abolish the question but turns it into one for the philosophy of history: why have the two theses, "The will is free" and "The will is unfree," become an antinomy? The historical origin of that reflection did not escape Kant, who expressly based the revolutionary claim of his own ethics on the delay in the reflection: "Man was seen to be bound to laws by his duty; but it occurred to no one that the only legislation to which man is subject is his own and yet universal, and that his only obligation is to act in line with a will that is his own but is also universally law-giving according to the ends of nature."[2] By no means, however, did it occur to Kant whether freedom itself—to him, an eternal idea—might not be essentially historic, and that not just as a concept but in its empirical substance.

Whole epochs, whole societies lacked not only the concept of freedom but the thing. To attribute the thing to them as an objective noumenon (even though totally hidden from the people concerned) would conflict with the Kantian transcendental principle—with the principle that is said to be founded in the subjective consciousness and would be untenable as the supposed consciousness at large if it were wholly lacking in any living person. Hence, probably, Kant's stubborn endeavor to demonstrate the moral sense as something that exists everywhere, even in the radically wicked. Otherwise he would have had to say that phases and societies in which there is no freedom are not only not rational but not human—and the adherent of Rousseau would scarcely have stooped to saying that.

Before the formation of the individual in the modern sense, which to Kant was a matter of course—in the sense meaning not simply the biological human being, but the one constituted as a unit by its own self-reflection,[3] the Hegelian "self-consciousness" —it is an anachronism to talk of freedom, whether as a reality or as a challenge. Likewise, freedom, which without impairment can only be achieved under social conditions of unfettered plenty, might be wholly extinguished again, perhaps without leaving a trace. The trouble is not that free men do radical evil, as evil is being done beyond all measure conceivable to Kant; the trouble is that as yet there is no world in which—there are flashes of this in

Brecht's work—men would no longer need to be evil. Evil, therefore, is the world's own unfreedom. Whatever evil is done comes from the world.

Society destines the individuals to be what they are, even by their immanent genesis. Their freedom or unfreedom is not primary, as it would seem under the veil of the *principium individuationis*. For the ego, as Schopenhauer explained by the myth of Maya's veil, makes even the insight into its dependence difficult to gain for the subjective consciousness. The principle of individualization, the law of particularity to which the universal reason in the individuals is tied, tends to insulate them from the encompassing contexts and thereby strengthens their flattering confidence in the subject's autarky. Under the name of freedom, their totality is contrasted with the totality of whatever restricts individuality. Yet the *principium individuationis* is by no means the metaphysically ultimate and unalterable, and thus it is not freedom either. Freedom is a moment, rather, in a twofold sense: it is entwined, not to be isolated; and for the time being it is never more than an instant of spontaneity, a historical node, the road to which is blocked under present conditions.

The individual's independence, inappropriately stressed by liberal ideology, does not prevail; nor is there any denying his extremely real separation from society, which that ideology misinterprets. At times the individual would oppose himself to society as an independent being, though a particular one—a being capable of rationally pursuing its own interest. In that phase, and beyond it, the question of freedom was the genuine question whether society permits the individual to be as free as it promises; and thus it was also the question whether society itself is as free as it promises. Temporarily, the individual looms above the blind social context, but in his windowless isolation he only helps so much more to reproduce that context.

No less indicative of the historic experience that inside and outside are unreconciled is the thesis of unfreedom. Men are unfree because they are beholden to externality, and this externality in turn consists also of men themselves. As perceived in Hegel's *Phenomenology,* it is only from that which has been divided from it, from that which is necessarily against it, that the subject acquires the concepts of freedom and unfreedom which it will then relate to its own monadological structure. The pre-philosophical consciousness is located this side of the alternative; to a subject that acts naïvely and opposes itself to its environment, its own conditioning is nontransparent.

To dominate this conditioning, consciousness must render it transparent. The thought, by means of its freedom, turns back to itself as to its subject, and its sovereignty also leads to the concept of unfreedom. The two concepts are not a simple antithesis; they are interwoven. No theoretical curiosity can make us aware of this; it is the nature-controlling sovereignty and its social form, dominion over people, that suggest the opposite to our consciousness: the idea of freedom. Its historical archetype was he who is topmost in hierarchies, the man who is not visibly dependent.

In the abstract universal concept of things "beyond nature," freedom is spiritualized into freedom from the realm of causality. With that, however, it becomes a self-deception. Psychologically speaking, the subject's interest in the thesis that it is free would be narcissistic, as immoderate as anything of the kind. There is narcissism even in Kant's arguments, for all his categorial localization of freedom in a sphere above psychology. According to his *Foundation for a Metaphysics of Morals,* everyone, including "the most arrant knave," need only be "shown examples of honest intent, of constancy in following good maxims, of compassion and of general good will," to wish that he too were so minded. He can expect no "gratification of desires" from this, "no condition that would satisfy any of his real or otherwise conceivable inclinations, but only a greater inner worth of his person. . . . But he believes that he is this better person when he puts himself on the standpoint of a member of the intelligible world—a move he is involuntarily compelled to make by the idea of freedom, i.e., independence of determining causes from the sensible world . . ."[4]

There is no effort Kant will not make to prove that this expectation of an enhanced inner personal worth, this supposed motivation behind the thesis of freedom, rests in turn upon the moral law—on the very objectivity to which, on the other hand, consciousness is said to rise only on grounds of that expectation. And yet he cannot make us forget that in our view of freedom the "practical use of common human reason"[5] is coupled with the need for self-exaltation, with the person's "worth." That immediate consciousness, the "common moral cognition of reason" which is the methodical starting point of Kant's *Foundation,* will find itself no less interested in denying the same freedom which it claims. The more freedom the subject—and the community of subjects—ascribes to itself, the greater its responsibility; and before this responsibility it must fail in a bourgeois life which in practice has never yet endowed a subject with the unabridged autonomy accorded to it in theory. Hence the subject must feel guilty.

What makes the subjects aware of the bounds of their freedom is that they are part of nature, and finally, that they are powerless against society, which has become independent of them. Yet the universality of the concept of freedom—a concept shared by the oppressed as well—recoils against dominion as freedom's model. Reacting to this recoil, those who have the privilege of freedom delight in finding others not yet ripe for freedom. They rationalize this persuasively by way of natural causality. The subjects are not only fused with their own physical nature; a consistent legality holds sway also in the psychological realm, which reflection has laboriously divided from the world of bodies. This feeling rose proportionally with the soul's definition as a unit. But a sense of unfreedom exists no more than does an immediately evident sense of freedom; it always requires either that socially perceived phenomena be reflected upon the subject—the oldest instance is the so-called Platonic psychology—or that objectifications be performed by psychological science, in whose hands its discovery, the life of the soul, becomes a thing among things and falls under the causality predicated by the world of things.

THE IMPULSE BEFORE THE EGO

The dawning sense of freedom feeds upon the memory of the archaic impulse not yet steered by any solid I. The more the I curbs that impulse, the more chaotic and thus questionable will it find the pre-temporal freedom. Without an anamnesis of the untamed impulse that precedes the ego—an impulse later banished to the zone of unfree bondage to nature—it would be impossible to derive the idea of freedom, although that idea in turn ends up reinforcing the ego. In spontaneity, the philosophical concept that does most to exalt freedom as a mode of conduct above empirical existence, there resounds the echo of that by whose control and ultimate destruction the I of idealistic philosophy means to prove its freedom. Through an apologia for its perverted form, society encourages the individuals to hypostatize their individuality and thus their freedom.

As far as such a stubborn delusion extends, it is solely in pathogenous states that a consciousness learns about its unfree side—in compulsion neuroses, for instance. They bid it act, within the circumference of its own immanence, in line with laws which the consciousness experiences as alien to the I; freedom is denied in its own native realm. Another metapsychological aspect of the pain of the neuroses is their destruction of a convenient image, "Free within, unfree without"—although in its pathic condition the subject will not come to see the truth conveyed by that condition, a truth which it can reconcile neither with its drives nor with its rational concerns. This truth content of neuroses is that the I has its unfreedom demonstrated to it, within itself, by something alien to it—by the feeling that "this isn't me at all." Neuroses are true in so far as they demonstrate the ego's unfreedom precisely where its rule over its inner nature fails.

Whatever falls under the unity of what traditional epistemology called "personal self-consciousness"—itself compulsive in nature, since all moments of that unity bear its stamp as that of a legality —all this seems free to the self-retrieving ego whose idea of freedom derives from the model of its own rule: first, from its rule over people and things, and then, internalized, from its rule over its entire concrete substance, which it commands by thinking it. This is not just the self-deception of immediacy blown up into an absolute. Only if one acts as an I, not just reactively, can his action be called free in any sense. And yet, what would be equally free is that which is not tamed by the I as the principle of any determination—that which, as in Kant's moral philosophy, strikes the I as unfree and has indeed been unfree to this day.

The progress of self-experience makes freedom as a datum problematical for this experience, and since the subject's interest in freedom will not dwindle, it sublimates freedom into an idea. Metapsychologically, this is verified by the psychoanalytical theory of repression. According to that theory—and dialectically enough —the repressing agent, the compulsive mechanism, is one with the I, the organon of freedom. In ourselves, by introspection, we discover neither a positive freedom nor a positive unfreedom. We conceive both in their relation to extramental things: freedom as a polemical counter-image to the suffering brought on by social coercion; unfreedom as that coercion's image. This is how little the subject is the "sphere of absolute origins," as it will be philosophizingly called; the very definitions that uphold its claim to sovereignty always need also what is said to need nothing but them, as those definitions are understood. What is decisive in the ego, its independence and autonomy, can be judged only in relation to its otherness, to the nonego. Whether or not there is autonomy depends upon its adversary and antithesis, on the object which either grants or denies autonomy to the subject. Detached from the object, autonomy is fictitious.

EXPERIMENTA CRUCIS

Consciousness cannot learn much about freedom from its self-experience, as witness the *experimenta crucis* of introspection. Not for nothing is the most popular one laid to an ass. Kant sticks to the same pattern in his attempt to show freedom by way of the decision to rise from a chair—a decision that would be more fitting in a play by Beckett. To decide cogently, empirically, so to speak, whether the will is free, situations must be rigorously cleansed of their empirical content; the determinants we can perceive in the conditions that are created for the thought experiment must be as few as possible. But in every less clownish paradigm the deciding subject is provided with rational reasons that would have to be chalked off as determinants. The *experimenta* are condemned to inanity by the principle on which decisions are supposed to be made, and this depreciates the decisions. Pure situations à la

Buridan are not apt to occur where they are not devised or brought about in order to demonstrate freedom. And even if something of the kind were discoverable anywhere, it would be irrelevant to any person's life and therefore ἀδιάφορον for freedom.

Some of Kant's *experimenta crucis* have greater pretensions, of course. They are dressed up as empirical evidence of the right to "introduce freedom into science," since "experience too confirms this order of concepts within us"[6]—whereas empirical evidence of something which in Kant's own theory is classified as supra-empirical ought to arouse his suspicions, rather, with the critical facts thus placed in the very sphere from which they are said to be removed as a matter of principle. And indeed, the example is not stringent. "Suppose one maintains that his carnal desire is quite irresistible for him if the beloved object and the opportunity for it were found. Ask him whether, if there were a gallows erected outside the house where he finds that opportunity, for hanging him as soon as he had slaked his lust—whether in this case he would not curb his desire. No need to guess about his answer. But ask him whether, if on the same instant pain of death his sovereign ordered him to bear false witness against an honest man, for whose ruin the prince wants a pretext—ask whether then, however great his love of life, he thinks it would be possible for him to overcome it. He may not dare say whether or not he would; but he must unhesitatingly admit the possibility. Therefore, in judging that he can do a thing because he feels he ought to do it, he comes to know within himself the freedom of which otherwise, without the moral law, he would have remained ignorant."[7]

That the thing can be done—this the man charged with "carnal desire" would presumably concede as readily as the victim of coercion by the tyrant whom Kant respectfully calls "his sovereign." It would probably be the truth if both men, mindful of the weight which self-preservation carries in such decisions, denied knowing how they would act in the real situation. In that situation, psychological moments like the "ego drive" and fear of death cannot fail to take forms differing from the improbable cogitative experiment that neutralizes them into unaffectively ponderable ideas. However consummate a man's integrity, there is no telling how he would act under torture; the situation—by then anything but fictitious—sets a limit upon what Kant takes for matters of course. His example does not, as he hoped, allow us to legitimize freedom by use in practice. The best we can do with it is shrug it off.

Another Kantian example, that of the cardsharp, is no more serviceable. "If a man has lost at cards he may feel anger at himself and his imprudence; but if he is aware of having cheated, he must—even though he has won thereby—despise himself when he compares his action with the moral law. This, then, must be something other than the principle of one's own happiness. To be obliged to say to myself, 'I am a knave although I have lined my pockets,' I need a standard of judgment that differs from applauding myself and saying, 'I am clever, for I have enriched myself.' "[8] Granting even that the cheat will reflect upon the moral law: whether or not he will despise himself is a crassly empirical question. He may be infantile and deem himself one of the chosen, above all bourgeois responsibilities; he may chuckle at the successful caper, with his narcissism shielding him from the alleged self-disdain; or he may have acted in accordance with a moral code approved among his kind. The pathos with which he would have to brand himself a knave is based on recognition of Kant's moral law—of the law Kant wants to base upon the example. In the group of all those covered by the concept of moral insanity, for instance, that law is suspended, yet they are by no means irrational; it is only metaphorically that they can be classed with the insane.

When any thesis about the *mundus intelligibilis* seeks comfort from the empirical world, it must put up with empirical criteria. And these criteria speak against the comfort, in line with the speculative thought's aversion to the so-called "example," as to something inferior. Kant's work is not lacking in displays of that aversion: "This is also the only great benefit of examples, that they sharpen the power of judgment. For as regards the accuracy and precision of intellectual insight, they commonly tend somewhat to impair this, rather, because they seldom adequately meet the conditions of the rule (as *casus in terminis*), and because, moreover, they often weaken the intellect's effort to understand the sufficiency of rules in general, independently of the particular circumstances of experience, and they therefore ultimately breed a habit of using rules like formulas more than as principles. Thus examples are the leading-strings of judgment, which he who lacks a natural gift for that power can never do without."[9]

Contrary to his own insight, Kant did not disdain to use examples in the *Critique of Practical Reason;* he needed them, one suspects, because empirical subreption was the only way to demonstrate the relation between existence and the formal moral law, and thus the possibility of the Imperative. This is the vengeance exacted by his philosophy: his examples are stabs at thin air. The absurdity of moral experiments may have its core in their coupling of incompatibles, in their undertaking to calculate things which are beyond the realm of calculability.*

THE ADDENDUM

Despite all this, the experiments show a moment which we may call the addendum, in line with the vague way it is experienced. The subject's decisions do not roll off in a causal chain; what

---

* The Kantian cogitative experiments are not unlike existentialist ethics. Kant knew well that good will is conveyed in the continuity of a lifetime rather than in isolated acts; but in the experiment, to make it prove what it should, he exacerbates good will into a choice between two alternatives. That continuity hardly exists any more—which is why Sartre, in a kind of regression to the eighteenth century, clings to the decision alone. Yet the alternative situation, which is supposed to demonstrate autonomy, is heteronomous before every matter of substance. Kant needs a despot for one of his exemplary situations of choice; analogously, many of Sartre's situations are derived from fascism and true as indictments of fascism, not as a *condition humaine.*

A free man would only be one who need not bow to any alternatives, and under existing circumstances there is a touch of freedom in refusing to accept the alternatives. Freedom means to criticize and change situations, not to confirm them by deciding within their coercive structure. Brecht, in defiance of his official creed, helped this insight along after a talk with students, when he followed up his doctrinal collectivistic piece on "Yes-sayer" with the deviating "Nay-sayer."

occurs is a jolt, rather. In traditional philosophy, this factual addendum in which consciousness externalizes itself is again interpreted as nothing but consciousness. It is supposed to intervene as if the intervention were somehow conceivable to the pure mind. Construed, to this end, is *quod erat demonstrandum:* that the subject's reflection alone is able, if not to break through natural causality, at least to change its direction by adding other motivational chains. The self-experience of the moment of freedom depends on consciousness; the subject knows itself to be free only insofar as its action strikes it as identical with it, and that is the case in conscious actions only. In those alone can subjectivity laboriously, ephemerally raise its head.

But the insistence on this was rationalistically narrowed. In that sense Kant—in keeping with his conception of practical reason as that which is truly "pure," that is, sovereign in relation to any material—kept clinging to the school overthrown by his critique of theoretical reason. Consciousness, rational insight, is not simply the same as a free act. We cannot flatly equate it with the will. Yet this precisely is what happens in Kant's thinking. To him, the will is the epitome of freedom, the "power" to act freely, the unifying characteristic of all acts conceived as free. Of the categories which "in the field of the supersensory" are "necessarily connected" with the "determining ground of the pure will," he teaches "that they always refer only to intelligent beings, and even in these only to the relation of reason to the will, and thus always only to practice."[10] It is through the will, he says, that reason creates its reality, untrammeled by the material, whatever its kind.

This may be what the formulations scattered throughout Kant's moral-philosophical writings converge upon. In the *Foundation for a Metaphysics of Morals,* the will is "conceived as a faculty to make oneself act according to the idea of certain laws."[11]* Later in the same book, the will is said to be "a sort of causality of living creatures, provided they are rational; and freedom would

---

* The "idea of certain laws" is tantamount to the concept of pure reason—defined by Kant, after all, as "the faculty of deriving cognition from principles."

be the quality of this causality, since it can be at work independently of alien causes that determine it."[12] The oxymoron "causality by freedom," appearing in the thesis of the Third Antinomy and explicated in the *Foundation,* owes its plausibility solely to the abstraction which has reason exhaust the will without a remainder.

In fact, freedom turns for Kant into a quality of the causality of living subjects because it lies beyond alien determining causes, and because it contracts into that necessity which coincides with reason. His view of the will as a "faculty of purposes"[13] in the *Critique of Practical Reason* takes its bearings from the concept of objective purposes, and yet the will is still interpreted as theoretical reason, since the purposes "are at all times determining causes of the faculty of desire according to principles."[14] To be conceived as principles, however, are solely the laws of reason, tacitly endowed with power to direct the faculty of desire, which in turn belongs to the sensible world. As the pure λόγος, the will becomes a no-man's-land between subject and object, antinomical in a manner not envisioned in the critique of reason.

And yet, it is at the outset of the self-emancipating modern subject's self-reflection, in *Hamlet,* that we find the divergence of insight and action paradigmatically laid down. The more the subject turns into a being-for-itself, the greater the distance it places between itself and the unbroken accord with a given order, the less will its action and its consciousness be one. The addendum has an aspect which under rationalistic rules is irrational. It denies the Cartesian dualism of *res extensa* and *res cogitans,* in which the addendum, as mental, is lumped with the *res cogitans,* regardless of the difference that separates it from the thought. The addendum is an impulse, the rudiment of a phase in which the dualism of extramental and intramental was not thoroughly consolidated yet, neither volitively bridgeable nor an ontological ultimate.

This also affects the concept of the will that contains so-called "facts of consciousness" (which at the same time, purely descriptively, are more than such facts—this lies hidden in the will's transition to practice). The impulse, intramental and somatic in one, drives beyond the conscious sphere to which it belongs just the same. With that impulse freedom extends to the realm of experience; this animates the concept of freedom as a state that would no more be blind nature than it would be oppressed nature. Its phantasm—which reason will not allow to be withered by any proof of causal interdependence—is the phantasm of reconciling nature and the mind. This is not as alien to reason as it would seem under the aspect of reason's Kantian equation with the will; it does not drop from heaven. To philosophical reflection it appears as downright otherness because the will that has been reduced to pure practical reason is an abstraction. The addendum is the name for that which was eliminated in this abstraction; without it, there would be no real will at all. It is a flash of light between the poles of something long past, something grown all but unrecognizable, and that which some day might come to be.

True practice, the totality of acts that would satisfy the idea of freedom, does indeed require full theoretical consciousness. In decisionism, which strikes out reason in the passage to the act, the act is delivered to the automatism of dominion: the unreflected freedom to which it presumes comes to serve total unfreedom. We have been taught this lesson by Hitler's Reich and its union of decisionism and social Darwinism, the affirmative extension of natural causality. But practice also needs something else, something physical which consciousness does not exhaust, something conveyed to reason and qualitatively different from it. The two moments are by no means separately experienced; but philosophical analysis has tailored the phenomenon in such a way that afterwards, in philosophical language, it simply cannot be put otherwise than as if something else were added to rationality.

Kant, by allowing no *movens* of practice but reason, remained under the spell of that faded theory against which he devised the primacy of practical reason as a complement. This is what ails his entire moral philosophy. The part of action that differs from the pure consciousness which in Kant's eyes compels the action, the part that abruptly leaps out—this is spontaneity, which Kant also transplanted into pure consciousness, lest the constitutive function of the "I think" be imperiled. In Kant's work, the memory of what has been eliminated survives only in the two-fold exegesis of an intramentally interpreted spontaneity. On the one hand it is thinking, an act of consciousness; on the other hand it is unconscious and involuntary, the heartbeat of the *res cogitans* and yet beyond it. Pure consciousness—"logic"—itself has come to be; it is a validity that has submerged its genesis. Its genesis lies in a moment which the Kantian doctrine skips: in the negation of the will, which according to Kant would be pure consciousness.

Logic is a practice insulated against itself. Contemplative con-duct, the subjective correlate of logic, is the conduct that wills nothing. Conversely, each act of the will breaks through the mechanical autarky of logic; this is what makes theory and prac-tice antithetical. Kant turns the matter upside down. Though the addendum may always be more sublimated with increasing con-sciousness, though indeed the concept of the will as something substantial and unanimous may only be formed in that increase —if the motor form of reaction were liquidated altogether, if the hand no longer twitched, there would be no will. What the great rationalistic philosophers conceived as the will is already, and without accounting for it, a denial of the will. The Schopenhauer of Book Four had every right to feel that he was a Kantian.

The fact that without a will there is no consciousness is blurred for the idealists by sheer identity, as if the will were nothing else but consciousness. In the most profound concept of transcenden-tal epistemology, the concept of productive imagination, the trace of the will invades the pure intellective function. Once that has happened, spontaneity is curiously skipped in the will. It is not merely reason that has genetically evolved from the force of human drives, as their differentiation; without the kind of willing that is manifested in the arbitrary nature of every thought act— the kind that furnishes our only reason to distinguish such an act from the subject's passive, "receptive" moments—there would be no thinking in the proper sense of the word. But idealism has taken an oath to the contrary and must not admit that, on pain of its own destruction. This explains the distortion as well as its proximity to the true facts.

THE FICTION OF POSITIVE FREEDOM

Freedom can be defined in negation only, corresponding to the concrete form of a specific unfreedom. Positively it becomes an "as if." It does so literally in the *Foundation for a Metaphysics of Morals:* "I am saying: Every creature that cannot act otherwise than under the idea of freedom is precisely therefore really free in a practical sense—i.e., all laws that are inseparably linked with freedom apply as much to that creature as if its will were declared free also in itself and in the valid form of theoretical philosophy."[15]

The aporetical character of this fiction—whose very weakness may be why the "I am saying" puts so much subjective stress on it—is illuminated by a footnote in which Kant apologizes for "regarding freedom as sufficient for our purpose if only rational creatures based their actions on its mere idea . . . lest I oblige myself to offer proof of freedom in its theoretical sense as well."[16] Yet he does envision creatures that "cannot act otherwise than" under that idea—in other words, real people—and these, according to the *Critique of Pure Reason,* are meant by that "theoretical intent" which lists causality in its table of categories. To warrant freedom to empirical human beings as if their will were demonstrably free even in theoretical philosophy, in the philosophy of nature—this takes an immense effort on Kant's part; for if the moral law were downright incommensurable to those people, there would be no point to the moral philosophy. It would be only too glad to shake off the fact that the Third Antinomy penalized both possible answers alike as boundary violations, ending in a draw. While Kant, in practical philosophy, rigorously proclaims the *chorismos* of what is and what ought to be, he is nonetheless compelled to resort to mediations. His idea of freedom turns into a paradox: it comes to be incorporated in the causality of the phenomenal world that is incompatible with the Kantian concept of freedom.

With the magnificent innocence that makes even his paralogisms superior to all sophistication, Kant utters this in the line about creatures unable to act otherwise than under the idea of freedom—creatures whose subjective consciousness is tied to that idea. Their freedom rests on their unfreedom, on their inability "to act otherwise," and at the same time it rests on an empirical consciousness whose *amour propre* might deceive it about its freedom as about innumerable other aspects of its psychological life. The being of freedom would be left to the accidents of spatial-temporal existence. Posited positively, as given or as unavoidable amidst given things, freedom turns directly into unfreedom.

But the paradoxical character of Kant's doctrine of freedom strictly corresponds to its location in reality. Social stress on freedom as existent coalesces with undiminished repression, and psychologically, with coercive traits. Kantian ethics, antagonistic in itself, has these traits in common with a criminological practice in which the dogmatic doctrine of free will is coupled with the urge to punish harshly, irrespective of empirical conditions. All the concepts whereby the *Critique of Practical Reason* proposes, in honor of freedom, to fill the chasm between the Imperative and mankind—law, constraint, respect, duty—all of these are repressive. A causality produced by freedom corrupts freedom into obedience.

Like the idealists after him, Kant cannot bear freedom without compulsion. Its mere undistorted conception fills him with that fear of anarchy which later urged the bourgeois world to liquidate its own freedom. We recognize this almost more in the tone than in the content of random phrasings in the *Critique of Practical Reason:* "A sense of the will's free submission to the law, a submission free and yet bound up with an unavoidable compulsion that is exerted, albeit by one's own reason only, upon all his inclinations—this is respect for law."[17] What became Kant's fearfully majestic a priori is what psychoanalysts trace back to psychological conditions. By causally explaining what it is that in idealism degrades freedom to a coercion not to be deduced, deterministic science really comes to the aid of freedom. That it does so is part of freedom's dialectics.

UNFREEDOM OF THOUGHT

Full-blown German idealism holds with a song from a famed romanticist anthology of the same period: "Thoughts are free." Since idealist doctrine takes all things there are for thoughts—thoughts of the Absolute—there is nothing that is not supposed to be free. But this notion would merely placate our sense of the fact that thoughts are anything but free. Before all social control, before all adjustment to conditions of dominion, the mere form of thoughts, the form of logical stringency, can be convicted of unfreedom. It can be shown that there is coercion both of what is being thought and of the thinker, who must extract the thought from himself by concentration. Whatever does not fit a judgment will be choked off; from the outset, thinking exerts that power which philosophy reflected in the concept of necessity. By way of identification, philosophy and society are interrelated in philosophy's inmost core. The presently universal regimentation of scientific thought externalizes this age-old relationship in modes of conduct and forms of organization.

And yet, without a coercive moment there could be no thinking. The antithesis of freedom and thought is no more removable by thinking than it is removable for thinking; it calls, rather, for self-reflection in thinking. Speculative philosophers from Leibniz to Schopenhauer were right to concentrate their efforts on causality. It is the crux of rationalism in that broader sense which includes Schopenhauer's metaphysics in so far as he was certain of his Kantian ground. The legality of the pure thought forms, the *causa cognoscendi,* is projected upon the objects as *causa efficiens.* Causality presupposes the formally logical principle—or better, perhaps, it presupposes noncontradictoriness, the principle of naked identity—as a rule for the material cognition of objects, even though the historical evolution may have taken the opposite course. Hence the equivocality of the word *ratio,* which means both reason and cause. Causality has to atone for this: according to Hume's insight, there is no immediate sense datum that might be cited for it. In this respect, causality is a dogmatic remnant in idealism, yet without it, idealism could not exercise the control it seeks over all there is. Freed from the compulsion of identity, thinking might perhaps dispense with causality, which is made in the image of that compulsion. Causality hypostatizes the form, as binding upon a content which on its own would not assume that form; a metacritical reflection would have to receive empiricism all over.

Opposed to this, Kant's entire philosophy stands in the sign of unity. This lends to it the character of a system, despite the heavy accentuation of "material" not derived from pure forms; Kant expected no less from a system than did his successors. The governing unity is the concept of reason itself, and eventually the logical reason of pure noncontradictoriness. Nothing is added to this in the Kantian doctrine of practice. The terminologically suggested difference between pure theoretical and pure practical doctrine; the difference between a formally logical and a transcendentally logical doctrine; finally the difference of the doctrine of ideas in the narrow sense—these are not differences within reason in itself. They are solely differences concerning its application, said either to have nothing to do with objects or to refer to the possibility of objects pure and simple, or—like practical reason—to create its objects, the free acts, out of itself.

Hegel's doctrine that logic and metaphysics are the same is inherent in Kant, though not yet thematical. To Kant, the objectivity of reason as such, the epitome of formal logical validity, becomes a haven for the ontology that has been fatally criticized in all material realms. This not only creates the unity of the three *Critiques;* it is as this very unifying moment that reason achieves the twofold character which later helped to motivate dialectics. Kant's reason is on the one hand the pure form of subjectivity, as distinct from thinking; on the other hand it is the totality of objective validities, the archetype of all objectivity. Its twofold character permits the turn taken by both Kantian philosophy and the German idealists: to teach what subjectivity has nominalistically sapped—the objectivity of truth and every content—and to teach it on the strength of the same subjectivity that has destroyed it. In reason, the two are said to be already one—in which case, of course, whatever anyone can mean by objectivity, anything opposed to the subject, will be submerged by abstraction in the subject, however unpalatable this may be to Kant.

But the structural bifurcation of the concepts of reason extends also to the concept of the will. In the name of spontaneity, of that which in the subject is not objectifiable at any price, the will is defined as nothing other than the subject—and yet, solid and identical like reason, it is objectified into a hypothetical but factual power amidst the factual-empirical world, and thus made commensurable with that world. Only the will's a priori ontical nature, which is extant like a quality, permits us, without being absurd, to make the judgment that the will creates its objects, the actions. It belongs to the world it works in. That we can say this of the will is the fee charged for the installation of pure reason as an indifferent concept. It has to be paid by the will, from which all impulses that refuse to be objectified are banned as heteronomous.

"FORMALISM"

An objection to Kant that may not weigh too heavily is immanent in his system: that the subdivision of reason by objects makes it depend, contrary to the doctrine of autonomy, on the extrarational it is supposed not to be. What comes to the fore in this discrepancy, despite Kant's intention, is the very thing he dispelled: reason's inner dependence upon what is not identical with it. Only, Kant does not go that far; the doctrine that reason is one and the same in all its alleged fields of application presupposes a firm dividing line between reason and its "what about." But since, in order to be any kind of reason, it necessarily refers to some such "what about," applicability becomes—against Kant's theory—determining for reason in itself as well.

There is a qualitative difference, for instance, between the role which the nature of objects plays in judgments about things to be done in practice and the role it plays in Kant's theoretical principles. In itself, reason is differentiated according to its objects; it must not be outwardly stamped on different objective realms as the same at all times, though with varying degrees of validity.

This also comes to extend to the doctrine of the will. The will is not χωρίς of its material, of society. If it were, the Categorical Imperative would be trespassing against itself; other people, being nothing but the material of the Imperative, would be used only as meant by the autonomous subject; they would not be ends also. This is the absurdity in the monadological construction of morals. Moral conduct is evidently more concrete than a merely theoretical one; yet it becomes more formal than theoretical conduct in consequence of the doctrine that practical reason is independent of anything "alien" to it, of any object.

True, the formalism of Kant's ethics is not merely damnable, as a reactionary German academic philosophy has been calling it from Scheler onward. Though failing to provide us with a positive casuistry for future action, this formalism humanely prevents the abuse of substantial-qualitative differences in favor of privilege and ideology. It stipulates the universal legal norm, and thus, despite and because of its abstractness, there survives in it something of substance: the egalitarian idea. The German critics who found Kantian formalism too rationalistic have shown their bloody colors in the fascist practice of making blind phenomena, men's membership or nonmembership in a designated race, the criteria of who was to be killed. The specious character of such concreteness—the complete abstraction of subsuming human beings under arbitrary concepts and treating them accordingly—does not erase the stain that has besmirched the word "concrete" ever since.

This does not void the criticism of abstract morality, however. With particular and universal still unreconciled, this morality suffices no more than does the allegedly material value ethics of norms that are eternal at short range. Picked as a principle, the appeal to either one does an injustice to the opposite. The depracticalization of Kant's practical reason—in other words, its rationalism—is coupled with its deobjectification; it must have been deobjectified before it can become that absolutely sovereign reason which is to have the capacity to work empirically irrespective of experience, and irrespective of the leap between action and deed. The doctrine of pure practical reason prepares for the re-translation of spontaneity into contemplation which occurred in the later history of the bourgeoisie and was consummated in political apathy, a highly political posture. The semblance of a noumenal objectivity of practical reason establishes its complete subjectification; it is no longer clear how its intervention across the ontological abyss may reach anything that is at all.

This is also the root of the irrational side of Kant's moral law, the root of what he called "given"—a term that denies all rational transparency and halts the advance of reflection. Since freedom, to Kant, amounts to reason's invariant identity with itself even in the practical realm, it loses what in common usage distinguishes reason from the will. Due to its total rationality, the will becomes irrational. The *Critique of Practical Reason* moves in a delusive context. It has the mind serve as a surrogate for action, which is to be nothing but the sheer mind. Thus freedom is sabotaged: its Kantian carrier, reason, coincides with the pure law. Freedom would need what Kant calls heteronomous. There would be no more freedom without some element of chance, according to the criterion of pure reason, than there would be without rational judgment. The absolute split between freedom and chance is as arbitrary as the absolute split between freedom and rationality. An undialectical standard of legality will always make some side of freedom seem contingent; freedom calls for reflection, which rises above the particular categories of law and chance.

THE WILL AS A THING

In the modern age, the concept of reason has been one of indifference. It was a compromise between subjective thinking reduced to its pure form—and thereby potentially objectified, detached from the ego—and the validity of logical forms divorced from their constitution (though this validity in turn would not be conceivable without subjective thought). Kant regards such objectivity as shared by human acts, the expressions of the will; and he accordingly calls them objects.* Their objectivity, copied

---

* "By a concept of practical reason I mean the conception of an object as a possible effect of freedom. Hence, to be an object of prac-

from the model of reason, ignores the *differentia specifica* of act and object.

The will, the cover concept of acts or their moment of unity, is analogously objectified. In what thus happens to it theoretically, however, there is some truth despite all flagrant contradictions. When we look at the individual impulses, the will is indeed independent, quasi-thinglike, insofar as the ego's principle of unity achieves some measure of independence vis-à-vis its phenomena in their quality of being "its." We can as well talk of a will that is independent and, to that extent, objective as we can talk of a strong ego or, in the language of olden days, of character. Even outside of Kant's construction, the will is that intermedium between nature and the *mundus intelligibilis* which Benjamin contrasts with fate.[18]

The individual impulses' objectification in the will that synthesizes and determines them is their sublimation, their successful, delaying, permanence-involving diversion from the primary goal of drives. Kant faithfully circumscribed this by the rationality of the will. It is this rationality that makes the will something other than its "material," the diffuse impulses. To stress a man's will means to stress the unifying moment of his actions, and that is the subordination of those actions to his reason. A common adjective for a libertine is "dissolute," dissolved; the language opts for morality as the unity of the person in accordance with the abstract rational law.

According to Kantian ethics, the subject's totality predominates over the moments it lives by—the moments which alone give life to the totality, although outside such a totality they would not make up a will. The discovery was progressive: it kept the judgment about particular impulses from being made casuistically any longer; it also put an inward end to the righteousness about works.

---

tical cognition as such means simply the will's relation to the act that would realize either the will or its opposite; and the judgment whether something is or is not an object of pure practical reason is merely the distinction of the possibility or impossibility of willing the specific act whereby, if we had the capacity (which must be judged by experience), a certain object would come to be." (Kant, *Kritik der praktischen Vernunft.* Works V, p. 57.)

This was an assist to freedom. The subject becomes moral for itself; it cannot be weighed by standards that are inwardly and outwardly particular and alien to the subject. Once the rational unity of the will is established as the sole moral authority, the subject is protected from the violence done to it by a hierarchical society—a society which (as still in Dante's case) would judge a man's deeds without any previous acceptance of its law by his own consciousness. Individual actions become venial. No isolated act is absolutely good or evil; their criterion is "good will," their unifying principle. An internalization of society as a whole replaces the reflexes of a feudal order whose structure splinters what is universal in mankind—the more so, the more solid it pretends to be. Kant's relegation of ethics to the sober unity of reason was an act of bourgeois majesty despite the false consciousness in his objectification of the will.

OBJECTIVITY IN THE ANTINOMY

According to Kant, both the assertion of freedom and that of unfreedom terminate in contradictions. Hence the controversy is called fruitless. Hypostatizing scientific-methodical criteria, Kant propounds it as self-evident that theorems which cannot be safeguarded from the possibility of their contradictory antithesis should be discarded in rational thinking.

After Hegel, this has been no longer tenable. The contradiction may lie in the thing itself; it may not, from the start, be attributable to procedure. The urgency of the concern with freedom suggests such objective contradictoriness. Kant, in demonstrating the necessity of the antinomies, disdained using the "pseudoproblem" as an excuse but was quick to bow to the logic of noncontradictoriness.*

---

* "For that which must needs impel us to go beyond the bounds of experience and of all phenomena is unconditionality, which reason necessarily and rightly requires of things-in-themselves, along with all that is conditioned, and thus completing the sequence of conditions. If it now turns out (assuming that our empirical cognition goes by

239

The Kantian transcendental dialectics is not wholly unaware of this. It is presented, of course, as a dialectics of sophistries after the Aristotelian model; but each thesis as well as each antithesis is noncontradictorily developed in itself. The antitheticality is not comfortably dismissed by any means; the point is, rather, to demonstrate its inevitability. It is said to be "soluble" only at a higher stage of reflection, as the hypostasis of logical reason toward things of whose being-in-itself it is ignorant, and on which it is therefore not entitled to pass positive judgments. That the contradiction is inescapable for human reason indicates that it is beyond that reason and its "logic." Substantially, this permits it to be possible for the carrier of reason, the subject, to be both free and unfree. Kant uses the means of undialectical logic to settle the contradiction by distinguishing between the pure subject and the empirical subject—a distinction in which the interrelation of the two concepts is disregarded.

The subject is to be unfree in so far as it is its own object and thus subjected to a lawful synthesis by the categories. To be able to act in the empirical world, the subject can indeed not be conceived otherwise than as a "phenomenon," and Kant certainly would not always deny this. The work on practical reason concurs with the work on the pure one in teaching that speculative criticism grants "to the objects of experience as such, and to our own subject among them, only the validity of phenomena."[19] Synthesis, the mediating process, cannot be subtracted from anything we positively judge. As the unifying moment of the thought it covers its every content and determines its neces-

---

the objects as things-in-themselves) that without contradiction the unconditional cannot be thought at all; and if on the other hand (assuming that our conception of things as they are given to us does not go by these things as they are in themselves, but that these objects as phenomena go by our mode of conception, rather) it turns out that the contradiction disappears, and that unconditionality will accordingly not be encountered in things when we know them, when they are given to us, but if we do not know them it will indeed be encountered in them as things-in-themselves—if this is the outcome, it shows our merely tentative initial assumption to be well founded." (Kant, *Kritik der reinen Vernunft*, Works III, p. 13f.)

sity. Even the talk of a strong ego as a firm identity, as the condition of freedom, would share that fate. It would have no power over the *chorismos*. In a Kantian sense the objectification of character could be localized only in the realm of the *constitutum*, not in that of the *constituens*. Otherwise, Kant would be committing the same paralogism of which he convicts the rationalists.

The subject is to be free, however, as it posits—"constitutes," in Kant's language—its own identity, the basis of its legality. That the *constituens* is to be the transcendental subject and the *constitutum* the empirical one does not remove the contradiction, for there is no transcendental subject other than one individualized as a unit of consciousness—in other words, as a moment of the empirical subject. The transcendental subject needs the irreducible nonidentity which simultaneously delimits the legality. Without that nonidentical element there would be neither identity nor an immanent law of subjectivity. Only for nonidentity is this a law; otherwise it is a tautology. The identifying principle of the subject is itself the internalized principle of society. This is why in the real subjects, in social beings, unfreedom ranks above freedom to this day. Within a reality modeled after the principle of identity there exists no positive freedom. Where men under the universal spell seem inwardly relieved of the identity principle, and thus of the comprehensible determinants, they are not more than determined, for the time being; they are less than determined. As schizophrenia, subjective freedom is a destructive force which incorporates men only so much more in the spell of nature.

DIALECTICAL DEFINITION OF THE WILL

A will without physical impulses, impulses that survive, weakened, in imagination, would not be a will. At the same time, however, the will settles down as the centralizing unit of impulses, as the authority that tames them and potentially negates them. This necessitates a dialectical definition of the will. It is the force that enables consciousness to leave its own domain and so to change what merely exists; its recoil is resistance.

Unquestionably, memories of this have always accompanied the transcendental rational ethics, as in the Kantian avowal of a given moral law independent of philosophical consciousness, for example. Kant's thesis is heteronomous and authoritarian, but it has an element of truth in its restriction of the purely rational character of the moral law. Strictly speaking, the one reason could be none but the unimpaired philosophical reason. The motif culminates in Fichte's formula that "the moral aspect is always self-understood."

As the bad conscience of its rationality, however, the will's irrationality becomes crumpled and false. Once it is held to be self-understood, excused from rational reflection, the self-understood character offers a refuge to the unelucidated remnant and to repression. To be self-understood is the mark of civilization: good, we say, is what is one, what is immutable, what is identical. What does not comply, any heritage of the pre-logical natural moment, will immediately turn into evil, into something as abstract as the principle of its opposite. Bourgeois evil is the post-existence of older things, of things that have been subdued but not wholly subdued.

Yet this evil is not absolutely evil, no more so than its violent counterpart. Each time, the judgment can only be made by a consciousness that will reflect the various moments in so far, and as consistently, as it has access to them. For the right practice, and for the good itself, there really is no other authority than the most advanced state of theory. When an idea of goodness is supposed to guide the will without fully absorbing the concrete rational definitions, it will unwittingly take orders from the reified consciousness, from that which society has approved. A will detached from reason and proclaimed as an end in itself, like the will whose triumph the Nazis certified in the official title of their party congresses—such a will, like all ideals that rebel against reason, stands ready for every misdeed. Good will may be self-understood, but in the mirage it grows obdurate, a historic sediment of the power which the will ought to resist. In contrast to its pharisaism, the irrational moment of the will condemns all moral aspects to fallibility as a matter of principle.

There is no moral certainty. Its mere assumption would be

immoral, would falsely relieve the individual of anything that might be called morality. The more mercilessly an objective-antagonistic society will comport itself in every situation, the less can any single moral decision be warranted as the right one. Whatever an individual or a group may undertake against the totality they are part of is infected by the evil of that totality; and no less infected is he who does nothing at all. This is how original sin has been secularized. The individual who dreams of moral certainty is bound to fail, bound to incur guilt because, being harnessed to the social order, he has virtually no power over the conditions whose cry for change appeals to the moral *ingenium*. It is for such decay—not of morality, but of the "moral aspect"—that the clever neo-German language after World War II hatched the name "overdemanding," an apologetical instrument of its own.

All conceivable definitions of the moral aspect down to the most formal, the unity of self-consciousness *qua* reason, were squeezed out of that "matter" with which moral philosophy did not want to dirty its hands. Today, morality has been restored to the heteronomy it loathes, and its tendency is to void itself. Without recourse to the material, no ought could issue from reason; yet once compelled to acknowledge its material in the abstract, as a condition of its own possibility, reason must not cut off its reflection on the specific material. Precisely this would make it heteronomous. Looking back, we see the positivity of the moral aspect, the infallibility which the subjective idealists attested to that aspect, unveiled as a function of a society still more or less closed, or at least of the appearance of such a society for a consciousness confined in it. This is what Benjamin may have meant by the conditions and limits of humanity. The primacy called for in the doctrines of Kant and Fichte, that of practical reason over theory—actually, of reason over reason—applies only to traditionalist phases whose horizon does not even admit the doubts which the idealists dreamed of resolving.

CONTEMPLATION

Marx received the thesis of the primacy of practical reason from Kant and the German idealists, and he sharpened it into a challenge to change the world instead of merely interpreting it. He thus underwrote something as arch-bourgeois as the program of an absolute control of nature. What is felt here is the effort to take things unlike the subject and make them like the subject—the real model of the principle of identity, which dialectical materialism disavows as such.

Yet as he extroverts the concept's immanent reality, Marx prepares for a recoil. The *telos* of due practice, according to him, was the abolition of the primacy of practice in the form that had prevailed in bourgeois society. It would be possible to have contemplation without inhumanity as soon as the productive forces are freed to the point where men will no longer be engulfed in a practice that want exacts from them, in a practice which then becomes automatic in them. To this day, the trouble with contemplation—with the contemplation that contents itself this side of practice, as Aristotle was the first to develop it as *summum bonum*—has been that its very indifference to the task of changing the world made it a piece of obtuse practice, a method and an instrumentality.

The possible reduction of labor to a minimum could not but have a radical effect on the concept of practice. Whatever insights were bestowed upon a practically freed mankind would differ from a practice that exalts itself ideologically and in one way or another keeps the subjects hustling. A reflection of that prospect falls on contemplation today. The current objection, extrapolated from the "Feuerbach Theses," that a happy spirit is impermissible amidst the growing misery of the exploding populations of poor countries, after the catastrophes that have occurred and in view of those that are impending—this objection has more against it than that it mostly makes a virtue of impotence. True, we cannot really enjoy the spirit any more, because a happiness bound to see through its own nonentity, through the borrowed time it has been granted, would be no happiness. Subjectively, too, it is undermined even where it keeps stirring. There is much to indicate that a knowledge crippled temporarily, at least, in its possible relation to practical change is not a blessing in itself either. Practice is put off and cannot wait; this is what ails even theory. But when a man can do nothing that will not threaten to turn out for the worst even if meant for the best, he will be bound to start thinking—and that justifies him as well as the happy spirit.

The horizon of such happiness need by no means be that of a transparent relation to a possible practice to come. There is always something inappropriate to dilatory thinking about practice, even when the postponements are due to naked coercion. Yet he who allows his thinking to be guided by the phrase *cui bono* may easily spoil everything. What will one day be imposed and bestowed upon a better practice can here and now—according to the warning of utopianism—be no more visualized by thought than practice, under its own concept, will ever be completely exhausted by knowledge. Without a practical visa, thought should go as much against the façade as possible, should move as far as it is capable of moving. A reality that insulates itself against traditional theory, even against that which has so far been the best, wants to do so for the sake of the spell that binds it; the eyes it casts upon the subject are so strange that the subject, mindful of its own failure, must not spare the effort of a reply.

Paradoxically, it is the desperate fact that the practice that would matter is barred which grants to thought a breathing spell it would be practically criminal not to utilize. Today, ironically, it profits thought that its concept must not be absolutized: as conduct, it remains a bit of practice, however hidden this practice may be from itself. Yet he who contrasts the literal, sensual happiness as something better with the impermissible one of the spirit, he misunderstands that once historic sublimation has an end, the detached sensual happiness will have a similarly regressive touch as the relationship of children to food, which disgusts the adult. Not to be like children in this sense is a bit of freedom.

STRUCTURE OF THE THIRD ANTINOMY

According to the results of transcendental analytics, the Third Antinomy would be cut off at the start: "Who told you to think up a downright first state of the world and thus an absolute beginning of the gradual sequence of phenomena, and to set limits upon boundless nature, so that your imagination might have a point to rest?"[20] However, Kant did not content himself with the summary diagnosis of the Antinomy as an avoidable mistake in the use of reason. Like the others, he carried it through. His transcendental idealism contains an anti-idealist prohibition against positing absolute identity. Epistemology is told not to act as though the immense, "infinite" content of experience might be obtained from positive definitions of reason in itself. He who violates this ban is said to be lapsing into the contradiction which common sense cannot bear.

This is a plausible proposition, but Kant keeps boring further. If reason acts the way for which he censures it, its own meaning and its unrestrainable cognitive ideal make it continue on the prohibited course as though yielding to a natural and irresistible temptation. Something whispers into reason's ear that the totality of things in being converges with it after all. For necessity, on the other hand, which in a manner of speaking is alien to all systems, the infinite process of reason's quest for conditions provides an authenticity, an idea of the absolute, without which truth—as opposed to cognition in the sense of a mere *adaequatio rei atque cogitationis*—would be unthinkable. That the process, and thus the antinomy, cannot be divorced from the same reason which in transcendental analytics, as critical reason, must suppress excesses of that kind—this unintentional bit of self-criticism demonstrates that as the organ of emphatic truth the critical approach contradicts its own reason. Kant presses for the necessity of the contradiction, and at the same time, to the higher glory of reason, he stops up the hole by juggling away the necessity said to derive from the nature of reason, by explaining it as due solely to a mistake in the use of the concepts, a mistake that we might correct.

To explain freedom, the thesis of the Third Antinomy not only talks about "causality through freedom"; it also refers to it as "necessary."[21] Accordingly, however unequivocally manifested its intent, Kant's own practical doctrine of freedom cannot be simply causal or anti-causal. He modifies or expands the concept of causality as long as he does not explicitly distinguish it from the one used in the antithesis. Contradictions pervade his theorem even before all the paradoxicality of the infinite. As a theory of valid scientific cognition, the *Critique of Pure Reason* has no way to treat its topics other than under the concept of law—not even those topics which are supposed to lie beyond legality.

KANT'S CONCEPT OF CAUSALITY

The famous, utterly formal Kantian definition of causality is that whatever happens presupposes a previous condition "upon which it inevitably follows in line with a rule."[22] Historically it was directed against the Leibniz school and its interpretation of the sequence of conditions as due to inner necessity, a being-in-itself. On the other hand, Kant's view differs from Hume's, holding that unanimous experience is not possible without the regularity of thought which Hume turned over to the accident of convention, and pointing out that in any particular spot Hume must talk causally in order to make plausible what as a convention he would make indifferent.

To Kant, however, causality becomes a function of subjective reason, and what it means is therefore more and more attenuated. It dissolves like a bit of mythology. Causality approximates the principle of reason as such, of thinking in line with rules. Judgments about causal connections turn into semi-tautologies: reason employs them to determine what it effects anyway, as the faculty of laws. That it prescribes nature's laws—or law, rather —denotes no more than a subsumption under rational unity. This unity, the principle of reason's own identity, is transformed from reason to the objects and palmed off, then, as their cognition. Once causality is as thoroughly disenchanted as it would be by tabooing the inner determination of objects, it will disintegrate in itself as well.

The only feature of Kant's rescue operation that lifts it above Hume's denial is that what Hume swept away is to Kant innate in reason—its necessary nature, so to speak, if not an anthropological accident. Causality is to arise, not in the objects and their relationship, but solely in inescapable subjective thought. Kant, too, is dogmatic about the thesis that a state of things might have something essential, something specific to do with the succeeding state of things; but it would be quite possible, in line with his conception, to devise legalities for successions without anything to remind us of a causal connection. The interrelation of objects that have passed through inwardness virtually turns here into something outward for the theorem of causality. The simplest meaning of the phrase that "something is the cause of something else" is ignored. A causality rigorously insulated against the interior of objects is no more than its own shell. The *reductio ad hominem* in the concept of law is a mere borderline value where the law has ceased to say anything about the objects; the expansion of causality into a concept of pure reason negates causality.

Kant's causality is one without a *causa*. As he cures it of naturalistic prejudice it dissolves in his hands. That consciousness cannot escape from causality, as its inborn form, is certainly an answer to the weak point in Hume's argument; but when Kant maintains that the subject *must* think causally, his analysis of the constituents, according to the literal sense of "must," is following the very causal proposition to which he would be entitled to subject only the *constituta*. If the constitution of causality by pure reason—which, after all, is supposed to be freedom—is already subject to causality, freedom is so compromised beforehand that hardly any place for it remains outside a consciousness complaisant toward the law.

In this entire antithetical construction, freedom and causality intersect. Kant's freedom, being the same as rational action, is also according to law, and free acts also "follow from rules." What has come out of this is the intolerable mortgage imposed on post-Kantian philosophy: that freedom without law is not freedom, that freedom exists only in identification with the law. Via the German idealists, this heritage has been passed on, with incalculably vast political consequences, to Friedrich Engels*; it is the theoretical source of the false reconcilement.

THE PLEA FOR ORDER

The end of the coercive epistemological character of causality would also end the claim to totality that will be made for causality as long as it coincides with the subjective principle. The very thing which in idealism can appear as freedom only in paradoxical form would then, substantially, become the moment that transcends the bracketing of the world's course with fate. If in causality we were looking for a definition of things themselves— no matter how subjectively conveyed—such specification would open the perspective of freedom as opposed to the undiscriminated One of pure subjectivity. It would apply to that which is distinguished from compulsion. Compulsion, then, would no longer be

---

* "Hegel was the first to present a correct picture of the relationship of freedom and necessity. To him, freedom is the insight into necessity. 'Necessity is blind only if it is not understood.' Freedom does not lie in dreams about independence of the laws of nature; it lies in the knowledge of these laws, and in the ability conferred by that knowledge, to make the laws work according to plan and to definite ends. This applies in regard to the laws of external nature as well as to those which regulate the physical and mental existence of man himself—two sets of laws which we can separate, at best, in imagination, but not in reality. Free will, therefore, means nothing other than the faculty of being able to decide with material knowledge. The freer a man's judgment in regard to a specific point in question, the greater, therefore, the necessity with which the content of his judgment will be determined; while the uncertainty based on ignorance, which seems to make an arbitrary choice among many different and contradictory possibilities of decision, demonstrates precisely thereby its unfreedom, its being dominated by the very object it ought to dominate. Freedom thus consists in our control, based upon our knowledge of the natural necessities, of ourselves and of external nature; it is thus necessarily a product of historic evolution." (Karl Marx/Friedrich Engels, *Werke*, Berlin 1962, vol. 20, p. 106.)

extolled as an act of the subject; its totality would no longer evoke an affirmative response. It would be stripped of its a priori power that was extrapolated from real compulsion. The chance of freedom increases along with the objectiveness of causality; this is not the least of the reasons why he who wants freedom must insist upon necessity.

Kant, however, calls for freedom and prevents it. The argument for the thesis of the Third Antinomy, the thesis of the absolutely spontaneous cause—a secularization of the free divine act of creation—is Cartesian in style: it applies so that the method will be satisfied. Complete cognition is set up as the epistemological criterion; we are told that without freedom "the sequence of phenomena even in the natural course is never complete on the side of the causes."[23] The totality of cognition, which is here tacitly equated with truth, would be the identity of subject and object. Kant restricts it as a critic of cognition and teaches it as a theoretician of truth. A cognition that has at its disposal as complete a sequence as Kant holds to be conceivable only under the hypostasis of an original act of absolute freedom —in other words, a cognition that no longer leaves any sensorily given thing outside—would be a cognition not confronted with anything unlike itself.

The critique of such identity would strike not merely at the positive-ontological apotheosis of the subjective causal concept, but at the Kantian proof of the necessity of freedom, a proof about whose pure form there is something contradictory anyway. That there must be freedom is the supreme *iniuria* committed by the lawmaking autonomous subject. The substance of its own freedom—of the identity which has annexed all nonidentity—is as one with the "must," with the law, with absolute dominion. This is the spark that kindles the pathos of Kant. He construes even freedom as a special case of causality. To him, it is the "constant laws" that matter. His timid bourgeois detestation of anarchy matches his proud bourgeois antipathy against tutelage. Here, too, society intrudes all the way into his most formal reflections. Formality in itself is a bourgeois trait: on the one hand, it frees the individual from the confining definitions of what has come to be just so, not otherwise, while on the other hand it has nothing to set against things as they are, nothing to base itself upon except dominion, which has been raised to the rank of a pure principle.

Hidden in the root of Kant's *Metaphysic of Morals* lies Comte's later sociological dichotomy between laws of progress and laws of order, along with the bias favoring the latter type. Order, on the strength of its legality, is to hold progress in check. We hear such overtones in a Kantian line from the proof of the antithesis: "Freedom (independence) from the laws of nature is indeed a deliverance from compulsion, but also from the guideline of all rules."[24] This guideline is to be "torn" by an "unconditional causality"—which is to say: by the free productive act; where this act is scientifically criticized in the antithesis, it has the epithet "blind"[25] bestowed on it by Kant, as the stubborn fact has elsewhere. The haste with which Kant thinks of freedom as the law above shows that he is no more scrupulous about it than his class has ever been. Long before it dreaded the industrial proletariat—in the economics of Adam Smith, for example—that class used to combine praise of individual emancipation with the apologia for an order in which, one heard, the "invisible hand" was taking care of both the beggar and the king, while even the free competitor in this order had to observe the—feudal—rules of "fair play."

Kant's popularizer* was not misrepresenting his philosophical mentor when he called order "heaven's bounteous daughter," nor when he emphasized in the same poem that "welfare can't thrive when peoples free themselves." Neither man would hear of it that the "chaos" which their generation saw in the relatively modest horrors of the French Revolution (the atrocities of the Chouans shocked them far less) was produced by a repression whose traits live on in those who rise against it. All the other German geniuses who had been constrained at first to hail that revolution could not vilify it fast enough, once Robespierre gave them a pretext; and the same sense of relief is perceptible in Kant's proof of the antithesis, when "legality" is praised at the expense of

---

* A reference to Friedrich Schiller. Quotes are from Schiller's poem *Die Glocke* (The Bell). —TRANS.

"lawlessness" and we actually hear the word "mirage of freedom."[26] Laws receive the encomiastic epithet "constant," which is to raise them above the dread specter of anarchy without allowing the suspicion to dawn that they precisely are the old evil of unfreedom. How much Kant is dominated by the concept of law shows in the fact that he cites it, as their supposedly higher unity, in arguing for the thesis as well as in arguing for the antithesis.

THE ANTITHETICAL ARGUMENT

The argument throughout the section on the antithetics of pure reason proceeds, as we know, *e contrario:* each thesis saddles the antithesis with the guilt of that transcendent use of causality which violates the doctrine of categories from the start. The causal category in the antithesis is said to transcend the bounds of possible experience; what is substantially ignored here is the fact that any consistent scientivism will guard against such metaphysical use of that category. To avoid the agnostic consequence of scientivism —with which the doctrine of theoretical reason sympathizes unmistakably—Kant sets up an antithesis that does not tally at all with the scientivistic position: freedom is won by knocking down a straw man made to measure. All that we have proved is that we must not look upon causality as positively given ad infinitum— a tautology, according to the tenor of the *Critique of Pure Reason,* to which the positivists would be the last to object. But by no means, not even in the argumentative context of the thesis, does it follow that the causal chain tears with the supposition of a freedom that is assumed as positively as the chain.

This paralogism is of incalculable import, because it permits the *non liquet* to be positively reinterpreted. Positive freedom is an aporetical concept, thought up to conserve a spiritual being-in-itself in the face of nominalism and scientification. At a central point of the *Critique of Practical Reason* Kant admitted what that book is all about: the saving of a residue. "Yet as this law inevitably covers all of the causality of things in so far as their existence is definable in time, we would (if this were also the way to conceive the existence of these things in themselves) have to reject the concept of freedom as void and impossible. Hence, if we would still save it, the only way left is for a thing's temporally definable existence—and consequently also for causality under the laws of natural necessity—to be assigned to the realm of mere appearance, while freedom has attributed to it the same character possessed by things-in-themselves."[27]

The construction of freedom admits to being inspired by what Goethe in *Elective Affinities* would later call the "saving urge," while in the first sentence, relegated to a quality of the intra-temporal subject, it was revealed as "void and impossible." It is the aporetical character of the construction, not the abstract possibility of the antithesis in the infinite, that speaks against the positive doctrine of freedom. The critique of reason apodictically bars all talk of a subject beyond space and time as an object of cognition. Initially this argument is still advanced in the philosophy of morals: "Even of himself, by the self-knowledge he has through inner sensation, man must not presume to know how he is in himself."[28] The Foreword to the *Critique of Practical Reason* repeats this, citing the *Critique of Pure Reason.*[29] Thereafter, Kant's stipulation that "objects of experience" must "nonetheless be based upon things-in-themselves"[30] sounds crassly dogmatic. Aporetical, however, is by no means only the question of the possibility of knowing what the subject is in and for itself; the subject's every thinkable definition, its every "noumenal" definition in the Kantian sense, is also aporetically questionable.

To share in freedom, according to Kant's doctrine, the noumenal subject would have to be extratemporal, "a pure intelligence in its temporally not definable existence."[31] The saving urge makes an existence of this noumenon—since nothing could be predicated of it otherwise—and yet it is to be undefinable in time. But if existence is given in any way, if it has not faded into a pure idea, its own concept will make it intratemporal. In the *Critique of Pure Reason,* in the "Deduction of Pure Intellectual Concepts" as well as in the chapter on schematism,* the subject's unity becomes a

---

* "This makes clear that what the schematism of the intellect amounts to, through the transcendental synthesis of imagination, is

pure form of time. It integrates the facts of consciousness, as those of the same person. There is no synthesis without an intratemporal interrelation of the synthesized moments; this interrelation would be a premise even of the most formal logical operations and of their validity. Accordingly, however, timelessness would not be attributable to an absolute subject either, so long as the name "subject" is to cover any thought whatever. If anything, it might be an absolute time, rather, that could be attributed to it.

It is unfathomable how freedom—which in principle is an attribute of temporal action and exclusively temporally actualized —should be predicated of something radically nontemporal; nor is it fathomable how such a nontemporal thing might take effect in the spatial-temporal world without turning temporal itself and straying into the Kantian realm of causality. What steps in as a *deus ex machina* is the concept of the "thing-in-itself." Arcane and indefinite, it marks a blind spot of the thought; its indefiniteness alone allows it to be used as an explanation, as needed. The only quality Kant would concede to the thing-in-itself is that it "affects" the subject. Yet in this activity it would be unceremoniously opposed to the subject; only an unredeemable speculation— nowhere performed by Kant either—might throw it together with the moral subject as another "being-in-itself."

Kant's cognitive critique does not permit him to summon freedom into existence; he helps himself by conjuring a sphere of existence that would indeed be exempt from that critique, but also from any judgment as to what it might be. His attempt to give a

---

nothing but the unity of all that is diverse in visuality in the inner sense—and thus, indirectly, the unity of apperception as a function corresponding to that inner sense of visuality (to a receptivity). Therefore, the schemata of pure intellectual concepts are the true and only conditions for giving to these concepts a relation to objects, and thus a meaning; and the categories have accordingly no other ultimate use than a possible empirical one, serving merely (by reasons of an a priori necessary unity, due to the necessary union of all consciousness in an original apperception) to subject phenomena to general rules of synthesis, and thus to fit them for consistent entwinement in an experience." (Kant, *Kritik der reinen Vernunft,* Works III, p. 138.)

concrete form to the doctrine of freedom, to ascribe freedom to living subjects, traps him in paradoxical assertions: "We may concede, then, that if we were capable of so profound an insight into a man's way of thinking, as shown in both inner and outer actions, that every last mainspring behind those actions were known to us, along with their every external cause—we may concede that in this case a man's future conduct would be calculable with the same certainty as a lunar or solar eclipse, and yet, at the same time, we may assert that man is free."[32]

That even in the *Critique of Practical Reason* Kant cannot do without such terms as "mainspring" is a matter of substantial relevance. In the attempt to give freedom the kind of intelligibility that is indispensable to a doctrine of freedom, the medium of his metaphors leads him inescapable to conceptions from the empirical world. "Spring" is a causal-mechanical concept. Yet even if the first clause were valid, the second would be nonsense. It would serve a single purpose: once man is empirically involved in total causality, to bring about his additional metaphysical involvement in a mythical context of fate, by saddling him in freedom's name with a guilt that would be no guilt if there were total determination. By culpability, determination would be reinforced all the way into the core of human subjectivity. With such a construction of freedom there is nothing left to do but to give up its supposed base in reason, and authoritatively to cow the man who strives in vain to conceive it. Reason itself is to Kant nothing but the lawmaking power. This is why, from the outset, he must present freedom as a "special sort of causality."[33] In positing it he takes it back.

ONTICAL AND IDEAL MOMENTS

In fact, what the aporetical construction of freedom rests upon is not the noumenal but the phenomenal. There, we can observe the moral law as given in the sense which seems to Kant, in spite of everything, like a warrant of freedom's existence. As the very word suggests, however, to be given is the opposite of freedom: it is naked compulsion, exerted in space and time. The Kantian freedom means the same as pure practical reason, the producer of its own objects; this, we are told, has to do "not with objects or their cognition, but with its own faculty to make those objects real (in line with their cognition)."[34] The absolute volitional autonomy implied therein would be the same as absolute rule of one's inner nature.

"To be consistent," Kant extols, "is a philosopher's greatest obligation, and yet most rarely encountered."[35] This not only turns the formal logic of pure consistency into the ultimate moral authority; it also subordinates each impulse to logical unity. This unity is given primacy over the diffuseness of nature, indeed over all the diversity of the nonidentical—for in the closed circle of logic that diversity will always seem inconsistent. Despite the resolution of the Third Antinomy, Kant's moral philosophy remains antinomical: his total conception will not let him visualize the concept of freedom otherwise than as repression.

Kant's every concretion of morality bears repressive features. Its abstractness is a matter of substance, eliminating from the subject whatever does not conform with its pure concept. Hence the Kantian rigorism. The hedonistic principle is argued against, not because it is evil in itself, but because it is heteronomous to the pure ego: "Insofar as the pleasure of the idea of a thing's existence is to be a determining cause of desire for the thing, it rests upon the subject's receptivity because it depends on the existence of an object; it thus belongs to the senses (feelings) and not to the intellect—which employs concepts to express how the idea relates to an object, but does not employ feelings to express how it relates to the subject."[36]

As he honors freedom, however, seeking to cleanse it of all impairments, Kant simultaneously condemns the person to unfreedom in principle. A person cannot experience this utterly tightened freedom otherwise than as a restriction of its own impulses. If in some passages (as in the magnificent Note Two to the Second Theorem from the "Principles of Practical Reason") Kant inclined to happiness after all, it was a case of humanity breaking through the norm of consistency. It may have dawned on him that without such exorability the moral law would be impossible to live by—that the pure rational principle of personality must converge with the principle of personal self-preservation, with the totality of a man's "interests," which include his happiness. On happiness, Kant takes as ambivalent a position as the bourgeois spirit as a whole, which would guarantee the pursuit of happiness to the individual and would have it forbidden by the ethics of labor.

Such sociological reflections are not introduced into Kant's apriorism classificatorily, from the outside. The constant recurrence of terms with a social content in the *Foundation* and in the *Critique of Practical Reason* may be incompatible with the aprioristic intent, but without this kind of metabasis the question of the moral law's compatibility with empirical man would reduce Kant to silence. It would be a surrender to heteronomy to admit that autonomy is beyond realization. By stripping those socially substantive terms of their plain meaning, by sublimating them into ideas for the sake of a systematic accord, one would not only be ignoring the text. It is the true source of moral categories which those terms herald with a force too great to be controlled by Kant's intention.

In the famous variant of the Categorical Imperative from the *Foundation*—"Act so that humanity, in your person as in every other person, will always be used also as an end, never just as a means"[37]—"humanity," the human potential in men, may well be meant only as a regulative idea; humanity as the principle of being human, not as "the sum of all men," is still unrealized. Even so, we cannot shake off the factual, substantive increment in the word: that every individual should be respected as a representative of the socialized human species, that he is not a mere function of the barter process. The difference of means and ends which Kant decisively stressed is a social difference; it is the difference between the subjects as merchandise, as labor power that can be managed so as to produce value, and the human beings who even in the form of such merchandise remain the subjects for whose sake the whole machinery is set in motion—the machinery in which they are forgotten and only incidentally satisfied. Without this perspective, the variant of the Imperative would be lost in a void.

As Horkheimer noted, however, Kant's "never just" is one of those majestically sober turns of speech designed not to spoil

Utopia's chance at realization. Empiricism, even in its reprobate form of exploitation, is accepted as a condition of better things —to the extent which Kant later unfolds in the philosophy of history, under the concept of antagonism. There we read: "The means which nature employs to develop all of its predispositions is their antagonism in society, provided this antagonism will eventually become the cause of a social order under law. By antagonism I mean the unsociable sociability of men, i.e., their tendency to enter into association and yet to put up a consistent resistance that keeps threatening to split this association. The predisposition for this evidently lies in human nature. Man tends to become socialized because he feels more human in that condition, i.e., he feels his natural predispositions unfold. But he also tends very much to become individualized (isolated) because, at the same time, he finds in himself the unsociable trait of wanting all things run according to his mind only, and because he therefore expects resistance everywhere, just as he knows himself inclined to resist others. This resistance is what awakens all the powers of man, what makes him overcome his innate laziness and —whether in quest of prestige, of power, or of possessions—to achieve for himself a rank among his fellows, whom he does not like too well but cannot do without, either."[38]

In spite of the most ethical mentality, the "principle of humanity as an end in itself"[39] is not something purely internal. It is a promissory note on the realization of a concept of man, and the only place of such a concept, such a social—albeit internalized —principle, is in every individual. Kant must have noticed the double meaning of the word "humanity," as the idea of being human and as the totality of all men; he introduced it into theory in a manner that was dialectically profound, even though playful. His subsequent usage vacillates between ontical manners of speech and others which refer to the idea. "Rational beings"[40] certainly means the living human subjects, but Kant's "universal realm of ends in themselves,"[41] which is to be identical with the rational beings, as certainly transcends them. He wants neither to cede the idea of humanity to the existing society nor to vaporize it into a phantasm. The tension keeps growing until the rupture occurs in Kant's ambivalence about happiness: on the one hand he defends it in the concept of "being worthy of happiness"; on the other hand he disparages it as heteronomous, as when he finds even "universal happiness"[42] an unfit law for the will.

Despite the categorical character of the Imperative Kant would not think of spotlessly ontologizing it, as witness the passage "that . . . the concept of good and evil must not be determined ahead of the moral law (which, it might seem, ought even to be based upon it), but only (as happens here) after that law and through it."[43] Good and evil are not beings-in-themselves as elements of a spiritual-moral hierarchy; they are posited by reason. This is how deeply nominalism continues to penetrate the Kantian rigorism. But as the moral categories are attached to self-preserving reason they cease being utterly incompatible with that happiness to which Kant so harshly opposed them. The modifications of his stand on happiness in the progress of the *Critique of Practical Reason* are not negligent concessions to the traditional ethics of property; instead, preceding Hegel, they are models of a motion in the concept. Intentionally or not, moral universality passes into society.

Documentary evidence of this is Note One to the fourth theorem in the work on practical reason. "Hence the mere form of a law that restricts the matter must be at the same time a reason to add this matter to the will—but it must not presuppose it. The matter, for example, may be my own happiness. If I attribute this to everyone (as indeed I may, in the case of finite creatures), it can become an objective practical law only when I include in it the happiness of others. The law to promote other people's happiness does thus not spring from the premise that this is an object for everyone's license; its source is simply that the form of universality —which reason needs as a condition for investing a maxim of self-love with the objective validity of a law—comes to be the determining cause of the will. This determining cause of the pure will was not the object (other people's happiness); it was solely the sheer legal form I used to restrict my inclination-based maxim, in order to give it the universality of a law and thus to fit it for pure practical reason. It was from this restriction alone, not from the addition of an external mainspring, that the concept of a duty —to extend the maxim of my self-love to the happiness of others—

could subsequently arise."[44] The doctrine that the moral law is absolutely independent, that it disregards empirical creatures, let alone the pleasure principle—this doctrine is suspended as the idea of the living is incorporated in the radical, general wording of the Imperative.

REPRESSIVE CHARACTER OF THE DOCTRINE OF FREEDOM

On the side, Kant's inwardly brittle ethics retains its repressive aspect. He glories in an unmitigated urge to punish.* It is not in his late works but in the *Critique of Practical Reason* that we find these lines: "Likewise, confront the man who is otherwise honest (or who this once will only mentally put himself in an honest man's place) with the moral law that makes him recognize the worthlessness of a liar—and his practical reason (in judging what he ought to do) will instantly depart from his advantage. It will unite with that which preserves his self-respect (with veracity); and the advantage, having been sundered and washed clean of all adjuncts of reason (which is solely and wholly on duty's side), will now be weighed by everyone so as, perhaps, to bring it into line with reason in other cases—excepting only where it might run counter to the moral law, which never departs from reason but enters into the closest union with it."[45]

In its contempt for pity, pure practical reason agrees with the "Grow hard!" of Nietzsche, its antipode: "Even this feeling of pity and tender-hearted compassion, if it precedes the reflection on duty and becomes a determining cause, is a burden upon the right-thinking. It confuses their considered maxims and makes them

---

* The opposite intent can still be found in the *Critique of Pure Reason,* in keeping with its tenor: "If legislation and government were arranged so as to accord with this idea, punishment would indeed become correspondingly rare; so it is entirely reasonable (as Plato claims) that if the first two were perfect there would be no need for anything like the third." (Kant, *Kritik der reinen Vernunft,* Works III, p. 248.)

wish to be rid of them and to be subject to laws of reason alone."[46] At times, the heteronomous admixture in the inner composition of autonomy grows into wrath at the same reason that is to be freedom's source. Then Kant sides with the antithesis of the Third Antinomy: "Where determination by natural laws ceases, however, all explication ceases also, and nothing remains but the defensive, i.e., repulsion of the objections of those who pretend to have looked more deeply into the essence of things and blithely declare freedom to be impossible."[47]

Obscurantism entwines with the cult of absolutely ruling reason. The constraint that issues from the Categorical Imperative, according to Kant, contradicts the freedom said to coalesce in it, as its supreme definition. This is largely why the Imperative, stripped of all empiricism, is put forth as a "fact"[48] that need not be tested by reason, despite the *chorismos* between idea and factuality. The antinomical character of the Kantian doctrine of freedom is exacerbated to the point where the moral law seems to be regarded as directly rational and as not rational—as rational, because it is reduced to pure logical reason without content, and as not rational because it must be accepted as given and cannot be further analyzed, because every attempt at analysis is anathema. This antinomical character should not be laid at the philosopher's door: the pure logic of consistency, its compliance with self-preservation without self-reflection, is unreasonable and deluded in itself. The *ratio* turns into an irrational authority.

SELF-EXPERIENCE OF FREEDOM AND UNFREEDOM

The contradiction dates back to the objective contradiction between the experience which consciousness has of itself and its relation to totality. The individual feels free in so far as he has opposed himself to society and can do something—though incomparably less than he believes—against society and other individuals. His freedom is primarily that of a man pursuing his own ends, ends that are not directly and totally exhausted by social ends. In this sense, freedom coincides with the principle of individuation. A freedom of this type has broken loose from primitive society; within an increasingly rational one, it has achieved a measure of reality. At the same time, in the midst of bourgeois society, freedom remains no less delusive than individuality itself.

A critique of free will as well as of determinism means a critique of this delusion. The law of value comes into play over the heads of formally free individuals. They are unfree, according to Marx's insight, as the involuntary executors of that law—the more thoroughly unfree the more rank the growth of the social antagonisms it took to form the very conception of freedom. The process of evolving individual independence is a function of the barter society and terminates in the individual's abolition by integration. What produced freedom will recoil into unfreedom. The individual was free as an economically active bourgeois subject, free to the extent to which the economic system required him to be autonomous in order to function. His autonomy is thus potentially negated at the source. The freedom of which he boasted had a negative side, which Hegel was the first to notice; it was a mockery of true freedom, an expression of the contingency of every individual's social fate. The real necessity involved in the kind of freedom praised by ultra-liberal ideology—in a freedom which the free had to maintain and to enforce with their elbows—this necessity was an image designed to cover up the total social necessity that compels an individual to be "rugged" if he wants to survive.

Thus even concepts abstract enough to seem to approach invariance prove to be historic. An example is the concept of life. While life keeps reproducing itself under the prevailing conditions of unfreedom, its concept, by its own meaning, presupposes the possibility of things not yet included, of things yet to be experienced—and this possibility has been so far reduced that the word "life" sounds by now like an empty consolation. But just as the freedom of the bourgeois individual is a caricature, so is the necessity of his actions. It is not the transparent necessity called for by the concept of law; it strikes every individual subject as an accident, rather, as a sequel to the mythical fate. Life has retained this negativity, an aspect that furnished the title of a Schubert piano piece for four hands: "Storms of Life." The anarchy in the production of goods is a manifestation of the social primitivity that vibrates in the word "life," in the use of a biological category for a thing that is social in essence.

If the social process of production and reproduction were transparent for the subjects, if the subjects determined that process, they would no longer be passively buffeted by the ominous storms of life. The so-called "life" would vanish, then, and so would the fatal aura with which the fin de siècle surrounded that word in the industrial age, to justify its wretched irrationality. The transiency of that surrogate occasionally casts its friendly shadows ahead: nineteenth-century novels about adultery are already waste paper— if we except the greatest products of that epoch, the ones that evoke its historic archetypes. Nor would a producer now dare to stage Hebbel's "Gyges"* for an audience whose ladies will not give up their bikinis. There is a touch of barbarism in this fear of anachronistic subject matter, this lack of aesthetic distance; and one day, if mankind does work its way out, the same fate will overtake everything that is today still viewed as life and merely fools us about how little life there is.

Until that time, the prevailing legality runs counter to the individual and his interests. Under the conditions of a bourgeois economy this is an unshakable fact; in such an economy there can be no answer to the question whether freedom or unfreedom of the will exists. And that economy in turn is a plaster cast of bourgeois society: the category of the individual—in truth, a historical category—deceptively exempts the question of free will from social dynamics and treats each individual as an original phenomenon. In keeping with the ideology of individualist society, freedom has been poorly internalized; this bars any cogent reply to the ideology. If the thesis of free will burdens the dependent individuals with the social injustice they can do nothing about, if it ceaselessly humiliates them with desiderata they cannot fulfill, the thesis of unfreedom, on the other hand, amounts to a metaphysically extended rule of the status quo. This thesis proclaims itself immu-

---

* *Gyges and His Ring,* German drama based upon a tale from Plato: a queen, outraged to learn that her royal husband let his favored courtier peer into her bedroom, gives the voyeur a choice of regicide or death. —TRANS.

table, and if the individual is not prepared to cower anyway, it invites him to cower because that is all he can do.

Determinism acts as if dehumanization, the totally unfolded merchandise character of the working capacity, were human nature pure and simple. No thought is given to the fact that there is a limit to the merchandise character: the working capacity that has not just an exchange value, but a use value. To deny free will outright means to reduce men unreservedly to the normal merchandise form of their labor in full-fledged capitalism. Equally wrong is aprioristic determinism, the doctrine of free will which in the middle of the merchandise society would abstract from that society. The individual himself forms a moment of the merchandise society; the pure spontaneity that is attributed to him is the spontaneity which society expropriates. All that the subject needs to do to be lost is to pose an inescapable alternative: the will is free, or it is unfree.

Each drastic thesis is false. In their inmost core, the theses of determinism and of freedom coincide. Both proclaim identity. The reduction to pure spontaneity applies to the empirical subjects the very same law which as an expanded causal category becomes determinism. Perhaps, free men would be freed from the will also; surely it is only in a free society that the individuals would be free. Along with outward repression, the inner one would disappear—probably after long periods of time, and with recidivism permanently threatening. Where traditional philosophy, acting in a spirit of repression, used to confound freedom and responsibility, responsibility would now turn into every individual's fearless, active participation in a whole that would no longer institutionalize the parts played, but would allow them to have consequences in reality.

The antinomy between the determination of the individual and the social responsibility that contradicts this determination is not due to a misuse of concepts. It is a reality, the moral indication that the universal and the particular are unreconciled. According to every psychological insight even Hitler and his monsters were slaves to their early childhood, products of mental mutilation; and yet, the few one managed to catch must not be acquitted lest the crime (justified to the unconscious of the masses by the failure of lightning to strike from heaven) be repeated ad infinitum. This is something not to be glossed over with artificial constructions such as a utilitarian necessity at odds with reason. Humanity comes to the individual only when the entire sphere of individuation, its moral aspect included, is seen through as an epiphenomenon. At times it is society as a whole which in despair about its situation stands for freedom—against the individuals, and for the freedom promised in a note which the unfreedom of the individuals dishonors.

On the other hand, in this age of universal social repression, the picture of freedom against society lives in the crushed, abused individual's features alone. Where that freedom will hide out at any moment in history cannot be decreed once for all. Freedom turns concrete in the changing forms of repression, as resistance to repression. There has been as much free will as there were men with the will to be free.

But freedom itself and unfreedom are so entangled that unfreedom is not just an impediment to freedom but a premise of its concept. This can no more be culled out as an absolute than any other single concept. Without the unity and the compulsion of reason, nothing similar to freedom would ever have come to mind, much less into being; this is documented in philosophy. There is no available model of freedom save one: that consciousness, as it intervenes in the total social constitution, will through that constitution intervene in the complexion of the individual. This notion is not utterly chimerical, because consciousness is a ramification of the energy of drives; it is part impulse itself, and also a moment of that which it intervenes in. If there were not that affinity which Kant so furiously denies, neither would there be the idea of freedom, for whose sake he denies the affinity.

THE CRISIS OF CAUSALITY

What happens to the idea of freedom seems to be happening also to its counterpart, the concept of causality: in line with a general trend of falsely voiding the antagonisms, the universal liquidates the particular from above, by identification. There are no quick conclusions to be drawn here from the crisis of causality in the natural sciences, where it expressly applies to the micro-realm only; on the other hand, Kant's formulation of causality in the *Critique of Pure Reason,* at least, are so large that presumably they would have room even for the purely statistical legalities. The natural sciences are content to handle causality with operational definitions that are inherent in their modes of proceeding; but for philosophy there can be no dispensation from accounting for causality, if more than an abstract repetition of natural-scientific methodology is to be accomplished. Natural science and philosophy have miserably come apart, and the need alone is not going to glue them together.

Yet the crisis of causality can also be seen in contemporary society, a field accessible to philosophical experience. Kant considered it the unquestionably rational method to trace every condition back to "its" cause, whereas the sciences—from which philosophy gets only farther away in its zeal to recommend itself as their advocate—are probably operating not so much with causal chains as with causal networks. But this is more than an incidental concession to the empirical ambiguity of causal relations. Even Kant would have to admit that an awareness of all the causal sequences that intersect in every phenomenon—instead of its being unequivocally determined by causality in the sequence of time—is essential to the category itself. It is a priori, in Kant's language: no single event is excepted from that diversity. The infinity of the enmeshed and intersecting makes it impossible to form such unequivocal causal chains as the Third Antinomy's thesis and antithesis equally stipulate.

It is impossible as a matter of principle, not just of practice. Even tangible historical investigations, which in Kant's case remained in a finite progression, involve horizontally, so to speak, that positive infinity which he criticized in the chapter on antinomies. Kant ignores this, as if he were transferring the uncomplicated surveyability of small town conditions to all possible objects. No road takes us from his model to the performance of causal determinations. Dealing with the causal relation exclusively as a principle, he thinks past the fact that in principle the relation is enmeshed. Conditioning this sin of omission is Kant's shift of causality into the transcendental subject. As a pure form of legality, causality becomes one-dimensional. Including the ill-reputed "interaction" in the table of categories is an ex post facto attempt to correct the deficiency; it is also an early sign of the dawning crisis of causality.

As the Durkheim school did not fail to notice, the schema of causality was as much a copy of the simple generational relation as that relation, to be explained, is in need of causality. Peculiar to causality is a feudal aspect, if not indeed—as in Anaximander and Heraclitus—an aspect of archaic legal vindictiveness. The process of demythologization has had a twofold effect upon causality, the legatee of the spirits held to be at work in things: demythologization has both confined causality and reinforced it in the name of the law. If causality is the true "unity within diversity" which led Schopenhauer to prefer it among the categories, there was as much causality throughout the bourgeois era as there was a system. The more unequivocal the circumstances, the easier was it to talk of causality in history. Hitler's Germany caused World War II in more exact fashion than the Kaiser's Germany caused World War I. But there is a recoil in the tendency. Eventually the system will reach a point—the word that provides the social cue is "integration"—where the universal dependence of all moments on all other moments makes the talk of causality obsolete. It is idle to search for what might have been a cause within a monolithic society. Only that society itself remains the cause.

Causality has withdrawn to totality, so to speak. Amidst its system it is no longer distinguishable. The more its concept heeds the scientific mandate to attenuate into abstractness, the less will the simultaneously ultra-condensed web of a universally socialized society permit one condition to be traced back with evidentiality to another single condition. Every state of things is horizontally and vertically tied to all others, touches upon all others, is touched by all others. The latest doctrine in which enlightenment used causality as a decisive political weapon is the Marxist one of superstructure and infrastructure: almost innocuously, it lags behind a condition in which not only the machineries of production, distribution, and domination, but economic and social relations and ideologies are inextricably interwoven, and in which living

267

people have become bits of ideology. Where ideology is no longer added to things as a vindication or complement—where it turns into the seeming inevitability and thus legitimacy of whatever is— a critique that operates with the unequivocal causal relation of superstructure and infrastructure is wide of the mark. In a total society all things are equidistant from the center; that society is as transparent, and its apologia as threadbare, as those who see through it are certain to die out.

Critics might use every industrial administration building and every airport to show to what extent the infrastructure has become its own superstructure. They need, on the one hand, a physiognomics of the total condition and of extensive single data, and on the other hand an analysis of economic structural changes; they no longer need to derive, from its causal conditions, an ideology which no longer has an independent existence and can no longer claim a truth of its own. It is a fact that the validity of causality disintegrates correlatively to the decline of the possibility of freedom, and this fact is a symptom of a transformation: a society that is rational in its means is transformed into that frankly irrational society which latently, in its ends, it has been for a long time. In the philosophy of Leibniz and Kant—in the separation of the final cause from the phenomenally applicable causality in the narrow sense, and in the attempt to combine the two—some of that divergence was felt, without getting to its root in the ends-and-means antinomy of bourgeois society.

But today's disappearance of causality signals no realm of freedom. Reproduced in total interaction, the old dependence expands. Its millionfold web prevents the rational penetration that is now due and close enough to touch—the penetration which causal thinking sought to promote in the service of progress. Causality itself makes sense only in a horizon of freedom. From empiricism it appeared to be protected, since without the assumption of causality a scientifically organized cognition seemed impossible; idealism had no stronger argument at its disposal. And yet, Kant's effort to raise causality as a subjective necessity of thought to the rank of a constitutive condition of objectivity was no more valid than its empiricist denial. Even he was forced to disavow that assumption of an inner connection of phenomena—the assumption without which causality turns into an "if-then" relation, losing precisely that emphatic legality, that "apriority," which the doctrine of its subjective-categorial nature seeks to conserve. Scientific developments subsequently realized the potential of the Kantian doctrine. Another expedient is to base causality on its immediate self-experience in motivation; psychology has since furnished substantial proof that this self-experience not only can but must be deceptive.

CAUSALITY AS A SPELL

If causality as a subjective principle of thought has a touch of the absurd, and yet there can be no cognition quite without it, the thing to do is to look in it for a moment that is not cogitative. Causality can teach us what identity has done to nonidentity. We are conscious of that when we are conscious of causality *qua* legality; a cognitively critical sense of causality is also a sense of the subjectively delusive aspects of identification. Upon reflection, causality points to the idea of freedom as the possibility of nonidentity. Objectively, in a provocatively anti-Kantian sense, causality would be a relation between things-in-themselves insofar—and only insofar—as they are subjugated by the identity principle.

Objectively and subjectively, causality is the spell of dominated nature. It has its *fundamentum in re* in identity, which as a mental principle simply mirrors the real control of nature. In reflecting upon causality, reason—which finds causality in nature wherever it controls nature—also grows aware of its own natural origin as the spellbinding principle. It is in such self-consciousness that a progressively enlightened mind parts company with the relapse into mythology to which it subscribed before reflecting. The reductive schema of enlightenment, "This is man," is stripped of its omnipotence as man recognizes himself as the object of his insatiable reductions. Causality, however, is nothing but man's natural origin, which he continues as control of nature. Once man, the subject, knows the moment of his own equality with nature, he will desist from merely equalizing nature with himself.

This is the secret and perverted truth content of idealism. For the more thoroughly the subject follows the idealistic custom to make nature equal to itself, the farther will it be removed from all equality with nature. Affinity is the point of a dialectics of enlightenment. It no sooner cuts completely through the affinity than it will recoil into delusion, into a conceptless execution from outside. Without affinity there is no truth; this is what idealism caricatured in the philosophy of identity. Consciousness knows as much about its otherness as it resembles that otherness; it does not know by striking out itself along with the resemblance. To define objectivity as the residue after the subject has been deducted is aping. Objectivity is the self-unconscious schema under which the subject brings its otherness. The less affinity to things it tolerates, the more ruthlessly will it identify.

But affinity is no positive, ontological individual definition either. When we turn it into intuition, into a truth directly, sympathetically known, the dialectics of enlightenment will grind it to bits as a relic, a warmed-up myth that agrees with dominion, with the mythology that reproduces itself from pure reason. Affinity is not a remnant which cognition hands us after the identifying schemata of the categorial machinery have been eliminated. Rather, affinity is the definite negation of those schemata. It is in such critique that we reflect on causality. What thinking performs in it is a mimicry of the spell of things, of the spell with which it has endowed things, on the threshold of a sympathy that would make the spell disappear. There is an elective affinity between the subjectivity of causality and the objects, a distant sense of what has happened to them at the subject's hand.

REASON, EGO, SUPER-EGO

The Kantian turn of the moral law into fact has a suggestive power because in the sphere of the empirical person Kant can actually cite such a datum to support his view. This helps to establish a connection—always problematic—between the intelligible and empirical realms. The phenomenology of empirical consciousness, not to mention its psychology, comes up against the very conscience which in Kantian doctrine is the voice of the moral law. The descriptions of its efficacy, notably those of the "constraint" it exerts, are not mere brainstorms; it was in the real compulsion of conscience that Kant read the coercive features he engraved in the doctrine of freedom. The empirical irresistibility of the super-ego, the psychologically existing conscience, is what assures him, contrary to his transcendental principle, of the factuality of the moral law—although, for Kant, conscience ought to disqualify factuality as the basis of autonomous morality, as much as it disqualifies the heteronomous drives.

Kant's refusal to allow any critique of conscience brings him into conflict with his own insight that in the phenomenal world all motivations are motivations of the empirical, psychological ego. This is why he removed the genetical moment from the philosophy of morals and substituted the construction of the intelligible character—a character which he described, to be sure, as initially given by the subject to itself.* But the temporal-genetical and nonetheless "empirical" claim of that "initially" is not redeemable. Every bit of knowledge we have of the genesis of character is incompatible with the assertion of such an act of original moral gestation. The ego that is supposed to perform it, according to Kant, is not something immediate. The ego itself is indirect. It has arisen; to speak in psychoanalytical terms: it has branched off from the diffuse energy of the libido. Not only all of the specific substance of the moral law refers constitutively to facts of existence, but so does its supposedly pure imperative form. This form presupposes the internalization of repression as

---

* "In judging the causality of free acts, we can therefore come only as far as the intelligible cause, but not beyond it; we can recognize that this cause might be free, i.e., determined independently of the realm of the senses, and that it might thus be the sensually unqualified qualification of phenomena. But why, in given circumstances, the intelligible character provides precisely these phenomena and this empirical character—that is a question so far beyond all powers of our reason, indeed beyond its every competence to ask, as if we were asking why the transcendental object provides our external sense perception with perception in space only, and not with some other kind." (Kant, *Kritik der reinen Vernunft*, Works III, p. 376f.)

much as the full development of the ego as the solid, identically maintained authority which Kant absolutizes as the necessary premise of morality.

No Kant interpretation that would object to his formalism and undertake to have the substance demonstrate the empirical moral relativity which Kant eliminated with the help of that formalism —no such interpretation would reach far enough. The law, even in its most abstract form, has come to be; its painful abstractness is sedimented substance, dominion reduced to its normal form of identity. Psychology has now concretely caught up with something which in Kant's day was not known as yet, and to which he therefore did not need to pay specific attention; with the empirical genesis of what, unanalyzed, was glorified by him as timelessly intelligible. The Freudian school in its heroic period, agreeing on this point with the other Kant, the Kant of the Enlightenment, used to call for a ruthless criticism of the super-ego as something truly heteronomous and alien to the ego. The super-ego was recognized, then, as blindly, unconsciously internalized social coercion.

Sandor Ferenczi,* with a caution that may be explained, perhaps, as fear of social consequences, wrote "that a real character analysis must do away temporarily, at least, with every kind of super-ego, including the analyst's. Eventually, after all, the patient must become free from all emotional ties that go beyond reason and his own libidinous tendencies. Nothing but this sort of razing of the super-ego as such can accomplish a radical cure. Successes that consist only in the substitution of one super-ego for another are still to be classified as successes of transference; they certainly do not serve the ultimate purpose of therapy, to get rid of the transference also."[49]

Reason—to Kant, the foundation of conscience—is here supposed to dissolve and refute it. For the unreflected rule of reason,

---

* In the following, Adorno quotes from *Bausteine zur Psychoanalyse,* a four-volume German collection of translation from Ferenczi's original Hungarian. Since the quoted passages are not included in the authorized English translation of Ferenczi's writings (*Contributions to Psychoanalysis,* trans. Ernest Jones), they have been rendered from the German. —TRANS.

the ego's rule over the id, is identical with the repressive principle, the principle which psychoanalysis, its criticism silenced by the reality principle of the ego, placed under the ego's unconscious sway. The separation of ego and super-ego, which the analytical topology insists upon, is a dubious affair; genetically, both of them lead equally to the internalization of the father image. The analytical theories about the super-ego, however bold their beginnings, will therefore flag in short order, lest they be obliged to spread to the coddled ego.

And indeed, Ferenczi promptly curbs his criticism: he is "fighting . . . only against the part of the super-ego that has become unconscious and is impervious to influence."[50] But this will not do—for, as in the case of the archaic taboos, the irresistibility which Kant found in the compulsion of conscience lies in such a turn to unconsciousness. If a state of universally rational actuality were conceivable, no super-ego would come into being. There have been attempts (by Ferenczi, and later by the psychoanalytical revisionists who subscribe, along with other healthy views, to that of a healthy super-ego) to divide it into two parts, a conscious one and a pre-conscious and therefore more harmless one; but these attempts are futile. The process that makes conscience an authority, a process of objectification and evolving independence, constitutes a forgetting and is thus alien to the ego.

Ferenczi agrees, emphasizing that "in his pre-conscious, a normal man continues to retain a sum of positive and negative models."[51] But if there is any concept that is heteronomous in the strict Kantian sense—psychoanalytically speaking: any that is libidinously bound—it is the concept of the model. It is the correlate of "normal man," whom Ferenczi respects likewise, of the man who actively and passively lends himself to every social repression. Psychoanalysis, clinging to its fatal faith in the division of labor, uncritically receives this view of normalcy from the existing society. As soon as it puts the brakes of social conformism on the critique of the super-ego launched by itself, psychoanalysis comes close to that repression which to this day has marred all teachings of freedom. How close, shows most clearly in passages like the following by Ferenczi: "So long as this super-ego is moderate and sees to it that one will feel as a civilized citizen and act accordingly, it is a useful institution that should be left alone. But pathological exaggerations of the super-ego formation . . ."[52]

The fear of exaggerations is the mark of the same civilized citizenry that will pay any price to keep the super-ego along with its irrationalities. How the normal and the pathic super-ego might be distinguished subjectively, by psychological criteria, is a question on which psychoanalysts, all too quick to see reason, are silent—as silent as the philistines are about the line between nationalism and that which they cultivate as natural national feelings. The only criterion of the distinction is its social effect, whose *quaestiones iuris* psychoanalysts declare to be without their competence. As Ferenczi puts it, contradicting his words, reflections on the super-ego are truly "metapsychological." A critique of the super-ego would have to turn into one of the society that produces the super-ego; if psychoanalysts stand mute here, they accommodate the ruling social norm. To recommend the super-ego on grounds of social utility or inalienability, while its own coercive mechanism strips it of the objective validity it claims in the context of effecting psychological motivations—this amounts to repeating and reinforcing, within psychology, the irrationalities which psychology braced itself to "do away with."

POTENTIAL OF FREEDOM

What has been going on in recent times, however, is an externalization of the super-ego into unconditional adjustment, not its sublimation in a more rational whole. The ephemeral traces of freedom which herald its possibility to empirical life tend to grow more rare; freedom comes to be a borderline value. Not even as a complementary ideology does one really dare to set it forth; the powers that be, by now administering even ideology with a firm hand, clearly have little faith in the continuing propagandistic appeal of freedom. Freedom is forgotten. Unfreedom is consummated in its invisible totality that tolerates no "outside" any more from which it might be broken. The world as it is becomes the only ideology, and mankind, its component.

Dialectical justice prevails there, too: it is meted out to the individual, the prototype and agent of a particularistic and unfree society. The freedom he must look forward to could not be his alone; it would have to be the freedom of the whole. A critique of the individual leads as far beyond the category of freedom as that category has been created in the unfree individual's image. The contradiction that for the individual sphere we can proclaim no free will, and thus no morality, while without them there is no preserving even the life of the species—this contradiction is not to be settled by imposing the octroi of so-called "values." Heteronomously posited like Nietzsche's "New Tables," they would be the opposite of freedom. But freedom need not remain what it was, and what it arose from. Ripening, rather, in the internalization of social coercion into conscience, with the resistance to social authority which critically measures that authority by its own principles, is a potential that would rid men of coercion. In the critique of conscience, the rescue of this potential is envisioned—not in the psychological realm, however, but in the objectivity of a reconciled life of the free.

Finally—though seeming to contradict its rigorous claim to autonomy—the convergence of Kantian morality with the ethics of property maintains the truth of a break not to be bridged by any conceptual synthesis: of the break between the social ideal and the subjective ideal of self-preserving reason. If it were charged that it is sheer subjective reason which absolutizes itself in the objectivity of the moral law, the indictment would be subaltern. What Kant puts into fallible and distorted words is what should be advanced as a social demand, with good reason. For good or ill, such objectivity goes on existing apart from the subjective sphere; it is not translatable into the subjective sphere of either psychology or rationality until the general interest and the particular one are in real accord. Conscience is the mark of shame of an unfree society.

Necessarily hidden from Kant was the arcanum of his philosophy: that in order to have the capacity with which he credits it, to constitute objectivities or to objectify itself in action, the subject on its part must always be objective also. Spooking in the transcendental subject, in the pure reason that interprets itself as objective, is the supremacy of the object—a moment without which the subject could not perform Kant's objectifying actions either. At the core, his concept of subjectivity bears apersonal features. Even that which is immediate, nearest, most assured to the subject, its own personality, requires mediation. There is no ego-consciousness without society, just as there is no society beyond its individuals. The postulates of practical reason which transcend the subject—God, freedom, immortality—imply a critique of the Categorical Imperative, of pure subjective reason. Without those postulates the Imperative would be unthinkable, all Kant's avowals to the contrary notwithstanding. Without hope there is no good.

AGAINST PERSONALISM

With direct violence erupting everywhere, our thought, unwilling to dispense with the protection of morality, is induced by nominalist trends to attach morality to the person, as to an indestructible property. Freedom, which would arise only in the organization of a free society, is sought precisely where it is denied by the organization of the existing society: in each individual. The individual would need freedom, but as he happens to be, he cannot guarantee it. Reflection on society does not occur in ethical personalism, no more than reflection on the person itself. Once detached entirely from the universal, the person cannot constitute a universal either; the universal is received in secret, then, from extant forms of rule.

In pre-fascist times, personalism and the prattle of "ties" got along quite well on a platform of irrationality. The person, as an absolute, negates the generality that is supposed to be read in it, and it creates a threadbare legal title for license. Its charisma is borrowed from the irresistibility of the universal, while the cogitative distress of coming to doubt the legitimacy of the universal makes the person withdraw to itself. Its principle, that of the unshakable unity which makes out its selfhood, defiantly repeats dominion in the subject. The person is the historically tied knot that should be freely loosened and not perpetuated. It is the ancient spell of the universal, entrenched in the particular. Whatever moral aspect is inferred from it remains as accidental as a direct Existenz.

Unlike the "personality" in Kant's antiquated manner of speaking, the person became a tautology for those left with nothing but the conceptless "being there" of their existence. The transcendence which some neo-ontologies hope to derive from the person exalts nothing but their consciousness. Yet their own consciousness would not be without that universal which their recourse to the person seeks to bar as an ethical ground. This is why the concept of the person as well as its variants—the "I-thou" relation, for example—have assumed the oily tone of unbelieved theology. We cannot anticipate the concept of the right human being, but it would be nothing like the person, that consecrated duplicate of its own self-preservation. From the viewpoint of a philosophy of history, this concept, which on the one hand assuredly presupposes a subject objectified into a character, presupposes on the other hand the subject's disintegration. Complete weakness of the ego, the subject's transition to a passive, atomistic, reflex-type conduct, is at the same time the well-earned judgment passed upon a "person" in which the economic principle of appropriation has become anthropological.

It is not the personal side of men that would have to be conceived as their intelligible character; it is what distinguishes them from their existence. In the person, this distinguishing element necessarily appears as nonidentity. Whatever stirs in a man contradicts his unity. Every impulse in the direction of better things is not only rational, as it is to Kant; before it is rational, it is also stupid. Men are human only where they do not act, let alone posit themselves, as persons; the diffuseness of nature, in which they are not persons, resembles the lineamentation of an intelligible creature, of that self which would be delivered from the ego. Contemporary art innervates some of this. The subject is the lie, because for the sake of its own absolute rule it will deny its own objective definitions. Only he who would refrain from such lies—who would have used his own strength, which he owes to identity, to cast off the façade of identity—would truly be a subject.

The ideological mischief of the person can be criticized immanently. According to that ideology it is substantiality that dignifies the person; but this substantiality does not exist. Without exception, men have yet to become themselves. By the concept of the self we should properly mean their potential, and this potential stands in polemical opposition to the reality of the self. This is the main reason why the talk of "self-alienation" is untenable. Despite—or perhaps on account of—the better days it has seen under Hegel and Marx,* that talk has become the stock in trade of apologists who will suggest in paternal tones that man has apostatized, that he has lapsed from a being-in-itself which he had always been. Whereas, in fact, he never was that being-in-itself, and what he can expect from recourses to his ἀρχαί is therefore nothing but submission to authority, the very thing that is alien to him. It is not only due to the economic themes of *Das Kapital* that the concept of self-alienation plays no part in it any more; it makes philosophical sense.

Negative dialectics does not come to a halt before the conclusive Existenz, the solid selfhood of the ego; nor will it halt before the ego's equally congealed antithesis, the "role" which serves the subjective sociology of our time as a nostrum, as the ultimate definition of socialization, analogous to the "self-being Existenz" of some ontologists. The concept of the role sanctions the bad, perverted depersonalization of today: unfreedom, which simply for a perfect adjustment's sake replaces the autonomy that was won laboriously and as if subject to recall, is less than freedom, not more. The hardships of the division of labor are hypostatized as virtues in the concept of the role. With this concept, the ego once again prescribes that which society condemns it to be: itself. The liberated ego, no longer locked up in its identity, would no longer be condemned to play roles either. The remnants of a division of labor which the radical curtailment of working hours might leave in society would lose the horror of

---

* "This 'alienation'—to remain intelligible to the philosophers—can of course be voided on two practical premises only." (Marx and Engels, *Die deutsche Ideologie,* Berlin 1960, p. 31.)

shaping the individuals throughout. The thinglike rigor of the self and its availability, its readiness to be committed to the socially desired roles, are accomplices. If identity is ever to pass into its otherness, it must not be denied abstractly even in the moral field, but must be preserved in resistance. The present condition is destructive: a loss of identity for the sake of abstract identity, of naked self-preservation.

DEPERSONALIZATION AND EXISTENTIAL ONTOLOGY

The duplicity of the ego has left its mark on existential ontology. Both the recourse to existence and the design of "intrinsicality" against the indefinite third person—the "one"—are metaphysical transfigurations of the idea of the strong, conclusive, "resolute" I; the effect of *Being and Time* was that of a personalist manifesto. But in Heidegger's interpretation of subjectivity as a mode of being, a mode superior to thought, personalism was already turning into its opposite. Linguistically this is indicated by the choice of apersonal terms for the subject, terms such as "existence" and "Existenz." What returns, unnoticed, in this usage is the idealistically German, civically pious predominance of identity beyond its carrier, the subject.

Depersonalization, the bourgeois devaluation of the individual whom one glorified in the same breath, was already the basis of the difference between subjectivity as the general principle of the individualized ego—between "egoity," in Schelling's language— and the individualized ego itself. The essence of subjectivity *qua* existence, a main theme of *Being and Time,* is like the remainder that is left of the person when it is no longer a person. The motives for this are not to be disdained. What is commensurable to the person's general conceptual extent, its individual consciousness, is always phenomenal as well, entwined in that transsubjective objectivity whose ground, according to both idealist doctrine and ontological doctrine, lies in the pure subject. Whatever an I can introspectively experience as "I" is also "not-I." Absolute egoity defies experience. Hence the difficulty (found by Schopen-hauer) of becoming aware of oneself.

The ultimate is not an ultimate. Hegel recognized this in the objective turn he gave to his absolute idealism, the equivalent of absolute subjectivity. But the more thorough the individual's loss of what used to be called his self-consciousness, the higher the rise of depersonalization. That to Heidegger, death came to be the essence of existence codifies the nullity of mere being-for-oneself.* In the sinister decision to depersonalize, however, we bow regressively to a doom we feel to be inescapable, instead of using the idea to point beyond the person, so that it may come into its own.

Heidegger's apersonality is a linguistic arrangement and won too easily, by simply leaving out what makes the subject a sub-ject. He thinks past the knot of the subject. An abstract attenua-tion of existence to its pure possibility would not unlock the perspective of depersonalization; only an analysis of the subjects existing in the world would do so. Heidegger's "analysis of exist-ence" does not go that far, which is why his apersonal *existentialia* can be attached to persons with so little effort. The micro-analy-sis of persons is unbearable to an authoritarian way of thinking; in selfhood it would strike at the principle of all dominion. Exist-ence generally, on the other hand, is apersonal and can be un-hesitantly treated as if it were superhuman and yet human.

In fact, as a functional context objectively preceding all the living, their overall condition moves toward apersonality in the sense of anonymity. This is as much deplored in Heidegger's lan-guage as that overall condition is affirmatively mirrored in his language, as supra-personal. Catching up with the horror of de-personalization would take an insight into the person's own reified side, into the limits placed upon egoity by equating the self with self-preservation. To Heidegger, ontological apersonality always remains the ontologization of the person without actually reaching

---

* Soon after the publication of Heidegger's chef d'oeuvre, its ob-jective-ontological implications and the recoil of objectless internality into negative objectivity could already be shown on Kierkegaard's concept of Existenz. (Cf. Theodor W. Adorno, *Kierkegaard,* Frank-furt 1962, p. 87ff.)

the person. There is a retroactive force in the cognition of what became of consciousness when its live side was abandoned: egoity has always been so thinglike. Dwelling in the core of the subject are the objective conditions it must deny for the sake of its unconditional rule. They are the conditions of that rule, and they are what the subject would have to get rid of. The premise of its identity is the end of compulsory identity. In existential ontology this appears in distortion only.

Yet nothing that fails to invade the zone of depersonalization and its dialectics can be intellectually relevant any longer. Schizophrenia is the truth about the subject, from the viewpoint of the philosophy of history. Heidegger, in touching upon the zone of depersonalization, unwittingly turns it into a parable of the administered world and, complementing the parable, into a desperately fortified definition of subjectivity. Its critique alone would yield an object for what Heidegger, under the name of "destruction," reserves to the history of philosophy. The things which Freud, the anti-metaphysician, taught about the id come closer to a metaphysical critique of the subject than Heidegger's metaphysics, which he does not want to be metaphysics. If the role, the heteronomy prescribed by autonomy, is the latest objective form of an unhappy consciousness, there is, conversely, no happiness except where the self is not itself. Historically, the subject has fought its way out of a state of dissociation and ambiguity, and if the immense pressure that weighs upon it hurls the self back into that state—into schizophrenia—the subject's dissolution presents at the same time the ephemeral and condemned picture of a possible subject. If its freedom, once upon a time, called a halt to the mythus, the subject would now win deliverance from itself as from the ultimate mythus. The subject's nonidentity without sacrifice would be utopian.

UNIVERSAL AND INDIVIDUAL IN THE PHILOSOPHY OF MORALS

In inveighing against psychology, Kant expresses not only the fear of losing the laboriously caught scrap of the intelligible world;

he expresses also the authentic insight that the moral categories of the individual are more than strictly individual. What manifests itself in them as universal, after the model of Kant's concept of the law, is secretly social. For all the oscillation of the concept of humanity in the *Critique of Practical Reason,* one of its major functions is that pure reason, being general, is valid for all rational beings; this is a point of indifference in Kant's philosophy. The concept of generality was obtained from the multiplicity of subjects and then made independent as the logical objectivity of reason, in which all single subjects—as well as, seemingly, subjectivity as such—will disappear. But Kant, on the narrow ridge between logical absolutism and empirical general validity, wants to return to that entity which the system's logic of consistency had banned before.

This is where the anti-psychological philosophy of morals converges with psychological findings of a later date. In revealing the super-ego as an internalized social norm, psychology breaks through its own monadological barriers. These in turn are social products. The objectivity of conscience vis-à-vis mankind is drawn from the objectivity of society, from the objectivity in and by which men live and which extends to the core of their individualization. Undividedly entwined in such objectivity are the antagonistic moments: heteronomous coercion and the idea of a solidarity transcending the divergent individual interests. The part of conscience that reproduces the tenaciously persisting repressive mischief of society is the opposite of freedom; it is to be disenchanted by evidence of its own determination.

The universal norm which conscience unconsciously appropriates, on the other hand, bears witness to whichever part of society points beyond particularity as the principle of its totals. This is its element of truth. The question of right or wrong in conscience cannot be answered succinctly because right and wrong lie in conscience itself and could not be separated by any abstract judgment: it takes the repressive form of conscience to develop the form of solidarity, in which the repressive one will be voided. To the philosophy of morals it is essential that the individual and society should be neither reconciled nor divided by a simple difference. The bad side of universality has declared itself in the socially unfulfilled claim of the individual. This is the supra-individual truth content of the critique of morality. But the individual inculpated by want, who comes to be his own be-all and end-all, will in turn fall into the delusion of individualist society and misconceive himself—a consequence which Hegel discerned, and discerned most acutely where he was lending a hand to reactionary abuses.

Society is in the wrong against the individual in its general claims, but it is also in the right against him, since the social principle of unreflected self-preservation—the very principle which makes up the bad universal—is hypostatized in the individual. Society metes out measure for measure. Encoded in the late Kantian sentence that everyone's freedom need be curtailed only insofar as it impairs soemone else's* is a reconciled condition that would not only be above the bad universal, the coercive social mechanism, but above the obdurate individual who is a microcosmic copy of that mechanism.

The question of freedom does not call for a Yes or No; it calls for theory to rise above the individuality that exists as well as above the society that exists. Instead of sanctioning the internalized and hardened authority of the super-ego, theory should carry out the dialectics of individual and species. The rigorism of the super-ego is nothing but the reflex response to the prevention of that dialectics by the antagonistic condition. The subject would be liberated only as an I reconciled with the not-I, and thus it would be also above freedom insofar as freedom is leagued with its counterpart, repression. How much aggression is so far inherent in freedom can be seen whenever, in the midst of general unfreedom, men act as if they were free.

In a state of freedom, the individual would not be frantically guarding the old particularity—individuality is the product of pressure as well as the energy center for resistance to this pressure—but neither would that state of freedom agree with the

----

* "Right is every act that can coexist—or whose maxim enables the freedom of everyone's license to coexist—with everyone's freedom, in line with a universal law." (Kant, *Metaphysik der Sitten,* Einleitung in die Rechtslehre, § C, Works VI, p. 230.)

283

present concept of collectivity. The fact that collectivism is directly commanded in the countries which today monopolize the name of socialism, commanded as the individual's subordination to society, this fact belies the socialism of those countries and solidifies antagonism. The complaints of "isolation" are as much manifestations of the ego's enfeeblement by a socialized society in which men are tirelessly rounded up, rendered both literally and metaphorically incapable of solitude, as they are signs of the truly unbearable chill spread over all things by the expanding barter relationship—a chill prolonged in the alleged people's democracies by authoritarian regimes and a ruthless disregard for needs of the subjects. The idea that a union of free men would constantly require them to flock together belongs to the conceptual circle of parades, of marching, flag-waving, and leaders' orations. These methods thrive for so long as society irrationally seeks to glue its compulsory members together; objectively they are not needed.

Collectivism and individualism complement each other in the wrong direction. Protests against both of them have been voiced by speculative philosophers of history from Fichte onward, in the doctrine of a state of consummate sinfulness and later in the doctrine of lost meaning. The modern world was equated with a de-formed one—whereas Rousseau, the initiator of retrospective hostility to one's own age, had struck the spark of this hostility on the last of the great styles; what he had abhorred was too much form, the denatured society. The time has come to give notice to the image of a world drained of meaning. From a cipher of longing, this image has degenerated into a slogan of order maniacs. Nowhere on earth is today's society "open," as apologists of scientivism certify it to be; but it is not de-formed anywhere either. The belief that forms have been lost arose from the devastation of cities and landscapes by planlessly expanding industry; it originated in a lack of rationality, not in its excess. Anyone who traces de-formation to metaphysical processes rather than to the conditions of material production is a purveyor of ideologies.

A change in the conditions of production might relieve the violent picture which the world shows to its violators. If supra-individual ties had vanished—they are far from having vanished —this in itself would not be bad at all; the truly emancipated works of twentieth-century art are certainly no worse than those that thrived in styles discarded by the modern age, for the best of reasons. Reversed as in a mirror is the experience that according to the state of consciousness, and of the material productive forces, men are expected to be free; that they expect themselves to be free; and that they are not free—while their radical unfreedom leaves them no such model of thought, of conduct, and (to use the most infamous term) of "value" as the unfree crave. The substance of the lament about lack of ties is a condition of society that simulates freedom without realizing it. There is a pale sort of freedom only in the superstructure; its perennial failure to succeed shifts the desire to unfreedom. This disproportion is probably what we express when we ask about the meaning of existence as a whole.

ON THE STATE OF FREEDOM

Black shrouds cover the horizon of a state of freedom that would no longer require either repression or morality, because drives would no longer have to be expressed in destruction. It is not in their nauseating parody, sexual repression, that moral questions are succinctly posed; it is in lines such as: No man should be tortured; there should be no concentration camps—while all of this continues in Asia and Africa and is repressed merely because, as ever, the humanity of civilization is inhumane toward the people it shamelessly brands as uncivilized.

But if a moral philosopher were to seize upon these lines and to exult at having caught the critics of morality, at last—caught them quoting the same values that are happily proclaimed by the philosophy of morals—his cogent conclusion would be false. The lines are true as an impulse, as a reaction to the news that torture is going on somewhere. They must not be rationalized; as an abstract principle they would fall promptly into the bad infinities of derivation and validity.

We criticize morality by criticizing the extension of the logic of consistency to the conduct of men; this is where the stringent logic of consistency becomes an organ of unfreedom. The impulse—naked physical fear, and the sense of solidarity with what Brecht called "tormentable bodies"—is immanent in moral conduct and would be denied in attempts at ruthless rationalization. What is most urgent would become contemplative again, mocking its own urgency. The theoretical meaning of the difference between theory and practice is that practice can no more be reduced to pure theory than it is χωρίς of it. The two cannot be glued together in a synthesis. What has not been severed lives solely in the extremes, in a spontaneously stirring impatience with argumentation, in the unwillingness to let the horror go on, and in the theoretical discernment, unterrorized by commands, that shows us why the horror goes on anyway, ad infinitum.

This contradiction alone is the stage of morality today, considering the real impotence of all individuals. Consciousness reacts spontaneously when it knows what is bad, without being content with that knowledge. The incompatibility of every general moral judgment with psychological determination—an incompatibility which nonetheless does not relieve us of the judgment that something is evil—comes from the objective antagonism, not from inconsistent thought. Fritz Bauer noted that the same types who find a hundred stale arguments for the acquittal of the torturers of Auschwitz favor a reintroduction of the death penalty. It is on this point that the latest stand of moral dialectics concentrates: the acquittal would be a barefaced injustice; but a just atonement would be infected with the principle of brute force, and nothing but resistance to that is humanity.

Benjamin forecast this dialectics in his remark that the execution of the death penalty might be moral, never its legitimation. If the men charged with torturing, along with their overseers and with the high and mighty protectors of the overseers, had been shot on the spot, this would have been more moral than putting a few on trial. The fact that they managed to flee, to hide out for two decades, effects a qualitative change in the justice that was missed at the time. Once a judicial machinery must be mobilized against them, with codes of procedure, black robes, and understanding defense lawyers, justice—incapable in any case of imposing sanctions that would fit the crimes—is falsified already, compromised by the same principle on which the killers were acting.

The fascists shrewdly exploit such objective madness with their devilishly insane reason. The historic basis of the aporia is that in Germany the anti-Fascist revolution failed, or rather, that in 1944 there was no revolutionary mass movement. The contradiction of teaching empirical determinism and yet convicting the normal monsters—according to those teachings, one should perhaps turn them loose—cannot be settled by superior logic. A justice that has been reflected upon theoretically ought not to shy away from this contradiction. Failure to make it conscious is a political factor that encourages the continuation of the torture methods for which the collective unconscious is hoping anyway. It looks forward only to their rationalization; this much of the theory of deterrence is certainly true. It is in admitting the rupture—the break between, on the one hand, a legal reason which for the last time accords to the guilty the honor of a freedom they do not deserve, and on the other hand, an insight into their real unfreedom—that the critique of identitarian thinking with its logic of consistency comes to be moral.

KANT'S "INTELLIGIBLE CHARACTER"

The construction of the intelligible character is Kant's way to connect existence with the moral law. The construction leans upon the thesis that "the moral law proves its reality"[53]—as if things that are given, things that exist, were legitimized by being given and existent. When Kant says further "that even outside the world of the senses, in freedom, the determining ground of this causality may be assumed as a quality of an intelligible being,"[54] the concept of a quality turns the intelligible being into a full-fledged "real" one that can be positively conceived in the life of the individual. Yet this, within the axiomatics of noncontradictoriness, runs counter to the doctrine that intelligibility is beyond the world of the senses.

Kant promptly and frankly recalls that doctrine. "The moral good, on the other hand, is supersensory as far as the object is concerned. Accordingly, nothing that corresponds to it"—and thus most certainly no "quality"—"can be found in any sense perception, and the power of judgment under laws of pure practical reason seems therefore to be subject to special difficulties resting upon the fact that a law of freedom is to be applied to actions as events which occur in the sensory world and thus belong to nature."[55]

In keeping with the spirit of the *Critiques,* the passage is directed not only against the ontology of good and evil as noumenal properties, stringently criticized in the *Critique of Practical Reason.* It also goes against the coordinated subjective faculty which is removed from the realm of phenomena, is said to assure that ontology, and bears a character of a downright supernatural sort. Objectively, one of the strongest motives behind Kant's attempt to save freedom by introducing the doctrine of the intelligible character (an utterly exposed, out-on-a-limb doctrine, resisting experience and yet conceived as a link to empiricism) was that the being of the will could not be inferred from phenomena, could not be defined by their conceptual synthesis either, but had to be presupposed as their condition—with the same drawbacks of a naïve realism of inwardness which Kant, in other cases of psychological hypostasis, destroyed in his chapter on paralogisms.

The precarious linkage is to be accomplished by proving that character is neither exhausted in nature nor absolutely transcendent to it—as its concept implies dialectically, by the way. Yet motivations without which there would be no such linkage have a psychological element, while the motivations of the human will, according to Kant, can "never be anything other than the moral law."[56] This is what the Antinomy prescribes for each possible answer. Kant elaborates it bluntly: "For how a law might immediately and by itself be a determining ground of the will (which is, after all, the essential factor in all morality)—this is a problem insoluble for human reason, and as one with the problem how there might be a free will. What we shall thus have to show, a priori, is not the ground on which the moral law in itself constitutes a mainspring; it is what, supposing the law is such a mainspring, it will bring about (one had better say: must bring about) in the human mind."[57]

Kant's speculation falls silent where it ought to start. He is resigned to simply describing immanent effective contexts—contexts which, had his purpose not overwhelmed him, he would not have hesitated to call delusive. Something empirical acquires a supra-empirical authority by stealth, by the strength of the affection it exerts. Kant deals with an "intelligible Existenz"[58] that exists without time, although according to him time has a part in constituting existence, and he treats it without being deterred by the *contradictio in adjecto,* without articulating it dialectically, indeed without saying what, if anything, one might conceive under that sort of Existenz. He goes farthest in discussing "the spontaneity of the subject as a thing-in-itself,"[59] a spontaneity of which, according to the *Critique of Pure Reason,* one could no more talk positively than of the transcendent causes of external sense phenomena; on the other hand, without an intelligible character there could be no moral action in the empirical realm, no intervention in that realm, and thus no morality.

Kant has to strive desperately for something prevented by the layout of his system. What helps him is that reason can intervene against the causal automatism of both physical and psychological nature, that it can create a new nexus. In the finished philosophy of morals he deigns to stop thinking of the intelligible realm— now secularized into pure practical reason—as absolutely different; in view of that discoverable influx of reason, however, this is by no means the miracle it would seem to be according to the abstract interrelation of Kant's basic theses. The prehistory of reason, that it is a moment of nature and yet something else, has become the immanent definition of reason. It is natural as the psychological force split off for purposes of self-preservation; once split off and contrasted with nature, it also becomes nature's otherness. But if that dialectics irrepressibly turns reason into the absolute antithesis of nature, if the nature in reason itself is forgotten, reason will be self-preservation running wild and will regress to nature. It is only as reflection upon that self-preservation that reason would be above nature.

No interpretive art would be able to remove the contradictions immanent in the definitions of the intelligible character. Kant does not say what it is, and how, on its own, it influences the empirical character; he does not tell us whether it is to be simply the pure act of positing the empirical character, or whether it is to go on beside it—a possibility that sounds sophistical but is not quite implausible for our self-experience. He is content to describe that influence as it appears in the empirical realm. If we conceive the intelligible character wholly χωρίς, as the word suggests, we cannot discuss it at all—no more than we can discuss the thing-in-itself, with which Kant cryptically equates the intelligible character in an utterly formal analogy, not even explaining whether it is "a" thing-in-itself, one in every person, the unknown cause of inner sense phenomena, or whether, as Kant says occasionally, it is "the" thing-in-itself, identical with all the rest, like Fichte's absolute I.

In exerting influence, such a radically severed subject would become a moment of the phenomenal world and subjected to its definitions, including causality. Kant, the traditional logician, should never permit one and the same concept to be both subject and not subject to causality.* Yet if the intelligible character

---

* A convenient rebuke to the concept of intelligibility is that mentioning unknown causes of phenomena positively, even in extreme abstraction, is forbidden. A concept of which simply nothing can be said is not one to operate with; it would equal nothing, and nothing would be its proper substance. This was one of the most effective arguments used against Kant by the German idealists, who wasted little time on Kant's and Leibniz's idea of the boundary concept.

Against Fichte's and Hegel's plausible critique of Kant we have to remonstrate, however. This critique follows the traditional logic, which prohibits—as idle—the discussion of whatever cannot be reduced to substantive contents which make out the substance of the concept in question. In their rebellion against Kant, the overzealous idealists forgot the principle they had been following against Kant: that consistent thinking forces us to construe concepts without any positively and definably given representative. For speculation's sake they denounced Kant as a speculator. They were guilty of the same positivism of which they accused him.

What survives in Kant, in the alleged mistake of his apologia for the thing-in-itself—the mistake which the logic of consistency from Maimon on could so triumphantly demonstrate—is the memory of the

were no longer χωρίς, it would no longer be intelligible either; in the sense of Kantian dualism, it would be contaminated by the *mundus sensibilis* and equally self-contradictory. Wherever Kant feels obliged to elaborate on the doctrine of the intelligible character, he must, on the one hand, base it on an act in time, on something empirical of the sort it is flatly supposed not to be; and on the other hand he must neglect the psychology he gets embroiled in.

"There are cases of people who from childhood on, even with an education that benefited others at the same time, show such early malice and keep increasing it so in adulthood that one takes them for born villains utterly incorrigible in their way of thinking; and yet their acts and omissions will be equally judged, their crimes equally censured as guilt, and even these censures deemed by themselves (the children) as well-founded as if—regardless of the hopeless natural disposition meted out to them—they remained just as responsible as any other human being. This could not happen if we did not presume that whatever springs from man's license (as every intentional act undoubtedly does) rests upon a free causality whose character, from early youth on, is expressed in its phenomena (the acts). These acts, by uniformity of conduct, indicate a natural context, but that context does not necessitate the will's ill-nature. It follows, rather, from the voluntary assumption of the evil and immutable principles which make it only more reprehensible and more deserving of punishment."[60]

Kant does not consider that the moral verdict on psychopaths might err. The allegedly free causality is relocated in early childhood—a most fitting shift, by the way, for the genesis of the super-ego. But it is foolish to attest to babies, whose reason is only just forming, the same autonomy that is attached to full-fledged

---

element which balks at that logic: the memory of nonidentity. This is why Kant, who surely did not misconceive the consistency of his critics, protested against them and would rather convict himself of dogmatism than absolutize identity (from whose meaning, as Hegal was quick to recognize, the reference to something nonidentical is inalienable). The construction of thing-in-itself and intelligible character is that of a nonidentity as the premise of possible identification; but it is also the construction of that which eludes identification.

reason. As moral responsibility is backdated from the adult's individual action to the dawn of its prehistory, an immoral pedagogical justice is administered to the under-age, in the name of their being of age. The processes which in the first years of life decide about the formation of ego and super-ego—or, as in the Kantian paradigm, about the failure of this formation—can evidently not be credited with apriority because of their priority in time; nor can we ascribe to their highly empirical content that purity which Kant's doctrine requires of the moral law. In his enthusiasm for the punishment deserved by infantile villains he leaves the intelligible realm only to cause mischief in the empirical one.

INTELLIGIBILITY AND THE UNITY OF CONSCIOUSNESS

Despite the ascetic reticence of Kant's theory, what he was thinking of when he conceived the intelligible character is not beyond conjecture. It was the unity of the person, the equivalent of the epistemological unity of self-consciousness. The backstage expectation of the Kantian system is that the supreme concept of practical philosophy will coincide with the supreme concept of theoretical philosophy: with the ego principle that makes for theoretical unity and tames and integrates the human drives in practice. The unity of the person is the stage of the doctrine of intelligibility. In the architecture of form-content dualism which runs through Kant's thinking, that unity is counted among the forms: in a dialectics that was unintended and remained unexplained until Hegel, the principle of particularization is a universal. In honor of universality, Kant draws a terminological line between personality and the person. He calls personality "the freedom and independence of the mechanism of nature as a whole, but viewed simultaneously as a power of a creature subject to peculiar pure, practical laws given by its own reason. In case of the person as part of the world of the senses, this means a creature subject to its own personality insofar as this belongs to the intelligible world at the same time."[61]

Personality, the subject as pure reason—as the suffix -*ity,* the index of a conceptual universal, signifies—is to subjugate the person, the subject as an empirical, natural, individual creature. What Kant meant by "intelligible character" was probably quite close to "personality" according to an older linguistic usage, where it "belongs to the intelligible world." Factual-psychological contents of consciousness are the premises, not only of the genesis, but of the sheer possibility of the unity of self-consciousness; this unity marks a zone of indifference between pure reason and spatial-temporal experience. That facts of consciousness would not exist without being determined in a single consciousness, not in some other picked at random, was glossed over in Hume's critique of the ego. Kant corrects this, but neglects the reciprocity: in criticizing Hume, he lets personality congeal to a principle beyond the individual persons, to their framework.

He conceives the unity of consciousness to be independent of any experience. There is a measure of such independence with respect to single, changing facts of consciousness, but not a radical independence of the existence of such facts, of there being any factual contents of consciousness whatsoever. Kant's Platonism (in *Phaedo,* the soul was something similar to the idea) is an epistemological echo of the eminently bourgeois affirmation of personal unity in itself, at the expense of its substance—an affirmation which ultimately left the name of personality to no one but the "strong man." The rank of the good is usurped by the formal achievement of integration, but this achievement is a priori anything but formal; it is substantial, the sedimented control of man's inner nature. The suggestion is that—regardless of the dubiety of "being oneself"—the more of a personality one is, the better he must be.

Great eighteenth-century novelists had their suspicions about that. Fielding's Tom Jones, the foundling, an "instinctual character" in the psychological sense, stands for the individual unmaimed by conventions and promptly turns comical. In Ionesco's *Rhinoceros* we heard the latest echo: the only man who demonstrates a strong ego by resisting the bestial standardization is an alcoholic and a failure at his trade; according to life's verdict, his ego is not all that strong. One might ask, despite Kant's example of the radically evil infant, whether an evil intelligible character would have been thinkable for him—whether evil, to him, did not lie in the fact that the formal unity miscarried. Where that unity does not exist at all, Kant would presumably talk no more of either good or evil than among the animals. Most likely, he conceived the intelligible character as a strong ego in rational control of all its impulses, the kind taught in the whole tradition of modern rationalism, notably by Leibniz and Spinoza, who found here, at least, a point they could agree upon.*

Great philosophy is set against the idea of a man not modeled after the reality principle, a man not set in himself. This puts Kant's cogitative strategy at an advantage: the thesis of freedom can be carried through on a course parallel to that of consistent causality. In the Kantian system the unity of the person appears as a formal a priori, but it is not that alone; against Kant's will—but favoring his *demonstrandum*—it is a moment of the subject's every content. Each of an individual's impulses is "his" impulse, just as he as a subject is the totality of these impulses, and thus their qualitative otherness. In the utterly formal region of self-consciousness the line is blurred. What can be predicated of this region, but not discriminated, is that which does not mutually exhaust each other: the factual content and the mediation, its connective principle.

It is in the indifferent concept of "personality" that extreme abstraction helps to vindicate a fact tabooed by traditional logic and its mode of argument but only the more real in dialectics: the fact that in our antagonistic world the individuals are antagonistic in themselves as well, that they are both free and unfree. In the night of indifference a glimmer of light falls on freedom as the noumenal personality, a Protestant kind of inwardness that is removed even from itself. The subject, according to Schiller's apothegm, is justified by what it is, not by what it does—as the Lutheran of yore was justified by faith, not by works. The in-

---

* Concerning the relationship between Kant's doctrine of will and that of Leibniz and Spinoza, cf. Johann Eduard Erdmann, *Geschichte der neueren Philosophie,* Stuttgart 1932, esp. Vol. 4, p. 128ff.

voluntary irrationality of the Kantian intelligible character, the undefinability forced upon it by the system, is a tacit secularization of the explicit theological doctrine of the irrationality of election by grace.

Conserved in progressive enlightenment, of course, this election becomes more and more oppressive. Once Kantian ethics had, so to speak, relegated God to the serving role of a postulate of practical reason—another thing forecast in Leibniz, and even in Descartes—it was difficult to conceive the intelligible character, which irrationally is the way it is, as anything but the same blind fate to which the idea of freedom takes exception. The concept of character has always oscillated between nature and freedom.[62] The more ruthlessly we equate the subject's absolute being-this-way with its subjectivity, the more impenetrable is the concept of that subjectivity. What once upon a time seemed to be election by grace, a divine decree, is scarcely conceivable any more as an election by objective reason—which would have to appeal to subjective reason, after all. Man's pure noumenality, devoid of any empirical substance and sought in nothing but his own rationality, does not permit us to make any rational judgment about why it worked in one case and failed in the next.

The authority, however, to which the intelligible character is tied—pure reason—is itself evolving and thus qualified, not absolutely qualifying. The idea of positing it outside of time as an absolute (an anticipation of the same Fichte with whom Kant was feuding) was far more irrational than the doctrine of Creation had ever been. It made an essential contribution to the alliance between the idea of freedom and real unfreedom. Irreducibly existent, the intelligible character is a conceptual duplication of that second nature in which society casts the characters of all its members anyway. Translated into judgments about real people, Kantian ethics knows but one criterion: how a man happens to be, so is his unfreedom. The primary intent of Schiller's apothegm surely was to manifest the disgust evoked by the subjection of all human circumstances to the barter principle, the evaluation of one act by comparison with another. Kant's moral philosophy announces the same motif in contrasting dignity with price. Yet in society as it ought to be, barter would be not only abolished but fulfilled: no man would be shortchanged about the yield of his labor.

There is no way to weigh an isolated action, and neither is there a good that is not externalized in action. An absolute state of mind, devoid of all specific interventions, would be bound to deteriorate to absolute indifference, to inhumanity. Objectively, Kant and Schiller both are preluding the odious concept of a freely suspended nobility which self-appointed elites can later attest to themselves at will, as their own quality. Lurking in Kantian ethics is a tendency to sabotage it. In that ethics, the totality of man comes to be indistinguishable from preestablished election. There is something sinister about the end of casuistic inquiry into the right and wrong of an action: it marks a transfer of jurisdiction to the compulsions of empirical society, which the Kantian ἀγαθόν sought to transcend. The categories "noble" and "mean," like all categories of the bourgeois doctrine of freedom, are intertwined with conditions of family and nature. Their natural origin breaks through once more, in late bourgeois society, as biologism and eventually as racism.

Under existing circumstances, the reconcilement of morality and nature as envisioned by Schiller (against Kant, and secretly in accord with him) is not so thoroughly humane and innocent as the philosophizing poet knew it to be. Nature, once equipped with meaning, substitutes itself for the possibility that was the aim of the intelligible character's construction. In Goethe's *kalokagathia* the ultimately murderous turnabout is unmistakable. We have a letter written by Kant about a portrait of himself, by a Jewish painter; in this letter he was already resorting to a maliciously anti-Semitic thesis later popularized by a Nazi, Paul Schultze-Naumburg.*

---

* "Heartfelt thanks, my most highly esteemed and beloved friend, for the disclosure of your kind sentiments toward me—duly received, along with your beautiful gift, on the day after my birthday! The portrait that was done, without my consent, by Herr Loewe, a Jewish painter, is indeed said by my friends to bear some degree of resemblance to me; but a connoisseur of paintings said at the first glance: A Jew will always paint another Jew, by tracing the nose as

Freedom is really delimited by society, not only from outside but in itself. We no sooner put it to use than we increase our unfreedom; the deputy of better things is always also an accomplice of worse ones. Even where men are most likely to feel free from society, in the strength of their ego, they are society's agents at the same time. The ego principle is implanted in them by society, and society rewards that principle although it curbs it. Kant's ethics was not yet aware of this dilemma, or else he was passing it by.

TRUTH CONTENT OF THE DOCTRINE OF INTELLIGIBILITY

If one dared to accord its true substance to the Kantian X of the intelligible character, the substance that will stand up against the total indeterminacy of the aporetical concept, it would probably be the historically most advanced, pointlike, flaring, swiftly extinguished consciousness inhabited by the impulse to do right. It is the concrete, intermittent anticipation of the possibility, neither alien to mankind nor identical with it. Men are not only the substrates of psychology. For they are not exhausted by the objectified control of nature which they reprojected—projected back upon themselves, from outward nature. They are things in themselves insofar as things are no more than they have made. To this extent, the world of phenomena is truly a semblance.

Hence the pure will of Kant's *Foundation* is not so very different from the intelligible character. There is a verse by Karl Kraus ("What has the world made of us") in which that will is pensively pondered; it is falsified by anyone who believes it to be in his possession. Negatively, it breaks through in the subject's painful perception that in their reality, in what became of them, all men are mutilated. What would be different, the unperverted essence, is withheld from a language that bears the stigmata of existence—there was a time when theologians would speak of the

he does— But enough of that." (From: *Kant's Briefwechsel*, vol. II, 1789–1794, Berlin 1900, p. 33.)

"mystical name." But the separation of the intelligible character from the empirical one is experienced in the eons-old block that shuts us off from the pure will, from the addendum: external considerations of every conceivable sort; manifold subaltern, irrational concerns of the subjects in a false society—in general, the principle of particular private interest, which in society as it is prescribes his action to every individual, bar none, and which is the death of all.

Inwardly, the block is extended in tendencies of obtuse egotism, and then in the neuroses. These, as we know, absorb an immense quantity of available human strength; acting on the line of least resistance and with the cunning of the unconscious, they prevent that right action which inevitably runs counter to hidebound self-preservation. And the neuroses have so much easier a time of it, are so much easier to rationalize, as the self-preserving principle in a state of freedom would be just as entitled to its due than would the interests of others, which it a priori interferes with. Neuroses are pillars of society; they thwart the better potential of men, and thus the objectively better condition which men might bring about. There are instincts spurring men beyond the false condition; but the neuroses tend to dam up those instincts, to push them back toward narcissistic self-gratification in the false condition. Weakness that will mistake itself for strength, if possible, is a hinge in the machinery of evil.

In the end, the intelligible character would be the paralyzed rational will. The part of it that is considered higher, on the other hand, the part deemed more sublime, unmarred by meanness, is essentially its own inadequacy, its inability to change the causes of its humiliation; it is denial stylized as an end in itself. And yet, among men there is nothing better than that character—the possibility to be another than one is, even though all are locked up in their selves and thus locked away even from their selves. The striking defeat in Kant's doctrine, the elusive, abstract side of the intelligible character, has a touch of the truth of the anti-image ban which post-Kantian philosophers—including Marx—extended to all concepts of positivity.

Like freedom, the intelligible character as a subjective possibility is a thing that comes to be, not a thing that is. It would be a betrayal to incorporate it in existence by description, even by the most cautious description. In the right condition, as in the Jewish *theologoumenon,* all things would differ only a little from the way they are; but not even the least can be conceived now as it would be then. Despite this, we cannot discuss the intelligible character as hovering abstractly, impotently above things in being; we can talk of it only insofar as it keeps arising in reality, in the guilty context of things as they are, brought about by that context. The contradiction of freedom and determinism is not, as Kant's understanding of his *Critiques* would have it, a contradiction between two theoretical positions, dogmatism and skepticism; it is a contradiction in the subjects' way to experience themselves, as now free, now unfree. Under the aspect of freedom, they are unidentical with themselves because the subject is not a subject yet—and its not yet being a subject is due precisely to its instauration as a subject. The self is what is inhuman.

Freedom and intelligible character are akin to identity and nonidentity, but we cannot clearly and distinctly enter them on one side or the other. The subjects are free, after the Kantian model, in so far as they are aware of and identical with themselves; and then again, they are unfree in such identity in so far as they are subjected to, and will perpetuate, its compulsion. They are unfree as diffuse, nonidentical nature; and yet, as that nature they are free because their overpowering impulse—the subject's nonidentity with itself is nothing else—will also rid them of identity's coercive character. Personality is the caricature of freedom. The basis of the aporia is that truth beyond compulsory identity would not be the downright otherness of that compulsion; rather, it would be conveyed by the compulsion. In the socialized society, no individual is capable of the morality that is a social demand but would be a reality only in a free society. The only social morality that remains would be at last to finish off the bad infinity, the vicious system of compensatory barter. But the individual is left with no more than the morality for which Kantian ethics—which accords affection, not respect, to animals[63]—can muster only disdain: to try to live so that one may believe himself to have been a good animal.

TWO

WORLD SPIRIT AND NATURAL HISTORY

An Excursion to Hegel

TREND AND FACTS

Most sensitively resisted by human "common sense," by the sound mind whose soundness is what ails it, is the preponderance of anything objective over the individuals, in their consciousness as well as in their coexistence. The preponderance can be experienced crassly day after day. One represses it as an unfounded speculation, so the individuals may continue to flatter themselves that their standardized notions are twice unconditional truths—so their delusions may be preserved from the suspicion of not being so and of their lives being doomed. Ours is an epoch that has been as relieved to shed the system of objective idealism as to discard the economic doctrine of objective values; and the theorems that are particularly topical in such an epoch are the ones said to be of no use to a spirit that seeks its own security and the security of cognition in the extant, in social institutions as the well-organized sums of immediate individual facts, or in the subjective character of their members.

The objective and ultimately absolute Hegelian spirit; the Marxist law of value that comes into force without men being conscious of it—to an unleashed experience these are more evident than the prepared facts of a positivistic scientific bustle which today extends to the native prescientific consciousness. Only, to the greater glory of objective cognition, that activity breaks men of the habit of experiencing the real objectivity to which they are subjected in themselves as well. If thinking people were capable of such experience and prepared for it, it would have to undermine their belief in facticity itself; it would have to make them go so far beyond the facts that the facts would lose their unreflected primacy over the universals which triumphant nominalism holds for nothing, for a subtractable adjunct tacked on by the classifying scientist.

There is a line in the initial deliberations of Hegel's *Logic*, to the effect that nothing in the world is not as mediated as it is immediate—and nowhere does this line endure more precisely than in the facts of which historiography is so proud. Of course, when the Gestapo knocks on a dissenter's door at six A.M. under Hitlerite fascism, it would be foolish to use epistemological refinements to deny that the individual to whom this happens is more directly affected than by the preceding power plays and by the installation of the party machine in every branch of administration, let alone by the historical trend that shattered the continuity of the Weimar Republic and does not show in any context other than in a conceptual one, and not compulsorily except in theoretical unfoldment. And yet, the brute fact of the governmental onslaught which fascism looses on the individual does depend on all those moments, however remote and currently irrelevant they may be to the victim.

It would take the most wretched nitpicking garbed as scientific acribia to blind us to the fact that the French Revolution, for all the abrupt concurrence of some of its acts, fitted into the overall course of bourgeois emancipation. That revolution would have been neither possible nor successful if in 1789 the key positions of economic production had not been already occupied by the bourgeoisie, if it had not already topped the absolutist crest of a feudalism that coalesced at times with the bourgeois interest. Nietzsche's scandalizing imperative. "What's falling ought to be pushed," serves ex post facto to codify an arch-bourgeois maxim. Probably all bourgeois revolutions were decided in advance by the historic upsurge of the respective class; an admixture of ostentation was then externalized in art, as classicistic decor. Even so, at the point of historic fracture, that trait would have scarcely been realized without the acute absolutist mismanagement and the financial crisis on which the physiocratic reformers foundered under Louis XVI. The specific privations of the masses of Paris, at least, presumably set off the movement, while in other countries, where the need was not so acute, the bourgeois emancipation process succeeded without a revolution and left the more or less absolutist form of government initially untouched.

One advantage of the infantile distinction of deeper cause and outward occasion is that it crudely registers the dualism of immediacy and mediation. The occasions are immediate; the so-called deeper causes are what mediates, what encompasses, what incorporates the details. As late as the most recent past, the preponderance of the trend could be read in the facts themselves. Specifically military acts such as the bombing raids on German cities functioned as slum clearing, retroactively integrated with that urban transformation which has long been observable around the globe, not in North America alone. Or: the strengthening of the family in the emergency situations of refugee life did temporarily slow down the tendency to anti-family developments, but it hardly stopped the trend; in Germany too, the number of divorces and that of incomplete families kept increasing. Even the Spanish conquests of old Mexico and Peru, which have been felt there like invasions from another planet—even those, irrationally for the Aztecs and Incas, rendered bloody assistance to the spread of bourgeois rational society, all the way to the conception of "one world" that is teleologically inherent in that society's principle.

The trend can never do without the facts, but ultimately such preponderance of it within the facts makes the oldfashioned line between cause and occasion look silly. The whole distinction, not just the occasion, is external because the concrete cause lies in the occasion. If courtly mismanagement was a lever of the uprisings in parts, even that mismanagement remained a function of the total picture of the absolutist "outgo" economy's lag behind the capitalist income economy. Moments which, as in the French Revolution, run counter to the historical entirety while doing only so much more to promote it—such moments derive their potency from that historical entirety alone. Even the lagging productive forces of one class lag only relatively, not absolutely, behind the advanced forces of the other class. One has to know all that to construe a philosophy of history, and it is for this reason as much as for any other that—visibly in the cases of Hegel and Marx already—the philosophy of history comes as close to historiography as historiography itself, the insight into the essence veiled by the facticity it qualifies, has come to be impossible save as philosophy.

CONSTRUCTION OF THE WORLD SPIRIT

Dialectics is not a variant of weltanschauung under this aspect either. It is not a philosophical position to be picked out from others on a sample chart. As the critique of the allegedly first philosophical concepts is a spur to dialectics, dialectics is a challenge from below. Experience alone, forcibly tailored to an obtuse concept of itself, excludes the emphatic concept as an independent even though mediated moment. If it is possible to argue against Hegel that absolute idealism defies what is, and that it thus recoils into the very positivism it was attacking as a philosophy of reflection, the dialectics due today would be the reverse: not just an indictment of the reigning consciousness, but the match of that consciousness. It would be a positivism which has been brought to itself—and which, of course, is thus negating itself.

The philosophical call for immersion in detail, a demand not to be steered by any philosophy from above or by any intentions infiltrated into it, was Hegel's one side already. Only, in his case the execution caught in a tautology: as by prearrangement, his kind of immersion in detail brings forth that spirit which from the outset was posited as total and absolute. Opposing this tautology was Benjamin's intent—developed by the metaphysicist in the preface to *Origins of German Tragedy*—to save inductive reasoning. When Benjamin writes that the smallest cell of visualized reality outweighs the rest of the world, this line already attests to the self-consciousness of our present state of experience, and it does so with particular authenticity because it was shaped outside the domain of the so-called "great philosophical issues" which a changed concept of dialectics calls upon us to distrust.

The primacy of totality over phenomenality is to be grasped in phenomenality, which is ruled by what tradition takes for the world spirit; it is not to be taken over as divine from this tradition which is Platonic in the broadest sense. The world spirit is; but it is not a spirit. It is the very negativity, rather, which Hegel shifted from the spirit's shoulders upon the shoulders of the ones who must obey it, the ones whose defeat doubles the verdict that the difference between them and objectivity is what is untrue and evil. The world spirit becomes independent vis-à-vis the individual acts from which so-called spiritual evolutions too are synthesized, as is the real total movement of society; and it becomes independent vis-à-vis the living subjects of those acts. It is over men's heads and through their heads, and thus antagonistic from the outset. The reflexive concept "world spirit" is disinterested in the living, although the whole whose primacy it expresses needs the living as much as they need it to exist.

It was such a hypostasis that was meant in a stoutly nominalistic sense by the Marxist term "mystified." Yet a dismantled mystification would not be pure ideology according to that theory either; it is equally a distorted sense of the real predominance of the whole. In thought, it appropriates the opaque and irresistible predominance of the universal, the perpetuated myth. Even philosophical hypostasis has its empirical content in the heteronomous conditions in which human conditions faded from sight. What is irrational in the concept of the world spirit was borrowed from the irrationality of the world's course, and yet it remains a fetishistic spirit. To this day history lacks any total subject, however construable. Its substrate is the functional connection of real individual subjects: "History does nothing, does not 'possess vast wealth,' does not 'fight battles'! It is man, rather, the real, living man who does all that, who does possess and fight; it is not 'history' that uses man as a means to pursue its ends, as if it were a person apart. History is nothing but the activity of man pursuing his ends."[1]

But history is equipped with those qualities because society's law of motion has for thousands of years been abstracting from its individual subjects, degrading them to mere executors, mere partners in social wealth and social struggle. The debasement was as real as the fact that on the other hand there would be nothing without individuals and their spontaneities. Marx stressed this antinominalist aspect time and again, though without admitting its philosophical consistency. "Only insofar as he is capital personified does the capitalist have historic value and that historical right to exist. . . . Only as a personification of capital is the capitalist respectable. As such a personification he shares the absolute enrichment drive with the hoarder of treasure. But what appears in the hoarder as an individual mania is in the capitalist an effect of the social mechanism, in which he is but a cog. Besides, the development of capitalist production necessitates a continuous increase of the capital invested in an industrial enterprise, and competition imposes on each individual capitalist the immanent laws of the capitalist mode of production as external coercive laws. It forces him to keep extending his capital in order to preserve it, and he can extend it only by means of progressive accumulation."[2]

"HARMONIZING WITH THE WORLD SPIRIT"

In the concept of the world spirit, the principle of divine omnipotence was secularized into the principle that posits unity, and the world plan was secularized into the relentlessness of what happens. The world spirit is worshipped like the deity, a deity divested of its personality and of all its attributes of providence and grace. It is the execution of a bit of enlightenment dialectics: the disenchanted and conserved spirit takes the form of a myth, or else it reverts to a shudder at something which is overpowering and at the same time devoid of qualities. Such is the essence of the feeling to be touched by the world spirit or to hear its murmur. It becomes a bondage to fate. Like the immanence of fate, the world spirit drips with suffering and fallibility. As total immanence is blown up into essentiality, the negativity of the world spirit becomes an accidental trifle.

Yet to experience the world spirit as a whole means to experience its negativity. This was the point of Schopenhauer's critique of the official optimism—a critique which remained as obsessive, however, as the Hegelian theodicy of "this world." That mankind lives only in total concatenation, that it may have survived only thanks to that concatenation, this did not refute

Schopenhauer's doubts whether to affirm the will to live. But upon that with which the world spirit harmonized there did at times fall the reflection of a fortune far beyond individual misfortune—in the relation between individual mental gifts and the state of history, for instance. If the individual mind is not, as it would please the vulgar separation of individual and universal, "influenced" by the universal, if it is selfmediated by objectivity, the objectivity is not always bound to be hostile to the subject; the constellation changes in the dynamics of history. In phases marked by a darkening of the world spirit, of the totality, even major talents cannot become what they are; in auspicious phases, as in the period during and directly after the French Revolution, mediocrities were lifted high above themselves. If man is in harmony with the world spirit precisely because he is ahead of his time, his very ruin as an individual is sometimes linked with a sense of not being in vain. Irresistible in the young Beethoven's music is the expression of the possibility that all might be well. However frail, the reconcilement with objectivity transcends the invariable. The instants in which a particular frees itself without in turn, by its own particularity, confining others—these instants are anticipations of the unconfined, and such solace radiates from the earlier bourgeoisie until its late period.

THE UNLEASHING OF PRODUCTIVE FORCES

Periods of harmony with the world spirit, of a happiness more substantial than the individual's, tend to be associated with the unleashing of productive forces, while the burden of the world spirit threatens to crush men as soon as their forces and the social forms they exist under come into flagrant conflict. Even this schema is too simple, however, and the talk of the rising bourgeoisie too shallow. Unfoldment and unleashing of productive forces are not antitheses in the sense of having to be assigned changing phases; rather, they are truly dialectical. The unleashing of productive forces, an act of the spirit that controls nature, has an affinity to the violent domination of nature. Temporarily that domination may recede, but the concept of productive force is not thinkable without it, and even less is that of an unleashed productive force. The very word "unleashed" has undertones of menace.

There is a passage in *Das Kapital:* "As a fanatic of value utilization, the exchange value ruthlessly compels mankind to produce for production's sake."[3] On the spot this strikes the fetish which the barter society makes of the production process; beyond that, however, it violates the presently universal taboo against doubting production as an end in itself. There are times when the technological productive forces, while scarcely impeded socially, work in fixed productive conditions without exerting much influence on those conditions. The unleashing of forces no sooner parts with the sustaining human relations than it comes to be as fetishized as the orders. Unleashing, too, is but an element of dialectics, not its magic formula.

In such phases the world spirit, the totality of the particular, may pass into that which it buries. Unless all signs deceive us, this is the signature of the present epoch. In periods when the living need the progress of productive forces, on the other hand, or are at least not visibly imperiled by those forces—in such periods the feeling of concordance with the world spirit will probably come to prevail, albeit with the apprehensive undercurrent that it is an armistice, and although the pressure of business will tempt the subjective spirit to defect overzealously to the objective one, like Hegel. In all of this, the subjective spirit also remains a historical category, a thing that has evolved, a changing, virtually transient thing. The still unindividuated tribal spirit of primitive societies, pressed by the civilized ones to reproduce itself in them, is planned and released by postindividual collectivism; the objective spirit is overpowering, then, as well as a barefaced swindle.

GROUP SPIRIT AND DOMINATION

If philosophy were what it was proclaimed to be in Hegel's *Phenomenology*—the science of the experience of consciousness—it could not, as Hegel does more and more, blithely dismiss the individual experience of the prevailing universal as an unreconciled evil and lend itself to the role of defending power from an allegedly higher vantage point. It is embarrassing to remember how inferiority prevails in committees, for instance, even if there is subjectively good will on the members' part; and this memory makes the preponderance of the universal evident as a disgrace not to be compensated for by citing the world spirit. The group's opinion dominates by way of adjustment to the majority of the group, or to its most influential members; more often yet, it dominates due to opinions that reign outside the group, in a more encompassing group, notably in one approved by the committee members. In the participants, the objective spirit of the class goes far beyond their individual intelligence. Their voice echoes that spirit even though they themselves—who may be defenders of freedom—feel nothing of it; intrigue plays a part only at critical points, as manifested criminality. The committee is a microcosm of the group of its members and eventually of their totality; this shapes the decisions in advance.

Such observations, which can be made everywhere, bear an ironic resemblance to those of formal sociology in Simmel's style. But their substance does not lie in socialization pure and simple, in empty categories such as that of the group. Instead—which formal sociology dislikes reflecting upon, in line with its definition—they are impressions of a social content; their invariance is a pure memento of how little the power of the universal has changed in history, how very much it always remains prehistoric. The formal group spirit is a reflective movement on material dominance. Formal sociology gets its right to exist from the formalization of social mechanisms, the equivalent of the dominance that progresses through the *ratio*. In agreement with this is the fact that the decisions of those committees, however substantial they may be in essence, are in most cases made from manifestly formal legal points of view. Compared with the class relationship, formalization is not more neutral. It is reproduced by abstraction, by the logical hierarchy of the stages of universality—and that the more bluntly, the more conditions of rule are made to disguise themselves as democratic procedures.

THE LEGAL SPHERE

And indeed, it was in the philosophy of law that Hegel, following *Phenemenology* and *Logic,* carried the cult of the world's course to extremes. In large measure, the law is the medium in which evil wins out on account of its objectivity and acquires the appearance of good. Positively it does protect the reproduction of life; but in its extant forms its destructiveness shows undiminished, thanks to the destructive principle of violence. While a lawless society will succumb to pure license, as it did in the Third Reich, the law in society is a preservative of terror, always ready to resort to terror with the aid of quotable statutes. Hegel furnished the ideology of positive law because in a society that was already visibly antagonistic the need for that ideology was most pressing.

Law is the primal phenomenon of irrational rationality. In law the formal principle of equivalence becomes the norm; everyone is treated alike. An equality in which differences perish secretly serves to promote inequality; it becomes the myth that survives amidst an only seemingly demythologized mankind. For the sake of an unbroken systematic, the legal norms cut short what is not covered, every specific experience that has not been shaped in advance; and then they raise the instrumental rationality to the rank of a second reality *sui generis.* The total legal realm is one of definitions. Its systematic forbids the admission of anything that eludes their closed circle, of anything *quod non est in actis.* These bounds, ideological in themselves, turn into real violence as they are sanctioned by law as the socially controlling authority, in the administered world in particular. In the dictatorships they become direct violence; indirectly, violence has always lurked behind them.

That the individual is so apt to find himself in the wrong when the antagonism of interests drives him into the legal sphere—this is not, as Hegel would persuade him, his own fault because he is too benighted to recognize his own interest in the objective legal norm and its guarantors. It is the fault of constituents of the legal sphere itself. Objectively true, however, remains the description which Hegel drafts as one of a supposedly subjective bias: "That the right and morality, and the real world of that which is right and moral, comprehend themselves in thought; that by means of thought they give themselves the forms of rationality—to wit, universality and distinctness—this, the law, is what that feeling which reserves its own discretion, that conscience which makes the right a matter of subjective conviction, will with good reason consider most hostile to itself. The form of the right as of a duty and a law strikes it as a dead, cold letter and a shackle; for it does not recognize itself in it, hence does not recognize itself as free, because the law is reason in the matter, and reason does not permit a feeling to warm itself by its own particularity."[4]

That the subjective conscience will "with good reason" consider objective morality most hostile to itself—this word of Hegel's looks like a philosophical slip of the pen. He is blurting out what he denies in the same breath. If the individual conscience actually regarded "the real world of that which is right and moral" as hostile because it does not recognize itself in it, no avowal would serve to gloss this over; for it is the point of Hegelian dialectics that conscience cannot act differently, that it cannot recognize itself in that real moral world. Hegel is thus conceding that the reconcilement whose demonstration makes out his philosophy did not take place. If the legal order were not objectively alien and extraneous to the subject, the antagonism that is inescapable for Hegel might be placated by better insight; but Hegel had far too thoroughly experienced its implacability to put his trust in that chance. Hence the paradoxon of his teaching and at the same time disavowing the reconcilement of conscience and the legal norm.

LAW AND EQUITY

Every positive, substantially elaborated doctrine of natural law leads to antinomies, and yet it is the idea of natural law which critically maintains the untruth of positive law. Today it is the reified consciousness that has been retranslated into reality and there augments domination. Even in its pure form, previous to class content and class justice, that consciousness expresses domination, the gaping difference between individual interests and the whole that is their abstract aggregate. From the outset, by subsumption of everything individual under the category, the system of selfmade concepts that serve a mature jurisprudence to cover up the living process of society is opting in favor of the order imitated by the system of classification. Aristotle's imperishable glory is to have proclaimed this, against the abstract legal norm, in his doctrine of εἰκότης, of equity.

The more consistently the legal systems are worked out, however, the greater their incapacity to absorb what essentially defies absorption. As a rule, the claim of equity—meant to be a corrective for the injustice in law—can be knocked down by the rational legal system as favoritism, as inequitable privilege. The tendency to do so is universal, of one mind with the economic process that reduces individual interests to the common denominator of a totality which remains negative because its constitutive abstraction removes it from those interests, for all its being composed of them at the same time. The universality that reproduces the preservation of life simultaneously imperils it in more and more menacing stages. The power of the self-realizing universal is not, as Hegel thought, identical with the nature of the individuals in themselves; it is always also contrary to that nature. The individuals are not only character masks, agents of value in a supposedly separate economic sphere. Even where they think they have escaped the primacy of economics—all the way into their psychology, the *maison tolérée* of uncomprehended individuality—they react under the compulsion of the universal. The more identical they are with it, the more unidentical with it are they as its helplessly obedient servants.

Expressed in the individuals themselves is the fact that the whole, the individuals included, maintains itself only through antagonism. There are innumerable times when unavoidable motives of self-preservation force people, even conscious people capable of criticizing the whole, to do things and to take attitudes which blindly help maintain the universal even though their consciousness is opposed to it. It is only because, to survive, they have to make an alien cause their own that there arises that appearance of reconcilement—an appearance which Hegelian philosophy, incorruptible in its recognition of the predominance of the universal, corruptibly transfigures into an idea. What shines as though it were above antagonisms is as one with the universal entanglement. The universal makes sure that the particular under its domination is not better than itself. That is the core of all the identity brought about to this day.

INDIVIDUALISTIC VEIL

A candid look at the predominance of the universal does all but unbearable psychological harm to the narcissism of all individuals and to that of a democratically organized society. To see through selfhood as nonexistent, as an illusion, would easily turn all men's objective despair into a subjective one. It would rob them of the faith implanted in them by individualistic society: that they, the individuals, are the substance. For the functionally determined individual interest to find any kind of satisfaction under existing forms, it must become primary in its own eyes; the individual must confuse that which to him is immediate with the πρώτη οὐσία. Such subjective illusions are objectively caused: it is only through the principle of individual self-preservation, for all its narrowmindedness, that the whole will function. It makes every individual look solely upon himself and impairs his insight into objectivity; objectively, therefore, it works only so much more evil. The nominalistic consciousness reflects a whole that continues by virtue of obdurate particularity. Literally it is ideology; socially, it is a necessary semblance.

The general principle is that of isolation. To the isolated, isolation seems an indubitable certainty; they are bewitched, on pain of losing their existence, not to perceive how mediated their isolation is. Hence the widespread popularity of philosophical nominalism. Each individual existence is to take precedence over its concept; the spirit, the consciousness of individuals, is to reside in individuals only and not to be just as much the supraindividual element synthesized in them, the element by which alone they are thinking. Stubbornly the monads balk at their real dependence as a species as well as at the collective aspect of all forms and contents of their consciousness—of the forms, although they are that universal which nominalism denies, and of the contents, though the individual has no experience, nor any so-called empirical material, that the universal has not predigested and supplied.

DYNAMICS OF UNIVERSAL AND PARTICULAR

Compared with epistemological reflection on the universal in individual consciousness, that consciousness is right in its refusal to be consoled about evil, sin, and death by references to the universal. What recalls this in Hegel is a doctrine that seems paradoxical in view of that of universal mediation, but is in fact magnificently paired with it: the doctrine of universally self-restored immediacy. But the nominalism that spread as a prescientific consciousness and is today, from that standpoint, once again commanding science, the nominalism that makes a profession of its naïveté (the positivistic tool kit does not fail to include pride in being naïve, a pride echoed by the category of the "everyday language")—this nominalism does not bother with the historic coefficient in the relationship of universal and particular.

A true preponderance of the particular would not be attainable except by changing the universal. Installing it as purely and simply extant is a complementary ideology. It hides how much of the particular has come to be a function of the universal—something which in its logical form it has always been. What nominalism clings to as its most assured possession is utopian; hence its hatred of utopian thinking, the thinking that conceives the difference from what exists. The bustle in the sciences would make believe that the objective spirit established by extremely real ruling mechanisms, the spirit which meanwhile is planning contents of consciousness for its reserve army too, is merely the sum of that army's subjective reactions. Yet those reactions have long been no more than afterbirths of a universal which solicitously fêtes men so as better to hide behind them, so as better to keep them in leash.

It is the world spirit itself that has switched on the subjectivistically obdurate conception of science, the conception which aims at an autarkic, empirically rationalistic system of science instead of comprehending a society that is objective in itself and dictated from above. The rebellion against the thing in itself, once critically enlightening, has turned into sabotage of cognition, although even the most crippled scientific concept formation shows surviving traces of the no less crippled thing. Kant's refusal in the amphiboly chapter to know the interior of things is the *ultima ratio* of the Baconian platform. The historic index of its truth was the revolt against scholastical dogmatics. Yet the motif capsizes where that which it bars to cognition is cognition's epistemological and real premise—where the knowing subject must reflect on itself as a moment of the universal that is to be known, without being quite like that universal.

It is absurd to prevent the subject's internal cognition of the very thing it dwells in, of the thing in which it has far too much of its own interior. In this respect Hegelian idealism was more realistic than Kant. When scientific concept formation comes to conflict as much within its ideal of facticity as with the ideal of plain reason, when it sets itself up as reason's antispeculative executor, its machinery has become unreason. Autocratically, method takes the place of what it ought to make known. The positivistic cognitive ideal of inwardly unanimous, noncontradictory, logically unimpeachable models is untenable due to the contradiction immanent in what is to become known—due to the antagonisms of the object. They are the antagonisms of the universal and particular in society, and the method denies them in advance of any content.

SPIRIT AS A SOCIAL TOTALITY

To experience that objectivity, which ranks ahead of the individual and his consciousness, is to experience the unity of a totally socialized society. Its closest kin in the sense of tolerating nothing outside it is the philosophical ideal of absolute identity. However fraudulently the promotion of unity to a philosophy may have exalted it at the expense of plurality, its supremacy, though not the *summum bonum* a victorious philosophical tradition since the Eleatics took it for, is an *ens realissimum*. It really has a touch of the transcendence which the philosophers praise in the idea of unity. While the unfolded bourgeois society—and the very earliest

unitarian thinking was already urban, rudimentarily bourgeois—
was made up of countless individual spontaneities of self-preserving individuals dependent on each other for self-preservation,
unity and the individuals were by no means in the balance claimed
for them by justifying theorems.

The nonidentity of unity and plurality does, however, have the
form that the One takes precedence as the identity of the system
which leaves nothing at large. Without individual spontaneities
unity would not have come into being, and as their synthesis it
was secondary; nominalism was a reminder of this. Yet as unity,
whether through the needs of the self-preservation of many or
merely due to irrational states of dominion abused as a pretext by
the many, came to be more and more tightly woven, all individuals
were caught up in unity on pain of destruction; they were "integrated" in it, to use Spencer's term, absorbed in its legality even
against their own better insight into their individual interest.
Gradually, then, this ended the progressive differentiation of which
Spencer could still dream that it necessarily accompanies integration. While the One and Whole takes shape in unchanged fashion,
solely due to the particularities it covers, it is taking shape in
ruthless disregard of those particularities.

What is realized by means of individuality and plurality is the
cause of the many, and again it is not their cause: they have less
and less control over it. Their totality is their otherness at the
same time; this is the dialectic carefully ignored by the Hegelian
one. Insofar as the individuals are at all aware of taking a back
seat to unity, its priority reflects to them the being-in-itself of the
universal which they encounter in fact: it is inflicted upon them,
all the way into their inmost core, even when they inflict it on
themselves. The line $\mathring{\eta}\theta o\varsigma$ $\mathring{\alpha}\nu\theta\rho\acute{\omega}\pi\omega$ $\delta\alpha\acute{\iota}\mu\omega\nu$—that the character of
men, as such always moulded by the universal, is their fate—has
more truth to it than the truth of a characterological determinism.
The universal by which every individual is determined at all, as
one of his particular kind, that universal is borrowed from what
is extraneous and therefore as heteronomous to the individual as
anything once said to have been ordained for him by demons.

The ideology of the idea's being-in-itself is so powerful because it is the truth, but it is the negative truth; what makes it

ideology is its affirmative reversal. Once men have learned about the preponderance of the universal, it is all but inescapable for them to transfigure it into a spirit, as the higher being which they must propitiate. Coercion acquires meaning for them. And not without all reason: for the abstract universal of the whole, which applies the coercion, is akin to the universality of thought, the spirit. And this in turn permits the spirit, in its carrier, to be reprojected on that universality as if it were realized therein, as if it had its own reality for itself. In the spirit, the unanimity of the universal has become a subject, and in society universality is maintained only through the medium of the spirit, through the abstracting operation which it performs in complete reality. Both acts converge in barter, in something subjectively thought and at the same time objectively valid, in which the objectivity of the universal and the concrete definition of the individual subjects oppose each other, unreconciled, precisely by coming to be commensurable.

In the name "world spirit" the spirit is affirmed and hypostatized only as that which it always was in itself. Durkheim (who was charged with metaphysics for that reason) recognized that what society worships in the world spirit is itself, the omnipotence of its own coercion. Society may find itself confirmed by the world spirit, because it actually has all the attributes which it proceeds, then, to worship in the spirit. The mythical adoration of the spirit is not pure conceptual mythology: it is the tender of thanks for the fact that in history's more highly developed phases all individuals have been living only by means of that social unit which the individuals did not exhaust, and whose prolongation takes them only closer to their doom. If today, without noticing it, they are literally granted their existence subject to annulment by the great monopolies and powers, this brings out only what has always been teleologically inherent in the emphatic concept of society. Ideology hypostatizes the world spirit because potentially it was already hypostatized. The cult of its categories, however— of the utterly formal ones of greatness, for example, which even Nietzsche accepted—this cult reinforces only the consciousness of the spirit's difference from everything individual, as if it were an ontological difference; it thus reinforces antagonism and the foreseeable calamity.

HISTORICAL REASON ANTAGONISTIC

It is not only now that compared with potential reason, with the total interest of the associating individual subjects it differs from, the reason of the world spirit is unreason. Like all his disciples, Hegel has been chided for equating logical categories with social ones and some from the philosophy of history; this was chalked up as a μετάβασις εἰς ἄλλο γένος, as that point of speculative idealism which had to break off in the face of the unconstruability of experience. Yet this very construction was doing justice to reality. The tit for tat of history as well as the totality-bound principle of equivalence in the social relation between individual subjects, both proceed according to the logicity which Hegel is said merely to interpret into them—except that this logicity, the primacy of the universal in the dialectic of universal and particular, is an *index falsi.* That identity exists no more than do freedom, individuality, and whatever Hegel identifies with the universal. The totality of the universal expresses its own failure.

What tolerates nothing particular is thus revealing itself as particularly dominant. The general reason that comes to prevail is already a restricted reason. It is not just unity within diversity, but as an attitude to reality it is imposed, a unity over something —and thus, as a matter of pure form, it is antagonistic in itself. Unity is division. The irrationality of the particularly realized *ratio* within the social totality is not extraneous to the *ratio,* not solely due to its application. Rather, it is immanent to it. Measured by complete reason, the prevailing one unveils itself as being polarized and thus irrational even in itself, according to its principle. Enlightenment is truly subject to dialectics: there is a dialectic taking place in its own concept.

Ratio is no more to be hypostatized than any other category. The transfer of the self-preserving interest from individuals to the species is spiritually coagulated with the form of the *ratio,* a form that is general and antagonistic at the same time. The transfer obeys a logic which the major bourgeois philosophy reproduced at such historic corners as Hobbes and Kant: without ceding the self-preserving interest to the species—in bourgeois thinking represented mostly by the state—the individual would be unable to preserve himself in more highly developed social conditions. This transfer is necessary for the individuals; all but inevitably, however, it puts the general rationality at odds with the particular human beings whom it must negate to become general, and whom it pretends—and not only pretends—to serve. The universality of the *ratio* ratifies the needfulness of everything particular, its dependency upon the whole, and what unfolds in that universality, due to the process of abstraction on which it rests, is its contradiction to the particular. All-governing reason, in installing itself above something else, necessarily constricts itself.

The principle of absolute identity is self-contradictory. It perpetuates nonidentity in suppressed and damaged form. A trace of this entered into Hegel's effort to have nonidentity absorbed by the philosophy of identity, indeed to define identity by nonidentity. Yet Hegel is distorting the state of facts by affirming identity, admitting nonidentity as a negative—albeit a necessary one—and misconceiving the negativity of the universal. He lacks sympathy with the utopian particular that has been buried underneath the universal—with that nonidentity which would not come into being until realized reason has left the particular reason of the universal behind. The sense of the wrong implied by the concept of the universal, a sense which Hegel chides, would deserve his respect because of the universality of wrong itself. When Franz von Sickingen, a condottiere at the outset of the modern age, lay mortally wounded and found the words "Naught sans cause" for his fate, he was expressing two things with the vigor of that age: the necessity of the social course of the world, which condemned him to perish, and the negativity of the principle of a course of the world in line with that necessity. With happiness, even of the whole, the principle is downright incompatible.

The empirical content of that dictum is more than the platitude that the causal theorem is generally valid. In that which happens to the individual person, the universal interdependence dawns upon that person's consciousness. Its seemingly isolated fate reflects the whole. What the mythological name of fate used to stand for is no less mythical when it has been demythologized into a secular "logic of things." It is burned into the individual as the figure of his particularization. Objectively, this motivated Hegel's construction of the world spirit. On the one hand it accounts for the emancipation of the subject: the subject must have stepped back from universality in order to perceive it in and for itself. On the other hand, the context of social individual acts must have been woven into a totality so continuous, so predetermining for the individual, as it had never been in the feudal age.

UNIVERSAL HISTORY

The concept of universal history, a concept whose validity inspired Hegelian philosophy in similar fashion as that of the mathematical natural sciences had inspired the Kantian one, became the more problematical the closer the unified world came to being a total process. On the one hand, a positivistically advancing historical science has splintered the conception of totality and unbroken continuity. The advantage which constructive philosophy enjoyed over that science was the dubious one of knowing less detail, an advantage easy enough to enter as "sovereign distance" on the credit side of the ledger; at the same time, of course, there was less fear of saying essential things, the things that are outlined at a distance only. On the other hand, advanced philosophy was bound to note the understanding between universal history and ideology,[5] and the discontinuous character of blighted life.

Hegel himself had conceived universal history as unified merely on account of its contradictions. The materialistic turnabout in dialectics cast the weightiest accent on insight into the discontinuity of what is not comfortably held together by any unity of spirit and concept. Yet discontinuity and universal history must be conceived together. To strike out the latter as a relic of metaphysical superstition would spiritually consolidate pure facticity as the only thing to be known and therefore to be accepted; it would do this exactly in the manner in which sovereignty, aligning facts in the order of the total march of One Spirit, used to confirm them as the utterances of that spirit.

Universal history must be construed and denied. After the catastrophes that have happened, and in view of the catastrophes to come, it would be cynical to say that a plan for a better world is manifested in history and unites it. Not to be denied for that reason, however, is the unity that cements the discontinuous, chaotically splintered moments and phases of history—the unity of the control of nature, progressing to rule over men, and finally to that over men's inner nature. No universal history leads from savagery to humanitarianism, but there is one leading from the slingshot to the megaton bomb. It ends in the total menace which organized mankind poses to organized men, in the epitome of discontinuity. It is the horror that verifies Hegel and stands him on his head. If he transfigured the totality of historic suffering into the positivity of the self-realizing absolute, the One and All that keeps rolling on to this day—with occasional breathing spells —would teleologically be the absolute of suffering.

History is the unity of continuity and discontinuity. Society stays alive, not despite its antagonism, but by means of it; the profit interest and thus the class relationship make up the objective motor of the production process which the life of all men hangs by, and the primacy of which has its vanishing point in the death of all. This also implies the reconciling side of the irreconcilable; since nothing else permits men to live, not even a changed life would be possible without it. What historically made this possibility may as well destroy it. The world spirit, a worthy object of definition, would have to be defined as permanent catastrophe. Under the all-subjugating identity principle, whatever does not enter into identity, whatever eludes rational planning in the realm of means, turns into frightening retribution for the calamity which identity brought on the nonidentical. There is hardly another way to interpret history philosophically without enchanting it into an idea.

ANTAGONISM CONTINGENT?

It is not idle to speculate whether antagonism was inherited in the origin of human society as a principle of *homo homini lupus,* a piece of prolonged natural history, or whether it evolved θέσει— and whether, even if evolved, it followed from the necessities of the survival of the species and not contingently, as it were, from archaic arbitrary acts of seizing power. With that, of course, the construction of the world spirit would fall apart. The historic universal, the logic of things that is compacted in the necessity of the overall trend, would rest on something accidental, on something extraneous to it; it need not have been. Not only Hegel, but Marx and Engels—whose idealism was hardly anywhere as pronounced as in relation to totality—would have rejected all doubts of the inevitability of totality. No one who means to change the world can help feeling such doubts, but Marx and Engels would have warded them off like fatal attacks on their own system rather than upon the ruling system.

Marx, of course, suspects all anthropology and carefully refrains from locating antagonism in human nature or in primitive times, which he paints according to the cliché of the Golden Age, rather; but this makes him only more stubborn in his insistence on the historical necessity of antagonism. Economics is said to come before dominion, which must not be deduced otherwise than economically. The argument is scarcely to be settled with the aid of facts; they fade away in the mists of primitive history. Probably, however, the interest in it was no more a concern with historical facts than once upon a time the interest in the social contract, which even Hobbes and Locke will hardly have regarded as really agreed upon.* It was a matter of deifying history, even to the atheistic Hegelians, Marx and Engels. The primacy of economics is to yield historically stringent reasons why the happy

---

* The imaginary social contract was so welcome to the early bourgeois thinkers because its fundament, its formal legal a priori, was the barter relationship of bourgeois rationality; yet it was as imaginary as the bourgeois *ratio* itself was in the nontransparent real society.

end is immanent in history. The economic process, we hear, produces the conditions of political rule and keeps overturning them until the inevitable deliverance from the compulsion of economics.

Yet the doctrinal intransigence in Engels' case, in particular, was precisely political. The revolution desired by him and Marx was one of economic conditions in society as a whole, in the basic stratum of its self-preservation; it was not revolution as a change in society's political form, in the rules of the game of dominion. Their point was directed against the anarchists. When Marx and Engels decided to translate even mankind's primal history, its original sin, so to speak, into political economy—although the concept of that very discipline, chained to the totality of the barter relationship, is a late phenomenon—the motive that swayed them was the expectation of revolution as directly imminent. They wanted the revolution to come next day; hence their acute interest in breaking up trends that would, they had to fear, be crushed like Spartacus once upon a time, or like the peasant uprisings.

Marx and Engels were enemies of Utopia for the sake of its realization. Their *imago* of the revolution put its stamp upon the image of the primal world; the overwhelming weight of the economic contradictions in capitalism seemed to call for its derivation from the accumulated objectivity of what had been historically stronger since time immemorial. They could not foresee what became apparent later, in the revolution's failure even where it succeeded: that domination may outlast the planned economy (which the two of them, of course, had not confused with state capitalism)—a potential whereby the antagonistic trend shown by Marx and Engels, the antagonism of economics toward mere politics, is extended beyond the specific phase of that economics. By its tenacious survival after the downfall of what had been the main object of the critique of political economy, dominion helped an ideology to a cheap triumph: the ideology that will deduce dominion either from such allegedly inalienable forms of social organization as centralization, for instance, or from forms of consciousness abstracted out of the real process—the *ratio*. This is the ideology which then, in open agreement or under crocodile tears, will prophesy dominion an infinite future, for as long as any organized society exists.

Against this there remains the vigorous critique of a politics fetishized into being-in-itself, or of a spirit bloated in its particularity. Touched upon by events of the twentieth century, however, is the idea of historic totality as a calculable economic necessity. Only if things might have gone differently; if the totality is recognized as a socially necessary semblance, as the hypostasis of the universal pressed out of individual human beings; if its claim to be absolute is broken—only then will a critical social consciousness retain its freedom to think that things might be different some day. Theory cannot shift the huge weight of historic necessity unless the necessity has been recognized as realized appearance and historic determination is known as a metaphysical accident. Such cognition is frustrated by the metaphysics of history. More in line with the catastrophe that impends is the supposition of an irrational catastrophe in the beginning. Today the thwarted possibility of something other has shrunk to that of averting catastrophe in spite of everything.

THE SUPRAMUNDANE CHARACTER OF THE HEGELIAN WORLD SPIRIT

By Hegel, however, notably by the Hegel of *Philosophy of History* and *Philosophy of Law,* the historical objectivity that happened to come about is exalted into transcendence: "This universal substance is not the mundane; the mundane impotently strives against it. No individual can get beyond this substance; he can differ from other individuals, but not from the popular spirit."[6]

The opposite of the "mundane," the identity to which the particular entity is unidentically doomed, would thus be supramundane. There is a grain of truth even to such ideology: the critic of his own popular spirit is also chained to what is commensurable to him, as long as mankind is splintered into nations. In the recent past the greatest, though mostly disparagingly garbed model of this has been the constellation between Karl Kraus and Vienna. But to Hegel, as always when he meets with something contrary, things are not that dialectical. The individual, he goes on, "may have more *esprit* than many others, but he cannot surpass the popular spirit. *Les esprits* are merely those who know about their people's spirit and know how to go by it."[7] With a malice that one cannot fail to hear in the use of the word *esprit,* the relationship is described far beneath the level of the Hegelian conception. "To go by it" would be literally nothing but to adjust. Like one confessing compulsively, Hegel deciphers his previously taught affirmative identity as a continuing break and postulates the submission of the weak to the more powerful. Euphemisms such as that in *Philosophy of History,* that in the course of world history "some individuals have been hurt,"[8] are involuntary approaches to a sense of nonreconcilement, and the trumpet call "Duty is the individual's liberation to substantial freedom"[9]—a common property of German thought, by the way—already defies distinction from its parody in the doctor scene from Büchner's *Woyzeck.*

What Hegel puts into philosophy's mouth is "that no power surpasses that of the good, of God, and keeps him from prevailing; that God is borne out; that world history represents nothing but the plan of Providence. God rules the world; the content of his rule, the execution of his plan, is world history; to comprehend this plan is the philosophy of world history; and its premise is that the ideal is accomplished, that only that which is in line with the idea has reality."[10] The world spirit seems to have worked in pretty cunning fashion when Hegel, as if to crown his edifying homily—to use Arnold Schönberg's phrase—apes Heidegger in advance: "For reason is the perceiving of the divine work."[11] The omnipotent thought has to abdicate and to make itself complaisant as mere perceiving.

To gild the heteronomy of the substantially universal, Hegel mobilizes Greek conceptions this side of experienced individuality. In such passages he vaults all historic dialectics and unhesitatingly proclaims that morality's form in Antiquity, the form which was first that of official Greek philosophy and then the one of German *Gymnasien,* is its true form: "For the morality of the state is not the moralistic, reflected one in which one's own convictions hold sway; this is more accessible to the modern world, while the true morality of Antiquity has its roots in every man's stand by his duty."[12]

The objective spirit takes revenge on Hegel. As memorial orator of Spartanism he anticipates the jargon of intrinsicality by a hundred years, with the term "stand by his duty." He stoops to offering victims decorative comfort without touching on the substantiality of the condition whose victims they are. What spooks there, behind his superior declarations, had previously been petty cash in the bourgeois till of Schiller, in whose "Song of the Bell" the *pater familias* burned out of house and home is not only sent wandering, i.e., begging, but told to do it merrily, to boot; for a nation—said to be worthless otherwise—Schiller prescribes joy in committing its all to its honor. The terror of good cheer internalizes the *contrainte sociale*.

Such exaggeration is not a poetic luxury. The idealistic social pedagogue must do something extra, since without the performance of additional and irrational identification it would be all too flagrant that the universal robs the particular of what it is being promised. Hegel associates the power of the universal with the esthetically formal concept of greatness: "These are a people's great men; they guide the people in accordance with the universal spirit. For us, the individualities disappear and are noteworthy only as those who realize the will of the popular spirit."[13] The blithely decreed disappearance of individualities—a negative which philosophy presumes to know as positive without any real change having occurred in it—is the equivalent of the continuing break. The power of the world spirit sabotages what a subsequent Hegelian passage extols in the individual: "That he is in line with his substance is due to himself."[14]

And yet the phrasing of the dismissal touches on serious matters. The world spirit is said to be "the spirit of the world as it explicates itself in human consciousness; men relate to it as individuals to the whole, which is their substance."[15] There Hegel is telling off the bourgeois conception of the individual, its vulgar nominalism. The very grimness with which a man clings to himself, as to the immediately sure and substantial, makes him an agent of the universal, and individuality a deceptive notion. On this, Hegel agreed with Schopenhauer; what he had over Schopenhauer was the insight that the abstract negation of individuality is not all there is to the dialectics of individuation and universality. The remaining objection, however—not just against Schopenhauer but against Hegel himself—is that the individual, the necessary phenomenon of the essence, the objective tendency, is right to turn against that tendency, since he confronts it with its externality and fallibility. This is implicit in Hegel's doctrine of the individual's substantiality "by way of himself." Yet instead of developing the doctrine, Hegel sticks to an abstract antithesis of universal and particular, an antithesis that ought to be unbearable to his own method.*

HEGEL SIDING WITH THE UNIVERSAL

Opposed to such a separation of substantiality and individuality, as much as to a narrowly immediate consciousness, is the insight of Hegelian logic into the unity of the particular and the universal, a unity which sometimes strikes him as identity. "Particularity, however, as universality, is such an immanent relation

---

* Among the positivists it was in Emile Durkheim's doctrine of collective spirit that Hegel's choice in favor of the universal was maintained and topped, if possible; in Durkheim's schema there is no more room for a dialectic of universal and particular even in the abstract. In the sociology of primitive religions, Durkheim made the substantial discovery that qualities, the things the particular is boasting of, have been imposed upon it by the universal. He designated to the universal both the delusion of the particular, as a mere mimesis, and the power that makes a particular of it in the first place: "Le deuil (qui s'exprime au cours de certaines cérémonies) n'est pas un mouvement naturel de la sensibilité privée, froissée par une perte cruelle; c'est un devoir imposé par le groupe. On se lamente, non pas simplement parce qu'on est triste, mais parce qu'on est tenu de se lamenter. C'est une attitude rituelle qu'on est obligé d'adopter par respect pour l'usage, mais qui est, dans une large mesure, indépendante de l'état effectif des individus. Cette obligation est, d'ailleurs, sanctionnée par des peines ou mythiques ou sociales." (Emile Durkheim, *Les formes élémentaires de la vie religieuse: Le système totémique en Australie*. Paris, 1912, *Travaux de l'Année sociologique*, p. 568.)

in and for itself, not by way of transition; it is totality in itself and simple definition, essentially a principle. It has no other definition than the one posited by the universal itself and resulting from the universal, as follows. The particular is the universal itself, but it is the universal's difference from or relation to something else, what it seems to be on the outside; but there exists nothing else from which the particular might differ, nothing but the universal itself. When the universal is defined, it is the particular; definition makes the difference; it differs only from itself."[16]

Immediately, then, the particular would be the universal, because it can find no definition of its particularity except by way of the universal only; without the universal, Hegel concludes in an ever-recurring mode, the particular is nothing. The modern history of the human spirit—and not that alone—has been an apologetic labor of Sisyphus: thinking away the negative side of the universal. The Kantian spirit still remembers it, as against necessity: Kant tried to confine necessity to nature. The Hegelian critique of necessity is removed by legerdemain. "The consciousness of the spirit must form in the world; the material, the soil, of this realization is nothing but the universal consciousness, the consciousness of a people. This consciousness contains and directs all of the people's purposes and interests; it makes up the people's rights, customs, religions. It is the substantial part of a people's spirit even if the individuals do not know it, even if it stands as a settled premise. It is like a necessity; the individual is raised in this atmosphere and knows of nothing else. Yet it is not merely education and a consequence of education; rather, this consciousness is developed by the individual himself, not taught to him: the individual has his being in that substance."[17]

The Hegelian phrasing "It is like a necessity" is very adequate to the preponderance of the universal; the "like"—suggesting the merely metaphorical character of such a necessity—fleetingly touches on the semblance character of that which is the most real of things. Doubts whether necessity is good are promptly knocked down with the avowal that, rain or shine, necessity is freedom. The individual, Hegel tells us, "has his being in that substance," in the universality which to him was still coinciding with the popular spirits. But its positivity itself is negative, and the more negative its bearing, the more positive it will be; unity gets worse as its seizure of plurality becomes more thorough. It has its praise bestowed on it by the victor, and even a spiritual victor will not do without his triumphal parade, without the ostentatious pretense that what is incessantly inflicted upon the many is the meaning of the world.

"It is the particular which fights each other to exhaustion, and a part of which is ruined. But it is precisely from struggle, from the fall of the particular, that the universal results. The universal is not disturbed."[18] It has not been disturbed to this day. And yet, according to Hegel, without the particular that defines it, as a thing detached from itself, there would be no universal either. There is only one way for Hegelian logic to succinctly identify a universal and an undefined particular, to equate cognition with the fact that the two poles are mediated; and that is for logic—which Hegel also views as an a priori doctrine of general structures—not to deal with the particular as a particular at all. His logic deals only with particularity, which is already conceptual.[19] Thus established, the logical primacy of the universal provides a fundament for the social and political primacy that Hegel is opting for.

This much should be granted to Hegel: not only particularity but the particular itself is unthinkable without the moment of the universal which differentiates the particular, puts its imprint on it, and in a sense is needed to make a particular of it. But the fact that dialectically one moment needs the other, the moment contradictorily opposed to it—this fact, as Hegel knew well but liked to forget on occasion, reduces neither moment to a $\mu\grave{\eta}$ $\check{o}\nu$. Stipulated otherwise would be the absolute, ontological validity of the logic of pure noncontradictoriness, which the dialectical demonstration of "moments" had broken through; ultimately stipulated would be the position of an absolute First—the concept—with the fact said to be secondary because according to idealistic tradition it "follows" from the concept. Of a particular, nothing can be predicated without definition and thus without universality, and yet this does not submerge the moment of something particular, something opaque, which that prediction refers to and is based upon. It is maintained within the constellation, else dialectics would end up hypostatizing mediation without preserving the moments of immediacy, as Hegel prudently wished to do everywhere else.

RELAPSE INTO PLATONISM

The immanent critique of dialectics explodes Hegelian idealism. Cognition aims at the particular, not at the universal. It seeks its true object in the possible determination of the difference of that particular—even from the universal, which it criticizes as nonetheless inalienable. But if the mediation of the universal by the particular and of the particular by the universal is reduced to the abstract normal form of mediation as such, the particular has to pay the price, down to its authoritarian dismissal in the material parts of the Hegelian system. "What man must do, what are the duties he has to fulfill to be virtuous, is easily told in a moral community—he has to do nothing other than is prescribed, expressed, and known to him in his circumstances. Probity is the universal that can be demanded of him, partly legally, partly morally. From the moral standpoint, however, it tends to appear as something subordinate, beyond which one ought to ask more of himself and of others; for the urge to be something particular is not contented by that which is in and for itself and universal. It is only in an exception that this urge will find the sense of intrinsicality."[20]

If Hegel had carried the doctrine of the identity of universal and particular farther, to a dialectic in the particular itself, the particular—which according to him is simply the mediated universal—would have been granted the same right as the universal. That he depreciates this right into a mere urge and psychologistically blackens the right of man as narcissism—like a father chiding his son, "Maybe you think you're something special"—this is not an individual lapse on the philosopher's part. Idealistically, there is no carrying out the dialectic of the particular which he envisions. Contrary to the Kantian *chorismos,* philosophy is not supposed to make itself at home in the universal as a doctrine of forms; it is to penetrate the content itself, rather, and this is why, in a grandiosely fatal *petitio principii,* reality is so arranged by philosophy that it will yield to the repressive identification with philosophy.

What is most true in Hegelian thinking, the sense of the particular without whose weight the concept of reality decays into a farce, leads to that which is most false. It removes the particular for which Hegel's philosophy is groping. The more insistently his concept strives for reality, the more benightedly is reality— the *hic et nunc* that should be cracked open as gilded nuts are cracked by children on a holiday—contaminated by him with the concept that covers it. "It is this very attitude of philosophy toward reality which the misconceptions affect, and so I come back to what I said before: that philosophy, because it means to fathom what is rational, means precisely therefore to grasp what is present and real, not to erect a Beyond said to be God knows where—or of which one can in fact say very well where it is, namely, in the error of empty, onesided rationalizing . . . When reflection, feeling, or whatever form the subjective consciousness may take, regards the present as vain, when it goes beyond the present and knows better, it is likewise vain and, being real only in the present, it is nothing but vanity. Conversely, if the idea is taken to be no more than just an idea, a conception held as an opinion, philosophy affords the insight that nothing but the idea is a reality. What matters, then, is that in the semblance of the temporal and transitory we may know the substance which is immanent, and the eternal which is present."21*

So Platonic, of necessity, is the dialectician's language. He will not admit that, from the viewpoint of logic as well as of the philosophy of history, the universal contracts into the particular until the latter breaks loose from the abstract universality that

---

* The cliché "only an idea" had already been criticized by Kant. "The Platonic republic has become proverbial as a supposedly striking instance of imagined perfection, which can be located only in an idle thinker's brain . . . One would do better, however, to pursue this thought some more, and (where the excellent man leaves us without assistance) to illuminate it by new efforts instead of putting it aside as useless, on the very wretched and harmful pretext that it is unfeasible." (Kant, *Kritik der reinen vernunft,* Works III, p. 247.)

has grown extraneous to it—while the universal he vindicates, as a higher objectivity, correlatively declines to a bad subjectivity, to the mean value of particularities. He who was set upon a transition of logic to time is now resigned to timeless logic.

DETEMPORALIZATION OF TIME

The simple dichotomy of temporality and eternity amidst and despite the Hegelian conception of dialectics conforms to the primacy of the universal in *Philosophy of History*. Just as the general concept, the fruit of abstraction, is deemed above time— and just as the loss which the subsumed suffers by the process of abstraction is entered in the profit column, as a draft on eternity—so are history's allegedly supratemporal moments turned into positiva. Hidden in them is the old evil, however. To agree to the perpetuation of the status quo is to discredit the protesting thought as ephemeral. Such an aboutface into timelessness is not extraneous to Hegel's dialectics and philosophy of history. As his version of dialectics extends to time itself, time is ontologized, turned from a subjective form into a structure of being as such, itself eternal.

Based on this are Hegel's speculations which equate the absolute idea of totality with the passing of everything finite. His attempt to deduce time, as it were, and to eternalize it as permitting nothing outside it is as much in line with this conception as with absolute idealism, which can no more resign itself to the separation of time and logic than Kant could to the separation of visuality and intellect. There again, by the way, Hegel, Kant's critic, was Kant's executor. When Kant turns time, as the pure visual form and premise of everything temporal, into an a priori, time on its part is exempted from time.* Subjective and objective

---

* "Time does not pass, but the existence of changeable things passes in it. Since time itself is immutable and enduring, what corresponds to it in phenomenality is the immutable in existence, i.e., substance, and it is by this alone that we can determine the sequence and simultaneity of the phenomena in time." (Kant, ibid., p. 137.)

idealism concur in this, for the basic stratum of both is the subject as a concept, devoid of its temporal content. Once again, as to Aristotle, the *actus purus* becomes that which does not move. The social partisanship of the idealists goes all the way down to the constituents of their systems. They glorify time as timeless, history as eternal—all for fear that history might begin.

For Hegel, the dialectic of time and temporality logically turns into a dialectic of time in itself.* It offers the positivists their favored point of attack. In fact, it would be bad scholasticism if dialectics were attributed to the formal concept of time, with every temporal content expurgated. In critical reflection, however, time is dialecticized as the internally mediated unity of form and content. Kant's transcendental esthetics would have no answer to the objection that the purely formal character of time as a "form of visuality," its "emptiness," has itself no corresponding visuality whatever. Kantian time defies every possible conception and imagination: to conceive it, we always have to conceive something temporal along with it, something to read it off on, something that permits its passage or its so-called flow to be experienced. The fact is that the conception of pure time does require that very conceptual mediation—the abstraction from all conceptions of time that can be carried out—from which Kant, for the sake of systematics, the disjunction of sensibility and intellect, wished and needed to relieve the forms of visuality.

Absolute time as such, bereft of the last factual substrate that is and passes in it, would no longer be what time, according to Kant, must inalienably be: it would no longer be dynamic. There is no dynamics without that in which it occurs. Conversely, however, a factuality without its place in the time continuum is not conceivable either. Dialectics carries this reciprocity into the most formal realm: of the moments essential to that realm, and

---

* "More closely, then, the real I itself belongs to time, with which—if we abstract from the concrete content of consciousness and self-consciousness—it coincides, being nothing but this empty motion of positing myself as something other and voiding this change, i.e., preserving therein myself, the I, and only the I as such. I is in time, and time is the being of the subject." (Hegel, Works 14, p. 151.)

opposed to each other, not one is without the other. Yet the reciprocity is not motivated by the pure form in itself that served to reveal it. A relationship of form and content has become the form itself. It is inalienably the form of a content—an extreme sublimation of the form-content dualism in detached and absolutized subjectivity.

An element of truth might even be squeezed out of Hegel's theory of time, provided one will not let logic produce time by itself, as he does; to be perceived in logic, instead, are coagulated time relations, as indicated variously, if cryptically, in *Critique of Pure Reason,* in the chapter on schematism in particular. Preserved likewise in the discursive *Logic*—unmistakeably in its conclusions—are time elements that were detemporalized as subjective thinking objectified them into pure legality; without such detemporalization, on the other hand, time would not have been objectified at all. As cognition of an element, it would be compatible with Hegel to interpret the link between logic and time by going back to something which current positivistic science considers pre-logical in logic. For what Hegel calls synthesis is not simply the downright new quality leaping forth from definite negation; it is the return of what has been negated. Dialectical progress is always a recourse as well, to that which fell victim to the progressing concept; the concept's progressive concretion is its self-correction. The transition of logic to time would like, as far as consciousness is able, to make up to time for the wrongs done to it by logic—by the logic without which, on the other hand, time would not be.

Under this aspect, the Bergsonian duplication of the concept of time is a bit of dialectics unaware of itself. In the concept of *le temps durée,* of lived duration, Bergson tried theoretically to reconstruct the living experience of time, and thus its substantial element that had been sacrificed to the abstractions of philosophy and of causal-mechanical natural science. Even so, he did not convert to the dialectical concept any more than science did. More positivistically than he knew in his polemicizing, he absolutized the dynamic element out of disgust with the rising reification of consciousness; he on his part made of it a form of consciousness, so to speak, a particular and privileged mode of cognition. He reified it, if you will, into a line of business. In isolation, the time of subjective experience along with its content comes to be as accidental and mediated as its subject, and therefore, compared with chronometric time, is always "false" also. Sufficient to elucidate this is the triviality that, measured by clock time, subjective time experiences invite delusion, although there would be no clock time without the subjective time experience which the clock time objectifies.

But the crass dichotomy of Bergson's two times does register the historic dichotomy between living experience and the objectified and repetitive labor process; his brittle doctrine of time is an early precipitation of the objective social crisis in the sense of time. The irreconcilability of *temps durée* and *temps espace* is the wound of that split consciousness whose only unity lies in being split. The naturalistic interpretation of *temps espace* can no more master this than the hypostasis of *temps durée*, in which the subject, flinching from reification, hopes in vain to preserve itself simply by being alive. The fact is that laughter—according to Bergson, the restoration of life from its conventional hardening —has long become the conventions' weapon against uncomprehended life, against the traces of something natural that has not been quite domesticated.

DIALECTICS CUT SHORT BY HEGEL

Hegel's transposition of the particular into particularity follows the practice of a society that tolerates the particular only as a category, a form of the supremacy of the universal. Marx designated this state of facts in a manner which Hegel could not foresee: "The dissolution of all products and activities into exchange values presupposes the dissolution of all fixed personal (historical) dependencies in production as well as the producers' universal dependence on each other. Every individual's production depends as much on the production of all others as the transformation of his product into food for himself has come to depend on the consumption of all others . . . This mutual interdependence is expressed in the constant necessity of exchange, and in the exchange value as universal mediator. The economists put it this way: Everyone pursues his private interest and thus unwillingly and unwittingly serves the private interests of all, the general interests. The joke is not that everyone's pursuit of his private interest will in effect serve the entirety of private interests, that is, the general interest; from this abstract phrase it might as well be inferred that everyone mutually inhibits the pursuit of the others' interest, and that, instead of general affirmation, the result of this *bellum omnium contra omnes* will be general negation. The point is, rather, that the private interest itself is already a socially determined interest, one that can be pursued only on the terms laid down by society and by the means provided by society —hence an interest tied to the reproduction of those terms and means. It is the interest of private persons; but its content as well as the form and means of realization are given by social conditions independent of them all."[22]

Such negative supremacy of the concept makes clear why Hegel, its apologist, and Marx, its critic, concur in the notion that what Hegel calls the world spirit has a preponderance of being-in-itself—that it does not (as would be solely fitting for Hegel) have merely its objective substance in the individuals: "The individuals are subsumed under social production, which exists as a doom outside them; but social production is not subsumed under the individuals who exercise it as their common capacity."[23] The real *chorismos* obliges Hegel, much against his will, to remodel his thesis of the reality of the idea. The theory does not admit this, but there are unmistakable lines about it in *Philosophy of Law:* "For the idea of the state one must not look to particular states or particular institutions; rather, the idea, this real God, must be contemplated by itself. Every state, although a man may call it bad according to the principles he holds, although he may find one or the other flaw in it, always contains the essential moments of its existence, especially if it is one of the developed states of our time. But because finding faults is easier than grasping the affirmative, one will easily fall into the error of letting specific sides make him forget the inner organism of the state itself."[24]

The tenor of the whole work is to dispute away the contradiction between idea and reality; but if the idea "must be contemplated by itself," not in "particular states," and that in principle, with an encompassing structure in mind, this resurrects the contradiction. In keeping with it is the ominous line that finding faults is easier than grasping the affirmative; today this has become the clamor for "constructive criticism," in other words, groveling criticism. Because the identity of idea and reality is denied by reality, ascertaining that identity nonetheless calls, so to speak, for an obsequious special effort on the part of reason; the "affirmative," the proof of positively accomplished reconciliation, is postulated, praised as a superior achievement of consciousness, because Hegel's pure eye witness does not suffice for such affirmation. The pressure which affirmation exerts on a balky reality acts tirelessly to strengthen the real pressure put upon the subject by the universal, its negation. The chasm between the two yawns the more visibly, the more concretely the subject is confronted with the thesis of the objective substantiality of morals.

In Hegel's late conception of education, this is described only as something hostile to the subject: "Absolutely defined, education is thus deliverance and the work on a higher deliverance, namely, the absolute point of transition to the infinitely subjective substantiality of morals, which is no longer immediate and natural but spiritual and likewise raised to the form of universality. —In the subject, this deliverance is the toil of striving against mere subjectivity of conduct, against immediate desire, as well as against the subjective vanity of sensation and the arbitrariness of liking. That it is this toil accounts for part of the disfavor it encounters. But it is by this educational toil that subjective volition gains in itself the objectivity which alone makes it worthy and capable of being the reality of the idea."[25]

Embroidering this is ὁ μὴ δαρείς, the Greek school maxim which Goethe—whom it fitted least of all—did not disdain to choose as a Hegelian-minded motto for his autobiography. Yet in trumpeting the truth about the identity it would like first to bring about, the classicist maxim admits its own untruth: literally that of birch rod pedagogy, and metaphorically, that of the unspeakable commandment to submit. Being immanently untrue, the maxim is unfit for the purpose entrusted to it; psychology, be-

WORLD SPIRIT AND NATURAL HISTORY

littled by the great philosophy, knows more about that than philosophy knows. Brutality is reproduced by men against whom it is practiced; the abused are not educated but repressed, rebarbarized. An insight of psychoanalysis—that civilization's repressive mechanisms transform the libido into aggression against civilization—cannot be extinguished any more. The man who has been educated by force will channel his aggressions by identifying with force, to pass it on and get rid of it; it is thus that subject and object are really identified according to the educational ideal of Hegel's philosophy of law. If a culture is no culture, it does not even want the people who are caught in its mill to be cultured.

In one of the most famous passages of *Philosophy of Law,* Hegel cites a line attributed to Pythagoras, to the effect that the best way morally to educate a son is to make him a citizen of a state with good laws.[26] This calls for a judgment whether the state itself and its laws are actually good. But to Hegel, order is good a priori; it does not have to answer to those living under it. Ironically, this confirms his subsequent Aristotelian reminiscence that "substantial unity is an absolute and motionless end in itself."[27] Motionless, the end stands in the dialectic that is supposed to produce it. It is thus devalued to an empty avowal that "freedom comes to its supreme right"[28] in the state; Hegel lapses into that insipid edification which he still despised in *Phenomenology.* He reiterates a cogitative cliché of Antiquity, from the stage at which philosophy's victorious Platonic-Aristotelian mainstream proclaimed its solidarity with the institutions, against their bases in the social process; all in all, mankind discovered society much later than the state, which is mediated as such but seems given and immediate to the governed.

Hegel's line "Whatever man is he owes to the state,"[29] that most obvious hyperbole, carries on the antiquated confusion. What induced the thesis is that the "motionlessness" he attributes to the general purpose might indeed be predicated of the institution, once it has hardened, but could not possibly be predicated of society, which is dynamic in essence. The dialectician confirms the state's prerogative to be above dialectics because—a matter he did not delude himself about—dialectics will drive men beyond bourgeois society. He does not put his trust in dialectics, does not look upon it as the force to cure itself, and disavows his own assurance that identity will produce itself in dialectics.

THE ROLE OF THE POPULAR SPIRIT

It could not escape Hegel's need for systematics that the metaphysic of reconciling universal and particular failed in its construction of reality, in the philosophy of history and law. He made an effort at mediation. His mediating category, the popular spirit, extends into empirical history. To the individual subjects it is said to be the concrete form of the universal, but the "specific popular spirit" on its part is called "merely an individual in the course of world history"[31]—an individuation higher in grade, but independent as such. It is precisely the thesis of this independence of popular spirits which Hegel uses to confer legality upon the rule of force over the individuals, in a way similar to Durkheim's later use of collective norms, and to Spengler's use of the soul of each culture. The more abundantly a universal is equipped with the insignia of the collective subject, the more completely will the subjects disappear in it. Yet that mediating category—which is not called mediation in so many words, by the way, but merely fulfills that function—lags behind Hegel's own concept of mediation. It does not hold sway in the matter itself, does not immanently determine its otherness; rather, it functions as a bridging concept, a hypostatized intermediary between the world spirit and the individuals.

By Hegel, the transitoriness of popular spirits is interpreted analogously to that of individuals, as the true life of the universal. In truth, however, it is the category of the people and their spirit itself that is transitory, not just its specific manifestation. Even if the torch of the Hegelian world spirit were actually carried further today by the newly emerging popular spirits, the danger is that they would reproduce the life of the human species on a lower level. Even in view of surveyable mankind, the Kantian universal of his period, Hegel's doctrine of a popular spirit was reactionary, a cultivation of something already perceived as particular. With his emphatic category of popular spirits he unhesitatingly goes in for the same nationalism whose sinister side he diagnosed in the student agitators of his day. His concept of the nation, the world spirit's changelessly changing carrier, turns out to be one of the invariants with which—paradoxically, and yet in keeping with its one aspect—his dialectical work is overflowing. Hegel's undialectical constants belie dialectics although there would be no dialectics without them, and they are as true as history is immutable, a bad infinity of guilt and atonement, running its course exactly as Heraclitus, Hegel's main witness, recognized and ontologically exalted it in archaic times.

But the nation, the term as well as the thing, is of more recent date. After feudalism perished, a precarious form of centralized organization was to tame the diffuse combines of nature so as to protect bourgeois interests. It was bound to become a fetish unto itself; there was no other way it might have integrated the individuals, whose economic need of that form of organization is as great as its incessant rape of them. And where the nation failed to accomplish the union that is the prerequisite of a self-emancipating bourgeois society—in Germany, that is—its concept becomes overvalued and destructive. To take in the *gentes,* the concept of the nation mobilizes additional regressive memories of its archaic root. As an evil ferment, these memories are apt to keep the individual—another late and fragile evolutionary product—down where his conflict with the universal is at the point of recoiling into rational critique of the universal. The irrational ends of bourgeois society could hardly have been stabilized by other than effective irrational means.

The specifically German situation of the immediate post-Napoleonic era may have deceived Hegel about the nature of his doctrine of the popular spirit. He failed to see what an anachronism it is, compared with his own concept of the spirit from whose progress a progressive sublimation, a deliverance from rudimentarily natural growth, cannot be excised. In his work, the popular spirit doctrine was already ideology, a false consciousness even though provoked by the need for Germany's administrative union. Masked and, as particularization, coupled with things as they happen to be, the popular spirits are proof against that reason whose memory is nonetheless preserved in the universal of the spirit. After the Kantian tract *On Perpetual Peace,* Hegel's eulogies of war can no longer hide behind a naive lack of historical experience. Even then, the *mores* he praised as substantial in popular spirits had hopelessly decayed into that body of customs which was then dug up in the age of dictatorships, to add an official historical touch to the individual's incapacitation. The mere fact that Hegel has to talk about popular spirts in the plural shows the obsoleteness of their alleged substantiality. It is negated as soon as we talk of many popular spirits, as soon as an international of nations is envisioned. After fascism, the concept reappeared.

POPULAR SPIRIT OBSOLETE

Its particularization into nations means that the Hegelian spirit no longer includes the material basis in the way in which it could at least claim to be doing as a totality. In the concept of the popular spirit it is an epiphenomenon, a collective consciousness, a stage of social organization, that is opposed as an entity to the real process of society's production and reproduction. That the spirit of a people can be realized, that it can be "turned into an extant world," says Hegel, "this is a feeling shared by all peoples."[32] Today it is hardly that, and wherever peoples are made to feel this way they come to grief. The predicates of that "extant world"—"religion, cults, customs, usages, art, constitution, political laws, the full extent of its institutions, its occurrences and deeds"[33]—have lost not only their self-evident character but that which Hegel took for their substantiality. His precept that individuals have to "align themselves, to form themselves according to the substantial being"[34] of their people, is despotic. Even in his day it was incompatible with the hypothesis—also outdated since —which we might call Shakespearean: that the historic universal is realized through individual passions and concerns, whereas in fact it is drilled into the individuals solely in the manner in which "healthy popular sentiments" are drilled into those caught in their machinery.

Hegel's thesis that no man can "vault the spirit of his people, no more than he can vault the globe,"[35] is a provincialism in the age of global conflicts and of a potential global constitution of the world. On few occasions did Hegel have to pay as high a toll to history as when he was conceiving history. But his thinking approached that point too; while hypostatizing the popular spirits, he relativized them in the sense of historical philosophy, as if he had deemed it possible for the world spirit some day to do without the popular spirits and to make room for cosmopolitism. "Each new popular spirit is a new step in the conquest of the world spirit, a step to win its consciousness and its freedom. A popular spirit's death is a passage to life—and not as in nature, where the death of one will bring another like it into existence. Rather, the world spirit advances from lower definitions to higher principles and concepts of itself, to more developed representations of its idea."[36]

Thus the idea, at least, of a world spirit that is to be "conquered," that is realized in the fall of the popular spirits and transcends them, would remain open. Yet world history can no longer be trusted to make progress in its passage from nation to nation, in a phase in which the victor is no longer bound to occupy the higher level that was probably always credited to him only because he was the victor. With that, however, Hegel's solace for the fall of nations comes to resemble the cyclical theories, down to Spengler. The philosophical decree about the becoming and passing of whole peoples or cultures drowns out the fact that history's irrational and unintelligible side came to be self-understood because things were never different; it deprives the talk of progress of its substance. And indeed, despite the well-known definition of history, Hegel failed to work out any theory of progress. The world spirit's Hegelian migration from one popular spirit to the next is the Migration of Nations blown up into metaphysics; the human steamroller of that migration is of course a prototype of world history itself, whose Augustinian conception coincided with the era of the Great Migration. The unity of world history which animates the philosopher to trace it as the path of the world spirit is the unity of terror rolling over mankind; it is the immediacy of antagonism. Concretely, Hegel did not go beyond nations except in the name of their incalculably reiterated destruction. The Schopenhauerian Richard Wagner's "Ring" is more Hegelian than would ever have occurred to Wagner.

INDIVIDUALITY AND HISTORY

What Hegel hypertrophically assigned to the popular spirits as collective individualities is withdrawn from individuality, from the individual human being. Complementarily, Hegel rates individuality both too high and too low.

It is rated too high in the ideology of great men, in whose favor Hegel retells the master class joke of the hero and his valet. The more opaque and alienated the prevailing universal's power, the fiercer the need of consciousness to make that power commensurable. This is where the geniuses must serve, the military and political ones in particular. Theirs is the publicity of larger-than-life size, derived from the very success which in turn is to be explained by individual qualities they mostly lack. Projections of the impotent longings of all, they function as an *imago* of unleashed freedom and unbounded productivity, as if those might be realized always and everywhere.

Contrasting with such ideological excess is Hegel's deficiency in the ideal; his philosophy has no interest in there being individuality at all. There the doctrine of the world spirit harmonizes with that spirit's own tendency. Hegel saw through both fictions, through that of individuality's historic being-for-itself as well as through the one of any direct immediacy, and he used the theory of the cunning of reason—a theory dating back to Kant's philosophy of history—to cast the individual as an agent of the universal, a role in which he had served well for centuries. In line with a consistent thought structure which simultaneously skeletalizes and revokes his conception of dialectics, Hegel conceived the relation as well as the mediation between individual and world spirit as invariant. He too was in bondage to his class, a class forced to perpetuate its dynamic categories lest it perceive the bounds of its continued existence.

Guiding Hegel is the picture of the individual in individualist society. It is adequate, because the principle of the barter society was realized only through the individuation of the several contracting parties—because, in other words, the *principium individuationis* literally was the principle of that society, its universal. And the picture is inadequate because, in the total functional context which requires the form of individuation, individuals are relegated to the role of mere executive organs of the universal. Along with his functions, the individual's own composition is subject to historic change. Compared with Hegel and his epoch, the individual has become irrelevant to a degree which no one could anticipate; the appearance of his being-for-himself has dissolved for all men as completely as Hegel's speculation had esoterically demolished it in advance.

A model of this is passion, the motor of individuality for Hegel as it was for Balzac. To the powerless, who find more and more narrowly prescribed what they can and cannot attain, passion becomes an anachronism. Adolf Hitler, tailored, as it were, after the classic bourgeois pattern of a great man, gave a parody of passion in his fits of weeping and carpet chewing. Even in the private realm, passion comes to be a rarity. The well-known changes in the erotic conduct of the young indicate the disintegration of the individual, whose ego no longer musters the strength for passion. Nor does he need that strength, because the integrating social organization sees to the removal of the patent obstacles that used to kindle passion and makes up for them by placing the controls into the individual, in the form of his adjustment at any price.

By no means has the individual thus lost all functions. Now as before, the social process of production preserves in the basic barter process the *principium individuationis,* private disposition, and thus all the evil instincts of a man imprisoned in his ego. The individual survives himself. But in his residue which history has condemned lies nothing but what will not sacrifice itself to false identity. The function of the individual is that of the functionless— of the spirit which does not agree with the universal and is therefore powerless to represent it. Only as exempt from the general practice is the individual capable of the thoughts that would be required for a practice leading to change. Hegel sensed the potential universality in individuation: "In their activity, the actors have finite purpose and special interests; but they also are knowing and thinking."[37]

The methexis wrought between each individual and the universal by conscious thinking—and the individual is no individual until he goes in for such thinking—transcends the contingency of the particular vis-à-vis the universal, the basis of both Hegel's and subsequently the collectivists' contempt for individuality. Experience and consistency enable the individual to see in the universal a truth which the universal as blindly prevailing power conceals from itself and from others. The reigning consensus puts the universal in the right because of the mere form of its universality. Universality, itself a concept, comes thus to be conceptless and inimical to reflection; for the mind to perceive and to name that side of it is the first condition of resistance and a modest beginning of practice.

THE SPELL

Human beings, individual subjects, are under a spell now as ever. The spell is the subjective form of the world spirit, the internal reinforcement of its primacy over the external process of life. Men become that which negates them, that with which they cannot cope. They do not even have to cultivate a taste for it any more, as for the higher thing which indeed it is, compared with them in the hierarchy of grades of universality. On their own, a priori, so to speak, they act in line with the inevitable. While the nominalist principle simulates individualization for them, they act as a collective. This much of Hegel's insistence on the universality of the particular is true: in its perversion, as impotent individualization at the universal's mercy, the particular is dictated by the principle of perverted universality. The Hegelian doctrine of the universal's substantiality in the individual adopts the subjective spell; what is presented there as metaphysically worthier owes this aura chiefly to its opaqueness and irrationality, to the opposite of the mind which metaphysics would have it be.

The basic stratum of unfreedom—one that in the subjects lies even beyond their psychology, which it extends—serves the antagonistic condition now threatening to destroy the subjects' potential to change it. Expressionism, a spontaneous form of collective reaction, jerkily registered some of that spell, which has since become as omnipresent as the deity whose place it is usurping. We do not feel it any more because hardly anything and hardly anyone escapes it far enough to make the difference show it. Yet mankind still keeps dragging itself along as in Barlach's sculptures and in Kafka's prose, an endless procession of bent figures chained to each other, no longer able to raise their heads under the burden of what is.[38] Mere entity, the opposite of the world spirit according to the highminded doctrines of idealism, is the incarnation of that spirit—coupled with chance, which is the form of freedom under the spell.*

The spell seems to be cast upon all living things, and yet it is probably not—as in Schopenhauer's sense—simply one with the *principium individuationis* and its mulish self-preservation. Something compulsive distinguishes animal conduct from human conduct. The animal species *homo* may have inherited it, but in the species it turned into something qualitatively different. And it did so precisely due to the reflective faculty that might break the spell and did enter into its service. By such self-perversion it reinforces

---

* Hegel's theory of the identity of chance and necessity (s.p. 357 below) retains its truth content beyond Hegel's construction. Under the aspect of freedom, necessity stays heteronomous even though predesigned by the autonomous subject. The Kantian empirical world is said to be ruled by the subjective category of causality, but precisely that removes it from subjective autonomy: to the individual subject, what is causally determined is absolutely accidental at the same time. Running its course in the realm of necessity, the fate of men is blind to them, "over their heads," contingent. The strictly deterministic character of the economic laws of social motion is just what condemns the members of society to chance, if their self-determination were truly deemed the criterium. The law of value and anarchy in the production of goods are one. Contingency is thus not only the form of a nonidentity mangled by causality; contingency itself coincides with the identity principle. And this principle—as merely posited, imposed upon experience, not arising from the nonidentical in experience—in turn carries chance in its inmost core.

the spell and makes it radical evil, devoid of the innocence of mere being the way one is. In human experience the spell is the equivalent of the fetish character of merchandise. The self-made thing becomes a thing-in-itself, from which the self cannot escape any more; in the dominating faith in facts as such, in their positive acceptance, the subject venerates its mirror image.

In the spell, the reified consciousness has become total. The fact of its being a false consciousness holds out a promise that it will be possible to avoid it—that it will not last; that a false consciousness must inevitably move beyond itself; that it cannot have the last word. The straighter a society's course for the totality that is reproduced in the spellbound subjects, the deeper its tendency to dissociation. This threatens the life of the species as much as it disavows the spell cast over the whole, the false identity of subject and object. The universal that compresses the particular until it splinters, like a torture instrument, is working against itself, for its substance is the life of the particular; without the particular, the universal declines to an abstract, separate, eradicable form. In *Behemot,* Franz Neumann diagnosed this in the institutional sphere: disintegration into disjoint and embattled power machineries is the secret of the total fascist state. In line with this is anthropology, the chemism of humankind. Resistless prey of the collective mischief, men lose their identity.

It is not altogether unlikely that the spell is thus breaking itself. For the time being a so-called pluralism would falsely deny the total structure of society, but its truth comes from such impending disintegration, from horror and at the same time from a reality in which the spell explodes. Freud's *Civilization and Its Discontents* has a substance that was scarcely in the author's mind: it is not only in the psyche of the socialized that aggressiveness accumulates into an openly destructive drive. Instead, total socialization objectively hatches its opposite, and there is no telling yet whether it will be a disaster or a liberation. An involuntary schema of this was designed by the philosophical systems; they too have been increasingly united in disqualifying their heterogeneities— whether called "sensation," "not-I," or whatever—down to that "chaos" whose name Kant used for heterogeneity at large. What some like to call *angst* and to ennoble as an existential is claustrophobia in the world: in the closed system. It perpetuates the spell as coldness between men, without which the calamity could not recur. Anyone who is not cold, who does not chill himself as in the vulgar figure of speech the murderer "chills" his victims, must feel condemned. Along with *angst* and the cause of it, this coldness too might pass. *Angst* is the necessary form of the curse laid in the universal coldness upon those who suffer of it.

REGRESSION UNDER THE SPELL

Whatever nonidentity the rule of the identity principle will tolerate is mediated in turn by the identitarian compulsion. It is the stale remnant left after identification has carved out its share. Under the spell, what is different—and the slightest admixture of which would indeed be incompatible with the spell—will turn to poison. As accidental, on the other hand, the nonidentical remnant grows abstract enough to adjust to the legality of identification. This is the sad truth of the doctrine expounded positively by Hegel: that chance and necessity are one. Substituting statistical rules for traditional causality ought to confirm that convergence. But the fatal common property of necessity and chance, a pair which Aristotle already ascribed to mere entity, is fate. It is located in the circle drawn by ruling class thought as well as in that which falls out of the circle, is bereft of reason, and acquires an irrationality converging with the necessity the subject posits.

The process of dominance keeps spewing undigested scraps of subjugated nature. If the particular is not to evaporate philosophically, into universality, it must not seclude itself in the defiance of chance. It is a reflection on the difference, not its extirpation, that would help to reconcile the universal and the particular. But Hegel pledges allegiance to extirpation, his pathos grants the world spirit the only reality, echoing a hellish laughter in heaven. The mythical spell has been secularized into compactly dovetailed reality. The reality principle, which the prudent heed in order to survive in it, captures them as black magic; they are unable and unwilling to cast off the burden, for the magic hides it from them and makes them think it is life.

Metapsychologically, the talk of regression is true. Without exception, what is called communication nowadays is but the noise that drowns out the silence of the spellbound. Individual human spontaneities, by now largely including the supposed opposition, are condemned to pseudoactivity and potential idiocy. Practiced from without, in brainwashing and kindred techniques, is an immanent anthropological tendency that is indeed motivated from without. The natural-historic norm of adjustment, with which Hegel agrees in the beer hall wisdom of having to sow one's wild oats, is the exact parallel of his: the schema of the world spirit as the spell. It may be that its experience, taboo among people, is projected upon animals by modern biology in order to exonerate the people who abuse the animals; the ontology of beasts apes the age-old, always newly repossessed bestiality of men.

In that sense too the world spirit contradicts itself, unlike Hegel's intention. The bestiality of self-preserving reason expels the spirit from the species that worships it. This is why, in all of its stages, the Hegelian metaphysic of the intellect comes so close to anti-intellectualism. In an unconscious society the mythical forces of nature reproduce themselves in expanded form, and so will the categories of consciousness produced by that society, including the most enlightened, inevitably grow delusive under the spell. Society and individual harmonize here as nowhere else. With society, ideology has so advanced that it no longer evolves into a socially required semblance and thus to an independent form, however brittle. All that it turns into is a kind of glue: the false identity of subject and object.

Due to the individuation principle itself, to each individual's monotonous confinement to his particular interest, the individuals, the ancient substrate of psychology, are also like one another, claimants to the dominant abstract universality as if it were their own cause. This is their formal a priori. Conversely, the universal to which they bow without feeling it yet is so tailored to their measure, so lacking in appeal to whatever in them is not like it, that they "freely bind themselves with ease and joy," as Schiller put it. Present ideology is no less a vessel to receive the psychology —always mediated already by the universal—of individuals than it is the ceaseless reproducer of the universal in the individuals.

Spell and ideology are one and the same. The fatal part of ideology is that it dates back to biology. Self-preservation, the Spinozist *sese conservare,* is truly a law of nature for all living things. Its content is the tautology of identity: what ought to be is what is anyway; the will turns back upon the willing; as a mere means of itself it becomes an end. This turn is already a turn to the false consciousness. If the lion had a consciousness, his rage at the antelope he wants to eat would be ideology.

The concept of ends, to which reason rises for the sake of consistent self-preservation, ought to be emancipated from the idol in the mirror. An end would be whatever differs from the subject, which is a means. Yet this is obscured by self-preservation, by its fixation of the means as ends which need not prove their legitimacy to any sort of reason. The more enhanced the forces of production, the less will the perpetuation of life as an end in itself remain a matter of course. The end, as a prey to nature, becomes questionable in itself while the potential of something other is maturing inside it. Life gets ready to become a means for that otherness, however undefined and unknown it may be; yet the heteronomous constitution of life keeps inhibiting it. Since self-preservation has been precarious and difficult for eons, the power of its instrument, the ego drives, remains all but irresistible even after technology has virtually made self-preservation easy; that power surpasses the one of the object drives whose specialist, Freud, misconceived it. Exertions rendered superfluous by the state of the productive forces become objectively irrational; hence the emergence of the spell as the metaphysic governing reality. The present stage of the fetishization of means as ends in technology points to a triumph of that trend, to the point of evident absurdity: models of conduct which were rational once and have since been outdated are conjured up without change by the logic of history. This logic is not logical any more.

SUBJECT AND INDIVIDUAL

"Subjectivity," Hegel puts it idealistically, "is the absolute form and the existing reality of substance, and the subject's difference from

349

it—as from its object, purpose, and power—is only the difference in form which has disappeared at the same time and with the same immediacy."[39]

Even to Hegel, after all, subjectivity is the universal and the total identity. He deifies it. But he accomplishes the opposite as well: an insight into the subject as a self-manifesting objectivity. There is an abysmal duality in his construction of the subject-object. He not only falsifies the object ideologically, calling it a free act of the absolute subject; he also recognizes in the subject a self-representing objectivity, thus anti-ideologically restricting the subject. Subjectivity as an existing reality of substance did claim precedence, but as an "existing," alienated subject it would be both objective and phenomenal. Yet this could not but affect the relation of subjectivity to concrete individuals as well. If objectivity is immanent to them and active in them, if it truly appears in them, an individuality which thus relates to the essence is far more substantial than one merely subordinated to the essence.

Hegel is silenced by such a consequence. He who seeks to liquidate Kant's abstract concept of form keeps nonetheless dragging along the Kantian and Fichtean dichotomy of transcendental subject and empirical individual. The lack of concrete definition in the concept of subjectivity is exploited as the benefit of higher objectivity on the part of a subject cleansed of chance; this facilitates the identification of subject and object at the expense of the particular. Hegel is here following an all-idealistic usage, but at the same time he is undermining his assertion of the identity of freedom and necessity. Due to its hypostasis as spirit, the subject, the substrate of freedom, is so far detached from live human beings that its freedom in necessity can no longer profit them at all. This is brought to light by Hegel's language: "As the state, the fatherland, makes out a community of existence, as man's subjective volition submits to the laws, the antithesis of freedom and necessity disappears."[40] No amount of interpretive skill would let us dispute away the fact that the word "submission" means the opposite of freedom. Its alleged synthesis with necessity bows to necessity and refutes itself.

DIALECTICS AND PSYCHOLOGY

Hegel's philosophy opens vistas of the loss involved in the rise of individuality, from the nineteenth century far into the twentieth—the loss in commitment, in that strength to approach the universal which individuality would need to come to itself. The decay of individuality that has become evident in the meantime is coupled with such a loss; the individual, who unfolds and differentiates himself by a more and more emphatic separation from the universal, is thus in peril of regressing to the accidental traits which Hegel adds up against him. Yet in so doing the restorative Hegel himself neglected both logic and coercion in the progress of individuation; citing instead an ideal composed of Greek model propositions and preluding the worst twentieth-century German reaction, he also neglected the forces which do not mature until individuality disintegrates.[41]

Again he is being unjust to his own dialectic. That the universal is not just a hood pulled over individuality, that it is its inner substance, this cannot be reduced to the platitude that prevailing human morals are encompassing. The fact ought to be tracked down in the center of individual modes of conduct, notably in human character—in that psychology which Hegel, agreeing with common prejudice, accuses of an accidentality since refuted by Freud. Granted, the Hegelian anti-psychologism does attain the cognition of the social universal's empirical precedence which Durkheim would express later, stoutly and untouched by any dialectical reflection.[42] Psychology seems the opposite of the universal, but under pressure it will yield to it, all the way into the cells of internalization; to this extent it is a real *constitutum*.[43] Yet objectivism, whether dialectical or positivistic, is as shortsighted in its view of psychology as it is superior to it. Since the reigning objectivity is objectively inadequate to the individuals, it is realized solely through the individuals—that is to say, psychologically.

Freudian psychoanalysis does not so much help to weave the appearance of individuality as it destroys it, as thoroughly as the philosophical and social concept. When the doctrine of the unconscious reduces the individual to a small number of recurring

351

constants and conflicts it does reveal a misanthropic disinterest in the concretely unfolded ego; and yet it reminds the ego of the shakiness of its definitions compared with those of the id, and thus of its tenuous and ephemeral nature. The theory of the ego as a totality of defense mechanisms and rationalizations is directed against the individual as ideology, against the same *hubris* of the self-controlled individual that was demolished by more radical theories of the supremacy of the object. Whoever paints a correct state of things, to meet the objection that he does not know what he wants, cannot disregard that supremacy, not even as supremacy over him. Even if he could imagine all things radically altered, his imagination would remain chained to him and to his present time as static points of reference, and everything would be askew. In a state of freedom even the sharpest critic would be a different person, like the ones he wants to change.

The chances are that every citizen of the wrong world would find the right one unbearable; he would be too impaired for it. To the consciousness of intellectuals who do not sympathize with the world spirit, this should add a dash of tolerance amidst their resistance. If a man will not be stopped from differing and criticizing, he is still not free to put himself in the right. Throughout the world, of course, no matter under which political system, such added indulgence would be ostracized is decadent. The aporia extends to the teleological concept of a happiness of mankind that would be the happiness of individuals; the fixation of one's own need and one's own longing mars the idea of a happiness that will not arise until the category of the individual ceases to be self-seclusive. Happiness is not invariant; to be always the same is the essence of unhappiness alone.

From the start, whatever happiness is intermittently tolerated or granted by the existing entirety bears the marks of its own particularity.[44] To this day, all happiness is a pledge of what has not yet been, and the belief in its imminence obstructs its becoming. This makes the anti-happiness phrases in Hegel's *Philosophy of History* truer than they were meant to be at the time: "Happy is what we call one who finds himself in harmony with himself. History too can be contemplated from the point of view of happiness; but history is not the soil for happiness. In history, times of happiness are empty pages. There is satisfaction in world history; but this is not what we call happiness, for it is the satisfaction of purposes standing above particular concerns. Purposes of significance in world history must be pursued by abstract volition, with energy. The world-historic individuals who pursued such ends did indeed satisfy themselves, but their aim was not to be happy."[45]

It certainly was not, but their renunciation—still confessed by Zarathustra—expresses the insufficiency of individual happiness compared with utopia. Happiness would be nothing short of deliverance from particularity as a general principle irreconcilable with individual human happiness here and now. But the repressive side of Hegel's position on happiness is not to be treated in his own fashion, as a quantité négligeable from a supposedly higher standpoint. However exigently he corrects his own historic optimism in the line that history is not the soil for happiness, he is transgressing when he seeks to establish that line as an idea beyond happiness. Nowhere is the latent estheticism of one for whom reality cannot be real enough as striking as it is here.[46] If times of happiness are to be history's empty pages—a dubious claim, by the way, considering such fairly happy periods as the European nineteenth century, which nevertheless did not want historic dynamism—this metaphor, in a book said to register deeds of greatness, suggests a concept borrowed unreflectively from educational conventions: the concept of world history as the grandiose.

A spectator intoxicated with battles, upheavals, and catastrophes is silent on whether the liberation he advocates, bourgeois style, would not have to free itself from that category. This is what Marx had in mind: he designated the sphere of politics, the quantity rigged up for contemplation, as ideology and as transitory. The thought's position toward happiness would be the negation of all false happiness. Sharply opposed to the all-governing view, it postulates the idea of an objectivity of happiness, as Kierkegaard conceived it negatively in his doctrine of objective despair.

"NATURAL HISTORY"

The objectivity of historic life is that of natural history. Marx, as opposed to Hegel, knew this and knew it strictly in the context of the universal that is realized over the subjects' heads: "Even if a society has found its natural law of motion—and the present work's ultimate goal is to unveil the law of modern society's economic motion—natural evolutionary phases can be neither skipped nor decreed out of existence . . . I certainly do not depict the figures of capitalist and landowner in any rosy light. But this is a matter of persons only insofar as they personify economic categories, insofar as they are carriers of specific class relationships and interests. I comprehend the development of society's economic formation of society as a process of natural history; less than any other does my standpoint permit holding the individual responsible for conditions whose social creature he remains, no matter how far he may subjectively rise above them."[47]

What is meant here is certainly not Feuerbach's anthropological concept of nature, against which Marx aimed dialectical materialism in the sense of a Hegelian reprise against the Left Hegelians.[48] The so-called law of nature that is merely one of capitalist society, after all, is therefore called "mystification" by Marx. "Actually expressed by the law of capitalist accumulation that has been mystified into a law of nature is thus only the fact that its nature excludes any decrease in the degree of labor's exploitation, or any increase in the price of labor, which might seriously threaten the constant reproduction of the capital proportion, and its reproduction on a constantly widened scale. It cannot be different in a mode of production that has the worker exist for the need to utilize existing values rather than the other way round, having objective wealth exist for the worker's need to develop."[49]

That law is natural because of its inevitable character under the prevailing conditions of production. Ideology is not superimposed as a detachable layer on the being of society; it is inherent in that being. It rests upon abstraction, which is of the essence of the barter process. Without disregard for living human beings there could be no swapping. What this implies in the real progress of life to this day is the necessity of social semblance. Its core is value as a thing-in-itself, value as "nature." The natural growth of capitalist society is real, and at the same time it is that semblance. That the assumption of natural laws is not to be taken *à la lettre*— that least of all is it to be ontologized in the sense of a design, whatever its kind, of so-called "man"—this is confirmed by the strongest motive behind all Marxist theory: that those laws can be abolished. The realm of freedom would no sooner begin than they would cease to apply.

By mobilizing Hegel's mediative philosophy of history, the Kantian distinction between a realm of freedom and a realm of necessity is transferred to the sequence of phases. Only to such a perverter of Marxian motives as Diamat—who prolongs the realm of necessity by avowing that it is the one of freedom—could it occur to falsify Marx's polemical concept of natural legality from a construction of natural history into a scientivistic doctrine of invariants. Yet this does not rob Marx's talk of natural history of any part of its truth content, i.e., its critical content. Hegel made do with a personified transcendental subject, albeit one already short of the subject; Marx denounces not just the Hegelian transfiguration but the state of facts it occurs to. Human history, the history of the progressing mastery of nature, continues the unconscious history of nature, of devouring and being devoured.

Ironically, Marx was a Social Darwinist: what the Social Darwinists praised, and what they would like to go by, is to him the negativity in which the chance of voiding it awakens. There is a passage from *Foundations of Political Economy* that leaves no doubt that his view of natural history was critical in essence: "Much as the whole of this motion appears as a social process, much as the single moments of this motion take their departure from the conscious will and from particular purposes of individuals—the totality of the process does appear as an objective context arising by natural growth. It is indeed due to the interaction of conscious individuals, but neither seated in their consciousness nor subsumed under them as a whole."[50]

Such a social concept of nature has a dialectic of its own. The thesis that society is subject to natural laws is ideology if it is hypostatized as immutably given by nature. But this legality is real as a law of motion for the unconscious society, as *Das Kapital,* in a phenomenology of the anti-spirit, traces it from the analysis of the merchandise form to the theory of collapse. The changes from each constitutive economic form to the next occurred like those of the animal types that rose and died out over millions of years. The fetish chapter's "theological quirks of merchandise" mock the false consciousness in which the social relation of the exchange value is reflected to contracting parties as a quality of things-in-themselves; but those quirks are also as true as the practice of bloody idolatry was once a fact. For the constitutive forms of socialization, of which that mystification is one, maintain their absolute supremacy over mankind as if they were divine Providence.

The line of the theories which would become a real power if they were to seize the masses—this line is already applicable to the structures that precede all false consciousness and assure social supremacy of its irrational nimbus, of the character of a continuing taboo and archaic spell, to this day. A flash of this struck Hegel: "It is downright essential that, although the constitution originated in time, it not be viewed as a product; for it is that, rather, which is flatly in and for itself, and is therefore to be considered divine and enduring and above the sphere of that which is produced."[51]

Hegel is thus extending the concept of φύσει to the one-time definition of the counterconcept of θέσει. Conversely, the name "constitution," bestowed on the historic world which mediated all natural immediacy, defines the sphere of the mediation—the historic sphere—as nature. The Hegelian phrase rests upon Montesquieu's polemic against the archaically unhistoric common theories of the state as a contract: the institutions of public law, it says, were not created by any conscious act of will on the part of the subjects. Spirit as a second nature is the negation of the spirit, however, and that the more thoroughly the blinder its self-consciousness is to its natural growth. This is what happens to Hegel. His world spirit is the ideology of natural history. He calls it world spirit because of its power. Domination is absolutized and projected on Being itself, which is said to be the spirit. But history, the explication of something it is supposed to have always been, acquires the quality of the unhistoric.

In the midst of history, Hegel sides with its immutable element, with the ever-same identity of the process whose totality is said to bring salvation. Quite unmetaphorically, he can be charged with mythologizing history. The words "spirit" and "reconcilement" are used to disguise the suffocating myth: "Accidents happen to that which is by nature accidental, and this very fate, then, is necessity —just as philosophy and the concept will always make the aspect of mere chance disappear and in it, as in appearance, will recognize its essence, necessity. It is necessary that the finite, possessions and life, be posited as accidental because this is the concept of finiteness. This necessity has the form of a force of nature, and everything finite is mortal and will pass."[52]

Nothing else had been taught by the Western myths of nature. In line with an automatism beyond the power of the philosophy of the spirit, Hegel cites nature and natural forces as models of history. They maintain their place in philosophy, however, because the identity-positing spirit identifies with the spell of blind nature by denying it. Looking into the abyss, Hegel perceived the world-historic derring-do as a second nature; but what he glorified in it, in villainous complicity, was the first nature. "The soil of the law at large is the realm of the spirit, and the law's closer location and point of departure is the will, which is free in the sense that freedom constitutes its substance and definition, and that the legal system is the realm of realized freedom, the world of the spirit brought forth from the spirit itself, as a second nature."[53]

But the second nature, philosophically raised again for the first time in Lukács' theory of the novel,[54] remains the negation of any nature that might be conceived as the first. What is truly θέσει— produced by the functional context of individuals, if not by themselves—usurps the insignia of that which a bourgeois consciousness regards as nature and as natural. To that consciousness nothing appears as being outside any more; in a certain sense there actually is nothing outside any more, nothing unaffected by mediation, which is total. What is trapped within, therefore, comes to appear to itself as its own otherness—a primal phenomenon of idealism.

The more relentlessly socialization commands all moments of human and interhuman immediacy, the smaller the capacity of men to recall that this web has evolved, and the more irresistible its natural appearance. The appearance is reinforced as the distance between human history and nature keeps growing: nature turns into an irresistible parable of imprisonment.

The youthful Marx expressed the unending entwinement of the two elements with an extremist vigor bound to irritate dogmatic materialists: "We know only a single science, the science of history. History can be considered from two sides, divided into the history of nature and the history of mankind. Yet there is no separating the two sides; as long as men exist, natural and human history will qualify each other."[55] The traditional antithesis of nature and history is both true and false—true insofar as it expresses what happened to the natural element; false insofar as, by means of conceptual reconstruction, it apologetically repeats the concealment of history's natural growth by history itself.

HISTORY AND METAPHYSICS

At the same time, the distinction of nature and history unreflectedly expresses that division of labor in which the inevitable one of scientific methods is unhesitatingly projected on the objects. The unhistoric concept of history, harbored by a falsely resurrected metaphysics in what it calls historicity, would serve to demonstrate the agreement of ontological thought with the naturalistic thought from which the ontological one so eagerly delimits itself. When history becomes the basic ontological structure of things in being, if not indeed the *qualitas occulta* of being itself, it is mutation as immutability, copied from the religion of inescapable nature. This allows us to transpose historic specifics into invariance at will, and to wrap a philosophical cloak around the vulgar view in which historic situations seem as natural in modern times as they once seemed divinely willed. This is one of the temptations to essentialize entity.

The ontological claim to be beyond the divergence of nature and history is surreptitious. A historicity abstracted from historic existence glosses over the painful antithesis of nature and history, an antithesis which equally defies ontologization. There too the new ontology is crypto-idealistic, once more requiring identity of the nonidentical, removing by supposition of the concept, of historicity as history's carrier rather than as history, whatever would resist the concept. But what moves ontology to carry out the ideological procedure, the reconciliation in the spirit, is that the real reconciliation failed. Historic contingency and the concept are the more mercilessly antagonistic the more solidly they are entwined. Chance is the historic fate of the individual—a meaningless fate because the historic process itself usurped all meaning.

No less delusive is the question about nature as the absolute first, as the downright immediate compared with its mediations. What the question pursues is presented in the hierarchic form of analytical judgment, whose premises command whatever follows, and it thus repeats the delusion it would escape from. Once posited, the difference of θέσει and φύσει can be liquidated, not voided, by reflection. Unreflected, of course, that bisection would turn the essential historic process into a mere harmless adjunct, helping further to enthrone the unbecome as the essence. Instead, it would be up to thought to see all nature, and whatever would install itself as such, as history, and all history as nature—"to grasp historic being in its utmost historic definition, in the place where it is most historic, as natural being, or to grasp nature, in the place where it seems most deeply, inertly natural, as historic being."[56]

The moment in which nature and history become commensurable with each other is the moment of passing. This is the central cognition in Benjamin's *Origins of German Tragedy*. The poets of the Baroque, we read there, envisioned nature "as eternal passing, in which the Saturnian eye of that generation alone recognized history."[57] And not just that generation's eye; natural history still remains the canon of interpretation for philosophers of history: "When history, in tragedy, makes its entrance on the stage, it does so as writing. The countenance of nature is inscribed 'History' in pictographs of passing. The allegorical physiognomy of nature's history, brought to the stage by tragedy, is really present as a ruin."[58]

This is the transmutation of metaphysics into history. It secularizes metaphysics in the secular category pure and simple, the category of decay. Philosophy interprets that pictography, the ever new Mene Tekel, in microcosm—in the fragments which decay has chipped, and which bear the objective meanings. No recollection of transcendence is possible any more, save by way of perdition; eternity appears, not as such, but diffracted through the most perishable. Where Hegelian metaphysics transfigures the absolute by equating it with the total passing of all finite things, it simultaneously looks a little beyond the mythical spell it captures and reinforces.

THREE

MEDITATIONS ON METAPHYSICS

1

AFTER AUSCHWITZ

We cannot say any more that the immutable is truth, and that the mobile, transitory is appearance. The mutual indifference of temporality and eternal ideas is no longer tenable even with the bold Hegelian explanation that temporal existence, by virtue of the destruction inherent in its concept, serves the eternal represented by the eternity of destruction. One of the mystical impulses secularized in dialectics was the doctrine that the intramundane and historic is relevant to what traditional metaphysics distinguished as transcendence—or at least, less gnostically and radically put, that it is relevant to the position taken by human consciousness on the questions which the canon of philosophy assigned to metaphysics. After Auschwitz, our feelings resist any claim of the positivity of existence as sanctimonious, as wronging the victims; they balk at squeezing any kind of sense, however bleached, out of the victims' fate. And these feelings do have an objective side after events that make a mockery of the construction of immanence as endowed with a meaning radiated by an affirmatively posited transcendence.

Such a construction would affirm absolute negativity and would assist its ideological survival—as in reality that negativity survives anyway, in the principle of society as it exists until its self-destruction. The earthquake of Lisbon sufficed to cure Voltaire of the theodicy of Leibniz, and the visible disaster of the first nature was insignificant in comparison with the second, social one, which defies human imagination as it distills a real hell from human evil.

Our metaphysical faculty is paralyzed because actual events have shattered the basis on which speculative metaphysical thought could be reconciled with experience. Once again, the dialectical motif of quantity recoiling into quality scores an unspeakable triumph. The administrative murder of millions made of death a thing one had never yet to fear in just this fashion. There is no chance any more for death to come into the individuals' empirical life as somehow conformable with the course of that life. The last, the poorest possession left to the individual is expropriated. That in the concentration camps it was no longer an individual who died, but a specimen—this is a fact bound to affect the dying of those who escaped the administrative measure.

Genocide is the absolute integration. It is on its way wherever men are leveled off—"polished off," as the German military called it—until one exterminates them literally, as deviations from the concept of their total nullity. Auschwitz confirmed the philosopheme of pure identity as death. The most far out dictum from Beckett's *End Game,* that there really is not so much to be feared any more, reacts to a practice whose first sample was given in the concentration camps, and in whose concept—venerable once upon a time—the destruction of nonidentity is ideologically lurking. Absolute negativity is in plain sight and has ceased to surprise anyone. Fear used to be tied to the *principium individuationis* of self-preservation, and that principle, by its own consistency, abolishes itself. What the sadists in the camps foretold their victims, "Tomorrow you'll be wiggling skyward as smoke from this chimney," bespeaks the indifference of each individual life that is the direction of history. Even in his formal freedom, the individual is as fungible and replaceable as he will be under the liquidators' boots.

But since, in a world whose law is universal individual profit, the individual has nothing but this self that has become indifferent, the performance of the old, familiar tendency is at the same time the most dreadful of things. There is no getting out of this, no more than out of the electrified barbed wire around the camps. Perennial suffering has as much right to expression as a tortured man has to scream; hence it may have been wrong to say that after Auschwitz you could no longer write poems. But it is not wrong to raise the less cultural question whether after Auschwitz you can go on living—especially whether one who escaped by accident, one who by rights should have been killed, may go on living. His mere survival calls for the coldness, the basic principle of bourgeois subjectivity, without which there could have been no Auschwitz; this is the drastic guilt of him who was spared. By way of atonement he will be plagued by dreams such as that he is no longer living at all, that he was sent to the ovens in 1944 and his whole existence since has been imaginary, an emanation of the insane wish of a man killed twenty years earlier.

Thinking men and artists have not infrequently described a sense of being not quite there, of not playing along, a feeling as if they were not themselves at all, but a kind of spectator. Others often find this repulsive; it was the basis of Kierkegaard's polemic against what he called the esthetic sphere. A critique of philosophical personalism indicates, however, that this attitude toward immediacy, this disavowal of every existential posture, has a moment of objective truth that goes beyond the appearance of the self-preserving motive. "What does it really matter?" is a line we like to associate with bourgeois callousness, but it is the line most likely to make the individual aware, without dread, of the insignificance of his existence. The inhuman part of it, the ability to keep one's distance as a spectator and to rise above things, is in the final analysis the human part, the very part resisted by its ideologists.

It is not altogether implausible that the immortal part is the one that acts in this fashion. The scene of Shaw on his way to the theater, showing a beggar his identification with the hurried remark, "Press," hides a sense of that beneath the cynicism. It would help to explain the fact that startled Schopenhauer: that affections in the face of death, not only other people's but our own, are frequently so feeble. People, of course, are spellbound without exception, and none of them are capable of love, which is why everyone feels loved too little. But the spectator's posture simultaneously expresses doubt that this could be all—when the individual, so relevant to himself in his delusion, still has nothing but that poor and emotionally animal-like ephemerality.

Spellbound, the living have a choice between involuntary ataraxy —an esthetic life due to weakness—and the bestiality of the involved. Both are wrong ways of living. But some of both would be required for the right *désinvolture* and sympathy. Once overcome, the culpable self-preservation urge has been confirmed, confirmed precisely, perhaps, by the threat that has come to be ceaselessly present. The only trouble with self-preservation is that we cannot help suspecting the life to which it attaches us of turning into something that makes us shudder: into a specter, a piece of the world of ghosts, which our waking consciousness perceives to be nonexistent. The guilt of a life which purely as a fact will strangle other life, according to statistics that eke out an overwhelming number of killed with a minimal number of rescued, as if this were provided in the theory of probabilities—this guilt is irreconcilable with living. And the guilt does not cease to reproduce itself, because not for an instant can it be made fully, presently conscious.

This, nothing else, is what compels us to philosophize. And in philosophy we experience a shock: the deeper, the more vigorous its penetration, the greater our suspicion that philosophy removes us from things as they are—that an unveiling of the essence might enable the most superficial and trivial views to prevail over the views that aim at the essence. This throws a glaring light on truth itself. In speculation we feel a certain duty to grant the position of a corrective to common sense, the opponent of speculation. Life feeds the horror of a premonition: what must come to be known may resemble the down-to-earth more than it resembles the sublime; it might be that this premonition will be confirmed even beyond the pedestrian realm, although the happiness of thought, the promise of its truth, lies in sublimity alone.

If the pedestrian had the last word, if it were the truth, truth would be degraded. The trivial consciousness, as it is theoretically expressed in positivism and unreflected nominalism, may be closer than the sublime consciousness to an *adaequatio rei atque cogitationis;* its sneering mockery of truth may be truer than a superior consciousness, unless the formation of a truth concept other than that of *adaequatio* should succeed. The innervation that metaphysics might win only by discarding itself applies to such other truth, and

it is not the last among the motivations for the passage to materialism. We can trace the leaning to it from the Hegelian Marx to
Benjamin's rescue of induction; Kafka's work may be the apotheosis of the trend. If negative dialectics calls for the self-reflection of
thinking, the tangible implication is that if thinking is to be true—
if it is to be true today, in any case—it must also be a thinking
against itself. If thought is not measured by the extremity that
eludes the concept, it is from the outset in the nature of the
musical accompaniment with which the SS liked to drown out the
screams of its victims.

2

METAPHYSICS AND CULTURE

A new categorical imperative has been imposed by Hitler upon
unfree mankind: to arrange their thoughts and actions so that
Auschwitz will not repeat itself, so that nothing similar will
happen. When we want to find reasons for it, this imperative is as
refractory as the given one of Kant was once upon a time. Dealing discursively with it would be an outrage, for the new imperative
gives us a bodily sensation of the moral addendum—bodily, because it is now the practical abhorrence of the unbearable physical
agony to which individuals are exposed even with individuality
about to vanish as a form of mental reflection. It is in the un-
varnished materialistic motive only that morality survives.

The course of history forces materialism upon metaphysics,
traditionally the direct antithesis of materialism. What the mind
once boasted of defining or construing as its like moves in the direction of what is unlike the mind, in the direction of that which eludes
the rule of the mind and yet manifests that rule as absolute evil. The
somatic, unmeaningful stratum of life is the stage of suffering, of
the suffering which in the camps, without any consolation, burned
every soothing feature out of the mind, and out of culture, the
mind's objectification. The point of no return has been reached in
the process which irresistibly forced metaphysics to join what it was
once conceived against. Not since the youthful Hegel has phi-

losophy—unless selling out for authorized cerebration—been able to repress how very much it slipped into material questions of existence.

Children sense some of this in the fascination that issues from the flayer's zone, from carcasses, from the repulsively sweet odor of putrefaction, and from the opprobrious terms used for that zone. The unconscious power of that realm may be as great as that of infantile sexuality; the two intermingle in the anal fixation, but they are scarcely the same. An unconscious knowledge whispers to the child what is repressed by civilized education; this is what matters, says the whispering voice. And the wretched physical existence strikes a spark in the supreme interest that is scarcely less repressed; it kindles a "What is that?" and "Where is it going?" The man who managed to recall what used to strike him in the words "dung hill" and "pig sty" might be closer to absolute knowledge than Hegel's chapter in which readers are promised such knowledge only to have it withheld with a superior mien. The integration of physical death into culture should be rescinded in theory—not, however, for the sake of an ontologically pure being named Death, but for the sake of that which the stench of cadavers expresses and we are fooled about by their transfiguration into "remains."

A child, fond of an innkeeper named Adam, watched him club the rats pouring out of holes in the courtyard; it was in his image that the child made its own image of the first man. That this has been forgotten, that we no longer know what we used to feel before the dogcatcher's van, is both the triumph of culture and its failure. Culture, which keeps emulating the old Adam, cannot bear to be reminded of that zone, and precisely this is not to be reconciled with the conception that culture has of itself. It abhors stench because it stinks—because, as Brecht put it in a magnificent line, its mansion is built of dogshit. Years after that line was written, Auschwitz demonstrated irrefutably that culture has failed.

That this could happen in the midst of the traditions of philosophy, of art, and of the enlightening sciences says more than that these traditions and their spirit lacked the power to take hold of men and work a change in them. There is untruth in those fields themselves, in the autarky that is emphatically claimed for them. All post-Auschwitz culture, including its urgent critique, is garbage. In restoring itself after the things that happened without resistance in its own countryside, culture has turned entirely into the ideology it had been potentially—had been ever since it presumed, in opposition to material existence, to inspire that existence with the light denied it by the separation of the mind from manual labor. Whoever pleads for the maintenance of this radically culpable and shabby culture becomes its accomplice, while the man who says no to culture is directly furthering the barbarism which our culture showed itself to be.

Not even silence gets us out of the circle. In silence we simply use the state of objective truth to rationalize our subjective incapacity, once more degrading truth into a lie. When countries of the East, for all their drivel to the contrary, abolished culture or transformed it into rubbish as a mere means of control, the culture that moans about it is getting what it deserves, and what on its part, in the name of people's democratic right to their own likeness, it is zealously heading for. The only difference is that when the apparatchiks over there acclaim their administrative barbarism as culture and guard its mischief as an inalienable heritage, they convict its reality, the infrastructure, of being as barbarian as the superstructure they are dismantling by taking it under their management. In the West, at least, one is allowed to say so.

The theology of the crisis registered the fact it was abstractly and therefore idly rebelling against: that metaphysics has merged with culture. The aureole of culture, the principle that the mind is absolute, was the same which tirelessly violated what it was pretending to express. After Auschwitz there is no word tinged from on high, not even a theological one, that has any right unless it underwent a transformation. The judgment passed on the ideas long before, by Nietzsche, was carried out on the victims, reiterating the challenge of the traditional words and the test whether God would permit this without intervening in his wrath.

A man whose admirable strength enabled him to survive Auschwitz and other camps said in an outburst against Beckett that if Beckett had been in Auschwitz he would be writing differently, more positively, with the front-line creed of the escapee. The escapee is right in a fashion other than he thinks. Beckett, and whoever else remained in control of himself, would have been broken in Auschwitz and probably forced to confess that front-line creed which the escapee clothed in the words "Trying to give men courage"—as if this were up to any structure of the mind; as if the intent to address men, to adjust to them, did not rob them of what is their due even if they believe the contrary. That is what we have come to in metaphysics.

3

DYING TODAY

And this lends suggestive force to the wish for a fresh start in metaphysics or, as they call it, for radical questioning—the wish to scrape off the delusions which a culture that had failed was papering over its guilt and over truth. But yielding to the urge for an unspoiled basic stratum will make that supposed demolition even more of a conspiracy with the culture one boasts of razing. While the fascists raged against destructive cultural bolshevism, Heidegger was making destruction respectable as a means to penetrate Being. The practical test followed promptly. Metaphysical reflections that seek to get rid of their cultural, indirect elements deny the relation of their allegedly pure categories to their social substance. They disregard society, but encourage its continuation in existing forms, in the forms which in turn block both the cognition of truth and its realization. The idol of pure original experience is no less of a hoax than that which has been culturally processed, the obsolete categorial stock of what is θέσει. The only possible escape route would be to define both by their indirectness: culture as the lid on the trash; and nature, even where it takes itself for the bedrock of Being, as the projection of the wretched cultural wish that in all change things must stay the same. Not even the experience of death suffices as the ultimate and undoubted, as a metaphysics like the one Descartes deduced once from the nugatory *ego cogitans*.

The deterioration of the death metaphysics, whether into advertisements for heroic dying or to the triviality of purely restating the unmistakable fact that men must die—all this ideological mischief probably rests on the fact that human consciousness to this day is too weak to sustain the experience of death, perhaps even too weak for its conscious acceptance. No man who deals candidly and freely with the objects has a life sufficient to accomplish what every man's life potentially contains; life and death cleave asunder. The reflections that give death a meaning are as helpless as the tautological ones. The more our consciousness is extricated from animality and comes to strike us as solid and lasting in its forms, the more stubbornly will it resist anything that would cause it to doubt its own eternity.

Coupled with the subject's historic enthronement as a mind was the delusion of its inalienability. Early forms of property coincided with magical practices designed to banish death, and as all human relations come to be more completely determined by property, the *ratio* exorcises death as obstinately as rites ever did. At a final stage, in despair, death itself becomes property. Its metaphysical uplifting relieves us of the its experience. Our current death metaphysics is nothing but society's impotent solace for the fact that social change has robbed men of what was once said to make death bearable for them, of the feeling of its epic unity with a full life.

In that feeling, too, the dominion of death may have been only transfigured by the weariness of the aged, of those who are tired of life and imagine it is right for them to die because the laborious life they had before was not living either, because it left them not even strong enough to resist death. In the socialized society, however, in the inescapably dense web of immanence, death is felt exclusively as external and strange. Men have lost the illusion that it is commensurable with their lives. They cannot absorb the fact that they must die. Attached to this is a perverse, dislocated bit of hope: that death does not constitute the entirety of existence—as it does to Heidegger—is the very reason why a man who is not yet debilitated will experience death and its envoys, the ailments, as heterogeneous and alien to the ego.

The reason, one may say nimbly, is that the ego is nothing but the self-preserving principle opposed to death, and that death therefore defies absorption in consciousness, which is the ego. But our experience of consciousness scarcely supports this view: in the face of death, consciousness does not necessarily take the form of defiance, as one would expect. Hardly any subject bears out Hegel's doctrine that whatever is will perish of itself. Even to the aging who perceive the signs of their debility, the fact that they must die seems rather like an accident caused by their own physis, with traits of the same contingency as that of the external accidents typical nowadays.

This strengthens a speculation in counterpoint to the insight of the object's supremacy: whether the mind has not an element of independence, an unmixed element, liberated at the very times when the mind is not devouring everything and by itself reproducing the doom of death. Despite the deceptive concern with self-preservation, it would hardly be possible without that mental element to explain the resistant strength of the idea of immortality, as Kant still harbored it. Of course, those powers of resistance seem to wane in the history of the species as they do in decrepit individuals. After the decline—long ratified in secret—of the objective religions that had pledged to rid it of its sting, death is now rendered completely and utterly alien by the socially determined decline of continuous experience as such.

As the subjects live less, death grows more precipitous, more terrifying. The fact that it literally turns them into things makes them aware of reification, their permanent death and the form of their relations that is partly their fault. The integration of death in civilization, a process without power over death and a ridiculous cosmetic procedure in the face of death, is the shaping of a reaction to this social phenomenon, a clumsy attempt of the barter society to stop up the last holes left open by the world of merchandise.

Death and history, particularly the collective history of the individual category, form a constellation. Once upon a time the individual, Hamlet, inferred his absolute essentiality from the dawning awareness of the irrevocability of death; now the downfall of the individual brings the entire construction of bourgeois existence down with it. What is destroyed is a nonentity, in itself and perhaps even for itself. Hence the constant panic in view of death, a panic not to be quelled any more except by repressing the thought of death. Death as such, or as a primal biological phenomenon, is not to be extracted from the convolutions of history;[1] for that, the individual as the carrier of the experience of death is far too much of a historical category. The statement that death is always the same is as abstract as it is untrue. The manner of people's coming to terms with death varies all the way into their physical side, along with the concrete conditions of their dying.

In the camps death has a novel horror; since Auschwitz, fearing death means fearing worse than death. What death does to the socially condemned can be anticipated biologically on old people we love; not only their bodies but their egos, all the things that justified their definition as human, crumble without illness, without violence from outside. The remnant of confidence in their transcendent duration vanishes during their life on earth, so to speak: what should be the part of them that is not dying? The comfort of faith—that even in such disintegration, or in madness, the core of men continuous to exist—sounds foolish and cynical in its indifference to such experiences. It extends, into infinity, a pearl of pompous philistine wisdom: "One always remains what he is." The man who turns his back on the negation of a possible fulfillment of his metaphysical need is sneering at that need.

Even so, it is impossible to think of death as the last thing pure and simple. Attempts to express death in language are futile, all the way into logic, for who should be the subject of which we predicate that it is dead, here and now? Lust—which wants eternity, according to a luminous word of Nietzsche's—is not the only one to balk at passing. If death were that absolute which philosophy tried in vain to conjure positively, everything is nothing; all that we think, too, is thought into the void; none of it is truly thinkable. For it is a feature of truth that it will last, along with its temporal core. Without any duration at all there would be no truth, and the last trace of it would be engulfed in death, the absolute.

The idea of absolute death is hardly less unthinkable than that of immortality. But for all its being unthinkable, the thought of death is not proof against the unreliability of any kind of meta-physical experience. The web of semblance in which men are caught extends to their imagined ways of tearing the veil. Kant's epistemological question, "How is metaphysics possible?" yields to a question from the philosophy of history: "Is it still possible to have a metaphysical experience?" That experience was never located so far beyond the temporal as the academic use of the word metaphysics suggests. It has been observed that mysticism—whose very name expresses the hope that institutionalization may save the immediacy of metaphysical experience from being lost altogether—establishes social traditions and comes from tradition, across the lines of demarcation drawn by religions that regard each other as heretical. Cabbala, the name of the body of Jewish mysticism, means tradition. In its farthest ventures, metaphysical immediacy did not deny how much of it is not immediate.

If it cites tradition, however, it must also admit its dependence upon the historic state of mind. Kant's metaphysical ideas were removed from the existential judgments of an experience that re-quired material for its fulfillment, yet the place he assigned to them, despite the antinomies, was in consistence with pure reason. Today, those ideas would be as absurd as the ideas expressing their absence are said to be, in a deliberately defensive classifica-tion. But if I will not deny that the philosophy of history has over-thrown the metaphysical ideas, and yet I cannot bear that over-throw unless I am to deny my own consciousness as well—then a confusion that goes beyond mere semantics tends straightway to promote the fate of metaphysical ideas to a metaphysical rank of its own. The secret paralogism is that despair of the world, a despair that is true, based on facts, and neither esthetic weltschmerz nor a wrong, reprehensible consciousness, guarantees to us that the hopelessly missed things exist, though existence at large has be-come a universal guilt context.

Of all the disgrace deservedly reaped by theology, the worst is the positive religions' howl of rejoicing at the unbelievers' despair. They have gradually come to intone their Te Deum wherever God is denied, because at least his name is mentioned. As the means usurp the end in the ideology swallowed by all populations on earth, so, in the metaphysics that has risen nowadays, does the need usurp that which is lacking. The truth content of the deficiency becomes a matter of indifference; people assert it as being good for people. The advocates of metaphysics argue in unison with the pragmatism they hold in contempt, with the pragmatism that dissolves metaphysics a priori. Likewise, despair is the final ideology, historically and socially as conditioned as the course of cognition that has been gnawing at the metaphysical ideas and cannot be stopped by a *cui bono*.

4

HAPPINESS AND IDLE WAITING

What is a metaphysical experience? If we disdain projecting it upon allegedly primal religious experiences, we are most likely to visualize it as Proust did, in the happiness, for instance, that is promised by village names like Applebachsville, Wind Gap, or Lords Valley. One thinks that going there would bring the fulfillment, as if there were such a thing. Being really there makes the promise recede like a rainbow. And yet one is not disappointed; the feeling now is one of being too close, rather, and not seeing it for that reason. And the difference between the landscapes and regions that determine the imagery of a childhood is presumably not great at all; what Proust saw in Illiers must have happened elsewhere to many children of the same social stratum. But what it takes to form this universal, this authentic part of Proust's presentation, is to be entranced in one place without squinting at the universal.

To the child it is self-evident that what delights him in his favorite village is found only there, there alone and nowhere else. He is mistaken; but his mistake creates the model of experience, of a concept that will end up as the concept of the thing itself, not as a poor projection from things. The wedding where Proust's narrator as a child gets his first look at the Duchess de Guermantes may have occurred just that way, with the same power over his later life, at a different place and time. Only in the face of absolute, indissoluble individuation can we hope that this, exactly this has existed and is going to exist; fulfilling this hope alone would fulfill the concept of the concept. But the concept clings to the promised happiness, while the world that denies us our happiness is the world of the reigning universal, the world stubbornly opposed by Proust's reconstruction of experience.

Happiness, the only part of metaphysical experience that is more than impotent longing, gives us the inside of objects as something removed from the objects. Yet the man who enjoys this kind of experience naïvely, as though putting his hands on what the experience suggests, is acceding to the terms of the empirical world—terms he wants to transcend, though they alone give him the chance of transcending. The concept of metaphysical experience is antinomical, not only as taught by Kantian transcendental dialectics, but in other ways. A metaphysics proclaimed without recourse to subjective experience, without the immediate presence of the subject, is helpless before the autonomous subject's refusal to have imposed upon it what it cannot understand. And yet, whatever is directly evident to the subject suffers of fallibility and relativity.

The category of reification, which was inspired by the wishful image of unbroken subjective immediacy, no longer merits the key position accorded to it, overzealously, by an apologetic thinking happy to absorb materialist thinking. This acts back upon whatever goes under the concept of metaphysical experience. From the young Hegel on, philosophers have been attacking objective theological categories as reifications, and those categories are by no means mere residues which dialectics eliminate. They are complementary to the weakness of idealistic dialectics, of an identitarian thought that lays claim to what lies outside thought—although there is no possible definition of something contrasted with thought as its mere otherness. Deposited in the objectivity of the metaphysical categories was not congealed society alone, as the Existentialists would have it; that objectivity was also a deposit of the object's supremacy as a moment of dialectics. The total liquefaction of everything thinglike regressed to the subjectivism of the pure act. It hypostatized the indirect as direct. Pure immediacy and fetishism are equally untrue. In our insistence on immediacy against reification we are (as perceived in Hegel's institutionalism) relinquishing the element of otherness in dialectics—as arbitrary a procedure as the later Hegel's unfeasible practice to arrest dialectics in something solid beyond it. Yet the surplus over the subject, which a subjective metaphysical experience will not be talked out of, and the element of truth in reity —these two extremes touch in the idea of truth. For there could no more be truth without a subject freeing itself from delusions than there could be truth without that which is not the subject, that in which truth has its archetype.

Pure metaphysical experience grows unmistakably paler and more desultory in the course of the secularization process, and that softens the substantiality of the older type. Negatively, that type holds out in the demand "Can this be all?"—a demand most likely to be actualized as waiting in vain. Artists have registered it; in *Wozzek,* Alban Berg gave the highest rank to bars that express idle waiting as music alone can express it, and he cited the harmony of those bars in the crucial caesuras and at the close of *Lulu.* Yet no such innervation, none of what Bloch called "symbolic intentionality," is proof against adulteration by mere life. Idle waiting does not guarantee what we expect; it reflects the condition measured by its denial. The less of life remains, the greater the temptation for our consciousness to take the sparse and abrupt living remnants for the phenomenal absolute.

Even so, nothing could be experienced as truly alive if something that transcends life were not promised also; no straining of the concept leads beyond that. The transcendent is, and it is not. We despair of what is, and our despair spreads to the transcendental ideas that used to call a halt to despair. That the finite world of infinite agony might be encompassed by a divine cosmic plan must impress anyone not engaged in the world's business as the kind of madness that goes so well with positive normalcy. The theological conception of the paradox, that last, starved-out bastion, is past rescuing—a fact ratified by the course of the world in which the *skandalon* that caught Kierkegaard's eye is translated into outright blasphemy.

5

"NIHILISM"

The metaphysical categories live on, secularized, in what the vulgar drive to higher things calls the question of the meaning of life. The word has a ring of *weltanschauung* which condemns the question. All but inevitably, it will fetch the answer that life makes whatever sense the questioner gives it. Not even a Marxism debased to an official creed will say much else, as witness the late Lukács. But the answer is false. The concept of sense involves an objectivity beyond all "making": a sense that is "made" is already fictitious. It duplicates the subject, however collective, and defrauds it of what it seemingly granted. Metaphysics deals with an objectivity without being free to dispense with subjective reflection. The subjects are embedded in themselves, in their "constitution": what metaphysics has to ponder is the extent to which they are nonetheless able to see beyond themselves.

Philosophems that relieve themselves of this task are disqualified as counsel. The activity of someone linked with that sphere was characterized decades ago: "He travels around giving lectures on meaning to employees." People who sigh with relief when life shows some similarity to life, for once—when it is not, as Karl Kraus put it, kept going only for production's and consumption's sake—will eagerly and directly take this for a sign of a transcendent presence. The depravation of speculative idealism into the question of meaning retroactively condemns that idealism which even at its peak proclaimed such a meaning, though in somewhat different words—which proclaimed the mind as the absolute that cannot get rid of its origin in the inadequate subject, and that satisfies its need in its own image.

This is a primal phenomenon of ideology. The very totality of the question exerts a spell that comes to naught before real adversity, all affirmative poses notwithstanding. When a desperate man who wants to kill himself asks one who tries to talk him out of it about the point of living, the helpless helper will be at a loss to name one. His every attempt can be refuted as the echo of a general consensus, the core of which appeared in the old adage that the Emperor needs soldiers. A life that had any point would not need to inquire about it; the question puts the point to flight. But the opposite, abstract nihilism, would be silenced by the counter-question: "And what are you living for?" To go after the whole, to calculate the net profit of life—this is death, which the so-called question of meaning seeks to evade even if the lack of another way out makes it enthuse about the meaning of death.

What might not have to be ashamed of the name of meaning lies in candor, not in self-seclusion. As a positive statement, the thesis that life is senseless would be as foolish as it is false to avow the contrary; the thesis is true only as a blow at the high-flown avowal. Nor is Schopenhauer's inclination to identify the essence of the world, the blind will, as absolutely negative from a humane viewpoint any longer fitting. The claim of total sub-sumption is far too analogous to the positive claim of Schopen-hauer's despised contemporaries, the idealists. What flickers up here again is the nature religion, the fear of demons, which the enlightenment of Epicurus once opposed by depicting the wretched idea of disinterested divine spectators as something better. Com-pared with Schopenhauer's irrationalism, the monotheism he at-tacked in a spirit of enlightenment has some truth to it also.

Schopenhauer's metaphysics regresses to a phase before the awakening of genius amidst the mute world. He denies the mo-tive of freedom, the motive men remember for the time being and even, perhaps, in the phase of total unfreedom. Schopenhauer gets to the bottom of the delusiveness of individuation, but his recipe for freedom in Book Four, to deny the will to live, is no less delusive—as if the ephemerally individualized could have the slightest power over its negative absolute, the will as a thing in itself; as if it could escape from the spell of that will without either deceiving itself or allowing the whole metaphysics of the will to get away through the gap. Total determinism is no less mythical than are the totalities of Hegel's logic.

Schopenhauer was an idealist *malgré lui-même*, a spokesman of the spell. The *totum* is the totem. Grayness could not fill us with despair if our minds did not harbor the concept of different colors, scattered traces of which are not absent from the negative whole. The traces always come from the past, and our hopes come from their counterpart, from that which was or is doomed; such an interpretation may very well fit the last line of Benjamin's text on *Elective Affinities*: "For the sake of the hopeless only are we given hope." And yet it is tempting to look for sense, not in life at large, but in the fulfilled moments—in the moments of present existence that make up for its refusal to tolerate anything outside it.

Incomparable power flows from Proust the metaphysicist because he surrendered to this temptation with the unbridled urge to happiness of no other man, with no wish to hold back his ego. Yet in the course of his novel the incorruptible Proust confirmed that even this fullness, the instant saved by remembrance, is not it. For all his proximity to the realm of experience of Bergson, who built a theory on the conception of life as meaningful in its concretion, Proust was an heir to the French novel of disillusionment and as such a critic of Bergsonianism. The talk of the fullness of life—a *lucus a non lucendo* even where it radiates—is rendered idle by its immeasurable discrepancy with death. Since death is irrevocable, it is ideological to assert that a meaning might rise in the light of fragmentary, albeit genuine, experience. This is why one of the central points of his work, the death of Bergotte, finds Proust helping, gropingly, to express hope for a resurrection—against all the philosophy of life, yet without seeking cover from the positive religions.

The idea of a fullness of life, including the one held out to mankind by the socialist conceptions, is therefore not the utopianism one mistakes it for. It is not, because that fullness is inseparable from the craving, from what the *fin de siècle* called "living life to the full," from a desire in which violence and subjugation are inherent. If there is no hope without quenching the desire, the desire in turn is harnessed to the infamous context of like for like—and that precisely is hopeless. There is no fullness without biceps-flexing. Negatively, due to the sense of nonentity, theology turns out to be right against the believers in this life on earth. That much of the Jeremiads about the emptiness of life is true. But that emptiness would not be curable from within, by men having a change of heart; it could only be cured by abolishing the principle of denial. With that, the cycle of fulfillment and appropriation would also vanish in the end—so very much intertwined are metaphysics and the arrangement of life.

Associated with the slogans of "emptiness" and "senselessness" is that of "nihilism." Jacobi first put the term to philosophical use, and Nietzsche adopted it, presumably from newspaper accounts of terrorist acts in Russia. With an irony to which our ears have been dulled in the meantime, he used the word to denounce the opposite of what it meant in the practice of political conspirators: to denounce Christianity as the institutionalized negation of the will to live.

Philosophers would not give up the word any more. In a direction contrary to Nietzsche's, they re-functioned it conformistically into the epitome of a condition that was accused, or was accusing itself, of being null and void. For thinking habits that consider nihilism bad in any case, this condition is waiting to be injected with meaning, no matter whether the critique of the meaning, the critique attributed to nihilism, is well-founded or unfounded. Though noncommittal, such talk of nihilism lends itself to demagoguery; but it knocks down a straw man it put up itself. "Everything is nothing" is a statement as empty as the word "being" with which Hegel's motion of the concept identified it—not to hold on to the identity of the two, but to replace it, advancing and then recurring again behind abstract nihility, with something definite which by its mere definition would be more than nothing.

That men might want nothingness, as Nietzsche suggests on occasion, would be ridiculous hubris for each definite individual will. It would be that even if organized society managed to make the earth uninhabitable or to blow it up. By "believing in nothingness" we can mean scarcely more than by nothingness itself; by virtue of its own meaning, the "something" which, legitimately or not, we mean by the word "believing" is not nothing. Faith in nothingness would be as insipid as would faith in Being. It would be the palliative of a mind proudly content to see through the whole swindle. The indignation at nihilism that has today been turned on again is hardly aimed at mysticism, which finds the negated something even in nothingness, in the *nihil privativum,* and which enters into the dialectics unleashed by the word nothingness itself. The more likely point, therefore, is simply moral defamation—by mobilizing a word generally loathed and incompatible with universal good cheer—of the man who refuses to accept the Western legacy of positivity and to subscribe to any meaning of things as they exist.

When some prate of "value nihilism," on the other hand, of there being nothing to hold on to, this cries for the "overcoming" that is at home in the same subaltern language sphere. What they caulk up there is the perspective whether a condition with nothing left to hold on to would not be the only condition worthy of men, the condition that would at last allow human thought to behave as autonomously as philosophy had always merely asked it to, only to prevent it in the same breath from so behaving. Acts of overcoming—even of nihilism, along with the Nietzschean type that was meant differently and yet supplied fascism with slogans —are always worse than what they overcome. The medieval *nihil privativum* in which the concept of nothingness was recognized as the negation of something rather than as autosemantical, is as superior to the diligent "overcomings" as the image of Nirvana, of nothingness as something.

People to whom despair is not a technical term may ask whether it would be better for nothing at all to be than something. Not even to this is there a general answer. For a man in a concentration camp it would be better not to have been born —if one who escaped in time is permitted to venture any judgment about this. And yet the lighting up of an eye, indeed the feeble tail-wagging of a dog one gave a tidbit it promptly forgets, would make the ideal of nothingness evaporate. A thinking man's true answer to the question whether he is a nihilist would probably be "Not enough"—out of callousness, perhaps, because of insufficient sympathy with anything that suffers. Nothingness is the acme of abstraction, and the abstract is the abominable.

Beckett has given us the only fitting reaction to the situation of the concentration camps—a situation he never calls by name, as if it were subject to an image ban. What is, he says, is like a concentration camp. At one time he speaks of a lifelong death penalty. The only dawning hope is that there will be nothing any more. This, too, he rejects. From the fissure of inconsistency that comes about in this fashion, the image world of nothingness as something emerges to stabilize his poetry. The legacy of action in it is a carrying-on which seems stoical but is full of inaudible cries that things should be different. Such nihilism implies the contrary of identification with nothingness. To Beckett, as to the Gnostics, the created world is radically evil, and its negation is the chance of another world that is not yet. As long as the world is as it is, all pictures of reconciliation, peace, and quiet resemble the picture of death. The slightest difference between nothingness and coming to rest would be the haven of hope, the no man's land between the border posts of being and nothingness. Rather than overcome that zone, consciousness would have to extricate from it what is not in the power of the alternative. The true nihilists are the ones who oppose nihilism with their more and more faded positivities, the ones who are thus conspiring with all extant malice, and eventually with the destructive principle itself. Thought honors itself by defending what is damned as nihilism.

6

KANT'S RESIGNATION

The antinomical structure of the Kantian system expressed more than contradictions in which speculation on metaphysical objects necessarily entangles itself. It expressed something from the philosophy of history. The powerful effect which *Critique of Pure Reason* exerted far beyond its epistemological substance must be laid to the faithfulness with which it registered the state of the experience of consciousness. Historiographers of philosophy see the achievement of the work primarily in the succinct separation of valid cognition and metaphysics. In fact, it first appears as a theory of scientific judgments, nothing more. Epistemology and logic in the broader sense of the word are concerned with exploring the empirical world under laws. Kant, however, does intend more. Through the medium of epistemological reflection he answers the so-called metaphysical questions in a far from metaphysically neutral way: they really must not be asked, he tells us. In that sense, *Critique of Pure Reason* anticipates both the Hegelian doctrine that logic and metaphysics are the same and the positivistic doctrine in which the questions everything depends upon are dodged by abolishing them and decided by indirect negation.

German idealism extrapolated its metaphysics from epistemology's fundamental claim to be the carrier of the whole. If we think it through to the end, it is precisely by its denial of objectively valid cognition of the absolute that the critique of reason makes an absolute judgment. This is what idealism stressed. Still, its consistency bends the motif into its opposite and into untruth. The thesis imputed to Kant's objectively far more modest doctrines on the theory of science is a thesis he had reason to protest against, despite its inescapability. By means of conclusions stringently drawn from him, Kant was—against himself—expanded beyond the theory of science. By its consistency, idealism violated Kant's metaphysical reservation. A thought that is purely consistent will irresistibly turn into an absolute for itself.

Kant's confession that reason cannot but entangle itself in those antinomies which he proceeds to resolve by means of reason was antipositivistic;* and yet he did not spurn the positivistic comfort that a man might make himself at home in the narrow domain left to reason by the critique of the faculty of reason, that he might be content to have solid ground under his feet. Kant chimes in with the eminently bourgeois affirmation of one's own confinement. According to Hegel's critique of Kant, letting

----

* "A dialectical thesis of pure reason must therefore have this element to distinguish it from all sophistical tenets: that it does not concern an arbitrary question posed to a certain random purpose only, but a question that must necessarily be encountered in the course of each human reason; and secondly, that in its antithesis it does not bear with it a mere artificial delusion which, once perceived, will fade at once, but a natural and inevitable delusion—one that even when it has ceased to deceive us is still delusive, although not deceptive, and can thus be rendered harmless but never expunged." (Kant, *Kritik der reinen Vernunft,* Works III, p. 290f.)

reason judge whether it had passed the bounds of possible experience, and whether it was free to do so, presupposes already that there is a position beyond the realms separated on the Kantian map, that there is a court of last resort, so to speak.* As a possibility of decision, and without accounting for it, the intellectual realm was confronted by Kant's topological zeal with the very transcendence on which he banned positive judgments.

German idealism came to vest this authority in the absolute subject "Mind," which was said to be producing the subject-object dichotomy and thus the limit of finite cognition. Once this metaphysical view of the mind has lost its potency, however, the delimiting intention ceases to restrict anything but the cognitive subject. The critical subject turns into a resigned one. No longer trusting the infinity of its animating essence, it goes against that essence to reinforce its own finiteness, to affix itself to the finite. That subject wants to be undisturbed all the way into metaphysical sublimation; the absolute becomes for it an idle concern. This is the repressive side of Criticism. Its idealist successors were as far ahead of their class as they were in rebellion against it.

Originally lurking in what Nietzsche still extolled as intellectual honesty is the self-hatred of the mind, the internalized Protestant rage at the harlot Reason. A rationality that eliminates imagination—still ranking high for the Enlightenment and for Saint-Simon, and drying up, complementarily, on its own—such a rationality is tainted with irrationalism. A change also occurs in the function of critique: it repeats the transformation of the bourgeoisie from a revolutionary class into a conservative one. An echo of this condition is the now world-wide and pervasive malice of a common sense proud of its own obtuseness. This malice argues, *e contrario,* for disregarding the boundary upon the cult

---

* "Usually . . . great store is set by the barriers to thought, to reason, and so forth, and those barriers are said to be impassable. Behind this contention lies unawareness that by its very definition as a barrier a thing is already passed. For a definite thing, a limit, is defined as a barrier—opposed to its otherness at large—only against that which it does not bar; the otherness of a barrier is its transcending." (Hegel, Works 4, p. 153.)

of which all are by now agreed. It is a "positive" malice, marked by the same arbitrariness of subjective arrangement which the common sense incarnated in Babbitt attributes to speculative thought.

Kant's metaphor for the land of truth, the island in the ocean, objectively characterizes the Robinson Crusoe style of the ivory tower, just as the dynamics of productive forces was quick enough to destroy the idyll in which the petty bourgeoisie, rightly suspicious of dynamics, would have liked to linger. The homeliness of Kant's doctrine is in crass conflict with his pathos of the infinite. If practical reason has primacy over the theoretical one, the latter, itself a mode of conduct, would have to approach the alleged capacity of its superior if the caesura between intellect and reason is not to void reason's very concept. Yet this is precisely the direction in which Kant is pushed by his idea of scientificality. He must not say so, and yet he cannot help saying so; the discrepancy, which in intellectual history is so easily put down as a relic of the older metaphysics, lies in the matter itself. Kant boasts of having surveyed the Isle of Cognition, but its own narrow selfrighteousness moves that isle into the area of untruth, which he projects on the cognition of the infinite. It is impossible to endow the cognition of finite things with a truth derived, in its turn, from the absolute—in Kantian terms, from reason—which cognition cannot reach. At every moment, the ocean of Kant's metaphor threatens to engulf the island.

7

RESCUING URGE AND BLOCK

That metaphysical philosophy, which historically coincides in essence with the great systems, has more glamour to it than the empiricist and positivist systems is not just a matter of esthetics, as the inane word "conceptual poetry" would have us believe. Nor is it psychological wish fulfillment. If the immanent quality of a type of thinking, the strength manifested in it, the resistance, the imagination, the unity of critique with its opposite—if all this is not an *index veri,* it is at least an indication. Even if it were a fact, it could not be the truth that Carnap and Mieses are truer than Kant and Hegel. The Kant of *Critique of Pure Reason* said in the doctrine of ideas that theory without metaphysics is not possible. The fact that it *is* possible implies that metaphysics has its justification, the justification advanced by the same Kant whose work effectively crushed metaphysics.

Kant's rescue of the intelligible sphere is not merely the Protestant apologetics known to all; it is also an attempted intervention in the dialectics of enlightenment, at the point where this dialectics terminates in the abolition of reason. That the ground of the Kantian rescuing urge lies far deeper than just in the pious wish to have, amidst nominalism and against it, some of the traditional ideas in hand—this is attested by the construction of immortality as a postulate of practical reason. The postulate condemns the intolerability of extant things and confirms the spirit of its recognition. That no reforms within the world sufficed to do justice to the dead, that none of them touched upon the wrong of death—this is what moves Kantian reason to hope against reason. The secret of his philosophy is the unthinkability of despair.

Constrained by the convergence of all thoughts in something absolute, he did not leave it at the absolute line between absoluteness and existence; but he was no less constrained to draw that line. He held on to the metaphysical ideas, and yet he forbade jumping from thoughts of the absolute which might one day be realized, like eternal peace, to the conclusion that therefore the absolute exists. His philosophy—as probably every other, by the way—circles about the ontological argument for God's existence; but his own position remained open, in a grandiose ambiguity. There is the motif of *"Muss ein ewiger Vater wohnen*—must live an eternal Father," which Beethoven's composition of Schiller's Kantian Hymn to Joy accentuated in true Kantian spirit, on the word "must." And there are the passages in which Kant—as close to Schopenhauer here as Schopenhauer later claimed— spurned the metaphysical ideas, particularly that of immortality, as imprisoned in our views of space and time and thus restricted on their part. He disdained the passage to affirmation.

Even according to Hegel's critique, the so-called "Kantian block," the theory of the bounds of possible positive cognition, derives from the form-content dualism. Human consciousness, says the anthropological argument, is condemned, as it were, to eternal detention in the forms it happens once to have been given. What affects those forms is said to lack all definition, to need the forms of consciousness to acquire definition. But the forms are not that ultimate which Kant described. By virtue of the reciprocity between them and their existing content, they too go through an evolution. Yet this cannot be reconciled with the conception of the indestructible block. Once the forms are elements of a dynamics—as would be truly in keeping with the view of the subject as original apperception—their positive appearance can no more be stipulated for all future cognition than any one of the contents without which they do not exist, and with which they change. The dichotomy of form and content would have to be absolute to allow Kant to say that it forbids any content to be derived only from the forms, not from the matter. If the material element lies in the forms themselves, the block is shown to have been made by the very subject it inhibits. The subject is both exalted and debased if the line is drawn inside it, in its transcendental logical organization. The naïve consciousness, to which Goethe too probably tended—that we do not know yet, but that some day, perhaps, the mystery will be solved after all—comes closer to metaphysical truth than does Kant's *ignoramus*. His anti-idealist doctrine of the absolute barrier and the idealist doctrine of absolute knowledge are far less inimical to one another than the adherents of both thought they were; the idealist doctrine, according to the train of thought of Hegel's *Phenomenology,* comes also to the net result that absolute knowledge is nothing but the train of thought of *Phenomenology* itself, and thus in no way a transcending.

Kant, who forbids straying into the intelligible world, equates the subjective side of Newtonian science with cognition, and its objective side with truth. The question how metaphysics is possible as a science must be taken precisely: whether metaphysics satisfies the criteria of a cognition that takes its bearings from the ideal of mathematics and so-called classical physics. Mindful of his assumption that metaphysics is a natural disposition, Kant poses the problem with reference to the "how" of generally valid and necessarily supposed cognition; but what he means is the "what" of that cognition, its possibility itself. He denies the possibility, measured by that scientific ideal.

Yet science, whose imposing results make him relieve it of further misgivings, is a product of bourgeois society. The rigidly dualistic basic structure of Kant's model for criticizing reason duplicates the structure of a production process where the merchandise drops out of the machines as his phenomena drop out of the cognitive mechanism, and where the material and its own definition are matters of indifference vis-à-vis the profit, much as appearance is a matter of indifference to Kant, who had it stenciled. The final product with its exchange value is like the Kantian objects, which are made subjectively and are accepted as objectivities. The permanent *reductio ad hominem* of all appearance prepares cognition for purposes of internal and external dominance. Its supreme expression is the principle of unity, a principle borrowed from production, which has been split into partial acts.

The moment of dominance in Kant's theory of reason is that is really concerns itself only with the domain in which scientific theses hold sway. Kant's confinement of his questioning to empirically organized natural science, his orientation of it by validity, and his subjectivist critique of knowledge are so entwined that none could be without the others. As long as the subjective inquiry is to be a testing of validities, cognitions which have no scientific sanction—in other words, which are not necessary and not universal—are second-rate; this is why all efforts to emancipate Kantian epistemology from the realm of natural science had to fail. We cannot supplement and make up within the identifying rudiment what that rudiment eliminates by nature; the most we can do is change the rudiment because we recognize its insufficiency. The fact, however, that the rudiment does so little justice to the living experience which cognition is—this fact indicates that the rudiment is false, that it is incapable of doing what it sets out to do, namely, to provide a basis for experience. For such a rigid and invariant basis contradicts that which experience tells us about itself, about the change that occurs constantly in the forms of experience, the more open it is, and the more it is actualized. To be incapable of this change is to be incapable of experience.

To Kant we can add no theorems of knowledge that were not developed by him, because their exclusion is central to his epistemology; the systematic claim of the doctrine of pure reason makes this exclusion unmistakable enough. The Kantian system is a system of stop signals. The subjectively directed constitutional analysis does not alter the world as it is given to a naïve bourgeois consciousness; rather, it takes pride in its "empirical realism." But it sees the height of the validity it claims as one with the level of abstraction. Obsessed with the apriority of its synthetic judgments, it tends to expurgate any part of cognition that does not bow to their rules. The social division of labor is respected without reflection, along with the flaw that has become strikingly clear in the two hundred years since: that the sciences organized by a division of labor have usurped an illegitimate monopoly on truth. Put in bourgeois and very Kantian terms, the paralogisms of Kant's epistemology are the bad checks that went to protest with the unfoldment of science into a mechanical activity. The authority of the Kantian concept of truth turned terroristic with the ban on thinking the absolute. Irresistibly, it drifts toward a ban on all thinking. What the Kantian block projects on truth is the self-maiming of reason, the mutilation reason inflicted upon itself as a rite of initiation into its own scientific character. Hence the scantiness of what happens in Kant as cognition, compared with the experience of the living, by which the idealistic systems wished to do right, even though in the wrong fashion.

Kant would hardly have denied that the idea of truth mocks the scientivistic ideal. But the discrepancy is by no means revealed only in view of the *mundus intelligibilis;* it shows in every cognition that is accomplished by a consciousness free of leading strings. In that sense the Kantian block is a phenomenon blaspheming against the spirit in which Hölderlin's late hymns philo-

MEDITATIONS ON METAPHYSICS

sophically outstripped philosophy. The idealists were well aware of this, but what was manifest to them came under the same spell which forced Kant to contaminate experience and science. Though many an idealistic stirring aimed at openness, the idealists would pursue it by extending the Kantian principle, and the contents grew even more unfree to them than to Kant. And this in turn invests the Kantian block with its moment of truth: it forestalled a mythology of the concept.

Socially there is good reason to suspect that block, the bar erected against the absolute, of being one with the necessity to labor, which in reality keeps mankind under the same spell that Kant transfigured into a philosophy. The imprisonment in immanence to which he honestly and brutally condemns the mind is the imprisonment in self-preservation, as it is imposed on men by a society that conserves nothing but the denials that would not be necessary any more. Once the natural-historic cares we share with beetles were broken through, a change would occur in the attitude which human consciousness takes toward truth. Its present attitude is dictated by the objectivity that keeps men in the state they are in. Even if Kant's doctrine of the block was part of a social delusion, it is still based as solidly as the factual rule of the delusion. The separation of the sensual and intellectual realms, the nerve of the argument in favor of the block, is a social product; by the *chorismos,* sensuality is designated as a victim of the intellect because, all arrangements to the contrary notwithstanding, the state of the world fails to content sensuality.

The social qualification of the sensual realm might well permit the split to disappear one day—whereas the idealists are ideologues, either glorifying the reconciliation of the unreconciled as accomplished or attributing it to the unreconciled totality. The idealistic efforts to explicate the mind as its own union with that which is not identical with it were as consistent as they were futile. Such self-reflection happens even to the thesis of the primacy of practical reason, a thesis which from Kant, via the idealists, leads straight to Marx. Moreover, the dialectics of practice called for the abolition of practice, of production for production's sake, of the universal cover for the wrong practice. This is the materialistic ground of the traits which in negative dialectics rebel against the official doctrinal concept of materialism. The elements of independence and irreducibility in the mind may well accord with the supremacy of the object. As soon as the mind calls its chains by name, the chains it gets into by chaining others, it grows independent here and now. It begins to anticipate, and what it anticipates is freedom, not entangled practice. The idealists made a heaven of the mind, but woe betide the man who had a mind.

8

MUNDUS INTELLIGIBILIS

Kant confronts the construction of his block with the positive construction of metaphysics in *Critique of Practical Reason*. He did not pass in silence over its moment of despair: "Even if a transcendental faculty of freedom may serve as a supplement, perhaps, to initiate changes in the world, this faculty would have to be solely outside the world, at least (although it always remains an audacious presumption to assume, outside the totality of all possible views, an object that cannot be given to any possible perception)."[2]

The parenthesis about the "audacious presumption" shows how skeptical Kant is of his own *mundus intelligibilis*. This formulation from the footnote to the Antithesis of the Third Antinomy comes close to atheism. What is so zealously postulated later is here called theoretically presumptuous; Kant's desperate reluctance to imagine the postulate as an existential judgment is strenuously evaded. According to the passage, it would have to be possible to conceive as an object of possible visuality, at least, what must at the same time be conceived as removed from all visuality. Reason would have to capitulate to the contradiction, unless the *hubris* of prescribing its own bounds had first irrationalistically narrowed reason's domain without tying it to those bounds objectively, as reason. But if—as by the idealists and also by the Neo-Kantians—visuality too were included in infinite reason, transcendence would be virtually cashiered by the immanence of the mind.

What Kant alludes to with respect to freedom would apply to God and immortality as well, only more so. For these do not refer to any pure possibility of conduct; their own concepts make them postulates of things in being, no matter of what kind. These entities need a "matter," and in Kant's case they would depend entirely upon that visuality whose possibility he excludes from the transcendent ideas. The pathos of Kantian intelligibility complements the difficulty of ascertaining it in any way, and if it were only in the medium of the self-sufficient thought designated by the word "intelligible." The word must not refer to anything real.

But the motion of *Critique of Practical Reason* proceeds to a positive *mundus intelligibilis* that could not be envisioned in Kant's intention. What ought to be—emphatically distinguished from what is—can no sooner be established as a realm of its own and equipped with absolute authority than the procedure will, albeit involuntarily, make it assume the character of a second existence. A thought in which we do not think something is not a thought. The ideas, the substance of metaphysics, are not visual, but neither could they be "airy nothings" of thought, lest they be stripped of all objectivity. The intelligible would be devoured by the very subject which the intelligible sphere was to transcend. A century after Kant, such flattening of the intelligible into the imaginary came to be the cardinal sin of the neo-romanticists of the fin de siècle, and of the phenomenological philosophy tailor-made to their measure.

The concept of the intelligible is not one of a reality, nor is it a concept of something imaginary. It is aporetical, rather. Nothing on earth and nothing in the empty heavens is to be saved by defending it. The "yes, but" answer to the critical argument, the refusal to have anything wrested away—these are already forms of obstinate insistence on existence, forms of a clutching that cannot be reconciled with the idea of rescue in which the spasm of such prolonged self-preservation would be eased. Nothing can be saved unchanged, nothing that has not passed through the portal of its death. If rescue is the inmost impulse of any man's spirit, there is no hope but unreserved surrender: of that which is to be rescued as well as of the hopeful spirit. The posture of hope is to hold lightly what the subject will hold on to, what the subject expects to endure. The intelligible, in the spirit of Kantian delimitation no less than in that of the Hegelian method, would be to transcend the limits drawn by both of these, to think in negations alone. Paradoxically, the intelligible sphere which Kant envisioned would once again be "appearance": it would be what that which is hidden from the finite mind shows to that mind, what the mind is forced to think and, due to its own finiteness, to disfigure. The concept of the intelligible is the self-negation of the finite mind.

In the mind, mere entity becomes aware of its deficiency; the departure from an existence obdurate in itself is the source of what separates the mind from its nature-controlling principle. The point of this turn is that the mind should not become existent in its own eyes either, to avoid an endless repetition of the eversame. The side of the mind that is hostile to life would be sheer depravity if it did not climax in its self-reflection. The asceticism which the mind demands of others is wrong, but its own asceticism is good; in its self-negation, the mind transcends itself—a step not so alien to Kant's subsequent *Metaphysics of Morals* as might be expected. To be a mind at all, it must know that what it touches upon does not exhaust it, that the finiteness that is its like does not exhaust it. The mind thinks what would be beyond it.

Such metaphysical experience is the inspiration of Kantian philosophy, once that philosophy is drawn out of the armor of its method. The question whether metaphysics is still possible at all must reflect the negation of the finite which finiteness requires. Its enigma animates the word "intelligible." The conception of that word is not wholly unmotivated, thanks to that independent moment which the mind lost by being absolutized, and which— as not identical with entity—it obtains as soon as we insist upon nonidentity, as soon as all there is does not evaporate in things of the mind. The mind, for all its indirectness, shares in existence, the substitute for its alleged transcendental purity. Although its moment of transcendent objectivity cannot be split off and ontologized, that moment is the unobtrusive site of metaphysical possibility.

The concept of the intelligible realm would be the concept of something which is not, and yet it is not a pure nonbeing. Under the rules of the sphere whose negation is the intelligible sphere, the intelligible one would have to be rejected without resistance, as imaginary. Nowhere else is truth so fragile. It may deteriorate into the hypostasis of something thought up for no reason, something in which thought means to possess what it has lost; and then again the effort to comprehend it is easy to confuse with things that are. If in our thinking we mistake thoughts for realities—in the paralogism of the ontological argument for the existence of God, which Kant demolished—our thinking is void. But the fallacy is the direct elevation of negativity, the critique of what merely is, into positivity as if the insufficiency of what is might guarantee that what is will be rid of that insufficiency. Even *in extremis* a negated negative is not a positive.

Kant called transcendental dialectics a logic of semblance: the doctrine of the contradictions in which any treatment of transcendent things as positively knowable is bound to become entangled. His verdict is not made obsolete by Hegel's effort to vindicate the logic of semblance as a logic of truth. But reflection is not cut short by the verdict on semblance. Once made conscious, the semblance is no longer the same. What finite beings say about transcendence is the semblance of transcendence; but as Kant well knew, it is a necessary semblance. Hence the incomparable metaphysical relevance of the rescue of semblance, the object of esthetics.

9

NEUTRALIZATION

In Anglo-Saxon countries Kant is often euphemistically called an agnostic. However little this leaves of the wealth of his philosophy, the awful oversimplification is not barefaced nonsense. The antinomical structure of the Kantian doctrine survives the resolution of the antinomies, and it can be crudely translated into a directive to thought: to refrain from idle questions. It is above the vulgar form of bourgeois skepticism, whose solidity is serious only about what one has safely in hand—though Kant was not utterly free of such states of mind either. His authority in Germany was surely strengthened far beyond the effect of his thoughts by the fact that in the Categorical Imperative, and indeed in the ideas of *Critique of Pure Reason,* that disdained sublimity was added with raised forefinger, as a bonus with which the bourgeoisie is as loath to dispense as with its Sunday, that parody of freedom from toil.

The element of noncommittal conciliatoriness in rigorism went rather well with the decorative tendency to neutralize all things of the mind. After the triumph of the revolution—or, where there was no revolution, after the imperceptible advance of general "bourgeoisation"—that tendency conquered the entire scenery of the mind, along with the theorems previously used as weapons of bourgeois emancipation. No longer needed for the interests of the victorious class, those theorems became uninteresting in a two-fold sense, as Spengler astutely noted in Rousseau's case. Society, for all its ideological praise of the spirit, subordinates the function of the spirit. The Kantian *non liquet* contributed to transforming the critique of feudalism's ally, religion, into that indifference which donned the mantle of humanity under the name of tolerance. The spirit, in the form of metaphysics no less than in the form of art, grows only more neutralized as the culture of which society prided itself loses its relation to any possible practice.

In Kant's metaphysical ideas that relation was still unmistakable. In those ideas bourgeois society sought to transcend its own limited principle, to void itself, as it were. Such a spirit becomes unacceptable, and culture turns into a compromise between its form of bourgeois utility and the side of it which in neo-German nomenclature is "undesirable" and projected into an unattainable distance. Material circumstances add their part. Capital, compelled to expand its investments, possesses itself of the spirit whose own inevitable objectifications spur it to transform them into property, into merchandise. Esthetics, by its disinterested approbation of the spirit, transfigures and debases it at the same time, satisfied to observe, to admire, and finally blindly and unrelatedly to revere all those things that were created and thought once upon a time, irrespective of their truth content. Objectively it is a mockery how the increasing merchandise character of culture estheticizes it for utility's sake. Philosophy becomes the manifestation of the spirit as a showpiece.

What Bernard Groethuysen traced back to the eighteenth and seventeenth centuries in religion—that the devil is no longer to be feared, and God, no longer to be hoped for—this expands beyond metaphysics, in which the memories of God and the devil live on even where it is a critical reflection on that fear and hope. What in a highly unideological sense ought to be the most urgent concern of men has vanished. Objectively it has become problematical; subjectively, the social network and the permanently overtaxing pressure to adjust leaves men neither the time nor the strength to think about it. The questions are not solved, and not even their insolubility is proven. They are forgotten, and any talk of them lulls them so much more deeply to their evil sleep. Goethe's fatal dictum that Eckermann need not read Kant because Kant's philosophy had done its job and entered into the universal consciousness—this line has triumphed in the socialization of metaphysical indifference.

The indifference of consciousness to metaphysical questions—questions that have by no means been laid to rest by satisfaction in this world—is hardly a matter of indifference to metaphysics itself, however. Hidden in it is a horror that would take men's breath away if they did not repress it. We might be tempted to speculate anthropologically whether the turn in evolutionary history that gave the human species its open consciousness and thus an awareness of death—whether this turn does not contradict a continuing animal constitution which prohibits men to bear that consciousness. The price to be paid for the possibility to go on living would be a restriction of consciousness, then, a means to shield it from what consciousness is, after all: the consciousness of death.

It is a hopeless perspective that biologically, so to speak, the obtuseness of all ideologues might be due to a necessity of self-preservation, and that the right arrangement of society would by no means have to make it disappear—although, of course, it is only in the right society that chances for the right life will arise. The present society still tells us lies about death not having to be feared, and it sabotages any reflection upon it. Schopenhauer, the pessimist, was struck by the fact how little men *in media vita* are apt to bother with death.* Like Heidegger a hundred years later, Schopenhauer read this indifference in human nature rather than in men as products of history. Both of them came to regard the lack of metaphysical sense as a metaphysical phenomenon. In any case, it is a measure of the depth reached by neutralization, an existential of the bourgeois consciousness.

This depth makes us doubt whether—as has been drilled into the mind by a romantic tradition that survived all romanticism—things were so very different in times allegedly steeped in metaphysics, in the times which the young Lukács called "replete with meaning." The tradition carries a paralogism with it. The truth of metaphysical views is not assured by their collective obligatoriness, by the power they exert over life in closed cultures. Rather, the possibility of metaphysical experience is akin to the possibility of freedom, and it takes an unfolded subject, one that has

---

* "Man alone bears the certainty of his death with him in abstract concepts; and yet—a fact that is very strange—this certainty can frighten him only at specific moments, when an occasion recalls it to his imagination. Reflection can do little against nature's powerful voice. The permanent condition holding sway in man, as in the unthinking animal, is an assurance sprung from the innermost feeling that he is nature, the world itself; due to this assurance, no man is notably troubled by the thought of certain and never distant death, but each one lives as if he had to live forever. Which goes so far that we might say: No one really has a living conviction of the certainty of his death, else no man's mood could differ so greatly from a condemned criminal's. We might say, rather, that everyone admits that certainty *in abstracto* and theoretically, but puts it aside like other theoretical truths that do not apply in practice, without the slightest acceptance of it into his living consciousness." (Schopenhauer, *Die Welt als Wille und Vorstellung I*, Works, ed. Frauenstädt, II, Leipzig 1888, p. 332 — *The World as Will and Idea,* trans. R. B. Haldane and J. Kemp, Humanities Press, New York 1964.

torn the bonds advertised as salutary, to be capable of freedom. The dull captive of socially authorized views on allegedly blessed times, on the other hand, is related to the positivistic believer in facts. The ego must have been historically strengthened if, beyond the immediacy of the reality principle, it is to conceive the idea of what is more than entity. An order that shuts itself up in its own meaning will shut itself away from the possibility above order.

Vis-à-vis theology, metaphysics is not just a historically later stage, as it is according to positivistic doctrine. It is not only theology secularized into a concept. It preserves theology in its critique, by uncovering the possibility of what theology may force upon men and thus desecrate. The cosmos of the spirit was exploded by the forces it had bound; it received its just deserts. The autonomous Beethoven is more metaphysical, and therefore more true, than Bach's *ordo*. Subjectively liberated experience and metaphysical experience converge in humanity. Even in an age when they fall silent, great works of art express hope more powerfully than the traditional theological texts, and any such expression is configurative with that of the human side—nowhere as unequivocally as in moments of Beethoven. Signs that not everything is futile come from sympathy with the human, from the self-reflection of the subjects' natural side; it is only in experiencing its own naturalness that genius soars above nature.

What remains venerable about Kant is that in his theory of the intelligible he registered the constellation of the human and the transcendent as no philosopher beside him. Before humanity opened its eyes, the objective pressure of the miseries of life made men exhaust themselves in their neighbor's shame, and the immanence of meaning in life is the cover of their imprisonment. Ever since there appeared something like organized society, a solidly built autarkic context, the urge to leave it has been weak. A child who has not been prepared already could not help noticing in his Protestant hymn book how poor and tenuous the part entitled "The Last Things" is in comparison with all the training exercises for what the faithful should believe and how they ought to behave. That magic and superstition might continue to flourish in religions has long been suspected, and the reverse of that suspicion is that the core, the hope for a Beyond, was hardly ever so important to the positive religions as their concept required. Metaphysical speculation unites with speculation in the philosophy of history; for the chance of the right consciousness even of those last things it will trust nothing but a future without life's miseries.

The curse of these miseries is that instead of spurring us beyond mere existence, they disguise existence and confirm it as a metaphysical authority. "All is vanity," the word with which immanence has been endowed by great theologians ever since Solomon, is too abstract to guide us beyond immanence. Where men are assured that their existence is a matter of indifference, they are not going to lodge any protest; as long as their attitude toward existence remains unchanged, the rest seems vain to them also. If one accuses entity of nonentity without differentiation, and without a perspective of possibility, he aids and abets the dull bustle. The bestiality which such total practice amounts to is worse than the original bestiality: it comes to be a principle unto itself. The Capuchin sermon of the vanity of immanence secretly liquidates transcendence as well, for transcendence feeds on nothing but the experiences we have in immanence. But neutralization, profoundly sworn to that immanence, has survived even the catastrophes which according to the clarion calls of the apologists were to have thrown men back upon their radical concerns.

For there has been no change in society's basic condition. The theology and metaphysics which necessity resurrected are condemned, despite some valiant Protestant resistance, to serve as ideological passports for conformism. No rebellion of mere consciousness will lead beyond that. In the minds of the subjects, too, a bourgeois society will choose total destruction, its objective potential, rather than rise to reflections that would threaten its basic stratum. The metaphysical interests of men would require that their material ones be fully looked after. While their material interests are shrouded from them, they live under Maya's veil. What is must be changeable if it is not to be all.

10

"ONLY A PARABLE"

Decades after Arnold Schönberg set Stefan George's "Rapture" to music, he wrote a commentary praising the poem as a prophetic anticipation of the feelings of astronauts. In this naïve reduction of one of his most important works to the level of science fiction he was involuntarily acting out the metaphysical need. The subject matter of that neo-romanticist poem, the face of a man setting foot on another planet, is beyond doubt a parable for something internal, for an ecstasy and exaltation recalling Maximinus. The ecstasy is not one in space, not even in the space of cosmic experience, although it must take its images from that experience. But precisely this shows the objective ground of the excessively earthly interpretation.

Taking literally what theology promises would be as barbarian as that interpretation. Historically accumulated respect alone prevents our consciousness from doing so, and like the symbolic language of that entire cycle, poetic exaltation has been pilfered from the theological realm. Religion *à la lettre* would be like science fiction; space travel would take us to the really promised heaven. Theologians have been unable to refrain from childishly pondering the consequences of rocket trips for their Christology, and the other way round, the infantile interest in space travel brings to light the infantilism that is latent in messages of salvation. Yet if these messages were cleansed of all subject matter, if their sublimation were complete, their disseminators would be acutely embarrassed if asked to say what the messages stand for. If every symbol symbolizes nothing but another symbol, another conceptuality, their core remains empty—and so does religion.

This is the antinomy of theological consciousness today. Getting along with it would be easiest for the anachronistic primitive Christianity of Tolstoy, a *successio Christi* here and now, with closed eyes and without reflection. Goethe's construction of Faust already has a touch of the antinomy. When Faust says *"Die Botschaft hör ich wohl, allein mir fehlt der Glaube*—I hear the message, yet I lack the faith," the depth of the emotions that hold him back from suicide is interpreted by him as a return of deceptively consoling childhood traditions. And yet he is saved into the Marian heaven. The dramatic poem leaves unsettled whether its gradual progress refutes the skepticism of the thinking adult, or whether its last word is another symbol (*"nur ein Gleichnis*— only a parable") and transcendence is secularized, in more or less Hegelian fashion, into a picture of the whole of fulfilled immanence.

Any man who would nail down transcendence can rightly be charged—as by Karl Kraus, for instance—with lack of imagination, anti-intellectualism, and thus a betrayal of transcendence. On the other hand, if the possibility, however feeble and distant, of redemption in existence is cut off altogether, the human spirit would become an illusion, and the finite, conditioned, merely existing subject would eventually be deified as carrier of the spirit. An answer to this paradox of the transcendent was Rimbaud's vision of a mankind freed from oppression as being the true deity. At a later date, the Old-Kantian Mynona undisguisedly mythologized the subject and made idealism manifest as *hubris*. With speculative consequences of this sort, science fiction and rocketry found it easy to come to an understanding. If indeed the earth alone among all heavenly bodies were inhabited by rational beings, the idiocy of such a metaphysical phenomenon would amount to a denunciation of metaphysics; in the end, men would really be gods—and what gods!—only under a spell that prevents them from knowing it, and without dominion over the cosmos. Luckily, the latter fact made such speculations null and void again.

All metaphysical speculations are fatally thrust into the apocryphal, however. The ideological untruth in the conception of transcendence is the separation of body and soul, a reflex of the division of labor. It leads to idolization of the *res cogitans* as the nature-controlling principle, and to the material denials that would founder on the concept of a transcendence beyond the context of guilt. But what hope clings to, as in Mignon's song, is the transfigured body.

Metaphysics will not hear of that. It will not demean itself to material things, and this is why it passes the line to an inferior faith in spirits. Between the hypostasis of a noncorporeal and yet individuated spirit—and what would theology have in hand without this?—and spiritualism, the mendacious assertion that purely spiritual beings exist, the only difference is the historical dignity clothing the concept of "spirit." The effect of this dignity is that power, social success, comes to be the criterion of metaphysical truth. The English language drops the German distinction between *Spiritismus*, the German word for spiritualism, and *Spiritualismus* —in German the doctrine of the spirit as the individual-substantial principle. The equivocation comes from the epistemological need which once upon a time moved the idealists to go beyond the analysis of individual consciousness and to construe a transcendental or absolute one. Individual consciousness is a piece of the spatial-temporal world, a piece without any prerogatives over that world and not conceivable by human faculties as detached from the corporeal world. Yet the idealistic construction, which proposes to eliminate the earthly remains, becomes void as soon as it wholly expunges that egoity which served as the model for the concept of "spirit." Hence the assumption of a nonsensory egoity—which as existence, contrary to its own definition, is nonetheless to manifest itself in space and time.

According to the present state of cosmology, heaven and hell as entities in space are simple archaicisms. This would relegate immortality to one of spirits, lending it a spectral and unreal character that mocks its own concept. Christian dogmatics, in which the souls were conceived as awakening simultaneously with the resurrection of the flesh, was metaphysically more consistent— more enlightened, if you will—than speculative metaphysics, just as hope means a physical resurrection and feels defrauded of the best part by its spiritualization. With that, however, the impositions of metaphysical speculation wax intolerably. Cognition weighs heavily in the scale of absolute mortality—something speculation cannot bear, something that makes it a matter of absolute indifference to itself. The idea of truth is supreme among the metaphysical ideas, and this is where it takes us. It is why one who believes in God cannot believe in God, why the possibility represented by the divine name is maintained, rather, by him who does not believe. Once upon a time the image ban extended to pronouncing the name; now the ban itself has in that form come to evoke suspicions of superstition. The ban has been exacerbated: the mere thought of hope is a transgression against it, an act of working against it.

Thus deeply embedded is the history of metaphysical truth— of the truth that vainly denies history, which is progressive demythologization. Yet demythologization devours itself, as the mythical gods liked to devour their children. Leaving behind nothing but what merely is, demythologization recoils into the mythus; for the mythus is nothing else than the closed system of immanence, of that which is. This contradiction is what metaphysics has now coalesced into. To a thinking that tries to remove the contradiction, untruth threatens here and there.

11

THE SEMBLANCE OF OTHERNESS

In spite of and, so to speak, absorbing the Kantian critique, the ontological argument for the existence of God was resurrected in Hegelian dialectics. In vain, however. In Hegel's consistent resolution of nonidentity into pure identity, the concept comes to be the guarantor of the nonconceptual. Transcendence, captured by the immanence of the human spirit, is at the same time turned into the totality of the spirit and abolished altogether. Thereafter, the more transcendence crumbles under enlightenment, both in the world and in the human mind, the more arcane will it be, as though concentrating in an outermost point above all mediations. In this sense, the anti-historical theology of downright otherness has its historical index. The question of metaphysics is sharpened into the question whether this utter tenuousness, abstractness, indefiniteness is the last, already lost defensive position of metaphysics—or whether metaphysics survives only in the meanest and shabbiest, whether a state of consummate insignificance will let it restore reason to the autocratic reason that performs its office without resistance or reflection.

The thesis of positivism is that even a metaphysics that has escaped to profanity is void. Even the idea of truth, on whose account positivism was initiated, is sacrificed. Credit is due to Wittgenstein for having pointed this out, however well his commandment of silence may otherwise go with a dogmatic, falsely resurrected metaphysics that can no longer be distinguished from the wordless rapture of believers in Being. What demythologization would not affect without making it apologetically available is not an argument—the sphere of arguments is antinomical pure and simple—but the experience that if thought is not decapitated it will flow into transcendence, down to the idea of a world that would not only abolish extant suffering but revoke the suffering that is irrevocably past.

To have all thoughts converge upon the concept of something that would differ from the unspeakable world that is—this is not the same as the infinitesimal principle whereby Leibniz and Kant meant to make the idea of transcendence commensurable with a science whose fallibility, the confusion of control of nature with being-in-itself, is needed to motivate the correcting experience of convergence. The world is worse than hell, and it is better. It is worse, because even nihility could not be that absolute as which it finally appears conciliatory in Schopenhauer's Nirvana. There is no way out of the closed context of immanence; it denies the world even the measure of sense accorded to it by the Hindu philosophem that views it as the dream of an evil demon. The mistake in Schopenhauer's thinking is that the law which keeps immanence under its own spell is directly said to be that essence which immanence blocks, the essence that would not be conceivable as other than transcendent. But the world is better than hell because the absolute conclusiveness which Schopenhauer attributes to the world's course is borrowed in turn from the idealistic system. It is a pure identity principle, and as deceptive as any identity principle.

As in Kafka's writings, the disturbed and damaged course of the world is incommensurable also with the sense of its sheer senselessness and blindness; we cannot stringently construe it according to their principle. It resists all attempts of a desperate consciousness to posit despair as an absolute. The world's course is not absolutely conclusive, nor is absolute despair; rather, despair is its conclusiveness. However void every trace of otherness in it, however much all happiness is marred by revocability: in the breaks that belie identity, entity is still pervaded by the ever-broken pledges of that otherness. All happiness is but a fragment of the entire happiness men are denied, and are denied by themselves.

Convergence, the humanly promised otherness of history, points unswervingly to what ontology illegitimately locates before history, or exempts from history. The concept is not real, as the ontological argument would have it, but there would be no conceiving it if we were not urged to conceive it by something in the matter. Karl Kraus, armored against every tangible, imaginatively unimaginative assertion of transcendence, preferred to read transcendence longingly rather than to strike it out; and he was not a romantically liberal metaphoricist. Metaphysics cannot rise again—the concept of resurrection belongs to creatures, not to something created, and in structures of the mind it is an indication of untruth—but it may originate only with the realization of what has been thought in its sign.

Art anticipates some of this. Nietzsche's work is brimful of anti-metaphysical invective, but no formula describes metaphysics as faithfully as Zarathustra's "Pure fool, pure poet." The thinking artist understood the unthought art. A thought that does not capitulate to the wretchedly ontical will founder upon its criteria; truth will turn into untruth, philosophy into folly. And yet philosophy cannot abdicate if stupidity is not to triumph in realized unreason. *Aux sots je préfère les fous*. Folly is truth in the form which men are struck with as amid untruth they will not let truth go. Art is semblance even at its highest peaks; but its semblance, the irresistible part of it, is given to it by what is not semblance. What art, notably the art decried as nihilistic, says in refraining from judgments is that everything is not just nothing. If it were, whatever is would be pale, colorless, indifferent. No light falls on men and things without reflecting transcendence. Indelible from the resistance to the fungible world of barter is the resistance of the eye that does not want the colors of the world to fade. Semblance is a promise of nonsemblance.

12

SELF-REFLECTION OF DIALECTICS

The question is whether metaphysics as a knowledge of the absolute is at all possible without the construction of an absolute knowledge—without that idealism which supplied the title for the last chapter of Hegel's *Phenomenology*. Is a man who deals with the absolute not necessarily claiming to be the thinking organ with the capacity to do so, and thus the absolute himself? And on the other hand, if dialectics turned into a metaphysics that is not simply like dialectics, would it not violate its own strict concept of negativity?

Dialectics, the epitome of negative knowledge, will have nothing beside it; even a negative dialectics drags along the commandment of exclusiveness from the positive one, from the system. Such reasoning would require a nondialectical consciousness to be negated as finite and fallible. In all its historical forms, dialectics prohibited stepping out of it. Willy-nilly, it played the part of a conceptual mediator between the unconditional spirit and the finite one; this is what intermittently kept making theology its enemy. Although dialectics allows us to think the absolute, the absolute as transmitted by dialectics remains in bondage to conditioned thinking. If Hegel's absolute was a secularization of the deity, it was still the deity's secularization; even as the totality of mind and spirit, that absolute remained chained to its finite human model.

But if our thought, fully aware of what it is doing, gropes beyond itself—if in otherness it recognizes something which is downright incommensurable with it, but which it thinks anyway— then the only shelter it will find lies in the dogmatic tradition. In such thoughts our thinking is estranged from its content, unreconciled, and newly condemned to two kinds of truth, and that in turn would be incompatible with the idea of truth. Metaphysics depends upon whether we can get out of this aporia otherwise than by stealth. To this end, dialectics is obliged to make a final move: being at once the impression and the critique of the universal delusive context, it must now turn even against itself. The critique of every self-absolutizing particular is a critique of the shadow which absoluteness casts upon the critique; it is a critique of the fact that critique itself, contrary to its own tendency, must remain within the medium of the concept. It destroys the claim of identity by testing and honoring it; therefore, it can reach no farther than that claim. The claim is a magic circle that stamps critique with the appearance of absolute knowledge. It is up to the self-reflection of critique to extinguish that claim, to extinguish it in the very negation of negation that will not become a positing.

Dialectics is the self-consciousness of the objective context of delusion; it does not mean to have escaped from that context. Its objective goal is to break out of the context from within. The strength required from the break grows in dialectics from the context of immanence; what would apply to it once more is Hegel's dictum that in dialectics an opponent's strength is absorbed and turned against him, not just in the dialectical particular, but eventually in the whole. By means of logic, dialectics grasps the coercive character of logic, hoping that it may yield—for that coercion itself is the mythical delusion, the compulsory identity. But the absolute, as it hovers before metaphysics, would be the nonidentical that refuses to emerge until the compulsion of identity has dissolved. Without a thesis of identity, dialectics is not the whole; but neither will it be a cardinal sin to depart from it in a dialectical step.

It lies in the definition of negative dialectics that it will not come to rest in itself, as if it were total. This is its form of hope. Kant registered some of this in his doctrine of the transcendent thing-in-itself, beyond the mechanisms of identification. His successors, however stringently they criticized the doctrine, were reinforcing the spell, regressing like the post-revolutionary bourgeoisie as a whole: they hypostatized coercion itself as the absolute. Kant on his part, in defining the thing-in-itself as the intelligible being, had indeed conceived transcendence as nonidentical, but in equating it with the absolute subject he had bowed to the identity principle after all. The cognitive process that is supposed to bring us asymptotically close to the transcendent thing is pushing that thing ahead of it, so to speak, and removing it from our consciousness.

The identifications of the absolute transpose it upon man, the source of the identity principle. As they will admit now and then, and as enlightenment can strikingly point out to them every time, they are anthropomorphisms. This is why, at the approach of the mind, the absolute flees from the mind: its approach is a mirage. Probably, however, the successful elimination of any anthropomorphism, the elimination with which the delusive content seems removed, coincides in the end with that context, with absolute identity. Denying the mystery by identification, by ripping more and more scraps out of it, does not resolve it. Rather, as though in play, the mystery belies our control of nature by reminding us of the impotence of our power.

Enlightenment leaves practically nothing of the metaphysical content of truth—*presque rien,* to use a modern musical term. That which recedes keeps getting smaller and smaller, as Goethe describes it in the parable of New Melusine's box, designating an extremity. It grows more and more insignificant; this is why, in the critique of cognition as well as in the philosophy of history, metaphysics immigrates into micrology. Micrology is the place where metaphysics finds a haven from totality. No absolute can be expressed otherwise than in topics and categories of immanence, although neither in its conditionality nor as its totality is immanence to be deified.

According to its own concept, metaphysics cannot be a deductive context of judgments about things in being, and neither can it be conceived after the model of an absolute otherness terribly defying thought. It would be possible only as a legible constellation of things in being. From those it would get the material without which it would not be; it would not transfigure the existence of its elements, however, but would bring them into a configuration in which the elements unite to form a script. To that end, metaphysics must know how to wish. That the wish is a poor father to the thought has been one of the general theses of European enlightenment ever since Xenophanes, and the thesis applies undiminished to the attempts to restore ontology. But thinking, itself a mode of conduct, contains the need—the vital need, at the outset—in itself. The need is what we think from, even where we disdain wishful thinking. The motor of the need is the effort that involves thought as action. The object of critique is not the need in thinking, but the relationship between the two.

Yet the need in thinking is what makes us think. It asks to be negated by thinking; it must disappear in thought if it is to be really satisfied; and in this negation it survives. Represented in the inmost cell of thought is that which is unlike thought. The smallest intramundane traits would be of relevance to the absolute, for the micrological view cracks the shells of what, measured by the subsuming cover concept, is helplessly isolated and explodes its identity, the delusion that it is but a specimen. There is solidarity between such thinking and metaphysics at the time of its fall.

NOTES

In this translation, as in the German original, Kant's Works are cited from the German Akademie-Ausgabe (Preussische Akademie der Wissenschaften, Berlin 1900ff.); Hegel's Works, from the Jubiläumsausgabe (Glockner, Stuttgart 1927ff.) except for *Reason in History* (from *Die Vernunft in der Geschichte*, 5th ed., Meiner, Hamburg 1955); the writings of Karl Marx and Friedrich Engels, from the new editions published since World War II (Marx, *Grundrisse der politischen Ökonomie*, Berlin 1953; Marx-Engels, *Die heilige Familie*, Berlin 1953; Marx, *Das Kapital*, Berlin 1955; Marx, *Kritik des Gothaer Programms*, ed. by Franz Borkenau, Frankfurt 1956). The sources of other citations appear in the respective Notes.

INTRODUCTION

1. Cf. Immanuel Kant, *Kritik der reinen Vernunft*, 2nd ed., Works III (Drittes Hauptstück der Transzendentalen Methodenlehre) — *Critique of Pure Reason*, trans. Norman Kemp Smith, Macmillan Co., New York 1929.
2. Cf. F. A. Trendelenburg, *Logische Untersuchungen*, Vol. I, Leipzig 1870, pp. 43ff., 167ff.
3. Cf. Benedetto Croce, *Lebendiges und Totes in Hegels Philosophie*, trans. K. Büchler, Heidelberg 1909, pp. 66ff., 68ff., 72ff., 82ff.
4. Cf. G. W. F. Hegel, Works 4, p. 78.
5. Cf. Theodore W. Adorno, *Zur Metakritik der Erkenntnistheorie*, Stuttgart 1956.
6. Hegel, Works 6 (*Heidelberger Enzyklopädie*), p. 28.
7. Kant, *Kritik der reinen Vernunft*, 1st ed., Works IV, p. 11.
8. Walter Benjamin, *Briefe*, Vol. 2, Frankfurt 1966, p. 686.
9. Cf. Karl Marx, *Das Kapital*, I, p. 621f.; Karl Marx/Friedrich Engels, *Kommunistisches Manifest*, Stuttgart 1953, p. 10.
10. Kant, *Kritik der reinen Vernunft*, 2nd ed., Works III, p. 109.
11. Cf. Ed. Zeller, *Die Philosophie der Griechen*, 2.1, Tübingen 1859, p. 390.
12. *The Philosophy of Plato* (Jowett translation), Modern Library, p. 311.

13. Hegel, Works 4, p. 402.
14. Hegel, Works 8, p. 217.
15. Cf. Hegel, Works 4, p. 291f.
16. Cf. Theodor W. Adorno, "Thesen über Tradition," *Inselalmanach für 1956,* p. 168.

PART ONE. Relation to Ontology

I. THE ONTOLOGICAL NEED

1. Martin Heidegger, *Aus der Erfahrung des Denkens,* Pfullingen 1954, p. 7.
2. Cf. Heidegger, *Vom Wesen des Grundes,* Frankfurt am Main 1949, p. 14 — *The Essence of Reasons,* trans. Terrence Malick, Northwestern University Press, Evanston 1969.
3. Heidegger, *Platons Lehre von der Wahrheit,* 2nd ed., Bern 1954, p. 76. — Plato's *Doctrine of Truth,* trans. J. Barlow, in *Philosophy in the Twentieth Century,* Vol. 3, New York 1962.
4. Heidegger, *Was heisst Denken?* Tübingen 1954, p. 57. — *What is Called Thinking?* trans. Fred D. Wieck and J. Glenn Gray, Harper & Row, New York 1968.
5. Ibid., p. 72f.
6. Kant, *Kritik der reinen Vernunft,* Works IV, p. 233.
7. Heidegger, *Einführung in die Metaphysik,* Tübingen 1958, p. 31. — *Introduction to Metaphysics,* trans. Ralph Manheim, Yale University Press, New Haven 1958.
8. Friedrich Nietzsche, *Gesammelte Werke,* Munich 1924, vol. 12, p. 182.
9. Cf. Heidegger, *Holzwege,* Frankfurt am Main 1950, p. 121ff.
10. Cf. Heidegger, *Sein und Zeit,* 6th ed., Tübingen 1949, p. 27. — *Being and Time,* trans. J. Macquarrie and E. Robinson, Harper & Row, New York 1962.
11. Heidegger, *Platons Lehre von der Wahrheit,* p. 119.
12. Cf. Theodor W. Adorno, *Zur Metakritik der Erkenntnistheorie,* Stuttgart 1956, p. 168.
13. Heidegger, *Platons Lehre von der Wahrheit,* p. 119.
14. Cf. Heidegger, *Sein und Zeit,* p. 35.
15. Cf. Adorno, *Zur Metakritik der Erkenntnistheorie,* p. 135ff.
16. Cf. Heidegger, *Einführung in die Metaphysik,* p. 155.
17. Ibid., p. 154f.
18. Cf. Theodor W. Adorno, *Drei Studien zu Hegel,* Frankfurt 1963, p. 127ff.
19. Heidegger, *Identität und Differenz,* 2nd ed., Pfullingen 1957, p. 47

—*Identity and Difference,* trans. Joan Stambaugh, Harper & Row, New York 1969.

20. Heidegger, *Platons Lehre von der Wahrheit,* p. 84.
21. Ibid., p. 75.
22. Ibid., p. 84.
23. Cf. Heidegger, *Vom Wesen des Grundes,* pp. 42, 47.
24. Cf. Kant, *Kritik der reinen Vernunft,* Works IV, p. 95.
25. Cf. Adolf Loos, *Sämtliche Schriften,* vol. 1, Vienna and Munich 1962, p. 278 and passim.

II. BEING AND EXISTENCE

1. Developed by Walter Benjamin, *Schriften I,* Frankfurt 1955, pp. 366ff., 426ff.
2. Cf. Max Horkheimer and Theodor W. Adorno, *Dialektik der Aufklärung,* Amsterdam 1947, p. 26 — *Dialectic of Enlightenment,* trans. John Cumming, Herder and Herder, New York 1972.
3. "Das geht aber/Nicht." Hölderlin, *Works* 2, ed. Friedrich Beissner, Stuttgart 1953, p. 190.
4. Cf. Hermann Schweppenhäuser, "Studien über die Heiderggersche Sprachtheorie," in *Archiv für Philosophie,* 7 (1957), p. 304.
5. Karl Jaspers, *Die geistige Situation der Zeit,* Berlin 1931 — *Man in the Modern Age,* trans. Eden and Cedar Paul, Routledge, London 1933.
6. Heidegger, *Sein und Zeit,* p. 11.
7. Cf. Part One, p. 70.
8. Karl Heinz Haag, *Kritik der neueren Ontologie,* Stuttgart 1960, p. 71.
9. Heidegger, *Sein und Zeit,* p. 42.
10. Heidegger, *Platons Lehre von der Wahrheit,* p. 68.
11. Ibid., p. 70f.
12. Ibid., p. 68.
13. Ibid., p. 75.
14. Hegel, Works 4, p. 110.
15. Cf. Werner Becker, "Die Dialektik von Grund und Begründetem in Hegels Wissenschaft der Logik" (Ph.D. diss., University of Frankfurt, 1964), p. 73.
16. Cf. Alfred Schmidt, "Der Begriff der Natur in der Lehre von Marx," *Frankfurter Beiträge zur Soziologie,* 11 (Frankfurt 1962), p. 22f.
17. Jaspers, *Philosophie,* 1932, 1955, vol. I, p. xx — *Philosophy,* trans. E. B. Ashton, University of Chicago Press, Chicago 1969.

18. Ibid., p. 4.
19. Ibid., p. xxiii, and Heidegger, *Uber den Humanismus,* Frankfurt am Main 1947, p. 17f. — "Letter on Humanism," trans. Edgar Lohner, in *Philosophy in the Twentieth Century,* vol. 3.
20. Heidegger, *Sein und Zeit,* p. 12.
21. Ibid., p. 13.
22. Jaspers, *Philosophie,* vol. I, p. 264.

PART TWO. Negative Dialectics. Concept and Categories.

1. Cf. Theodor W. Adorno, *Zur Metakritik der Erkenntnistheorie,* Stuttgart 1956, p. 97 and passim.
2. Cf. *Weltgeist und Naturgeschichte,* passim.
3. Cf. Hegel, Works 4, p. 543.
4. Ibid., p. 98ff.
5. Ibid., p. 543.
6. Cf. Walter Benjamin, *Ursprung des deutschen Trauerspiels,* Frankfurt am Main 1963, p. 15ff.
7. Max Weber, *Gesammelte Aufsätze zur Religionssoziologie,* Frankfurt am Main 1947, p. 30.
8. Ibid.
9. Ibid., p. 4ff.
10. Cf. Karl Marx, *Kritik des Gothaer Programms,* Frankfurt am Main 1956, p. 199ff.
11. Cf. Alfred Schmidt, "Der Begriff der Natur in der Lehre von Marx," in *Frankfurter Beiträge zur Soziologie,* 11 (Frankfurt 1962), p. 21.
12. Cf. Kant, *Kritik der reinen Vernunft,* Works III, p. 93ff.
13. Cf. Walter Benjamin, *Deutsche Menschen, Eine Folge von Briefen,* afterword by Theodor W. Adorno, Frankfurt am Main 1962, p. 128.
14. Cf. Marx, *Das Kapital,* vol. I, p. 514.
15. Walter Benjamin, *Passagenarbeit* (manuscript), vol. 6.

PART THREE. Models

I. FREEDOM

1. Aristotle, *Metaphysics,* Book A, 983 b.
2. Kant, *Grundlegung zur Metaphysik der Sitten,* Works IV, p. 432 — *Foundations of the Metaphysics of Morals,* trans. Lewis W. Beck, Liberal Arts Press, New York 1959.
3. Cf. Max Horkheimer and Theodor W. Adorno, *Dialektik der*

Aufklärung, Amsterdam 1947, p. 106 — *Dialectic of Enlightenment*, trans. John Cumming, Herder and Herder, New York 1972.
4. Kant, *Grundlegung zur Metaphysik der Sitten*, p. 454f.
5. Ibid., p. 454.
6. Kant, *Kritik der praktischen Vernunft*, Works V, p. 30.
7. Ibid.
8. Ibid., p. 37.
9. Kant, *Kritik der reinen Vernunft*, Works III, p. 97.
10. Kant, *Kritik der praktischen Vernunft*, p. 56f.
11. Kant, *Grundlegung*, p. 427.
12. Ibid., p. 446.
13. Kant, *Kritik der praktischen Vernunft*, p. 59.
14. Ibid.
15. Kant, *Grundlegung*, p. 448.
16. Ibid.
17. Kant, *Kritik der praktischen Vernunft*, p. 80.
18. Cf. Walter Benjamin, *Schriften I*, Frankfurt am Main 1955, p. 36f.
19. Kant, *Kritik der praktischen Vernunft*, p. 6.
20. Kant, *Kritik der reinen Vernunft*, p. 311.
21. Ibid.
22. Ibid., p. 308.
23. Ibid., p. 310.
24. Ibid., p. 309.
25. Ibid., p. 311.
26. Ibid.
27. Kant, *Kritik der praktischen Vernunft*, p. 95.
28. Kant, *Grundlegung*, p. 451.
29. Cf. footnote 19.
30. Kant, *Kritik der praktischen Vernunft*, p. 6.
31. Ibid., p. 114.
32. Ibid., p. 99.
33. Kant, *Kritik der reinen Vernunft*, p. 309.
34. Kant, *Kritik der praktischen Vernunft*, p. 89.
35. Ibid., p. 24.
36. Ibid., p. 22.
37. Kant, *Grundlegung*, p. 429.
38. Kant, *Idee zu einer allgemeinen Geschichte in weltbürgerlicher Absicht*, Works VIII, p. 20f. — *Idea for a Universal History with Cosmopolitan Intent*, trans. Carl J. Friedrich, Modern Library, New York 1949.
39. Kant, *Grundlegung*, p. 430.

40. Ibid., p. 447.
41. Ibid., p. 462.
42. Kant, *Kritik der praktischen Vernunft,* p. 36.
43. Ibid., p. 62f.
44. Ibid., p. 34f.
45. Ibid., p. 92f.
46. Ibid., p. 118; cf. Horkheimer and Adorno, *Dialektik der Aufklärung,* p. 123ff.
47. Kant, *Grundlegung,* p. 459.
48. Kant, *Kritik der praktischen Vernunft,* p. 31; cf. Horkheimer and Adorno, *Dialektik der Aufklärung,* p. 114.
49. Sandor Ferenczi, *Bausteine zur Psychoanalyse,* Bern 1939, vol. III, p. 394f.
50. Ibid., p. 398.
51. Ibid.
52. Ibid., p. 435.
53. Kant, *Kritik der praktischen Vernunft,* p. 48.
54. Ibid., p. 67.
55. Ibid., p. 68.
56. Ibid., p. 72.
57. Ibid.
58. Ibid., p. 99.
59. Ibid.
60. Ibid., p. 99f.
61. Ibid., p. 87.
62. Cf. Benjamin, *Schriften I,* p. 36ff.
63. Cf. Kant, *Kritik der praktischen Vernunft,* p. 76.

II. WORLD SPIRIT AND NATURAL HISTORY

1. Karl Marx and Friedrich Engels, *Die heilige Familie,* Berlin 1953, p. 211.
2. Marx, *Das Kapital,* Vol. I, p. 621f.
3. Ibid., p. 621.
4. Hegel, Works 7, p. 28f.
5. Cf. Walter Benjamin, *Schriften I,* Frankfurt am Main 1955, p. 494ff.
6. Hegel, *Die Vernunft in der Geschichte,* 5th ed., Hamburg 1955, p. 60.
7. Ibid.
8. Ibid., p. 48.
9. Hegel, Works 7, p. 230.

NOTES

10. Hegel, *Die Vernunft in der Geschichte*, p. 77.
11. Ibid., p. 78.
12. Ibid., p. 115.
13. Ibid., p. 60.
14. Ibid., p. 95.
15. Ibid., p. 60.
16. Hegel, Works 5, p. 43f.
17. Hegel, *Die Vernunft in der Geschichte*, p. 59f.
18. Ibid., p. 105.
19. Cf. esp. Part One, Being and Existence.
20. Hegel, Works 7, p. 231.
21. Ibid., p. 32ff.
22. Marx, *Grundrisse der Kritik der politischen Ökonomie*, Berlin 1953, p. 73f.
23. Ibid., p. 76.
24. Hegel, Works 7, p. 336.
25. Ibid., p. 268f.
26. Ibid., p. 235.
27. Ibid., p. 329.
28. Ibid.
29. Hegel, *Die Vernunft in der Geschichte*, p. 111.
30. Cf. Oskar Negt, "Strukturbeziehungen zwischen den Gesellschaftlehren Comtes und Hegels," in *Frankfurter Beiträge zur Soziologie*, 14 (Frankfurt am Main 1964), p. 49 and passim.
31. Ibid., p. 72.
32. Ibid., p. 67.
33. Ibid.
34. Ibid.
35. Ibid., p. 95.
36. Ibid., p. 73.
37. Ibid., p. 95.
38. Cf. Benjamin, *Schriften II*, Frankfurt am Main 1955, p. 197.
39. Hegel, Works 7, p. 234f.
40. Hegel, *Die Vernunft in der Geschichte*, p. 115.
41. Cf. Theodor W. Adorno, *Versuch Über Wagner*, Berlin and Frankfurt am Main, 1952, p. 195.
42. Cf. Emil Durkheim, *Les règles de la méthode sociologique*, 13th ed., Paris 1956, p. 100f.; cf. Adorno, "Notiz über sozialwissenschaftliche Objektivität," in *Kölner Zeitschrift für Soziologie und Sozialpsychologie*, 17, no. 3 (1965), p. 416ff.
43. Cf. Durkheim, *Les règles*, p. 104.

415

44. Cf. Herbert Marcuse, *Zur Kritik des Hedonismus,* in *Zeitschrift für Sozialforschung,* VII, (Paris 1939), p. 55f.
45. Hegel, *Die Vernunft in der Geschichte,* p. 92f.
46. Cf. Adorno, *Drei Studien zu Hegel,* Frankfurt am Main 1963, p. 154f.
47. Marx, *Das Kapital,* vol. I, p. 7f.
48. Cf. Alfred Schmidt, "Der Begriff der Natur in der Lehre von Marx," in *Frankfurter Beiträge zur Soziologie,* 11 (Frankfurt am Main 1962), p. 15.
49. Marx, *Das Kapital,* vol. I, p. 652f.
50. Marx, *Grundrisse,* p. 111.
51. Hegel, Works 7, p. 375.
52. Ibid., p. 434.
53. Ibid., p. 50.
54. Cf. Georg Lukács, *Die Theorie des Romans,* Berlin 1920, p. 54ff.
55. Marx, *Deutsche Ideologie,* in *MEGA,* Part I, vol. V (Berlin 1932), p. 567.
56. Adorno, *"Die Idee der Naturgeschichte,"* Kant Society lecture given in Frankfurt, July 1932.
57. Walter Benjamin, *Ursprung des deutschen Trauerspiels,* Frankfurt am Main 1963, p. 199.
58. Ibid., p. 197.

III. MEDITATIONS ON METAPHYSICS

1. Cf. Heinrich Regius, *Dämmerung,* Zurich 1934, p. 69f.
2. Kant, *Kritik der reinen Vernunft,* Works III, p. 313.